Anyone who wants to know  *ows are distributed and exploited can l* k.

Pixar . nager, EVP,
cer *Wall•E*

m Morris,

The entertainment industry is an industry with ongoing challenges with constant change. Jeff provides a road map to see where you are going by understanding where you started.

—Louis Feola, President,
Paramount Famous Productions

Ulin expertly depicts the fluid nature of content creation and distribution in a concise and understandable way. There's never been a better insider's look at the choices and challenges that studio executives face every day.

—Gary Marenzi,
President, MGM Worldwide Television

Jeff Ulin's broad spectrum of expertise, spanning all aspects of motion picture and television distribution, from theatrical to home entertainment to new media and television licensing, render him uniquely qualified to illuminate the business side of the entertainment business.

—Hal Richardson,
President of Paramount Worldwide Television

Jeff Ulin's book is a must read for practitioners, academics and potential investors in the new media space. Having worked in all segments of the industry, Ulin brings together a unique combination of experience and analytical rigor to deconstruct the driving forces of an industry in dynamic change.

—Pablo Spiller,
Jeffrey A. Jacobs Distinguished Professor of Business
and Technology, Haas School of Business.

This is the book that everyone in the business has been waiting for—Jeff's seen it all, and has written a must-read book for those wanting to understand the jigsaw of media distribution and in what ways the web is influencing how, when and where money is made.

—Michael Uslan,
Executive Producer, *Batman, Batman Begins, The Dark Knight*

Every Silicon Valley start-up working with Hollywood needs to know what Jeff knows. With his knowledge, you're better able to fast forward the future of online video. Without it, you risk being stuck on pause.

—Kevin Yen,
Director, Strategic Partnerships YouTube

The Business of Media Distribution

Monetizing Film, TV, and Video Content

Jeff Ulin

ELSEVIER

AMSTERDAM • BOSTON • HEIDELBERG • LONDON
NEW YORK • OXFORD • PARIS • SAN DIEGO
SAN FRANCISCO • SINGAPORE • SYDNEY • TOKYO
Focal Press is an imprint of Elsevier

Focal Press is an imprint of Elsevier
30 Corporate Drive, Suite 400, Burlington, MA 01803, USA
Linacre House, Jordan Hill, Oxford OX2 8DP, UK

Library of Congress Cataloging-in-Publication Data
Application submitted

British Library Cataloguing-in-Publication Data
A catalogue record for this book is available from the British Library.

ISBN: 978-0-240-81200-7

For information on all Focal Press publications
visit our website at www.elsevierdirect.com

10 11 12 13   5 4 3 2 1

Printed in the United States of America

Working together to grow
libraries in developing countries

www.elsevier.com | www.bookaid.org | www.sabre.org

ELSEVIER   BOOK AID
             International   Sabre Foundation

Dedication

For Eve, Charlie, Teddy and the dogs

Contents

viii

xi

xii

Acknowledgment

First, and most importantly, I would like to thank my family, including my wife Eve and sons Charlie and Teddy. I spent many long hours writing, and deeply appreciate their tolerance and patience.

As noted at the outset of the book, the business side of the entertainment business is often apprentice-based in terms of learning. Beyond family and friends, there are a lot of people I would like to thank for their help, either for being willing to bounce ideas off of, contribute quotes, or review sections, as well as educating me (and serving as mentors, past and present) and simply offering encouragement: David Anderman, Tonik Barber, David Barron, Eric Besner, Chris Carvahlo, Ed Catmull, Alex Collmer, Jason Donnell, Mike Dunn, Marion Edwards, Louis Feola, Jeff Fino, Bill Gannon, Alexander Goethal, Lynne Hale, Jim Hedges, Michael Hoff, Carrie Hurwitz, Barry Jossen, Jayant Kadambi, Jack Kennedy, Cathy Kirkman, Michael Knobloch, Michael Kohn, Josh Kramer, Kevin Kurtz, Peter Levinsohn, Michael Lopez, George Lucas, Rich Lyons, Gary Marenzi, Jamie McCabe, Jim Morris, Sean McGinn, Jim Mullany, Ned Nalle, Daniel Paul, Tom Quinn, Gordon Radley, Hal Richardson, Curtis Roberts, Howard Roffman, Craig Sherman, Pablo Spiller, Eric Stein, Steve Swassey, Michael Uslan, Pedro de Vasconsoles, Kul Wadhwa, Tom Warner, Jim Ward, Tom van Wavern, Blair Westlake, Catherine Winder, and Kevin Yen

And, of course, everyone at Elsevier/Focal, including especially Elinor Actipis, Chris Simpson, and Paul Gottehrer.

CHAPTER 1

Market Opportunity and Segmentation—The Diverse Role of Studios and Networks

 More content from this chapter is available on www.businessofmediadistribution.com

Introduction

This book provides an overview of how the business side of the television and motion picture industry works. By the end of the text, readers will gain a practical understanding of how a film, television, or video project moves from concept to making money. Stars make the headlines, but marketing and distribution convert content into cash. To explain how the system works, this book charts the path entertainment content takes from development to financing to distribution, and attempts to demystify the submarkets through which a production is exhibited, sold, watched, rented, or otherwise consumed. In summary, this book explains the process by which a single idea turns into a unique piece of entertainment software capable of generating over a billion dollars and sustaining cash flow over decades. I will also attempt to put into context the growing array of Internet and other new media opportunities for content, exploring the emergence of digital-based distribution systems and the blurring of lines with traditional outlets.

With the potential of generating great wealth also comes great risk, and motion picture studios today can be seen as venture capitalists managing a specialized portfolio. In contrast to traditional venture capitalist investments, though, film investors risk capital on a product whose initial value is rooted in subjective judgment. Valuing creativity is tough enough, but investing in a film or TV show often asks people to judge a work before they can see it—literally a step back from the famous pornography standard "I know it when I see it." Bets are accordingly hedged by vesting vast financial responsibility over productions in people who have developed successful creative track records. Focusing too much attention, though, on creative judgment as opposed to marketing and financial acumen risks failure, and managers who can balance competing creative and business agendas often become the corporate stars. Analysts seeking trends may promote "content is king," but in the trenches success tends to be linked with marrying creative and sales skills.

As a result of this mix, there is no defined career path to breaking into the business or rising to success within it. Unlike attending law school and rising to partner, or business school and aspiring to investment banking, leaders in the film and TV world are an eclectic group hailing from legal, finance, producing, directing, marketing, and talent management backgrounds. Without a clear educational starting point or defined career path, how do these leaders and entrepreneurs learn the so-called "business"?

Beyond what I hope will be a "we wish we'd had this book" reply, the simplest answer is that many executives learn by some form of apprenticeship. As an alternative to starting in the mailroom, which will always remain both a legendary and real option for breaking into the entertainment business, this book will equip readers with a basic understanding of the economics and business issues that affect virtually every TV show and film. Behind every program or movie is a multi-year tale involving passion, risk, millions of dollars, and hundreds of people. In fact, every project is akin to an entrepreneurial venture where a business plan (concept) is sold, financing is raised, a product is made and tested (production), and a final product is released.

While this sounds simple enough, the potential of overnight wealth, a culture of stars, and the power of studios and networks serve to throw up barriers to entry that segment the industry and make the entertainment production and distribution chain unique. The emergence of online and digital distribution is changing the equation, enabling cheaper, faster production and new ubiquitous and simultaneous access to content; whether sustainable business models evolve to efficiently monetize content to launch on these new platforms, or these outlets simply serve as a supplementary access point for content is the question of the day.

What is certain, however, is that to understand these new avenues one has to understand the historical landscape. Traditional media (film/TV/video) still accounts for over 90% of all media revenues and the success of online/digital ventures will be tied to how opportunities relate to existing revenue streams. The exploitation of media is a symbiotic process, where success is achieved by choreographing distribution across time and distribution outlets to maximize an ultimate bottom line. Media conglomerates have developed a fine-tuned system mixing free and paid-for access (TV vs. theaters), varying price points (DVD sales and rentals, pay TV, video-on-demand), and windows driving repeat consumption — a system that will generate far more money (and therefore sustain higher budgets) than an ad hoc watch-for-free-everywhere-now structure. It is because the Internet offers the chance to dramatically broaden exposure, lower costs, and target finely sliced demographics that the two systems are both attractive and struggling to merge in a way that ensures expansion rather than contraction of the pie.

Market Opportunity and Segmenting the Market

A reference to the "film and TV market" is a bit of a misnomer, because these catchall categories are actually an aggregation of many specialty markets, each with its nuances and particular market challenges. The rest of the chapters of this book detail exploitation patterns common across product categories, such as how a property is distributed into standard channels, while this chapter first outlines the range of primary markets and niche businesses. I will also try to highlight differing risk factors and financials that are explored in greater detail later in the book, but here I want to focus on the diversity of the market and how it can be segmented. In fact, the simple process of segmentation illustrates the diversity of the business and how studios can be defined as an almost mutual fund-like aggregation of related businesses with differing investment and risk profiles. It is because of this range of activities and the way a studio can be characterized that business opportunities tend to be "silo specific"; a successful business plan in the entertainment industry is likely to focus on limited or niche risk profiles and financials. Except for the launch of DreamWorks (which ultimately retrenched to primarily focus on film production), it is rare for any entity to try and tackle the overall market from scratch.

Defining Studios by Their Distribution Infrastructure

There are a finite number of major studios (i.e., Sony, Disney, Paramount, Universal, Warner Bros., Fox, and MGM), and the greatest power that the studio brings to a film is not producing. Rather, studios are financing and distribution machines that bankroll production, and then dominate the distribution channels to market and release the films they finance.

Accordingly, the most defining element of a studio is its distribution arm — this is how studios make most of their revenue, and is the unique facet that distinguishes a "studio" from a studio look-alike. Sometimes a company, such as Lionsgate or Miramax in its original iteration (when run independently by Bob and Harvey Weinstein), will have enough scale that it is referred to as a "mini-major." This somewhat fluid category generally refers to a company that is independent, can offer broad distribution, and consistently produces and releases a range of product; again, though, what largely distinguishes a mini-major from simply being a large production company is its distribution capacity. Any company, studios included, can arrange financing: there are plenty of people that want to invest in movies. In this regard, the film business is no different than any other business. Is the production bank financed, risk/VC financed, or funded by private individuals? (See Chapter 3 for discussion of production financing.)

What is different with studios is that they will not invest (generally) in a film without obtaining and exercising distribution rights. This is because they are first and foremost marketing and distribution organizations, not banks. Sure, they buy properties, hire stars, and finance the films they elect to make; however, to some extent this can be viewed as a pretext to controlling which properties they distribute and own (or at least control). If the project looks like a hit, it is captive and the studio through its exclusive control of the distribution chain can maximize the economic potential of the property. If the property fails to meet creative expectations, however, the studio has options from writing it off and not releasing the property, to selling off all or part of the rights as a hedge, to rolling the dice with a variety of release strategies.

So beyond money, which anyone can bring, and creative production, which an independent can bring, what is it about distribution that separates studios?

What Does Distribution Really Mean?

Distribution in Hollywood terms is akin to sales; however, it is more complicated than a straightforward notion of sales given the nature of intellectual property and the strategies executed to maximize value over the life of a single property. Intellectual property rights are infinitely divisible, and distributing a film or TV show is the art of maximizing consumption and corresponding revenues across exploitation options. Whereas marketing focuses on awareness and driving consumption, distribution focuses on making that consumption profitable. Additionally, distribution is also the art of creating opportunities to drive repeat consumption of the same product. This is managed by creating exclusive or otherwise distinct periods of viewing in the context of ensuring that the product is released and customized worldwide.

In contrast to a typical software product, the global sales of which are predicated on a particular release version (e.g., Windows 98), a film is released in multiple versions, formats, and consumer markets in each territory in the world.

Figure 1.1 represents what I will call "Ulin's Rule": content value is optimized by exploiting the factors of time, repeat consumption (platforms), exclusivity, and differential pricing in a pattern taking into account external market conditions and the interplay of the factors among each other.

Launching content via online distribution presents monetization challenges because simultaneous, non-exclusive, flat-priced access

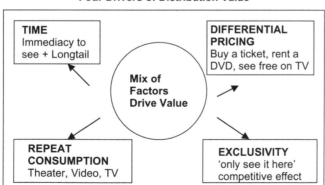

Figure 1.1

---

does not allow the interplay of the Ulin Rule factors: use of online platforms tend only to drive value by exploiting the time factor. To earn the same lifetime value on the Internet for a product that would otherwise flow through traditional markets, not only must initial consumption expand to compensate for a decline caused by cutting out markets in the chain (or reduced because a driver such as exclusivity is removed), but also it must compensate for the cumulative effect of losing the matrix of drivers that have been honed to optimize long-term value. When thinking about Internet opportunities and different distribution platforms, keep in mind these elements and ask whether the new system is eliminating one or more of the factors: if the answer is yes, then there is likely a tug-of-war between the old media and new media platforms, with adoption slowed as executives struggle for a method of harmonizing the two that does not shrink the overall pie.

Range of Activities — Distribution Encompasses Many Markets

To accomplish the feat of releasing a single property in multiple versions and formats to a variety of consumer markets a huge infrastructure is needed to manage and customize the property for global release. The following is a sample listing of release markets, versions, and formats:

Specialized Markets Where a Film is Seen
- Movie theatres
- Video and DVD
- Pay television
- Pay-per-view television/video-on-demand (PPV/VOD)
- Free and cable television
- Hotel/motel
- Airlines
- Non-theatrical (colleges, cruise ships)
- Internet/portable devices

Formats
- Film prints (35 mm, 70 mm, 16 mm)
- Digital master for D-cinema
- Videocassette
- DVD

- Formatted (and often edited) for TV broadcast (video master)
- Compressed for Internet/download

Versions
- Original theatrical release
- Extended or special versions for video/DVD (e.g., director's cut)
- Wide screen versus pan and scan aspect ratios
- Accompanied by value added material (commentary, deleted scenes, trailers)

The need for different markets, formats, and even versions creates a complex matrix for delivery of elements. Moreover, as technology affords more viewing platforms, the combinations grow by a multiple; for example, because DVD was additive to video (at least initially), the product SKUs increased by a factor of this doubling of the distribution channel times the number of versions released. Take this formula and compound it by all major territories in the world, and the complications of supplying consumer demand involve complex logistics.

The following illustrates this point. Assume a studio or producer has a family genre movie, such as Harry Potter or *Spiderman*, that will be released "wide" in all traditional release channels in all major markets in the world. How many different versions of the film do you think need to be created, marketed, sold, and delivered? The number can quite easily equal 150 versions, and possibly even more. The chart below assumes:

7

- The movie is initially released in theatres, in at least 20 major markets around the world.
- The movie is released worldwide in the home video market on DVD and VHS, and that consumers are offered a range of formats, such as a letterbox version (a "widescreen" version that leaves black on the top and bottom of the screen) and a "pan and scan" version that is reformatted from the theatrical aspect ratio to fill up a traditional square television screen. (Note: VHS releases are largely phased out, but the analogy remains as there will be Blu-ray and traditional DVD skus.)
- The film is released into major pay TV markets worldwide (channels may have different specs).
- The film is edited for broadcast on major network TV channels.
- The property is compressed for Internet/download viewing.

- Miscellaneous other masters, with different specs, are needed for ancillary markets such as airlines.

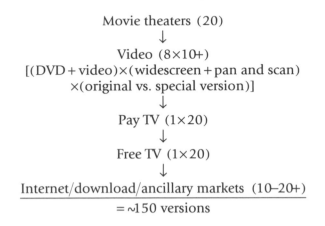

Movie theaters (20)
↓
Video (8×10+)
[(DVD + video)×(widescreen + pan and scan)
×(original vs. special version)]
↓
Pay TV (1×20)
↓
Free TV (1×20)
↓
Internet/download/ancillary markets (10–20+)

= ~150 versions

Overhead

Not every element above adds significant new complexity, but to manage just this part of the distribution chain, which represents only a portion of the distribution channels, requires significant overhead. Within each of the primary divisions (theatrical, pay TV, free TV, video) there are several key functions that need to be staffed. Typically there is dedicated sales, marketing, and finance staff plus general management; to the extent there is a formula, every subsidiary office in an overseas territory would replicate this general structure.

To extrapolate cost, let us assume 10 people per office with an average salary of $100,000, and that salary costs represent ~60% of the office's budget, with SG&A expenses accounting for the other ~40%. That would represent a budget of ~$1.7M per office. Assuming 12 offices, this represents $20M of overhead per year for a film or video division; the United States remains the largest and most fiercely competitive market in the world, with overhead costs that can represent a significant portion of the worldwide overhead numbers.

Arguably, the foregoing is a conservative snapshot, for upwards of 1,000 people can be employed worldwide at a major studio across the divisions comprising the distribution chain. To illustrate the size, simply take a key individual territory as an example. A major operation in France could easily have 50+ people depending on structure and product flow with an organizational infrastructure as

8

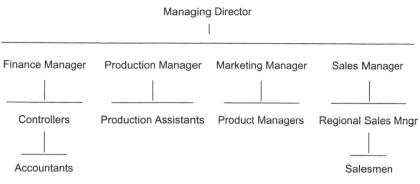

Finance Manager   Production Manager   Marketing Manager   Sales Manager

Controllers   Production Assistants   Product Managers   Regional Sales Mngr

Accountants   Salesmen

Figure 1.2

seen in Figure 1.2 (excluding personal assistants/administrative support).

Usually the largest number of people are in the sales area, and in a geographically dispersed area with hundreds or even thousands of individual accounts to cover could comprise half of the overall headcount. (Note: In some cases there could also be dedicated legal, although legal and business affairs tend to operate at headquarters.)

Pipeline

The overhead required to run the distribution apparatus cannot be justified without a sufficient quantity of product to market and sell. This relationship is fairly straightforward: the more titles released, the greater the revenue, the easier to amortize the cost of the fixed overhead. Stated simply, if there is $50M in distribution overhead, an independent releasing 5 films/year would need to amortize $10M/film, whereas a larger studio releasing 25 pictures would need to recoup only $2M/picture in overhead costs.

Studio distribution is the organization and function that matches the content pipeline with the challenge of delivering that content to every consumer on the planet — multiple times.

Complexity + Overhead + Pipeline = Studio Distribution

The above infrastructure and needs are the underbelly of the studio system, and what studios do better than anyone else is market and distribute film product to every nook and cranny of the world.

Need for Control

The other piece of the equation is control, which requires a more hands-on distribution approach than would otherwise be acceptable in an OEM or purely licensed world. Control can be viewed in terms of a negative or positive perspective. The need for control in a negative sense exists as a watchdog feature, providing security to producers and investors and others associated with the project and assuring that the project is looked after properly. Control in a positive sense means that proper focus can be brought to distribution, thereby increasing the revenue potential on a particular project. Arguably, in the Hollywood context, these can be of equal importance.

Negative Control

Films are very individual with stars, producers, and directors so vested in the development, production, and outcome that they have enormous influence over detailed elements of release and distribution. When travel was less ubiquitous than it is today, and revenues from international markets were a nice sprinkling on top of United States grosses, attention may not have been as significant; however, when a top star or director is likely to hear about (or even see) what has happened to their film in Germany or Japan, they will generally want the same rules applied in local markets as in Hollywood and New York. The only way to police this is on the ground control, making it less likely to cede supervisory control in major markets to mere licensees. How can the studio boss look his most important supplier in the face and pledge "we'll take care of you" if he has passed the baton locally?

Executives will not risk their careers on "he'll never know about it," and the danger of discovering non-compliance has ratcheted up with every improvement in communications technology. If an advertisement that requires Tom Hanks' approval is improperly handled in Spain, a competitor could take a picture of it on his cell phone and transmit it to his agent in Los Angeles over a wireless Internet connection instantly. If you were counting on Mr. Hanks for your next picture, or if this were even a breach of your contract for a current picture in release, would you risk it?

Positive Control

By positive control I simply mean that focus will usually lead to incremental revenue. Subdistribution or agency relationships by their nature yield control to third parties, and studios tend to have direct offices handling distribution in their major markets. Only with this level of oversight can a distribution organization push its agenda and maneuver against its competitors who are invariably releasing titles of their own at the same time and to the same customers. This direct supplier–customer relationship is what studios offer to their clients — a global matrix of relationships and focus that an independent without the same level of continuous product flow cannot support.

The Independent's Dilemma

An independent may not care as much about some or all of these issues, for it may have less entrenched relationships or be more willing by its very nature to take on certain risks. It still has to release its product via all the key distribution channels (e.g., theatrical, TV, video) and into as many territories as possible around the world. To raise money it may make strategic sense to license rights, which may then have the consequence of ceding an element of control and potential upside — an advance guarantee, a slightly different fee, a recognition that less direct control may forfeit revenues at the margin, all may greatly outweigh the burden of carrying the extra overhead. In essence, they can beat over 70% of the system, but they cannot match the pure strength and reach of the studio distribution infrastructure. And to many people, and especially on big movies with powerful producers and directors behind them, a pitch of "almost as good" simply is not good enough.

Joint Ventures

The pressure to fill a pipeline and bring down per title releasing costs while guaranteeing the broadest possible release is great, and even defining of what makes a studio. Despite the fact, however, that costs come down in a linear progression relative to titles released, the total overhead is still a very large number. Such a large number, in fact, that it has frequently led to the formation of joint ventures. A joint venture may only need an incremental amount of extra overhead, if any, while perhaps doubling or tripling the throughput of titles. In the above studio case, a joint venture could easily increase the title flow from 25 to 60, bringing down the per recoupment number in the above scenario to under $1M per title to cover the overhead.

Studio joint ventures grew in the 1980s with the globalization of the business. The number of titles a studio released fell within a relatively static range, and even a significant percentage increase in product still meant a finite number of major films (e.g., 20 or 30). What

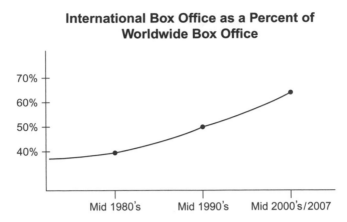

International Box Office as a Percent of Worldwide Box Office

Mid 1980's   Mid 1990's   Mid 2000's/2007

Figure 1.3   Data by permission of SNL Kagan, a division of SNL Financial LC, estimates. All rights reserved.

changed dramatically was the importance of the international markets. In the early 1980s, the international box office as a percentage of the worldwide box office was in the 40% range, then grew to over a 50% share by the mid-1990s, and by the mid-2000s had grown to 64% (64% in each of 2006 and 2007 pursuant to the most recent report from the Motion Picture Association of American, MPAA).[1] The splits, of course, are picture dependent (and in extreme cases films such as Sony's *The Da Vinci Code* can have an international share >70%), but the overall trend is clear, especially for box office hits with international stars and franchise recognition.[2]

When individual territories outside the United States started to represent the potential, and then the actual return, of tens of millions of dollars, the studios needed to build an infrastructure to manage and maximize the release of its product abroad. Moreover, this matured market by market. First, the growth of the international theatrical market warranted the expansion. Shortly thereafter, with the explosive growth of the videocassette market in the 1980s and 1990s, including in the 1990s the expansion of major United States retailers such as Blockbuster to international markets, studios needed to mirror theatrical expansion on the video side. Distribution of videocassettes (now DVDs) and of movies into theatres utilizes the same underlying product and target consumers, but the similarities stop there; the differences of marketing a live event in theatres versus manufacturing a consumer product required different manufacturing, delivery, and marketing and with it a different management infrastructure.

12

Three studios joined together to form United International Pictures, better known in the industry by its acronym UIP. Headquartered in London, UIP was historically a joint venture among Paramount Pictures, Universal Pictures, and MGM (MGM later dropped out, but the volume of titles remained high as DreamWorks titles were put through the venture). The three parties shared common overhead in the categories described above: general management, finance, marketing, sales, and legal. Additional efficiencies were gained by sharing office space and general sales and administrative budget cost lines.

What was not shared is perhaps more interesting—the parties shared costs, but did not share revenues. A cost-sharing joint venture is a peculiar instrument of fierce competitors in the film community. Natural adversaries came together for two common goals: protection of intellectual property and the need to establish sales and marketing beachheads around the globe for as little overhead as possible. Both goals could be completely fulfilled without sharing revenues on a per product or aggregate basis; perhaps more important, the structure of the business likely would not have permitted the sharing of revenues even if this was a common goal. Because each film has many other parties tied to it, with complicated equity, rights, and financial participation structures, it is unlikely that all the parties that would need to approve the sharing of such revenues would ultimately agree to do so.

Why, for example, would Ron Howard, Imagine Films, and Universal all agree to share revenues on its film *Apollo 13* with Paramount or MGM? Similarly, why would Paramount Pictures and Tom Cruise want to share revenues on *Mission Impossible* with Universal or MGM? The simple answer is they would not and they do not. Every one of these parties, however, has a vested interest in the films released under a structure that (1) minimizes costs and therefore returns the greatest cash flow, (2) protects the underlying intellectual property and minimizes forces such as piracy that undermine the ability to sell the property and generate cash, and (3) maximizes the sales opportunities.

Once this formula is established, it is relatively easy to replicate for other distribution channels. UIP, for example, spun off a separate division for pay television (UIP Pay TV), a market which exploded in the early 1990s. The same theatrical partners joined forces to lower overhead and distribute product into established and emerging pay TV markets worldwide.

Additionally, two of these partners, Paramount and Universal, teamed up for videocassette distribution and formed CIC Video

13

(where I once worked, based in UIP House in London). CIC, similar to UIP and UIP Pay TV, set up branch operations throughout the world headquartered in the UK. Table 1.1 is a representative chart of countries served by direct subsidiary offices:

Table 1.1 Countries Served by Direct Subsidiary Offices/Territory

Australia	Malaysia
Brazil	Mexico
Denmark	New Zealand
France	Norway
Germany	South Africa
Holland/The Netherlands	South Korea
Hong Kong	Spain
Italy	Sweden
Japan	United Kingdom

In addition to direct offices, the venture would service licensees in countless other territories. These are examples of territories typically managed by studios as licensee markets: Argentina, Chile, Colombia, Czech Republic, Ecuador, Finland, Greece, Hungary, Iceland, Indonesia, Israel, Philippines, Poland, Portugal, Singapore, Taiwan, Thailand, Turkey, Uruguay, and Venezuela. (Note: This is not an exhaustive list.) Whether it makes sense to operate a subsidiary office or even to license product into a territory at all depends on factors including market maturity, economic conditions, size of the market, and the status of piracy/intellectual property enforcement. Many of the largest developing markets, which historically have been licensee territories throughout most of the span of the era of joint ventures, including Russia, China, and India, are being transitioned by studios into direct operations. The most noteworthy currently is Russia, where the economic growth propelled the theatrical market from insignificant to among the top 10 worldwide markets in just a few years.

UIP and CIC, although among the longest lasting and most prominent joint ventures (UIP was formed in 1981), are simply examples and many other companies similarly joined forces in distribution (e.g., CBS and Fox formed CBS/FOX, partnering to distribute product on videocassette worldwide).

Demise of Historic Joint Ventures

None of UIP, CIC, UIP Pay TV, or CBS/FOX Video exist today in their grand joint venture forms. First, UIP Pay TV was disbanded in the mid 1990s, then the video venture CIC was largely shuttered by 2000, and finally UIP's theatrical breakup was announced in 2005 and implemented in 2006 (though the partners still distribute via the venture in limited territories). Why did this happen?

The answer is rooted in part in economics and part in ego. The economic justification in several instances was less compelling than when the ventures were convenient cost-sharing vehicles enabling market entry and boosting clout with product supply. In the case of pay television, for example, the overhead necessary to run an organization was nominal when compared to a theatrical or video division. Most countries only had one or two major pay TV broadcasters; accordingly, the client base worldwide was well under 50 and the number of significant clients was under 20.

This lower overhead base coupled with growing pay TV revenues made the decision relatively easy. Additionally, given the limited stations/competition, and the desire to own part of the broadcasting base, the studios started opportunistically launching joint or wholly owned local pay TV networks. Over time, services such as Showtime in Australia or LAP TV in Latin America, both of which are owned by a consortium of studios, became a common business model. Fox was among the most aggressive studios, replicating its successful SKY model in the UK and owning or acquiring significant equity stakes in the largest number of pay TV services worldwide. The Fox family of global pay networks grew to include the following major services:

15

- BSkyB — UK
- Star — Asia (including Southeast Asia, India, Mideast, China/ Hong Kong)
- Sky Italia — Italy
- LAP TV — partner interest in Latin American service
- Showtime — Australia, partner interest in Australian service

The logic behind the breakups of CIC and UIP are a bit more complicated, and are seemingly grounded as much in politics as economics. In both instances the companies called on thousands of clients and the range of titles from multiple studios virtually ensured the entity of some of the strongest and most consistent product flow in the industry — a fact that is critical in a week in, week out business. A video retailer is more likely to accept better terms and take more units from one of its best suppliers, knowing that a blockbuster it is likely to want will always be just around the corner. This strength of product flow, however, also turned out to be a problem with local competition authorities.

UIP was forced to defend anti-competitive practices allegations for years, and formally opposed an investigation by the European Union Commission (Competition Authority) in Brussels that threatened sanctions and even the breakup of the venture. Some argue that the EU Commission's claims were politically bolstered by member states with protectionist legislation and quotas for locally produced product. In the end, UIP was successful in its defense, but the company was always a political target and forced to be on guard. While CIC was not similarly subject to an EU Commission inquiry, as a sister company it was always conscious of the issues.

In addition to theoretical arguments regarding anti-competitive behavior given market leverage, these types of joint ventures were always in the spotlight for specific claims. One of the most active watchdogs has been the competition authority in Spain. In 2006 the studios were fined by the Spanish authorities on a theatrical claim. *Variety* reported: "In the biggest face-off in recent years between Hollywood and Spanish institutions, Spain's anti-trust authorities have slammed a Euros 12 million ($15.3 million) fine on the sub-branches of Hollywood's major studios in Spain for cartel price fixing and anti-competitive co-ordination of other commercial policies."[3] Cases like this only make operators of a joint venture among studios all that more paranoid.

Competition concerns aside, these ventures always had the maverick studio boss looming over them, wary that their film was somehow disadvantaged by treatment of a competitive partner's title. The defense to this type of attack is that there will always be a competitive film, and better it be in the family so the headquarters can work to maximize all product; at least in a venture it is theoretically easier to schedule releases and allocate resources so that one studio's product is not directly against another partner's product (although, in practice, pursuant to antitrust/competition rules studios cannot share release dates). Ultimately, no matter what argument is made the concern comes down to focus: every studio wants its big title pushed at the expense of everything else, and this is hard (at least by perception) to achieve in a joint venture. As the markets matured, and the international theatrical and video markets continued to grow as a percentage of worldwide revenues, many studio heads wanted unfettered control and dedication.

Many have argued that the breakup of these ventures simply for dedication and control is economic folly. These joint ventures had

16

been releasing major studio hits for decades without discriminating one over the other. In fact, they could not discriminate for the partners were always wary of this and any significant diverting of focus or resources to one partner versus another would not be tolerated. Moreover, focus/dedication would have to yield a return that recovered 100% of the overhead now borne by the studio that had been allocated to its partner(s) previously. In a 50/50 joint venture that means recouping an equivalent of 100% more than it needed to previously (e.g., if $20M in total overhead, the studio now needed to recoup the full $20M rather than only $10M), and in a partnership with 3 parties it was even worse. These are pure bottom line sums, for direct picture costs were already allocated by title. It is for this reason that politics comes into the equation. Clearly not all product will have an uplift to cover the additional overhead costs, but by the same measure never again will an executive of Studio X be fearful that he left money on the table for a major release because resources were diverted to a competitor's film.

Branding and Scale Needs; Online Giving Rise to New Era of Joint Ventures?

Perhaps the Internet and new digital delivery systems are fostering a new era of joint ventures. Today global reach need not be achieved in an iterative fashion by rolling out international subsidiaries; rather, given unprecedented online adoption rates (e.g., YouTube, Facebook), companies are competing in a kind of virtual land grab and teaming up for services that offer instant scale.

As discussed in Chapter 7, NBC/Universal and Fox partnered in 2008 to launch Hulu; by combining the breadth of programming from these two networks/studios, the on-demand service was able to offer diversified, premium content on a scale to support a new distribution platform. (Note: The joint venture expanded in 2009 when ABC became a third partner.) Similarly looking to innovate within the on-demand space, Paramount, MGM, and Lionsgate in 2008 formed the joint venture Studio 3 Networks, branding its distribution service "epix." Set to launch in Q4 2009, epix bills itself as a "next-generation premium entertainment brand, video on demand and Internet service" leveraging diversified content from its partners and providing multi-platform access to satisfy the new consumer who insists on viewing content anywhere, anytime.[4] Both of these services followed the major studios' initial foray into the online space, where MovieLink and CinemaNow were launched as joint ventures to download films, but for a variety of reasons never achieved hoped-for adoption levels (see Chapter 7).

Studios as Defined by Range of Product

Although I will continue to argue that the distribution capacity and capability of a studio in fact defines a studio, this is not the popular starting point. Most look at a studio as a "super producer," with the financial muscle to create a large range of product. Given consolidation of most TV networks into vertically integrated groups, this range of product is further diversified by primary outlet (e.g., made for film, TV, online). Although I may refer in some of the examples below to only one category, such as film, the premise often holds across media types, which accentuates the distribution diversity under the broader media groups.

Quantity

It is instructive to compare a studio to an independent on two basic grounds: quantity of product and average product budget. On these two statistics alone, it would be easy to segment studios. From a pure quantity standpoint, studios have the greatest volume of product. MPAA member companies collectively tend to release in the range of 200 new feature films per year, and while the total number of independent films released is roughly double that number (~400/year in each of 2006 and 2007 for a total of roughly 600 films/year released in the United States), the independent releases tend to be on a much smaller scale and capture only a sliver of the total box office receipts (even if, as of late, they are capturing more of the awards glory). (Note: A good example of a top independent, often releasing pictures gaining recognition at film festivals, is Samuel Goldwyn Films.)

Viewed from the standpoint of an independent producer, which companies tend to be dedicated to the output of individuals (e.g., a producer or director), even the largest and longest tenured independents are limited to the number of films their key players can handle in a given period. New Regency, headed by Arnon Milchan, and Imagine, led by Brian Grazer and Ron Howard, are two of the largest and most consistently producing independents over the last several years. These two companies, respectively, have distribution output deals with Fox and Universal. Imagine, which released *Changeling* and *Frost/Nixon* in 2008, and *Angels and Demons* in 2009 (its follow-up to the 2007 *The Da Vinci Code*), only released one film, *American*

Gangster, in 2007. New Regency, which released a staggering eight pictures in 2008, including *Marley & Me, Meet Dave, Jumper,* and *What Happens in Vegas,* released less than half that quantity (three films) in 2007.

The point regarding quantity becomes self-evident and simple— only a larger organization that aggregates talent can produce on this larger scale. By corollary, to aggregate talent (e.g., producers and directors) the same organization needs to defer to talent on many issues, including the physical production of films. Coming full circle, the consequence of this aggregation is the resulting scale to take on different risks, including maintaining distribution overhead.

Range of Labels and Relationships
Range of Labels
One simple way to boost output is to create a number of film divisions. Almost all of the studios have availed themselves of this strategy, which segments risks into mini-brands and labels that usually have very specific parameters. These parameters are often defined by budget limit, but can also be differentiated by type of content. Fox, for example, created Fox Searchlight, which specializes in lower budget fare, and similarly Universal created Focus; these are examples of smaller labels that take advantage of part of the larger studio infrastructure, but otherwise are tasked with a certain quantity output at lower budget ranges to diversify the studio's overall portfolio.

19

Divisions and smaller labels are not strictly limited, though, to lower budget films. Disney, for example, diversified into (1) Walt Disney Pictures, which is generally limited to family and animated fare; (2) Touchstone, which is generally a releasing-only arm; (3) Hollywood Pictures; and (4) Miramax (when run by the Weinsteins, was a large, internally diversified studio releasing a comparable number of pictures in a year to the balance of the sister Disney labels).

Table 1.2 is a chart of some of the specialty labels under studio umbrellas and examples of the pictures made and/or released. (Note: Given the glut of films in the market, studios have started to re-trench and absorb their smaller or specialty labels into larger divisions with Warners and Paramount, respectively, closing Warner Independent and Paramount Vantage in 2008.)[5]

Taking a snapshot from a couple of years ago at the height of specialty labels, with the exception of Paramount (where DreamWorks' pictures—prior to its separation and move to Disney—accounted

Table 1.2 Specialty Labels Under Studio Umbrellas

Studio	Labels	Example of Films in Sub-Label
Sony	Columbia	
	Revolution	
	Screen Gems	
	Sony Classics	*Friends with Money*
	Tristar	
Fox	20th Century Fox	
	Fox 2000	
	Fox Searchlight	*Little Miss Sunshine, The Last King of Scotland*
	Fox Atomic	
	Fox Walden*	*Journey to the Center of the Earth*
Disney	Walt Disney Pictures	All Pixar releases (e.g., *Finding Nemo*)
	Touchstone	
	Miramax	*The Queen*
	Hollywood Pictures	
Warners	Warner Bros.	
	New Line	*Lord of the Rings Trilogy*
	Warner Independent	*March of the Penguins, Good Night and Good Luck*
Paramount	Paramount	
	DreamWorks	
	MTV/Nickelodeon	
	Paramount Vantage	*Babel, An Inconvenient Truth*
Universal	Universal	
	Focus Features	*Brokeback Mountain*
	Rogue	

*Walden was originally with Disney, where it produced *The Chronicles of Narnia*

for a substantial percentage of the studio's overall box office), the principal arm rather than the specialty labels accounted for greater than two-thirds of the studios' overall domestic box office. Fox was a typical example. Table 1.3 is a breakdown of its total $1.56 billion 2006 domestic box office.[6]

Range of Relationships
In addition to subsidiary film divisions that specialize in certain genres or budget ranges or simply add volume, studios increase output

Table 1.3 Breakdown of Fox Domestic Box Office

Label/Releasing Arm	Division BO	% of Total Studio BO
20th Century Fox	1.1 Billion	72
Fox 2000	$272 M	17
Fox Searchlight	$162 M	10
Fox Atomic	$7 M	1

via "housekeeping" deals with star producers and directors. Studios will create what are referred to as "first look" deals where they pay the overhead of certain companies including funding offices (e.g., on the studio lot) in return for a first option on financing and distributing a pitched property. (See the online supplemental material for a discussion of first look deals and puts.)

Range of Budgets

Studios produce and finance projects within a wide range of budgets, with the distribution pattern creating a bell-type curve bounded by very low and very high budgets at the extremes; the average in this case represents the majority of output, expensive product in any other industry, but in studio terms mid-range risk. An example of a high budget label is Paramount's former relationship with DreamWorks, where DreamWorks had the freedom to independently greenlight movies with budgets up to $85 million, and reportedly up to $100 million if Steven Spielberg was directing.[7]

Low Budget It is possible to produce a film for under $1M, as the proliferation of film festivals demonstrates. Technology has also brought the cost of filmmaking down making it accessible to a wider range of filmmakers. Easy access to digital tools and software for editing are revolutionizing the business. Studios have the choice of commissioning lower budget films directly, or as discussed above, creating specialty labels focusing on this fare. Although there is no per se ceiling for low budget, the category implies a budget of under $10M, and generally refers to under $5M or $7M.

Under the Radar What is truly under the radar is a moving target. With the cost of production escalating, films under $30M and especially under $20M have a different risk profile and can be categorized as so-called "under the radar." It may often be easier to jumpstart a film in this range, and some studios will allow stars to dabble in this category for a project perceived as more risky (e.g., out of character). I do not mean to imply that this is a trivial sum, or that making a project in this range is easy. Rather, executives tacitly acknowledge that in the budget hierarchy there is a category between low and high budget that sometimes receives less scrutiny.

High Budget   High budget is now a misnomer, for a typical budget is in fact high and people search for terms that differentiate the extremes, such as when a film costs more than $100M. Accordingly, it is in this very wide range of somewhere above the then-current perceived cutoff for a higher level of scrutiny or approval matrix to authorize (so called under the radar where the project is in a lower risk category) and $100M that most films today fall. According to MPAA statistics, the average cost of a major MPAA member studio movie in 2007 was $70.8M.[8]

Franchise or Tentpole Budget   There is no formal range for this term of art, but when someone mentions "tentpole" the budget is invariably >$100M, sometimes > $200M, and the studio is making an exception for a picture that it believes can become (or extend) a franchise. Moreover, a tentpole picture has the goal of lifting the whole studio's fortunes, from specific economic return to driving packages of multiple films to intangible benefits. These are big bet and often defining films, properties that are targeted for franchise or award purposes. Modern day epics fall into this range with *Titanic* leading the way. In other cases films with a perceived "can't-fail" audience may justify an extraordinary budget, such as franchise sequels: Warner Brothers with Harry Potter, Sony with Spiderman, and Disney with Pirates of the Caribbean. *Variety*, discussing the extraordinary number of big budget tentpole sequels in the summer of 2007, noted that "five key tentpoles have an aggregate budget of $1.3 billion," and continued: "Production costs continue to climb precipitously at the tentpole end, with *Spider-Man3*, Pirates 3 (*Pirates of the Caribbean: At Worlds' End*), and *Evan Almighty* redefining the outer limits of spending. Last year's discussion of how far past $200 million *Superman Returns* may have gone seems quaint by comparison."[9] (Note: Other major sequels for the summer of 2007 included Shrek3 (*Shrek the Third*), Fantastic 4 2 (*Rise of the Silver Surfer*), Die Hard 4 (*Live Free or Die Hard*), Harry Potter 5 (*Harry Potter and the Order of the Phoenix*), Bourne 3 (the *Bourne Ultimatum*) and *Rush Hour 3*.)

This category of if-we-make-it-they-will-come blockbusters are drivers for the studios. There is frequently guaranteed interest and PR, cross-promotion opportunities galore, sequel and franchise potential, pre-sold games and merchandise, etc. Additionally, as discussed in other chapters, these tentpole pictures stake out certain prime weekends and holiday periods (Memorial Day, Christmas, Thanksgiving) for release and virtually guarantee the sale of other pictures in TV packages of films.

Why there is this range of budgets is again economically driven. All films can succeed or fail beyond rational expectations. Higher budget films cost more because "insurance" factors are baked in: a star, a branded property, groundbreaking or spectacular special effects, and action sequences are all assumed to drive people to the theater (although, as discussed in Chapter 3, the highly variable nature of box office success is generally not tempered by such factors). With the extra costs come extra risks, as well as the need to share the upside with the stars/people/properties that are making it expensive in the first place. Accordingly, every studio dreams of the film that will cost less and break through — perhaps less glitzy, but driving more profits to the bottom line. Every studio would take ten *My Big Fat Greek Weddings* or *Slumdog Millionaires* over an expensive action hero film. (In fact, the film *Last Action Hero* starring Arnold Schwarzenegger was Sony/Columbia's big bet in 1993, but significantly underperformed at the box office with a domestic take of $50M against a reputed budget of close to $90M, as famously chronicled in the book *Hit & Run* in the chapter "How They Built the Bomb.")[10]

The Internet Wrinkle The Internet is allowing people to experiment with production at costs that are in cases so low that it is redefining what low budget means. It is hard to compare most online production to other media because the current format generally is short-form. As people continue to experiment, whether producing content intended only for Web viewing or hoping to utilize the medium for lower cost pilots that can then migrate to TV, it will be interesting to see whether budgets rise to match quality expectations of other media or whether the Internet will sustain a different cost structure linked to new and evolving online content categories (see Chapter 3).

Pipeline and Portfolio
Range of Genre and Demographic
While economics drive a portfolio strategy in terms of budget range, marketing drives the product mix in terms of sales. Accordingly,

23

product targeted at different genres is produced to satisfy a variety of consumer appetites:

- Action
- Romance
- Comedy
- Thriller
- Drama
- Historical or reality based stories
- Kids and family
- Musical
- Adult entertainment

These categories may seem obvious because they have become so ingrained. Simply check out the shelf headings at your local video store or read film critics reviews—descriptions are peppered with Dewey decimal system type verbiage to categorize films. If the film is not easy to peg, then use a crossover term such as chick flick, or combine phrases such as "action thriller" or "romantic comedy." Retailers' creative labeling of shelves/sections and endless categories for awards further add to the lexicon of segmentation.

At some level, the categories become self-fulfilling, and demand is generated to fill the niche pipeline. How many romantic comedies do we have? If the studio cannot supply the genre, it starts to become more of a niche player, which can start to affect perceptions, relationships, and ultimately valuations. Categories come into and out of vogue (e.g., musicals), and about the only category where it has always been accepted to opt out is adult entertainment.

Range of Type/Style

If a portfolio strategy is not complicated enough, then draw a matrix combining different types of budget, genres, and relationships, and then layer on styles and types. Films distributed today include live action movies, traditional animation, computer graphics generated, etc.

These categories are more technical or process driven, but serve to create yet another level of specialization or segmentation. For a studio, it is not enough to stop at the "kids market." Conscious decisions need to be made about a portfolio within this limited category—how many titles, what budget range, how many animated vs. live action, is there a range of budgets within the animation category, etc.

Other Markets — Video, Online, etc.

This proliferation of product cutting across every possible style and range has served to create outlets and demand for product beyond what is released in theatres or produced for TV. Demand in the children's market, linked to the growth of home viewing starting with videocassettes, spawned the "made for video" business. At a video store, it is nearly impossible to discern whether sequels or spinoffs from films and name brands (*Aladdin 2, The Scorpion King 2, Lion King 1.5, American Pie 4*) were made for the movie or video market. (Note: The growth of this segment, and specific economics, are discussed in more detail in Chapter 5.)

Finally, online is expanding the production palate with producers creating original product that ranges from features to shorts. In theory, distributing original Internet content should fall outside the studio system, for any producer with a Web site can stream content to anyone; hence, with the Internet enabling independence why pay, or team, with a studio? The reason is that accompanying the near zero barrier to entry with Internet distribution (bandwidth/site infrastructure is still needed) is the challenge of infinite competition and clutter. Accordingly, not only are networks and studios beginning to produce their own content, but they will start to affiliate with independents that need marketing assistance (and/or financing, as costs increase with talent inevitably demanding more in relation to growing revenues, or higher quality thresholds are sought). In fact, associating with a brand is one of the easiest ways to rise above clutter and attract viewers, and there is every reason to expect that over time studios/networks will add a portfolio of Internet originals complementing the diversity found today in traditional media platforms.

25

Brand Creation versus Brand Extension

Finally, in terms of looking at the creation of product to fill the studio pipeline one needs to look at the desire to find a branded property. Everyone is looking for that "sure thing," and a property with built-in recognition and an assumed built-in audience theoretically lowers risk and gives marketing a jump start.

Aside from the new idea, there are four treasure troves of ideas that serve as the lifeblood of Hollywood: the real world, books and comics, sequels, and spin-offs. I will only mention the real world in passing, given the obvious nature of creating dramas either set in historical settings or adaptations of real-life events (e.g., *Saving Private Ryan, The Pianist, Erin Brockovich, The Queen*). However, it is worth noting that the explosion of user-generated content on the Internet is defining an entirely new source of material that producers are trying to exploit as well as migrate to other media.

Books and comics are the largest source of branded fare. In fact, try to find a bestseller with a strong lead character today that is not being adapted for the screen. The following list is a very small sampling:

Book	Film
Jurassic Park	*Jurassic Park*
Harry Potter	Harry Potter movies
Tom Clancy books	*The Hunt for Red October*
John Grisham books	*Pelican Brief, The Firm*
Jane Austen novels	*Pride and Prejudice*
The Da Vinci Code	*The Da Vinci Code*
Tolkien Series	Lord of the Rings movies

Comic	Film
Batman	Batman series of films
Spiderman	*Spiderman 1, 2, 3*
X-Men	*X-Men, X2, X3, Origins: Wolverine*
Superman	Superman series of films

Brand Extension: Sequels

Sequels are a relatively new phenomenon looking over the last 100 years of film in that these rights, while reserved by the studios, were not considered very valuable until the success of *Jaws* and *Star Wars* in the 1970s proved otherwise. George Lucas recognized the inherent value of sequels with *Star Wars*, and by retaining sequel and related rights to the original property built the most lucrative franchise in movie history. It only takes someone else making a billion dollars before others catch on, and today rights in sequels and spin-offs are cherished and fiercely negotiated for upfront.

A successful film can become a brand overnight, and since the 1980s, and especially the 1990s, the mantra has been once a movie reaches a certain box office level executives immediately start thinking about making a sequel. The following are some prominent examples:

Original Film	Sequel(s)
Jaws	*Jaws 2, 3....*
Rocky	*Rocky II, III...Rocky Balboa*
Star Wars	*The Empire Strikes Back* (V), *Return of the Jedi* (VI); Episodes I, II, III
Raiders of the Lost Ark	*Indiana Jones and the Temple of Doom, Indiana Jones and the Last Crusade, Indiana Jones and the Kingdom of the Crystal Skull*
Jurassic Park	*Jurassic Park: The Lost World,* and *Jurassic Park III*
Terminator	*Terminator 2, 3, Terminator Salvation*
The Mummy	*The Mummy Returns, The Mummy: Tomb of the Dragon Emperor*
Home Alone	*Home Alone 2, 3, 4*
The Matrix	*The Matrix Reloaded* and *The Matrix Revolutions*
Pirates of the Caribbean: The Curse of the Black Pearl	*Dead Man's Chest, At World's End*
Spider-Man	*Spider-Man 2* and *3*
Die Hard	*Die Hard 2, Die Hard with a Vengeance, Live Free or Die Hard*
Harry Potter series	*Harry Potter 2, 3, 4...*

Sequels have become such a successful formula — of course they are not a guarantee, witness *Babe 2 Pig in the City* — that they have given birth to "prequels" and simultaneously produced sequels. Sequels used to be thought about in terms of what happens next: do they live, do they live happily ever after, what's the next adventure...? Because movies are fantasy based and have no boundaries, prequels are now becoming popular. In these movies the audience learns how a character grew up — often without the famous actors from the original films even appearing. The recent *Star Wars* prequels (*The Phantom Menace, Attack of the Clones,* and *Revenge of the Sith*) serve as the most striking examples, absent stars such as Harrison Ford, Mark Hamill, and Carrie Fisher.

Additionally, with expensive films and effects, producers have started making more than one film in a series simultaneously to amortize costs. *The Matrix Reloaded* and *The Matrix Revolutions*, for example, were made together and were released six months apart in 2003 in the summer and at Christmas. *The Lord of the Rings* trilogy was greenlit by New Line Cinema to be made as a production bundle, and Disney committed to making both Pirates of the

Caribbean 2 and 3 at the same time, thus being able to keep the cast and crew together (and presumably achieving certain production efficiencies).

Brand Extension: Spin-Offs

The classic spin-off is when a character from one film/property is used to launch an ancillary franchise. In television, one of the best examples is *Frasier*. The Frasier character, played by Kelsey Grammer, appeared in *Cheers*, and when *Cheers* wound down the network launched *Frasier* as a new series. As most TV watchers know, Frasier was a pompous psychiatrist who was among the cast of support characters who regularly hung out at the Boston-based bar on the earlier *Cheers*. In the new show, the premise was that he has moved home to Seattle and practices psychiatry via hosting a local radio call-in show. The difference between a sequel and a spin-off should be quite clear. A sequel to *Cheers* would be, for example, a *Cheers* movie or *Cheers* reunion show where we saw what happened down the road.

An example of a movie spin-off would be *The Scorpion King*. *The Scorpion King* stars the villain from *The Mummy*, but does not continue with the other main characters nor does it continue the quest or love interests pursued by the hero/main character in *The Mummy* or *The Mummy Returns* played by Brendan Fraser. In fact, the distinction between *The Mummy Returns* versus *The Scorpion King* paints a good distinction between a sequel (the former) and a spin-off (the latter). (Note: Not having worked on these, it is possible that in the specific contracts for these films that they were not treated this way and were negotiated differently.)

Brand Extension: Remakes

A remake provides another category of brand extension, albeit one that is used less frequently than a sequel or spin-off. An example of a remake is *Sabrina*, where a classic film is remade with new lead actors and actresses. The original film, starring Audrey Hepburn, Humphrey Bogart, and William Holden, was remade using the same lead characters, same principal story line, and same general locations, but the former cast is now updated with Julia Ormond, Harrison Ford, and Greg Kinnear.

Remakes are less common for a simple reason: it is natural for audiences to compare the remake with the original, and if the original is strong enough that it is worthy of remaking then the new film better be strong enough to stand up to the original. Still, the formula of starting with a classic and substituting current stars seems a formula

28

and risk often worth taking. Again, this is a classic example of brand extension with another variation on risk analysis.

Crossover to Other Markets: Sequels and Spin-Offs

Finally, there is the catchall crossover category where properties migrate across media.

- Films spawn TV shows (e.g., *MASH*, *My Big Fat Greek Life*, *The Young Indiana Jones Chronicles*)
- TV series spawn films (e.g., *Star Trek*, *Miami Vice*, *The Flintstones*)
- Games spawn films (e.g., *Lara Croft — Tomb Raider*)

Sometimes a property becomes so successful and spawns so many permutations that it is nearly impossible to distinguish what came from what. The original *Star Trek* series certainly led to the success of spin-off series such as *Star Trek: The Next Generation*, but with further spin-offs and sequel movies from both the original series and spin-off series the boundaries become blurred (and becoming more so all the time, with a prequel to the *Star Trek* series, simply titled *Star Trek*, released theatrically in summer 2009). Maybe this is like the show's mantra of "to go where no one has gone before" because the cumulative weight of episodes and movies has led to a Star Trek franchise that is bigger than the sum of its parts and almost unique in the business. It is, in fact, an example of brand extension where the brand has outgrown its origin and taken on a life of its own. (It certainly seemed that way when I attended a Royal Premiere in London of a new Star Trek film starring the cast of the TV series *Star Trek: The Next Generation*, and an actress playing an alien doctor sat next to Prince Charles during the playing of "God Save the Queen." If this is not an example of the international reach of brand extension then I don't know what is.)

29

Windows and Film Ultimates: Life Cycle Management of Intellectual Property Assets

While the following discussion focuses on film, most original linear media has now found additional sales windows outside of its launch platform. TV shows are now released on video, downloaded, seen on cable, watched in syndication, and more recently accessed online. The ability to adapt linear video content to multiple viewing platforms — at different times and for differentiated prices — is the essence of the

Ulin's Rule continuum, which allows distributors to maximize the lifetime value of a single piece of intellectual property. A property such as *Star Wars* or Harry Potter can generate revenues in the billions of dollars over time, taking advantage of multiple consumption opportunities that at once expand access to those who did not view the production initially and entice those who did watch to consume the show/film again and again. This unique sales cycle is the envy of games producers, who have still not innovated material downstream sales platforms, as well as the challenge of the day for how best to utilize the Web. The following overview focuses on film, but highlights the key points of consumption that all media needs either to leverage, or compete with, depending on where one sits in the chain.

Film: Primary Distribution Windows

It is common to tie up the rights to a movie for five or more years shortly after it has been released in theatres, and in cases before the movie is even released. In some cases, movie rights may be committed for more than ten years. Carving out exclusive shorter periods of exploitation ("windows") during these several years creates the time-sensitive individual business segments that form the continuum of film distribution.

Typically, a film will be launched with a bang in theaters, with the distributor investing heavily in marketing; the initial theatrical release engine then fuels downstream markets and revenues for years to come. After theatrical release, the film will be exclusively licensed for broadcast, viewing, or sale in a specified limited market for a defined length of time. The following are the primary windows and rights through which films have historically been distributed:

- Theatrical
- Video and DVD
- Pay television
- Free television
- Hotel/motel
- Airline
- PPV/VOD
- Non-theatrical
- Cable and syndication

The above are the main distribution outlets, and do not represent the full reach of exploitation of the rights in a film. For example, rights to create video games and merchandising are not listed above, as they are labeled ancillary exploitations (See Chapter 8).

Film Revenue Cycle

The following depicts the film revenue cycle:

Theatrical → Hotel PPV → Home Video →
Residential VOD → Pay TV → Free TV

The length of each of these windows and whether they are exclusive or have a period of non-exclusive overlap with other rights is relatively standard, but far from fixed. With the advent of new technologies and platforms there have been more window shifts in the last 5 years than probably in the prior 25 (see below, including sections Shifting Windows and New and Changing Windows, regarding recent shifts and experiments in window patterns). Because intellectual property rights are, in theory, infinitely divisible, the crux of the economics is what layering will maximize the ultimate return on the property. Everyone in a segment is fearful of a different right cannibalizing its space, and accordingly the language of windows and distribution is all about holdbacks, exclusivity, and the term to exploit the rights. As a general rule, distribution is all about maximizing discrete periods of exclusivity. This is the heart of the clash with Internet opportunities, for the greatest successes of the Web tend to be tied to free and ubiquitous access.

The succeeding chapters will discuss the relevant windows in all of these categories, and the economic influences that have caused the windows to evolve into their jigsaw places in the pattern. As a brief overview here, the windows above can be summarized as follows (see also Figure 1.4):

31

Theatrical: 1–3 months, with a holdback of 6 months to home video.

Hotel VOD/PPV: Short window, 2–3 months, prior to home video.

Home Video: Continuous window, with holdback of 6 months before pay TV and shorter holdback (1+ months) before residential VOD.

Residential VOD: Historically 3+ months post video, but given online pressures now accelerating and often simultaneous with or 30 days post video.

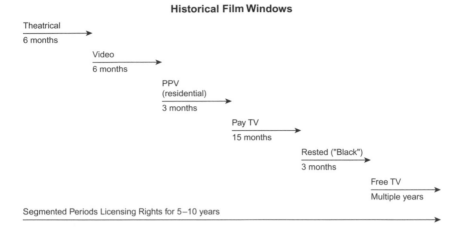

Historical Film Windows

Theatrical
6 months

Video
6 months

PPV
(residential)
3 months

Pay TV
15 months

Rested ("Black")
3 months

Free TV
Multiple years

Segmented Periods Licensing Rights for 5–10 years

Figure 1.4

> Pay TV: 1–1.5 years, sometimes with multiple windows, between video and free TV, with an 18-month holdback to free TV. Often includes a "black" period following the pay window where the property cannot be exploited and is "rested."
>
> Free TV: Multiple year window, with length, holdbacks, and carve-outs for secondary pay windows deal dependent, and also dependent on the type of Free TV outlet (e.g., network vs. cable vs. syndication).

International Variations

In the United States, and in most countries, windows are negotiated between parties and freely movable — no laws could stop a producer from releasing a movie on DVD on the same date as its theatrical release. In fact, 2929 Productions has done just this and espouses this release strategy (see below). However, a few countries regulate windows to create order and to protect the local film industry.

France is the best known example, and the windows for video, pay and free TV exploitation relative to theatrical release are all set by law: pay TV may not show a picture prior to 18 months following its theatrical release in the territory, a movie may not be released on DVD prior to 6 months following the local theatrical release, and there is a three-year holdback from theatrical to free TV. Accordingly, while an American studio that releases a hit movie in the middle of the summer, such as *Pirates of the Caribbean* by Disney over July 4th, will make sure the DVD comes out for the fourth quarter holiday gift giving period domestically, the studio cannot take advantage of the Christmas traffic in France.

Life Cycle and Ultimates

Assuming one entity controls all the distribution rights and has autonomy to set the property's exploitation, then the goal will be life cycle management to maximize the return on the property through its various windows. This is obviously harder than it sounds; in big corporations divisions often run autonomously and even compete with each other. Moreover, divisions and individuals who are compensated by quarterly or annual performance may be unwilling to look at the big picture if that means sacrificing their revenue for the sake of another division — especially if a current revenue stream is secure, and other revenue streams are either speculative or still subject to performance. Would you jeopardize a bonus or meeting your department's financial goals to preserve a downstream upside for which neither you nor your department would directly financially benefit?

Accordingly, senior management needs to set priorities and set boundaries and rules governing the exploitation of windows. From a macro and accounting perspective, companies and owners of intellectual property assets need to project the revenue over this life cycle; the sum total amount expected through all relevant windows over a defined period (which period could be a planning cycle internally, or may be a specific defined length of time as required by accounting standards) is called the film's ultimate and, as discussed in the online supplemental material to Chapter 10, is required for tax purposes in amortizing film costs and expenses.

Shifting Windows

Collapsed Windows and Protecting Windows

2929 Entertainment, the maverick entertainment company founded and run by billionaires Mark Cuban and Todd Wagner (formerly having started Broadcast.com and selling it to Yahoo!), has created a vertically integrated chain combining production financing (via its Magnolia Pictures), theatrical exhibition (by its Landmark Theatre chain), and TV (via its HD Net movie channel). They have backed various directors/producers such as Steven Soderberg and George Clooney, and have lobbied for "day-and-date" release across multiple distribution platforms, including video and theatrical. 2929 Entertainment's so-called triple bow in movie theaters, cable, and on DVD of Steven Soderberg's *The Bubble* in January 2006 was the first test and proved little: "With grosses of some $72,000 from 32 theatres, most owned by Cuban and Wagner's Landmark Theatres, the results of the much-watched experiment showed that simultaneous release may be better at selling DVDs than movie tickets."[11]

Despite this first trial, Todd Wagner and others have publicly spotlighted the inefficiencies in the market, and in so doing made a number of interesting points. In particular he has questioned: (1) Why would you want to spend marketing money twice, first to launch a movie theatrically and then for video—wouldn't it be more efficient and therefore profitable to combine spending and release a video simultaneously? (2) Why should consumers who may not want to see a movie in theatres, or did not have the time to see it in theatres (as theatrical runs are becoming shorter and shorter), or couldn't afford to take the family to see it in the theatre, have to wait 6 months to see it on video? Wouldn't it be nice to be part of the water cooler conversation while the film is in release and is topical?

Some of these arguments are sacrilegious to various industry segments, not to mention counter to the Ulin's Rule value matrix (especially regarding repeat consumption). Most theatre owners predict the end to their business if they do not have a protected window, and a consumer could on the same day choose to buy a movie on PPV/VOD or rent it on video rather than seeing it in the theatre. The greatest power of windows is the marketing pitch "only available here," a message that is diluted if not fully undermined when exclusivity is lost; moreover, for a distributor initial consumption must expand enough to offset the loss driven by collapsing repeat consumption windows (e.g., DVD), a proposition that is both risky and unproven. Nevertheless, with 2929 Entertainment's strategy, and general flux in historical windows with the advent of new technologies and shifting consumption (e.g., growth of residential and online VOD), an interesting experiment is being played out that at its core challenges the pillars on which the studio system is based.

New and Changing Windows

2929 Entertainment's strategy is not an isolated example: distributors are considering changing windows all the time. In early 2006, for example, Fox announced the introduction of a premium hi-def VOD window just 60 days after a film's theatrical release.[12] At around the same time IFC Entertainment announced "IFC in Theaters" to debut select independent films via Comcast's On Demand service on the same day that the movies were theatrically released in cinemas.[13]

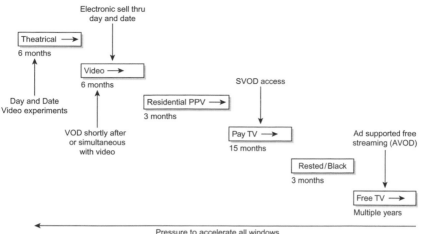

Windows in Flux

Theatrical ⟶
6 months

Electronic sell thru
day and date

Video ⟶
6 months

Day and Date
Video experiments

Residential PPV ⟶
3 months

SVOD access

VOD shortly after
or simultaneous
with video

Pay TV ⟶
15 months

Ad supported free
streaming (AVOD)

Rested/Black
3 months

Free TV ⟶
Multiple years

← Pressure to accelerate all windows

Figure 1.5

A test that extended windowing challenges to the Internet realm
was ClickStar's (a company backed by Intel and actor Morgan
Freeman) attempt to pioneer the downloading of feature films. In
part to combat Internet piracy and avoid illegal downloads of films,
Clickstar announced plans to make its films simultaneously available
for Internet download with theatrical release.[14] Clickstar experiment-
ed with a couple of broadband day-and-date releases, partnering with
AOL, for example, to release *Lonely Hearts* (featuring an ensemble
cast with stars such as John Travolta and James Gandolfini). The
company did not succeed with the dual release strategy, and rumors
existed that theaters would not support the product given the windowing. Whether in fact windowing tussles were the prime causal
factor (as opposed, for example, to the films themselves), the notion
of on-demand Internet premieres, which may have seemed futuristic
just a couple of years ago, is now not only feasible, but potentially
poses one of the greatest threats to movie windows by any technology
recently created. The question is no longer whether this can happen,
but rather what is the appropriate window for Internet access.

As typified by the Clickstar example, quiet boycotts by competitive
chains to Landmark's 2929 Entertainment releases, and cinemas
refusing to book movies when DVD releases are accelerated too close
to the theatrical premiere (as happened with Fox's *Night at the Museum*
when major chains in the UK and Germany boycotted the film in the
face of the planned DVD release in mid-April after its Christmas

35

theatrical launch),[15] changing windows is always a gamble, with the length of an exclusive theatrical run among the most sensitive elements. As highlighted by *Business Week*: "Windows preservation needs to be disciplined," says former Paramount Entertainment Chairman Jonathan L. Dolgen. "The value of the big screen is what starts everything."[16]

What no one questions today, however, is that the increased variety of windows is creating more competition than ever before, and as a corollary leading to the compression of windows, acceleration of revenues (with most films now staying in theaters only a handful of weeks), and greater risk. Moreover, as discussed throughout this book, new technologies and distribution platforms are not only causing window juggling (e.g., on-demand access), but threatening to undermine the entire window system and with it the fundamental economic underpinnings of the business.

Television: Channels Defined by Range and Quantity of Product Plus Reach and Specialization

Distribution is obviously very different in the TV arena, as a network or cable channel is the distribution channel itself rather than a conduit to decentralized points where consumers view a product (i.e., movie theatres). Accordingly, the question "what is a network" has a more tangible answer than what is a "studio" (and further falls more into the regulatory and legal area). Chapter 6 discusses this line in more detail, and for the purposes here I will limit the analysis to the parallel issues such as range and differentiation of product and how segmentation plays out and even defines channels in the TV world.

Defining Networks by Product, Reach, and Range of Budgets

Aside from the technical or legal definitions, networks like studio entities are defined by diversity, quantity, and reach. Marketing, scheduling, and affiliating a common trademark across the breadth of disparate content then help create a wraparound brand, leveraging goodwill to enable cross-promotion and awareness.

By diversity, I mean that programming, while specialized at times, caters to the overall audience and covers a broad spectrum: news, kids, sports, talk shows, dramas, sitcoms, etc. A channel could fulfill legal and FCC bells and whistles for carriage, time devoted to education, and other criteria, but the consumer base would not equate it with a so-called broadcast network without the rhythm of a morning show followed by soaps followed by daytime and kids followed by news followed by primetime followed by late night... that defines the viewing public's day. In essence, networks are defined by their diversity rather than specialization, with specialization limited to style, feel, and demographic targeting.

If this description is accurate, it poses a challenge in translating the network brand to the Internet where the linear rhythm and differentiated programming by time period disappear. In a VOD world the brand becomes more a symbol of quality, the "network seal of approval" a filter from clutter. Even if one views the Web as the great equalizer, removing the power of the gatekeeper for those with time to select content via discovery, there are a lot of people who trust that gatekeeper to deliver programming true to a brand they trust.

In terms of reach, the footprint needs to capture a critical mass of households, which in network terms means national coverage. What is "national," and whether coverage needs to be via terrestrial over the air broadcast rather than via cable or satellite are issues for legislative fodder. Finally, regarding quantity, consumers associate networks with unparalleled numbers of original programs, in essence putting them at the vanguard of entertainment (see Chapter 6 for detailed discussion of network hours, definition of reach, etc.)

The point I am trying to make is that absent the formal definitions, networks and studios are remarkably similar. They stand out against independents or pretenders because they have an indisputable edge in terms of ability to reach viewers and in the quantity and diversity of product that they supply to viewers. Like the studios, the desire for hits and the cost of filling the pipeline rationally leads to diversification of product across budgets, genres, and suppliers. The same issue of brand creation versus brand extension applies, with the same economic forces driving the choices. Also, the desire to tie up talent and secure first looks at the hoped-for next hit shows is the same. Even the portfolio strategy defined by type (e.g., live action vs. animation) is similar in the decision process.

What principally differs is how the genres are defined, how product specialization has uniquely evolved in the TV market, how product specialization and cable have come to drive niche channels, and how product distribution infrastructure is important but not defining in TV (on this last point, the same forces that led to joint ventures internationally in theatrical and video generally did not exist in TV, given the limited points of sale).

Television Genres: Defined by Time Slots

Television is now a 24/7 medium, and programming is primarily driven by ratings. Accordingly, product is developed to cater to the audience that is most likely to be watching during a specific period of the day—a driving force, and constraint, that is wholly absent in defining genres in the film world.

In the left column below I have repeated the genres highlighted for motion pictures, and in the right column I have listed key genres for TV:

Film/Motion Pictures	Television
Action	Morning
Romance	Daytime
Comedy	Soap
Thriller	Primetime
Drama	Kids
Historical or reality-based stories	News
Kids and family	Late night
Musical	Sports
Adult entertainment	Movies

It is actually quite interesting to see side-by-side two industries that are so closely aligned, and the difference in the driving categories for programming. Of course, this is an oversimplification, but the larger point holds true: TV is time based, and each time segment has its own demographics and related ratings targets.

Product Differentiation within Time Slots

Networks' product portfolio strategies therefore deal with setting line-ups by days of the week. A station will rarely, for example, target all drama or all comedy and instead diversify its portfolio by targeted evenings. This is self-evident from simply looking over TV listings, where a viewer will pick out an evening of sitcoms (e.g., NBC's former Thursday night lineup anchored by *Friends*, or current lineup of *30 Rock* and *The Office*) or a pairing of favorite dramas.

Bundling like-type shows also allows a hit show to create a halo effect providing a strong lead-in or lead-out for surrounding series. When a new show following a hit fails to retain a threshold percentage of its lead-in audience then almost inevitably it will be in trouble, sending programmers scurrying to juggle time slots and better hold the audience (see Chapter 6).

Range of Budgets

Ratings and advertising dollars spent are the lifeblood of TV and ultimately determine budgets. As is obvious, space with less demand, and fewer eyeballs, necessitates lower budget content targeted at a smaller, often niche audience; in fact, outside of primetime hours, one of the great challenges of TV is how to fill up the rest of the space. A range of budgets is a natural outgrowth of time segmentation, and the only real issue is how elastic are budgets within already predefined budget ranges. A network may pay millions of dollars a half hour for a primetime show versus another primetime show with a modest budget, but both of these shows will fall within the same high budget primetime category and be viewed independently from budgets for daytime fare.

39

Product Portfolio Strategy: Brand Extension versus Brand Creation

Brand Extension and Brand Creation

The same concept discussed above with respect to film applies to TV, but less frequently, or perhaps less overtly. While it is easy to list a series of books that are translated into movies, the same task is harder in TV. The trend is strong when it comes to classic kids' comics and properties (e.g., Spiderman, Batman, X-men), but far fewer adult series are spawned from books and other media.

Economically, it is not obvious why this is the case; TV could similarly benefit from a large launch bolstered by high pre-awareness of the subject. The reason therefore seems to lie more in the format, as TV given its rigid time periods is inherently more formulaic and less forgiving. A compelling series, with full story arc and punctuated cliffhangers, needs to be told in a repeatable pattern in 22 minutes (for a commercial half hour slot) or approximately 44 minutes (for an hour program).

The quick pace of comedies with strong fanciful hyperbolic characters tends to lend itself to this structure, but generally novels do not. The books that do tend to be translated are those with strong characters in a genre that already works well on TV, such as a detective series. Robert Parker's private detective was successfully brought to TV in the series *Spenser: For Hire* — yet even it seems an exception in the category. Most new TV series, and the vast majority of hits, are truly fresh properties that depend more on the associated creative talent (including the cast) than on an existing brand. Table 1.4 compares some of the top movies versus TV shows from a couple of years ago and the difference is clear:

Table 1.4   Sources of Top TV Shows and Movies

Top Films and Source	Top TV Shows and Source
Pirates of the Caribbean (theme park)	*24* (original)
Harry Potter (book)	*The Closer* (original)
X-Men 3 (comic)	*The Office* (original, TV remake)
The Da Vinci Code (book)	*Survivor* (original)
	American Idol (original format)

40

What serves as fodder for TV are new concepts to drive an old formula. The sitcom with the seemingly mismatched husband and wife, the new reality series, the hospital drama, the disease-of-the-week TV movie, the new cop show, the sexual tension (she/he never meets the right guy/girl) sitcom — these formulas work, and much to the disdain of TV critics that pine for something out of the mold, network TV is much more dependent on mining old formulas than mining brands.

Segmenting Driving Specialized Cable Channels

The ultimate portfolio strategy is not only to segment properties within a network, but have enough critical mass of product to further segment properties into specialty channels. The maturation of the cable market in the 1980s created additional shelf space leading to a proliferation of specialty cable channels in the 1990s. By the year 2000 a market that 25 years before was defined by the big three networks (ABC, CBS, and NBC) plus public television and limited UHF local stations had dedicated channels that few could have imagined (see Table 1.5):

Table 1.5 TV Channel Demographics/Specialties

Demographic/Specialty	Channel
Kids	Nickelodeon
	Noggin
	Cartoon Network
	The Disney Channel
	ABC Family
	PBS Kids Sprout
General sports	ESPN, ESPN2
	Comcast Sports Net
	Fox Sports Net
Golf	The Golf Channel
Weather	The Weather Channel
Women	Lifetime
	Oxygen
Animals and nature	Animal Planet
	Discovery Channel
News and finance	CNN
	CNN FN
	MSNBC
	Fox News Channel
Shopping	
	Home Shopping Network (HSN)
Food	The Food Network
Travel	The Travel Channel
Comedy	Comedy Central
Independent film/classics	The Sundance Channel
	IFC
	AMC
Science fiction	The Sci-Fi Channel
Music related	MTV
	VH1
History	The History Channel

I refer to the above channels as "channels" rather than networks for they generally fail the diversity test and have a limited scope of original programming, even if national carriage satisfies reach and around-the-clock programming satisfies duration. At heart, these are genre specific channels that program to limited demographics. Because the majority of the above channels are owned by their parent networks and studios, however, the individual channels can be seen as part of a portfolio strategy within large media groups.

In terms of influence, it had long been assumed that cable channels, because of their narrow focus, could not compete head on with networks. That is generally true in terms of overall ratings, but within specific demographics the genre can overwhelm network clout. The kids' area is perhaps the strongest example. Nickelodeon has become such a powerful brand that for years it has consistently beaten network ratings in key children's time slots. The force of 24/7 kids shows and cartoons is in fact so strong that I have had network executives bemoan that they cannot compete—the cross-promotion opportunities and targeted marketing dollars are so large next to what a network can muster with only a few hours a week dedicated to the kids demographic that the network is often put in a position that it accepts second class status and is fighting for incremental rather than leadership share.

Additionally, as further discussed in Chapter 6, cable networks are increasingly moving to develop original programming. Recent examples include dramas on F/X such as *The Shield*, *Rescue Me*, and *Nip/Tuck*, as well as *The Closer* and *Saving Grace* on TNT, *Battlestar Galactica* on Sci-Fi, and *Psych* and *Burn Notice* on USA. In cases, these shows can draw ratings directly competing with networks; ratings for *The Closer* (especially within specified advertiser demographics) can equal or surpass traditional network shows.

Television Windows and Life Cycle Revenues

The concepts of windows and life cycle revenues discussed above regarding film also apply to original television programming.

In terms of windows, TV series will have an exclusive run on a broadcaster and then may be licensed into several "aftermarkets." Additional markets include:

- Cable — if launch on network or pay TV (e.g., *Sex and the City* on TNT post HBO)
- Syndication — licensed market-by-local-market if enough episodes are available to strip; usually requires a minimum of 65 episodes
- Video —TV series are licensed by "seasons" for consumption on DVD
- Download/Internet—TV series available for download on iTunes plus other services
- PPV/VOD — TV series available after initial broadcast either for free or purchase, such as free-on-demand via Hulu

(Chapters 6 and 7 describe these windows in more detail.) Unlike the film revenue cycle where windows are set in a fairly rigid and consistent time frame, windows for TV are more dependent on success and aggregating sufficient episodes for licensing into downstream markets. However, if one assumes a hit series for which there are at least 65 episodes, the window pattern may appear as follows:

TV broadcast → Residential VOD/PPV → Internet re-broadcast →
Video release → Downloads → Syndication

These windows are shifting, with residential VOD, for example, accelerated, and new models for "catch up" tested on the Internet, including free Internet VOD (via streaming; again, see Chapters 6 and 7). Interestingly, some of the experiments are proceeding faster in Europe, where certain services are allowing viewers to buy next week's episode early on a VOD basis; some broadcasters are even offering a "season pass" whereby a subscriber pays for the ability to watch all episodes of a series prior to their TV debut (with the restriction that the most one can skip ahead is to see the next new episode early).

43

Are the Current Shifts in Windows Forewarning the Collapse of the Window Construct?

Given how the studios and networks have historically controlled the pipeline for product, both in terms of content creation and distribution, it is interesting to ponder whether current Internet-driven shifts in content creation will force similar shifts in distribution patterns. The open nature of the Web has led to a democratization of content such that virtually anyone can post anything. Will this inevitably force distribution to follow in such a way that we will eventually see a world without so-called windows? I asked Blair Westlake, Corporate VP of Media and Entertainment for Microsoft, and former Universal Pictures senior executive, how he viewed this clash, as he has a unique perspective interacting among all the major studios and media players:

While the Internet offers virtually unlimited capability to deliver and access content—beyond anything we have ever seen before—with broadband speeds even permitting delivery of high-definition quality, a far cry from just a few years ago where the viewing screen was several inches, "democratization of content" has impediments many have underestimated creeping to the surface.

The common refrain we are hearing today from traditional distributors such as cable MSOs is "we're not paying you (content owner) for something you're giving away for free on the Internet." Sound familiar to the newspaper business? Except in that case, it was the consumer saying "why should I subscribe/pay for a newspaper when I can get the same news, faster, online, for free?" Newspapers didn't have anyone "monitoring" their every move the way cable channel providers do. Maybe if newspapers had, we wouldn't see the demise of as many print publications (e.g., The Christian Science Monitor, Hearst saying it will close the Seattle Post-Intelligencer if it doesn't find a buyer, etc.), which has only just begun. Even release/availability "windows" are "baked" into how media can be distributed, thanks primarily to agreements (e.g., pay TV output deals with HBO, Showtime, Starz) in place, which limit distribution "flexibility" by the content owners for a very long period. Of course, without those deals, much of the content would either be scaled back in production quality or never made, so it's a trade-off. My prediction is that the windows will fall away and the business models, the amount the consumer pays (or very targeted advertising accompanying the programming), will dictate how, when, and where you see content.

(TV) Life Cycle and Ultimates

Life cycle management is just as important with a TV series as with a film, because a successful TV series can run in repeats/syndication indefinitely. However, the "long-tail" of syndication is giving way to the long tail of the Internet, with downward revenue pressures from more diverse and earlier exposure. Accordingly, planning is more complex in an area that was already challenging for planners that needed to estimate whether a show would even survive enough seasons to reach a critical episode threshold for syndication. In terms of ultimates, the same concept applies in that financial planners need to aggregate all potential revenue streams—a process that has also become much more complex with the relatively new trend of releasing TV series on DVD and the new technology windows emerging (TV series VOD and downloads did not exist prior to 2006).

Internet and New Media

Throughout this book I will discuss the impact of online and new media exploitation avenues on traditional revenue streams — all of which goes into the calculus of ultimates and what value can be derived from an individual piece of content. Given the dynamic times and excitement around new platforms, delivery methods, points of access, and even new types of content there is a tendency to hype new media over the existing system. However, the evolution of so-called convergence can only be understood in the context of grasping the nuances of how the current, finely honed, systems of distribution work to maximize revenue potential. New media and online-enabled opportunities are part of the overall fabric, and as certain platforms reach or move past their consumption peaks (e.g., DVD sales and revenues) distribution executives need to carefully balance what is incremental revenue, whether they risk trading higher margin for lower margin sales, and whether new media opportunities even hold the potential of being substitutional for the billions of dollars now seemingly at risk. I asked long-time TV veteran Hal Richardson, currently President, Paramount Worldwide Television Distribution, and former DreamWorks Head of Television Distribution, for his perspective on old versus new media, and he provided an excellent summary of the relative growth and maturation curves:

For the past 25 years the two largest and most important ancillary revenue streams for motion picture distribution have been home entertainment (VHS cassettes and DVDs) and television (the licensing of movies to pay television and broadcast and/or basic cable networks). These distribution activities deliver tens of billions of dollars in revenue annually to motion picture producers and distributors. These distribution businesses are mature and year-on-year revenue growth has begun to flatten, or even decline marginally with respect to home entertainment. It can be argued the increased availability of motion pictures through digitally delivered alternatives may have accelerated the flattening of the growth curve for traditional ancillary distribution. In addition, at least so far, the incremental additional revenue generated through new media distribution (download to own, DTO; electronic sell through, EST; transactional video-on-demand, TVOD; subscription video-on-demand, SVOD;, and free video-on-demand, FVOD) delivers a very small fraction of the revenue generated by traditional ancillary distribution. In other words, the flattening of the growth in old media distribution is not even close to being replaced by the incremental revenue generated by new media digital distribution. Therefore, the trick, which all distributors of motion pictures will need to master, is how to prudently manage the continuing maturation of traditional ancillary distribution while continuing to enfranchise the unquestioned potential inherent in digital distribution through new media; all within the context of continuing to grow the overall revenue generated by this continuingly evolving array of opportunities for consumers to enjoy motion pictures.

Online Impact

Given this interplay of old and new media, at the end of each chapter (excluding Chapter 7) I will summarize some of the key ways in which the Internet and new media applications are influencing the area discussed. While challenging in this introductory overview chapter to distill select trends, I nevertheless want to highlight the following:

- Online and new media applications, such as downloads and VOD, are dramatically influencing and changing the historical windowing patterns of films and TV.
- The notion of what is a "network" is an intriguing question in the online space, as the trademark brands that are grounded in linear programming tailored to defined time periods struggle for relevancy in an inherently VOD environment.
- Studios, whose strength is unparalleled distribution infrastructure and reach, are grappling with how to retain dominance in an online world where infrastructure needs are now commoditized and minimized, and where a sole producer with a Web site can achieve equal reach.
- The diversity of production and portfolio strategies that define studios and networks remain just as important in an online world, but the question remains whether online and

new media outlets will prove an expansion of the portfolio or come to turn the whole system on its head.

- Content distribution joint ventures, which were formed to defray costs in establishing global beachheads for distributing film, TV, and video, and then declined when international markets grew to the size of justifying control of local operations, are back in vogue in the online space. The breadth of content enables instant scale in branding new on-demand platforms (plus, a single access point affords the potential of global reach).

CHAPTER 2

Intellectual Property Assets Enabling Distribution—The Business of Creating, Marketing, and Protecting an Idea

48

More content from this chapter is available on
www.businessofmediadistribution.com

The process of creating a property for production and sale, though often perceived as more fun than building a standard widget, is still very much a business proposition. Being an art, there are exceptions and patrons who may ignore the commercial aspects; however, the production business is predominantly a for-profit endeavor. This means business choices are made even at the root stages of creating content. (Note: For an interesting perspective on "art for art's sake" and the conflict between creative endeavors vs. business, see Richard Caves' book *Creative Industries*.)

This chapter will explore some of the business choices surrounding the development process (e.g., What should be made and why? Can we sell it?) as well as address the business and art of marketing and selling an idea (aka, pitching). While nuances are different, the principles of selling creative ideas are no different than any other business. What differs are the risk factors, as captured famously by Oscar-winning screenwriter William Goldman's famous rule about the correlation between a developed idea and commercial success: "Nobody knows anything."[1]

Finally, it is the underlying nature of intellectual property that allows pieces of content to be divided and licensed in a myriad of ways, enabling the distribution side of the business. The essence of distribution is then figuring out how best to carve up and exploit rights in a way that maximizes the return on the whole. Given that the parceling and licensing out of rights derives from the underlying intellectual property rights and rules governing their exploitation, it is important to understand some of the fundamentals of how the legal framework functions to authorize, foster, and protect a vibrant market for content.

The Development Process

In a sense, development and distribution are the bookends to exploiting media content. Development kicks off the cycle, and can be likened, in part, to product development. First, an idea or product is roughed out and analyzed. After beating up the idea a bit, a decision will be made to archive the idea or invest in a prototype. The prototype will be built, and likely go through a few iterations of refinement before testing. Finally, after testing and debugging the assembly line the product will be marketed and shipped. Unfortunately, the analogy is far from perfect because a creative good is subject to infinite variance and the outcome is largely unknown until the property is produced and then distributed for viewing.

Further underlying the challenge of development and the "nobody knows" principle is the concept of creative products as experience goods (see Chapter 3 for further discussion), such that an individual cannot truly know if he likes something until he consumes it. If you accept this proposition then development and distribution may be less bookends than the blind leading the blind. This, I would argue, is where economic what ifs and reality clash, for there are no doubt methods to improve the odds: I digress a bit below into issues of pitching and marketing ideas because methodology matters, I describe certain breaks with orthodoxy because some have figured out a way to beat the supposed impossible system (e.g., Pixar), and I relate distribution because it is stuck with optimizing the result in the face of waiting for the consumptive verdict on the experience good.

Development in Stages

With a creative business, the first stage of development is generating a range of ideas for projects. This could mean that a single individual

49

originates concepts, or in the case of an organization, such as a network or studio, development executives take pitches from so-called "creatives." Whatever the context, a variety of ideas will rise to the top, and there is a winnowing out of concepts until finalists are selected. Once there is a choice regarding which to pursue, the so-called development process begins in earnest: an idea is taken from concept to script (the prototype). Once the script is written it will need refinement, which can mean many drafts and may even require fresh blood in the form of different writers (redesigning and refining the prototype). Once the script is ready, the similarities stop because it just is not possible to test a script.

The TV industry has solved the problem with the concept of a pilot, which pushes the prototype concept out one step. Pilots are still risky and expensive, but clearly short of the full investment of a 13 or more episode commitment. There is no exact parallel in film, although executives try to review and test at relevant stages. Dailies and rough cuts are scrutinized, and decisions made to fix problems as soon as possible even if that means re-shooting; on occasion, directors will also utilize animatics to rough out the story (see further discussion in the section Mock-ups and Storyboards). Online is more akin to TV and pilots can be created, although the medium is still so new that everyone is struggling to figure out what content works best and whether the medium is better adapted to testing content for other media (e.g., TV) or for creating new forms of self-sustaining online properties.

Development in the Context of Distribution

I talk about development for the same reason that William Goldman laments that writers are infrequently consulted or involved after tendering a script, even though it is their blueprint and nuance that grounds the project. The quandary is why do elements so inextricably interdependent become so separated in the production chain? It is a peculiar Hollywood (and perhaps more generally creative production) practice that first the executive producer, then the writer, then the director knows best; as the responsibility baton is passed, judgment and authority over the whole tend to be transferred too, often disenfranchising a key guiding force. Perhaps this explains the passion over credits (and the need for public thank yous), which at a root level ensures that each contribution continues to be valued. In the continuum of segmenting value (or input), distribution and marketing rarely have input at the development stage, even though each represents the beginning and end of the chain and is ultimately dependent upon one another. Is there a way to fix the chain, or is William Goldman correct that inherent in the creative process "nobody knows" and so no one is worse off from a system which may allow somewhat isolated inputs in an otherwise collaborative endeavor? Can it not be argued that this structure jeopardizes the whole while fostering a culture of plausible deniability by being able to blame the producer or "suits" on failure (it was the product, marketing screwed it up, they didn't know how to handle it...)?

Vesting Control with the Director, and Pixar Breaking the Mold

Sometimes a radical break with orthodoxy can lead to success, and here and later in the chapter I will cite Pixar as an exception driving true innovation. I was honored to have Ed Catmull, president and co-founder of Pixar, speak at my Media & Entertainment class at the Haas School of Business (Berkeley), and asked him the straightforward question: What, if anything, does Pixar do differently that has led to the unbroken streak of hit after hit? After all, no one in the history of the motion picture business has a batting average anywhere near that of Pixar's, starting with *Toy Story* and continuing with every film since. His answer was at once simple and earthshaking: Pixar, he described, essentially greenlights people, not projects, and puts its faith in directors to come up with a story and see it through. In an article titled "How Pixar Fosters Collective Creativity" in the *Harvard Business Review*, Mr. Catmull punctuated this very point:

We believe the creative vision propelling each movie comes from one or two people and not from either corporate executives or a development department. Our philosophy is: You get great creative people, you bet big on them, you give them enormous leeway and support, and you provide them with an environment in which they can get honest feedback from everyone.[2]

Directors such as Brad Bird (*The Incredibles*), Andrew Stanton (*Finding Nemo*), or John Lasseter (*Toy Story*) will know the next picture is "theirs" and proceed with a mini-team to develop a handful of ideas from which one is chosen. Of course, there is debate over ideas, and the ability to beat up concepts and refine as a team, but Pixar's ability to build up a "creative brain trust" (as Catmull puts it) that can check egos and collaborate with brute honesty for the benefit of the whole is no doubt unique. Clearly there are multiple factors at play, but one common thread rarely mentioned or given credence is the continuous link from concept to completion.

I always hear a similar theme from luminary directors such as George Lucas, a vocal proponent of protecting the director's vision, and he is, of course, right as long as the director acts responsibly. The problem is that ceding too much control to a director without the ability to manage the budget has often been the bane of Hollywood. For those who want to read the ultimate business management disaster story, Steven Bach's classic *Final Cut* recounts how director Michael Cimino's *Heaven's Gate* (made following his multiple Oscar winning film *The Deer Hunter*) virtually brought down United Artists' studio (note the book's subtitle: *Art, Money and Ego in the Making of Heaven's Gate, the Film that Sank United Artists*).

Is There an Optimal Feedback Loop?

Coming back to distribution: Is it not possible to create a better relationship among distribution, marketing, and development than already exists, or innovate a new methodology much as Pixar has achieved at least on the development front? On the one hand any creative executive will bristle at so-called "suits" telling them what to do — often rightly so. But there is a difference between input and decision, and as long as the creative executives have final say would it be productive for them to have input from those people responsible for selling what they plan to make? Would any other business decide to put a new product into production without direct feedback from the people responsible for bringing it to market? At some level, this is the filter that is supposed to be provided by studio heads, but they have their own predilections and may have scant experience on the sales and marketing side. When I was CEO of the animation studio Wild Brain (producer of multiple TV series), I stayed relatively hands-off from the development meetings, but once a slate was recommended I used to refer to myself as the "are you out of your mind" filter. The issue was am I the best person to fill that role, or is that a fair expectation for anyone?

There are, obviously, plenty of examples of trying to create a productive feedback loop, and the challenge is balancing the yin and yang of these different sources of studio power. I was fortunate enough to create a TV show that became a hit on Disney Channel, a preschool animated series called *Higglytown Heroes* (featured on Playhouse Disney). When Disney was evaluating the rough idea, and then after focus testing a trial, it involved a number of divisions, most notably merchandising. The question was could this lead to successful toys, etc. As described in Chapter 8, merchandising can be a driver for production, and in the case of children's and in particular animated fare, this is often the case. Here is an example of the end-sellers becoming involved at the outset, so that the whole team is vested in success. However, is the tail wagging the dog here, and as creative executives will argue should merchandising and similar considerations be driving or diluting the creative, when an equal argument can be made that too much input like this will homogenize creativity and doom a production? Not an easy call, but again I would argue that constructive input is always a good factor as long as lines are drawn. It is the ability to balance such factors and make the correct call that is the art of surviving as a studio chief.

Is Online Different?

Development for original online media, while talked about as new, has been around for more than ten years. Again, referring back to Wild Brain, in the late 1990s the studio produced a range of online original animated series in flash (Figure 2.1) — many of which premiered on Cartoon Network's online Web Premiere Toons.

The difference with online "series" then and now tends to be length, as Web original series are generally only a few minutes long, tailored to the surfing mentality of online viewers, and originally limited due to connectivity concerns and bandwidth costs for streaming.

Also similar today is the tendency to view these shorts as a live development test: successful series may be picked up as TV series, and the total development costs are relatively small, because a company can produce multiple Web series for less than the cost of a TV pilot. While there are instances of pickups, such as *Sophia's Diary* by UK's Channel 5 from online and social networking site Bebo (in development for TV by Sony Pictures International TV) where the series had become an online sensation, this is still an infrequent exception, and most Internet fare is targeted and designed for a different viewing experience. Time will tell — as others such as Fox Television Studios, ABC, and cable networks target Web series as pilot fodder — whether convergence applies and Web series become a viable laboratory for traditional TV.

54

Figure 2.1

Although lower development costs on the Web are an advantage, the lower investment may also prove an impediment to shows being picked up on TV. This is because an inexpensive show without the budget to attract top talent may only be able to pull in limited revenues from nascent Web advertising. This too will evolve, with top directors and producers starting to test the Web experience. Marshall Herskovitz and Ed Zwick (*Thirtysomething*) produced *Quarterlife*, an original online series debuting on MySpace, which then was touted as the first high-profile Web series to make the jump to broadcast when it was picked up by NBC. After a disappointing launch, however, the show was quickly canceled.[3] Another trial is ABC's *In the Motherhood*, starring Leah Remini (former star of *King of Queens*) and Jenny McCarthy (MTV), which in March 2009 tried to make the leap from Web series to network sitcom. The online series, which was reputedly higher cost than typical Web fare, combined top talent with a Web-sponsorship angle, as the successful online series was backed by Unilever and Sprint and produced by WPP's entertainment affiliate Mindshare Entertainment.[4]

Other experiments will continue, Web series will on occasion cross over, but the struggle in part is symptomatic of the premise discussed above: the Web is a different medium with its own viewership quirks. Producers, whether those starting with the Web or those with success in other media trying to adapt, are challenged when figuring out how to make an online original successful, let alone strike a chord that will create equal or greater success in the longer form, linear, and largely formulaic outlet of broadcast television.

What is undoubtedly clear is that the Web, which has a barrier to entry of virtually zero, fosters an extraordinary variety of creativity. With no gatekeepers anyone can post just about anything. Moreover, in the flat world of the Internet ideas can come from anywhere, and individuals can be influenced by trends and ideas in a virtual world. Great artistic movements have often dovetailed with the congregation of like-minded creators in a location, such as the art schools in Paris. Today an individual interested in X no longer needs to travel to Y to be part of the Z movement, and can be tapped into ideas and influenced by a circle of friends who have never met in person. We are truly at ground zero of this new melting pot, which in theory should spur innovation.

A fascinating corollary to this unparalleled access to global peers and elimination of filters to express creative concepts is that the content can be critiqued by anyone, with a feedback loop of favorites, top picks, etc., rising to the top from online voting and metrics. Figure 2.2 shows a form of network effect, where popularity is driven from the masses in an inverted pyramid from the historical development process:

55

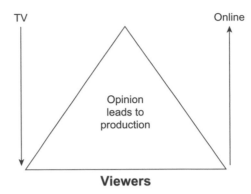

Development Executive

TV

Online

Opinion
leads to
production

Viewers

Figure 2.2

Development Guidelines

When there is a filter, and so-called gatekeepers, there will typically be a series of questions asked in selecting an idea/concept to develop. What those questions are, however, is not formalized: No standard checklist exists, and unquestionably lots of executives go on their "gut." If that does not sound scary, it should. The online supplemental material outlines a number of threshold questions (e.g., is the idea sustainable, or so-called "big enough"?) that illustrate the filtering process that film executives may employ, and an idea that can run this gauntlet will improve its odds of moving from concept to production. The supplementary material also addresses the related issue in selecting projects of market timing, where questions such as "is the genre hot?" or "is there a growing demographic?" are addressed.

Development Costs

Development costs money, both in terms of hard costs and labor. A typical development department would have the following line items in its budget:

- People/overhead
- Fund for writers
- Fund for acquisitions/options
- Legal costs for negotiating deals
- Travel and entertainment costs

- Marketing costs
- Rent, phones, and general office costs

More important, it is a department of all costs and no revenues — *development is a pure overhead category.*

The ratio of properties produced to those developed is never 1 : 1, and in fact the ratio can vary dramatically from company to company. A 5 : 1 or 10 : 1 ratio is not extraordinary, and it is easy to see how costs can mount quickly. This is especially true once projects enter script stages, where screenwriters cost at minimum tens of thousands of dollars a draft, and often in the hundreds of thousands (even reaching sums in the millions with superstar writers). I have been involved with projects that were greenlit after development costs ranging from under $100,000 to several millions, and no one was trying harder in one scenario versus another. In all cases, the unspoken focus remains on ROI, with higher development costs justified by the belief that certain "proven" talent will more likely lead to a project's success.

The development process requires many stars to align, including the clicking of the underlying creative, the satisfying of various egos and executives, and the luck of timing. Simply put, there is no magic formula. What most outsiders perceive as relatively easy, to insiders is recognized as a very difficult, often frustrating and time-consuming process. As Jim Morris, former president of Industrial Light & Magic and producer of Pixar's *Wall-E* (as well as General Manager of Pixar Animation Studios) told me, "I've never met a director who was trying to make a bad movie."

Mock-Ups and Storyboards

In the quest to implement systems that reduce costs and risks, and stage phases before full production costs are committed, directors are always seeking new tools or systems. As noted previously, the concept of pilots tempers risk in TV, but there is no similar scheme in film production. Certain projects, though, and especially animated features, lend themselves to mock-ups. Detailed storyboards together with temporary voice tracks can be pieced together to gain a sense of timing and story — it is at this stage of "putting it up on reels" that the producer can gain a glimpse of whether the characters, humor, etc., are working as intended. Additionally, this can become a milestone after which approval of the more labor-intensive and expensive production phase of full animation and lighting a film may be greenlit. With technological advances, this process can now be computerized and it is possible

57

to construct an animatic for any type of film. While on occasion this may prove helpful with effects intensive projects where concepts are difficult to visualize, it is not utilized in most instances given the dependence of live action films on actors' performances.

Optioning Properties

An option has evolved as the standard means of acquiring film and television properties. Not unlike an option in other markets, an option in the media context represents an economic compromise balancing issues of time, exclusivity, value, and uncertain conditions of moving a project forward.

Accepting the proposition that with books, comics, and life stories there is a limitless source of ideas for projects, the market has developed to value these ideas while putting constraints on the time an acquirer can take to turn the property into a film or TV show. The owner of a book, for example, may be thrilled that someone wants to turn it into a film, but also wants assurance that if it entrusts that process to producer X they will deliver. What happens if the producer starts working on a script but the script does not progress as hoped for, or worse the producer (if not a studio or network) is unable to secure financing and distribution? Months or years can pass, and there needs to be a mechanism in place to dissolve the relationship and help find a new partner.

58

Efficiency of Options

Producers who develop properties are ultimately middlemen. They are an efficient source of developing content for studios and networks in that they scour the world for interesting ideas. Producers, together with agents who package creative talent and properties, then bring other talent into the mix evolving and ultimately transforming the idea into a production; however, producers know that for every project produced their office is littered with many more properties that died along the way or are in limbo. In essence, a producer acquires a property believing they can then add value to it and sell it to a third party who will distribute and finance the production (even if they contribute financing, they will ultimately need a broadcast or distribution partner). Because the odds are significantly against any optioned project actually making it to production, the producer acquiring the property wants to invest as little up front in the option as possible.

The option market functions as efficiently as other option markets, governed by the simple principle of supply and demand. If a property is not famous and/or has limited exposure, few people are likely to be competing for the rights; the option price will be low, and in cases can even be zero. For a book by a well-known author, who has had other properties successfully translated to film, the price can be in the millions. The elasticity of the price is then tempered by factoring in subjective elements such as (1) is there other value in the parties working together, such that it is worth lowering or raising a fee to close the deal, (2) is there a strong belief that the party has a better chance of securing financing and distribution, therefore increasing the odds this project will make it to production, and (3) is there a synergy between the parties or related products or divisions?

Options effectively balance this time–money–uncertainty continuum by carving out a middle ground protecting both property creators and acquirers from respective downsides (predominantly time on the creator side, and risked capital on the acquirer side). The option agreement also sets out a formal agreement for success, ensuring who has what rights and financial stake assuming the project moves forward to production and release or broadcast.

At a certain point, the option holder needs to make a commitment to buy or release the property. All option contracts have a "purchase price," and the option holder has the right to acquire defined rights in the property (usually all rights, including copyright ownership) by paying an agreed sum before the expiration of the option period. This is where real money is paid. While option payments are often in the low thousands of dollars, purchase prices tend to be in the hundreds of thousands or millions of dollars: this is the transfer of ownership. (See the online supplementary material for a short overview of option contracts.)

Marketing Ideas (aka Pitching)

There are no set rules or formulas for pitching an idea, but there are certain conventional practices that seem to have evolved. This is ultimately not magic, but pure marketing. How do you grab someone else's attention, get them excited about an idea, and convince them that your idea is the one worthy of their time and investment?

Also, movies and television are consumed in a short period relative to the time it takes to read a book. Accordingly, at some level, they are formulaic to ensure that the audience has been sucked in and brought through a roller coaster of emotion within a short period of time. The online supplemental material delves into a bit more detail on the strategy of setting up pitches, who should make the pitch, and what materials may be appropriate. In the next section, I will simply address the rhythm of how story beats are crafted and provide an example illustrating some of the threshold questions a development executive may need to navigate on the road to greenlighting a project.

Rhythm of the Story, Walk Me through the Story

All films have what are referred to as story beats, which are a very rough equivalent to acts in plays or musicals. They define the pace and the emotional arc that the story takes us through. In marketing a story, a good creative executive should be able to address the following items when explaining and trying to sell his concept.

What are the main story beats? The creative executive should try to make sure that a story has enough twists and turns and depth to satisfy the following type of hierarchy:

- Once upon a time ...
- And every day ...
- Until one day ...
- And because of this ...
- And because of that ...
- Until finally ...
- And ever since then ...

What are the main plot points? Namely, what are the dramatic twists that change the direction of the story and/or character? Think about how many times you have seen a movie and things are going along fine until ... someone dies, someone is attacked, someone is kidnapped, or something precious is stolen. Then something needs to be found or someone saved or avenged—we are drawn into the story.

Toy Story as an Example

- *What is it about?*—In two or three sentences, whose story is it and what happens? It is a story about a boy's favorite toy, a cowboy doll named Woody (and all the toys are alive!). When Woody loses his leader-of-the-toys role and is abandoned in favor of the newfangled spaceman toy, Buzz Lightyear, Woody

60

ousts Buzz. Woody ultimately redeems himself and reclaims his cherished position by leading the other toys to rescue Buzz from the jeopardy Woody has put him in.

- *Make me care: What is the lead character's goal?* — Woody is driven to make Billy (the boy) love him and be his favorite toy — Woody wants to be left on Billy's pillow and taken on trips, not thrown in the closet to gather dust.
- *Who are the lead characters? What is the personality of the lead characters?* — Woody is a lovable jokester. Buzz Lightyear is a haughty by-the-book Mountie in space gear who you know has a soft spot (because, after all, he is a toy).
- *What's the core conflict?* — Who is the villain, or who or what opposes the protagonist? Buzz Lightyear threatens Woody's position (stature, life, etc.)
- *What changes?* — How has the key character grown/transformed, what lessons have been learned, what are the consequences for the story's arc? Woody comes to like and respect Buzz, not view their relationships as a "me against him" contest for Billy's attention: there is room for both.
- *Who is it for?* — What is the target demographic? Kids of all ages.
- *What's the best analogy for the story?* — Is it like Superman meets … (the more original, the harder it is to come up with something).
- *Who would you cast?* — Who would make your perfect lead, friend, villain? It would be Tom Hanks as Woody, Tim Allen as Buzz Lightyear.
- *What is the setting?* — Where does it take place? It takes place in a stylized, animated version of an American suburb.
- *What's the tone and style?* — Is it a comedy, or is it action… is it a live-action mix? It is a comedy adventure, produced entirely in computer graphics animation.
- *Can you capture the spirit with a one-line premise?* — What if all your toys were alive?
- *What are the two (or more) driving plot points?* — What spins the audience around from Act I to Act II, and Act II to Act III?
  1. Buzz arrives on the scene, instantly upsetting Woody's world and security
  2. Buzz is put in jeopardy: left behind outside the house and needs to be rescued
  3. Woody to the rescue

61

Protecting Content: Copright, Piracy, and Related Issues

Ideas in their raw form are not protectable. It is only when they are committed to writing or a tangible form of expression that they transform from a thought or verbal description to a concrete expression of that idea that is afforded copyright protection. The following is not meant to be a legal primer, but a brief introduction to the main vehicles used to protect the expression of creative content. Most critically, by properly protecting an idea one creates property, namely a piece of intellectual property—it is the development and exploitation of individual pieces of intellectual property around which the entire film and television business is based.

Copyright

Copyrights are the primary and historical method by which intellectual property in the film and television business is protected. The idea of copyrights is rooted in the United States Constitution, which states: "The Congress shall have Power…To promote the Progress of Science and useful Arts, by securing for limited Times to Authors and Inventors the exclusive Right to their respective Writings and Discoveries."[5]

Copyright Law Basics

The specific copyright law is contained in federal law, which covers both what can be copyrighted and what rights are granted by copyright. In terms of the "what," the law enumerates several categories of "works of authorship" and specifically includes "motion pictures and other audiovisual works"—a category that easily encompasses film, video, television, etc.[6]

In terms of the rights affixing to copyrighted works, the law then defines a bundle of exclusive rights that an author possesses by owning the copyright to his or her work. These rights include the right to copy, distribute, perform, and display works, together with the right to make derivative works (e.g., sequels); more important, these are the rights that enable the licensing and exploitation of movies and TV shows (all video-based content), and ground the distribution side of the business. As codified, the specific language of the law grants copyright owners the right:

1. to reproduce the copyrighted work in copies or phonorecords;
2. to prepare derivative works based upon the copyrighted work;
3. to distribute copies or phonorecords of the copyrighted work to the public by sale or other transfer or ownership, or by rental, lease or lending;
4. in the case of literary, musical dramatic, and choreographic works, pantomimes, and motion pictures and other audiovisual works, to perform the copyrighted work publicly; and
5. in the case of literary, musical, dramatic, and choreographic works, pantomimes, and pictorial, graphic, or sculptural works, including the individual images of a motion picture or other audiovisual work, to display the copyrighted work publicly.[7]

There are, of course, nuances to the application of these general principles (e.g., international applications), but a detailed discussion of copyright law is far beyond the scope of this book; however, I do at least want to mention the doctrine of fair use. Basically, "fair use" is an exception category that expressly allows certain uses of a copyrighted work without the permission of the owner, including for criticism, news reporting, teaching, and research.[8] Moving from this high-level description to a practical set of rules is more complicated, as the law includes a set of factors by which fair use can be judged, such as how much of the work is used/copied in relation to the whole, and what is it being used for. A body of case law has evolved dealing with the enumerated factors and how they are to be balanced; nevertheless, it is easy to imagine the complications and arguments arising in the fair use context, and how case law has had to evolve to define mind-boggling permutations. Simply pose the question: What is news?

The final two points I want to highlight regarding copyright regard length of protection and divisibility of content. In terms of length, the duration of copyright protection has changed over time due to amendments in the act, with studios and other owners of key brands lobbying for extensions. An extension in 1998 was at the time jokingly referred to as the Mickey Mouse extension, due in part to vigorous lobbying efforts by Disney, which faced Mickey Mouse entering the public domain. (Note: Copyright for movies is now generally for the life of the author +70 years, or in the case of corporate authorship the earlier of 95 years after publication or 120 years after creation.) Perhaps the most important element of copyright ownership in terms of distribution is that intellectual property is divisible; namely, any

63

or all of the exclusive rights vested in the copyright owner may be transferred or licensed separately. Hence, the licensing of various rights, such as rights for TV exhibition or video distribution, are grounded in copyright and enable the distinct licenses that embody the windowing of content. Moreover, it is the infinite permutations of licenses that create the different distribution rights discussed throughout this book.

Grant of Rights and Digital Complications

In the context of digital rights and new technology, it is interesting to note the evolution of the language "whether now known or hereafter devised," which is frequently used in a grant of rights. This language developed as a direct result of technology. Methods of exploitation continue to be invented that creators of content could not have envisioned when producing the original work. When David Lean made *Lawrence of Arabia*, the studio could never have anticipated that one day that film would not only be shown in theaters and possibly TV, but that it would be viewed on videocassettes, DVDs, over the Internet, and by digital file sharing. Inevitably, when a new delivery medium generates significant revenues, people will argue that this area was not covered by the original contract or grant of rights and is reserved. This argument was quite common when the videocassette market emerged. Accordingly, this catchall language grew to protect against rights that the original owner might later claim were reserved, because the rights/market never existed at the time of the grant.

Nature of Copyright Allows Segmenting Distribution Rights; Licensing Content Rights is Complicated

Coming back to an earlier point, revenues are derived from multiple distribution streams (theaters, TV, video, merchandising, online, etc.) and it is the ownership of copyright and the nature of intellectual property that allows rights and revenues to be segmented and applied separately to each of those distribution streams. The copyright owner of a film could in theory parcel off each possible distribution right to a different party, creating one license for pay TV, one for free TV, one for film clips, one for a soundtrack album, and on and on. In fact, it is this divisibility that allows the interplay of factors outlined in Ulin's rule discussed in Chapter 1, where the value of a single asset is a function of maximizing value by balancing time, differential pricing options, exclusivity, and multiple platforms for repeat consumption.

Complicating the challenge of segmenting rights into bits are the dual factors that licenses can be bounded in multiple ways (e.g., exclusive vs. non-exclusive, in perpetuity vs. limited periods of time, worldwide vs. in discrete territories) and that third parties often retain stakes in or approvals over the use of the content being licensed. While at one level there is an owner (who may or may not be the creator) and a consumer, between the two is a labyrinth of rights, inputs, and approvals. Licensing content is fundamentally complicated (Figure 2.3):

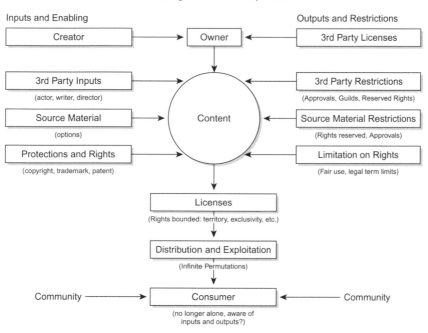

Figure 2.3

65

Copyright in the Digital Age — New Laws and Evolving Boundaries

The 1998 Digital Millennium Copyright Act (DMCA) represents a major overhaul of copyright law, and among its several provisions was an attempt to promote Internet access by insulating carriers from claims based upon content they helped transport but did not screen/review. An ISP or phone company would be reluctant to carry messages and content over its lines or network if it could be sued by someone based upon carried content. The section of the DMCA that provides for the limitation of liability — in fact a bar on monetary damages — for copyright infringement (a so-called "safe harbor") has been thrust into the public spotlight by a $1B suit by Viacom against YouTube (see also discussion in Chapter 7).

The practical application of the law has been to insulate service providers from liability from third party postings on Web sites (which have recently grown exponentially with user-generated content, and social networking sites), and YouTube and others argue that as long as they are acting to "take down" infringing content when placed on notice they should be able to avail themselves of the law's safe harbor protections. A variety of cases are testing the boundaries of the law, and at the crux of many debates is the line of what is fair use and what is infringing. The debate is not new. Elements of this line have been challenged in the digital space before, such as in the context of peer-to-peer file sharing services.

Peer-to-Peer File Sharing, Piracy, and the Seminal Supreme Court Grokster Case

It is in the file sharing space — first highlighted in the music industry by Napster, and then in the film space by Grokster, Morrpheus, Kaaza, and other similar services — where peer-to-peer file sharing services raised novel copyright issues. At stake was whether certain activities were non-infringing legitimate copyright activities or pirate activities that could result in damages or even criminal penalties.

Peer-to-peer networks allow disparate computer users to share electronic files of content. Peer-to-peer systems differ from other systems in that they are not funneled through a central server, but rather operate by sharing information directly between the different computers tapped into the system. If a popular file, such as a copy of a movie not yet publicly available, is on a computer then others who are notified of the availability can start swapping bits to download and simultaneously share that file. The advantages are speed, as data is parceled out in bits, and cost since there are no central bandwidth or server storage costs; in fact, it is the free access and remarkable efficiency of the systems that led them to grow so rapidly. Peer-to-peer networks and technology grew so fast that some articles estimated that upwards of one-third of all Internet traffic in 2006 utilized Bit Torrent, a highly efficient peer-to-peer technology initially created by its whiz kid founder as a publishing tool.

Anxious to avoid the chaos and downturn experienced in the music industry (which, to some extent can be bounded as the time between when Napster skyrocketed until Apple's iTunes offered a legal and compelling download alternative), the studios acting through their trade organization, the Motion Picture Association of America (MPAA), were keen to resolve the legal landscape and prevent a Napster-type scenario in the film and video business. (Note: P2P and piracy issues are global concerns, and the MPAA works in concert with its sister arm, the Motion Picture Association (MPA), whose focus is international markets.) There was a sense of urgency, for as broadband penetration continued to increase there was a belief that it was simply a matter of time before compression and storage enabled larger video files to be downloaded quickly and easily. Fortunately, for the film and TV business, a major Supreme Court case (Grokster — see next) clarified the field and curtailed the spread of illegal peer-to-peer video file sharing before some of the technology issues improved enough to enable simple mass market adoption.

The seminal case addressing the peer-to-peer issue, supported by the MPAA, was *Metro-Goldwyn-Mayer Studios v. Grokster, Ltd.* (popularly known as the Grokster Case). A unanimous Supreme Court decision (June 2005) prohibited the Grokster service, and sent notice to peer-to-peer services that encouraged illegal downloads that they would be held accountable and shut down. The services could not argue they were a neutral bystander while culpability rested with the actual users downloading files. Justice Souter, in delivering the opinion, summarized: "We hold that one who distributes a device with the object of promoting its use to infringe copyright, as shown by clear expression or other affirmative steps taken to foster infringement, is liable for the resulting acts of infringement by third parties."

The Grokster case also revisited elements of the famous Sony Betamax case, which enabled the videocassette industry, and the upgraded technological iterations including DVD which followed. In Chapter 5 the landmark Supreme Court case of *Sony Corp. of America v. Universal City Studios, Inc.* is discussed in the context of permitting home use copying via VCRs. The underlying issue in that case was whether Sony, a manufacturer of VCRs, was liable for infringement when VCR owners used their VCRs to tape copyrighted programs. The court held no, arguing that "time shifting" (recording a program to view at a later time) was a fair and non-infringing use; in essence, the video industry was saved by the Supreme Court's reasoning that because a VCR was capable of "commercially significant non-infringing uses" Sony (e.g., manufacturers) was not liable for copyright infringement.

This history is important, because in the Grokster case the Supreme Court had to revisit elements of Sony to assess whether peer-to-peer copying represented a similar fair and non-infringing use. In finding in favor of the studios, it first set the moral or value equation, noting "The more artistic protection is favored, the more technological innovation may be discouraged; the administration of copyright law is an exercise in managing the trade-off."[9] In a sense, it was an easy case because the facts showed "a purpose to cause and profit from third-party acts of copyright infringement";[10] in an opinion so politically charged, the court likely did not want to stray further than necessary, and in some ways took the easy path in relying on somewhat egregious facts tipping the scales in favor of defining the activities as infringement.

In so doing, however, the implications were clear and the path was set. The real world does not wait like law school professors to argue the nuances: Grokster had lost, induced copyright violations via peer-to-peer file sharing were considered illegal, and services like Grokster were henceforth branded pirates.

Beyond Sony and Grokster

The Web knows no geographic boundaries, and accordingly Grokster can be seen as merely a starting point in a global battle to curb Internet piracy. As discussed briefly next, and also touched on in Chapter 7, the MPAA and MPA work on enforcement and education worldwide, trying to defeat safe havens. This is a particularly challenging problem, because a few individuals with powerful servers (e.g., capable of tracking which computers have downloaded file elements), can literally set up anywhere and cause significant damage from remote locations.

Beyond enforcement/piracy issues, permutations of content distribution in the digital realm continue to lead to new debates and novel issues. The next iteration of copyright debate arose not in the download/file sharing medium, but in the area of digital access to streaming video on services such as YouTube (e.g., applying the DMCA's notice and takedown provisions to user postings of third-party copyrighted content, which had grown in scale, as highlighted by the earlier mentioned lawsuit filed by Viacom against YouTube/Google; see also related discussion in Chapter 7). This and other pending cases may set new boundaries in the evolution of copyright law — a process that is likely to be ongoing for years, with questions about display, access, storage, and copying all pushing the edge of legal doctrine that is struggling to keep pace with the changes enabled by new digital and online applications. Simply ponder the following: Where should lines of ownership and fair use be drawn in the context of video mash-ups?

Trademarks

Trademarks complement copyright in the context of protecting a film or TV property: Whereas copyright will protect the whole as well as fundamental elements, trademarks serve to protect elements of the property that identify the brand, and in turn can brand specific products that have distinct value as a result of the association with the brand. For example, the movie *Toy Story* is the subject of copyright protection, but the name of a key character (e.g., Buzz Lightyear) will be separately protected to brand a Buzz Lightyear action figure toy or a *Toy Story* T-shirt featuring a cast of characters. Trademarks are denoted by a word, name, or symbol that identifies the source of a good and differentiates it from another good; consumers are accustomed to seeing a "TM" notice, indicating a property claim on the item. For a detailed discussion of trademarks, an easy reference guide can be found at the United States Patent and Trademark Office's Web site.[11]

Trademarks as Anchor of a Merchandising Program
Trademarks in the entertainment arena are very important when a property is used to sell commercial merchandise (see Chapter 8 for a discussion of merchandising). Batman action figures, Mickey Mouse T-shirts, Lord of the Rings puzzles, and Star Wars toy light sabers are all examples of merchandise where the product is branded by its association to the related film or film character. The trademark on the merchandise, in the form of a word, name, or symbol, indicates to the customer the source of that product.

The online supplemental material includes a brief discussion of the administration of a trademark program, together with a short overview of patents and their application in the production/distribution realm.

Piracy and Fighting Illegal Copying and Downloads

Piracy is a fancy word for copyright theft, and historically piracy of content was limited to illegal copies of prints and tapes. Namely, anti-piracy efforts were focused on stopping people from going into theaters and camcording a film to make copies, or from obtaining a copy (legally or illegally) of a videocassette and replicating that copy without a license for additional sale. The digital age creates a plethora of new piracy categories from making digital copies to sharing files. The MPAA and film studios mince no words about equating piracy with theft:

> Movie pirates are thieves, plain and simple. Piracy is the unauthorized taking, copying or use of copyrighted materials without permission. It is no different from stealing another person's shoes or stereo, except sometimes it can be a lot more damaging. Piracy is committed in many ways, including Internet piracy, copying and distribution of discs, broadcasts, and even public performances.[12]

Digital theft has grown so rapidly that MPAA member studios' losses from illegal downloads is starting to approach bootlegged piracy losses. An MPAA sponsored study in 2006 found that of an overall estimated $6.1B loss to MPAA studios in 2005 $3.8B was from "hard goods" piracy such as illegally manufactured or copied DVDs, but that ~$2.3B was lost to Internet piracy such as illegal downloads.[13] In fact, Internet piracy has grown so quickly that the prior categories have been collapsed into so-called "hard goods" piracy from what had previously been segmented into categories of bootlegging and illegal copying.

It is impossible to overstate the industry's concern over illegal downloading, hence the MPAA's stance in the Grokster case. When Warner Bros. released *Batman: The Dark Knight* (2008), despite robust advance efforts to protect prints and keep the film from illegal streaming sites, media measurement firm BigChampagne, as cited in a *New York Times* article titled "New Wave of Pirates Plunders Hollywood," estimated that the movie had been illegally downloaded more than seven million times worldwide by the end of the year of release; the same article referenced the MPAA as claiming that digital theft now accounts for about 40% of industry losses attributable to piracy.[14] There is little doubt that established losses as a result of illegal downloads and streaming will soon surpass, and in time dwarf, losses from so-called hard goods piracy (if in fact this has not already happened).

Fighting Piracy

The MPAA is the principal agent for fighting piracy, and all of its member Hollywood studios contribute a percentage of film revenues to fund the organization generally. A sizeable portion of the MPAA's budget is then specifically targeted toward bolstering copyright laws and funding global anti-piracy efforts. Many of the MPAA's employees in its anti-piracy efforts are former law enforcement officers who have experience planning raids and working with local, national, and international law enforcement agencies.

The MPAA fights piracy by employing a variety of tactics. In its own words, from the "Piracy and the Law" tab on the MPAA's Web site, the organization notes that "it takes a multi-pronged approach to fighting piracy, including educating people about the consequences of piracy, supporting the prosecution of Internet thieves, assisting law enforcement authorities to root out pirate operations, and encouraging the development of new technologies (e.g., encryption) that foster legal Internet and digital media uses."[15] (See Figure 2.4.) In a form of technology battling with technology, to counter piracy studios and other content suppliers are employing a range of tactics beyond encryption, including embedding markers into product (e.g., watermarking), and requiring digital rights management (DRM) systems (see Chapter 7 for a further discussion of DRM). Additionally, altering windows to release product day-and-date is at once a market response to the reality of piracy as well as an attempt to blunt its impact.

As noted above, the losses incurred from quantifiable piracy are staggering and are made that much worse when factoring in opportunity costs from markets that have either not matured or are simply unavailable due to piracy factors. Most of the market in China and Russia is lost to piracy. Given that these are two of the fastest growing major economies in the world, and present some of the greatest upside for growth to the Hollywood studios and networks, the efforts to fight piracy there are among the highest priority items of the MPA. China and Russia have begun to mature on the theatrical side, with both countries posting some of the largest market gains for box office revenue in the world; video and TV, however, continue to lag behind, especially in China, elevating intellectual property and piracy to key issues in trade negotiations at the political/government level.

How to turn a pirate market into a legitimate market is obviously a tricky equation. To succeed against legitimate distribution pirate prices need to be lower—the essence of piracy is earlier or at least simultaneous access and lower prices. Lower prices, though, mean lower margins, not to mention limited distribution to the extent major retail channels enforce stocking legitimate product. If you can show a pirate a way to improve distribution and increase margins, as a simple business proposition they will start seeing that working with

71

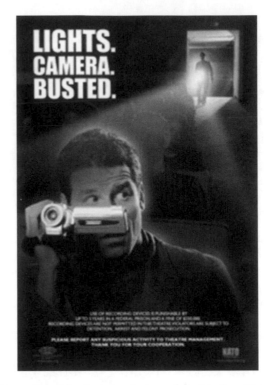

LIGHTS.
CAMERA.
BUSTED.

USE OF RECORDING DEVICES IS PUNISHABLE BY
UP TO 3 YEARS IN A FEDERAL PRISON AND A FINE OF $250,000
RECORDING DEVICES ARE NOT PERMITTED IN THE THEATRE VIOLATORS ARE SUBJECT TO
DETENTION, ARREST AND FELONY PROSECUTION.

PLEASE REPORT ANY SUSPICIOUS ACTIVITY TO THEATRE MANAGEMENT
THANK YOU FOR YOUR COOPERATION.

Figure 2.4   Reproduced by the permission of the Motion Picture Association of America

the rights owners will yield more money. Like a diplomat talking to the enemy, product suppliers sometimes need to work with pirates to help convert them. This is what started happening in select markets, with key suppliers first accelerating windows to start competing with pirates (starting to erode their market share) and then working with the so-called pirates to establish new, and higher sustainable price points. Through this process, markets can start to evolve legitimate distribution.

Online Impact

- The lower cost to produce original online content has led to the use of the Web for online pilots; these pilots can be tested both for Web use and potential crossover to television.

- Online is the fastest and largest growing area of piracy. This has created industry action to contain peer-to-peer file sharing services enabling the illegal copying of content; efforts to thwart digital piracy have also led to tagging content in new ways (e.g., watermarks), accelerating breadth and timing of releases, and putting focus on DRM and encryption technologies.
- The Web is enabling increased risk taking, as less is at stake given lower entry costs in online programming; the net result is lower and fewer barriers to entry and the democratization of content.
- There is an increased pool of creativity from the flat world and global Internet access: development no longer needs to be local; an artist need not go to an enclave to network, interact, and absorb trends; anyone can receive feedback from anywhere (the next hit could come from a kid in New Delhi as easily as from Hollywood).
- The Web provides an instant feedback loop: voting for "best" creates a pyramid effect, forcing up and validating favored content via a type of instant network effect.
- The evolution of the Internet is pushing the boundaries of copyright laws, with new digital applications continuously creating novel issues (e.g., where should lines of fair use be drawn in the context of mash-ups?).

73

CHAPTER 3

Financing Production: Studios and Networks as Venture Capitalists

Overview

This chapter will discuss how film and television projects are financed, including how the money is raised and secured and what piece of the pie parties retain for their investment. I will argue that to a large degree Hollywood studios are simply specialized venture capitalists with the return on investment (ROI) strategy premised on limited but large bets. The discussion of traditional film and TV financing is in stark contrast to original Internet production, which today remains heavily dependent on venture capital or other private backing given the nascent (though growing) video advertising market and speculative returns.

Standard Hollywood movies have become extraordinarily expensive: the average cost of a studio released film is now greater than $70M, and when then adding marketing and distribution costs the sunk cost per project typically exceeds $100M[1]; moreover, all studios have a certain number of event or so-called tentpole pictures per year whose total production and marketing costs will be well in excess of $100M. In fact, as highlighted in Chapter 1, certain pictures can even have budgets exceeding $200M. In 2005, Universal's *King Kong* directed by Peter Jackson was reported to have a budget of $207M.[2] In 2006, *Variety* reported *Superman Returns* from Warners passed $200M as well, and by 2007 multiple pictures (e.g., *Spider-Man 3, Pirates of the Caribbean 3*) were reputedly cresting this mark.[3]

TV financing costs are tempered by the ability to stage commitments (e.g., pilot, episode commitment by season), and while the risks are therefore smaller, the numbers for network shows and movie-like pay TV series (e.g., *Sopranos, Rome*) can nevertheless be in the tens of millions across a season.

Principal Methods of Financing Films

As with any other business, there are innumerable ways of financing the production and release of a film. The following is a snapshot of the most common financing schemes, with each category discussed in detail later in this chapter.

The first and perhaps oldest method to fund production is via studio financing, where a major studio simply foots the bill itself. Even when a studio pays, however, there are often issues about how it raises the money and whether it reduces the risk by syndicating a portion of the financing or selling off parts. A second form of financing involves schemes pursuant to which independent producers secure capital either to co-finance or fully fund a picture; this can involve bank financing, pre-sales, completion bonds, negative pickup structures, and complicated debt and equity slate financings.

Another scenario employed by independent producers, though limited to a subset of extremely wealthy and powerful producers (and as a corollary successful), is simply to shoulder all the risk and self-finance pictures. This is the scenario sometimes referred to as a distribution rental model such as the deal between Lucasfilm and Fox for the Star Wars prequels, the much speculated about deal between Pixar and Disney (before Disney acquired Pixar in 2006), and DreamWorks' new relationship with Disney.

Finally, in an apt analogy to the venture capital world, productions can sometimes have "angel" financing, where a wealthy third party entity or individual may simply underwrite a production. This was the case with Bob Zemekis's *Polar Express* which, as discussed in more detail later, was significantly underwritten by real estate mogul Steve Bing.

A level of complexity is introduced in most financings because the structure is rarely a pure form of the methods previously described. Co-productions, for example, are a common vehicle to share risk and can take place within any one of the structures; moreover, the term co-production itself is much ballyhooed and little understood. It can mean anything from a sharing of rights to a legal structure tied to formal government subsidies and tax schemes.

75

Principal Methods of Financing Online Production

There is not much to summarize in this area because there are no well-developed models in the online space akin to film and TV. Today, the principal method of financing online production is to secure funding from friends and family or venture capitalists (VC) willing to advance funds against a stake in the Web site/production company. Very few companies are breaking even in the space, and the VCs are betting on building up sites and "mini-channels" rather than focusing on funding a specific individual piece of content. Sites like Funnyordie.com (Will Ferrell and Sequoia Capital backed), comedy.com (Dean Valentine, former Prexy UPN), Heavy.com, and MyDamnChannel.com are seemingly content aggregation plays that likely rest on the strategy that the brand/site will be worth more than the sum of its parts. Accordingly, we can surmise that the goal, as with all VC-type investments, is an IPO or sale based on future multiples rather than value based on a piece of content's current cash flow. The online space is better understood if one views the space as a clear playing field in which entrepreneurs are launching hundreds of new networks, each vying for reach and brand adoption.

The other strategy is for the larger media groups to fund online sister divisions, attempting to incubate new content that may create crossover synergies as well as developing self-sustaining niche channels and hits. Examples of this include Disney/ABC's Stage 9 digital production unit (which has since been folded back into ABC) and AOL's backing of shows like *Kate Modern* (which was originally part of Bebo before AOL's 2008 acquisition of the site). Funding for shows in affiliated divisions is advanced by the larger company, and then recouped by revenues garnered through advertising, sponsorships, and product placements. (see also Chapter 9 for a discussion of product placements vs. promotional partners). Bebo's *Kate Modern* may be an example of trends to come, in that the funding was secured up-front via embedded product placements (e.g., character wears a particular shoe brand) and sponsorships; this secure funding tempers the dependence on impression-based advertising revenues. *Kate Modern* producer, LG15 Studios, started the trend with its prior online hit *Lonelygirl 15*, where pursuant to a deal with Neutrogena it integrated cosmetic products into the story.[4] The sponsorship model was taken to a new level with *Kate Modern*, where sponsors included Microsoft, Procter & Gamble, Warners Music, Paramount, and Orange; the UK's *Guardian* reported that these sponsors each paid up to

£250,000 for placement in the show, with each sponsor paying "... based on the amount its brand is integrated into the storyline, which includes monitoring the number of times it appears in the video and is mentioned in the script."[5]

Additionally, and importantly, the growth of video advertising with significantly higher CPMs than display ads is making online programming more akin to traditional TV, and for the first time creates a landscape where original programming can garner direct advertising revenues with the potential of covering production costs. As video ads become more common, and views are expanded by syndicating content offsite to capture more eyeballs (i.e., producers don't care if you watch the show on their site or MySpace as long as they capture a material share of video ad revenues wherever you watch), then online will become parallel to traditional TV. The question will be then one of ratings, with metrics tied to views, impressions, and engagement (e.g., click-throughs, text messages) vs. ratings points, and the strength of content setting market prices for CPM rates.

Currently, however, there appears to be a disconnect between CPM rates for TV and online, with content owners often claiming premium content is undervalued online, while online networks in contrast assert that the same content is priced at a premium to offline media. Although this should be a simple comparison, in fact the two positions are difficult to reconcile because the rates are priced independently and each has different advantages and disadvantages. In the case of offline, the "live" effect of programming and its scale in simultaneously reaching a mass audience commands a premium despite the relative inefficiency of targeting a diffuse (even if generally demographically targeted) audience without direct online-like metrics to track delivery. With online, the advertising can focus delivery and virtually track one-to-one relationships that should command a premium; however, online content's value is diluted relative to offline because the same scale of mass delivery is only reached (if at all) in fragmented impressions over a long period of time (e.g., 10 million people may be reached over a week or month, rather than simultaneously). Accordingly, given the still immature online market, valuing what advertising rates should be when similar (if not identical) content is delivered online via free streaming versus the rate for free television delivery is not as straightforward as it may appear.

Arguably, as referenced in Chapter 6, online is more comparable in delivery to TV syndication, and over time some convergence in valuation between these markets may emerge. Even then the parallels are not exact, in that TV syndication tends to be focused on local pricing (as advertising may be sold market by market), while online syndication of premium content on the Web is not only local, but potentially global. In the end, to some degree the analogy between the experiences (which are not identical) is like comparing apples and oranges, while recognizing there are strong correlations (both fruits and healthy) as well as differentiating nuances (green and red apples, mandarin oranges). With all these moving parts, it is not surprising that producers of original online content struggle to build monetization models against budgets and have launched shows with the relative certainty of sponsorships driven by product placements.

I asked Jayant Kadambi, founder and CEO of YuMe networks, one of the top ten online advertising platforms and networks, and a leader in the video advertising space, whether he thought we would soon see convergence between online and offline pricing, or whether the markets would continue to set rates independently. He advised:

Providing a comparison or correlation between online media spending and offline media spending will only help increase the scale, reach, and breadth of online advertising. If an offline advertiser spends $100,000 to reach an audience and receives a GRP of 52, then the natural question before the advertiser spends $100,000 online is what is the GRP equivalent. Think about purchasing an apple in the US for $1.00. Intuitively, we know whether that is expensive or not. If we spend 400 Drachma for an apple in Greece, the immediate reaction is to convert back to USD to see if it's expensive. So, whether there is convergence in the pricing models between online and offline will eventually be influenced by the net value the advertiser sees in each medium. But there definitely will be correlation models between the two media outlets.

Variety of Financing Methods as a Response to Difficulty and Risks in Predicting Success of Experience Goods

As a premise to discussing financing, it is important to digress into certain economic theories that lurk behind the allocation of risk and the disproportionate importance that marketing has in the media and entertainment business. Film and television are classic experience goods, as distinct from ordinary goods. An experience good is a product that the consumer cannot accurately or fully assess until consuming it, whether that is via watching a film or TV show or reading a book.[6] Given the nature of creative goods — that nobody knows what will be a success — and the fact that you cannot really know whether you will like a property until you digest it yourself, it is natural for us to look for signals and references to make better bets before investing our time. These references and signals can come from sources as disparate as award recognition, critics' picks, and word of mouth (or blogs, a new media form of word of mouth). In the end, we are all searching for a trusted source that improves the odds we will make a good choice. The problem is that a good choice is highly personal, and mapping external sources of information regarding a creative good onto an internal measurement, while having to choose among a dizzying range of product (sometimes referred to as infinite variance) from which we will pick a small sample to spend time with (consume), seems an almost impossible proposition.

The issue is made more complex when one considers that the external signals are imperfect. Statistics show that awards are often poor predictors of commercial success, with trends and voting pool demographics (which the consumer is not likely to share) skewing results. One only needs to look at the disconnect recently between best picture Oscar nominations and commercial success to see the pattern. Of the top 15 box office films of 2008 (including the top five, *Batman — The Dark Knight*, *Iron Man*, *Indiana Jones and the Kingdom of the Crystal Skull*, *Hancock*, and *Wall-E*) none were nominated for best picture (though this comparison, to be fair, should exclude *Wall-E* which won for Best Animated Feature). In contrast, of the pictures nominated for best picture Oscars in 2008 and 2009, only one picture each year (respectively, *Juno* and *The Curious Case of Benjamin Button*) had a United States box office greater than $100 M. Perhaps this lack of correlation is a function of the line between movies as an art form versus a commercial endeavor; industry-sponsored awards shows tend to focus on underlying skills and performance attributes, which subset of inputs are simply another source of signals. When art and entertainment value do overlap, though, such as with a blockbuster that is also a best picture winner, then this may be one of the few cases where signals are clear.

Critics are another source of information, but this information is only as good as your personal mapping to a critic's choice: How often have we said I disagree with that opinion, or were disappointed with a recommendation? Accordingly, we tend to try and adjust the critics' picks by integrating bias, countering with whether there is a better correlation to types of films they have liked where we agree, etc. Additionally, as also discussed in Chapter 9, it is unclear whether online sources of information that aggregate reviews (e.g., rottentomatoes.com) and social networking sites that exponentially disseminate opinions, actually improve personal decision making or interject a cacophonous web of biases requiring more sophisticated (or perhaps arbitrary) filtering. Even affinity for actors might pique interest, but it does not help that much (even your favorite actors can be in a clunker).

Finally, word of mouth is the mother of all external signals, and it is the watercooler buzz and positive recommendations that marketers so covet. The danger here is that trends follow herd behavior, and experience goods inherently lend themselves to bandwagon and cascade effects. This is because even with imperfect information (needing to consume the good yourself to really know if you agree with the pack/like it) consumers have to balance internal and external inputs without knowing which judgment is correct. Richard Caves illuminates the problem by what almost seems like a riddle. If you see John buying good X, and you have an independent sense you will like X, you will follow your hunch and go with the flow (and the same pattern holds in reverse with rejection). But what happens if your internal sense differs from the external recommendation and the signals cross each other out? What do you do? If we were to assume the outcome is determined by a coin flip, it can start a trend — if heads you buy, then you agree with John and the next consumer will see two positive signals even though in reality there was only one. The problem cascades such that a trend can appear even though the sum of the individual collective gut picks may come out the other way.[7] This helps explain, at least in part, how it is easy to wonder how everyone loved or hated such and such and yet you felt just the opposite coming out of the theater.

Combining the factors of information cascades, infinite variance, experience goods, and imperfect signals, it is no wonder that success of product is highly variable, risk is extreme, and that assorted financing schemes have evolved to try and combat the problem. In trying to solve the question whether there are strategies that may temper the risk inherent with movies, and sampling over 2,000 films, economists Arthur de Vany and David Walls concluded that box office revenues have infinite variance and that they do not converge on an average because the mean is dominated by extreme successes (block-busters). As far as mitigating risk, they conclude it is impossible:

We conclude that the studio model of risk management lacks a foundation in theory or evidence. Revenue forecasts have zero precision, which is just a formal way of saying that "anything can happen." Movies are complex products and the cascade of information among film-goers during the course of a film's theatrical exhibition can evolve along so many paths that it is impossible to attribute the success of a movie to individual causal factors. In other words, as Goldman said, "Nobody knows anything."[8]

It is because risk cannot be fully mitigated that participants (studios, producers) have evolved varying financing mechanisms as a way of distributing that risk. I will also argue in Chapter 9 that the nature of experience goods underlies the importance of marketing, which can help signaling and at least try to influence a positive cascade of information.

Challenge Exacerbated in Selecting which Product to Produce

The previous section focuses on the process by which consumers grapple with experience goods in making decisions, but the related challenge of financing is to predict that very outcome before the experience good is even made. The ultimate challenge of financing is that someone is asked to judge this creative value proposition at a root sage without adequate inputs to make the decision required. This is a nearly impossible task. Additionally, it helps explain why the development process is so murky, protracted, subject to second-guessing, and littered with projects that "almost got made."

This quandary is also, in part, why so much emphasis is placed on backing those with successful track records; it is also why some executives continue to seek a repeatable system to implement and become frustrated realizing that indeed some development/production elements are formulaic (e.g., plot points and acts in a script, needing conflict and character growth) and yet the formulas do not necessarily lead to success. Alas, as noted in Chapter 2, there are no golden rules nor right answers in selecting creative goods before they are produced. If experience goods were merely widgets, then an assembly line would work. However, because creative goods are subject to infinite variety, and nobody knows with certainty what will work—especially at the root stage before a project is infused with its creative spark—what is most coveted and compensated is creative talent backers believe will infuse a project with pixie dust.

Studio Financing

Classic Production–Financing–Distribution Deal

This is the standard deal where a producer brings a developed picture to a studio, and the studio agrees to fund production and marketing costs as well as distribute the film. The difference between this structure and a pure in-house production is that in an in-house production the studio has already acquired the property and then simply greenlights the project, engaging a producer on a work-for-hire basis. While a production–financing–distribution (PFD) deal may entail an assignment of the underlying rights to the studio in return for agreeing to move forward, typically the deal starts with an independent producer who has acquired the rights to a property, developed it, attached key talent, and then so-called "sets it up" at the studio. This is also the stage where agents often play a critical role, by specializing in "packaging" talent (and take a packaging fee), such that a studio is presented with a turnkey project ready to produce.

In return for financing production and distribution, the studio typically acquires all copyright and underlying rights in and to the property, as well as worldwide distribution rights in all media in perpetuity (Note: There may be select guild mandated reservations of rights). While this may sound extreme, the studio is shouldering all the financial risk and the producer will be making both up-front fees in the budget as well as have a backend participation tied to a negotiated profits definition (see Chapter 10). Accordingly, this is the classic risk–reward scenario, where full financing vests the distributor with the upside and ownership.

Studio Financing of Production Slate; Studio Co-productions

Regardless of whether a studio enters into a PFD agreement or some other structure on a particular picture, from a macro standpoint studios need a strategy to finance their overall production slate. The simplest and oldest method of financing is via bank credit facilities covering a slate of films. As the business continues to grow riskier and more complex, however, studios have sought a variety of methods to secure production financing, acknowledging that they need to cede some upside to offset the enormous risks taken.

Co-productions
When a studio wants to offset risk it will often enter into a co-production relationship with another studio. In such a case, each studio will agree what percentage of the budget it will contribute, and will in turn keep certain exclusive distribution rights. The simplest and most frequently used mechanism is to split domestic and foreign rights. Sometimes this scenario arises when the project involves talent tied to different studios, and the only way to move forward is sharing. This occurred, for example, on *War of the Worlds* (2005) directed by Steven Spielberg and starring Tom Cruise. Tom Cruise had an overall production deal at Paramount, Steven Spielberg was tied to DreamWorks (before the Paramount acquisition of DreamWorks, and subsequent split and deal with Disney), and the picture was produced/released as a Paramount and DreamWorks picture.

The foregoing is an example of a co-production planned from the inception of shooting. Sometimes, however, during production a studio will become nervous with escalating costs and decide to limit its risk by selling off a piece. The most famous example of this is the film *Titanic*. The movie was originally a Fox production, but as costs spiraled and the studio became increasingly nervous (at the time there was even talk that the whole studio could be in jeopardy if the film bombed given the investment) Fox elected to sell off part of the film to Paramount. It was rumored that Paramount invested a fixed sum, allowing the picture to be completed, and ended up with a 50% share of the picture even though its investment was ultimately less than 50% of the costs. With the film going on to break all box office records, the deal made by then studio head John Dolgin was regarded as one of the shrewdest of its day.

A more detailed discussion of co-productions follows, but it is discussed here as a financing mechanism by a studio to spread risk or marry talent, as opposed to the later strategy where a co-production is a necessary vehicle to raise the money for production in the first place. (Note: Studios can also employ the same strategy as discussed in the section Independent Financing; namely selling select rights or markets. This was a strategy frequently employed by Paramount in the 1990s when the international rights to many of its films were sold off to hedge risk.)

Debt and Equity Financings

Another mechanism by which a studio will finance films is via stock or other equity/debt offerings. Pixar, for example, went public and was able to use its proceeds to co-finance its pictures with Disney. DreamWorks Animation's public offering similarly allowed it to finance films and secure below market distribution fees, and ultimately remain independent when its parent, DreamWorks SKG, was sold to Paramount (December 2005). This is a difficult strategy because (1) there are off-the-top offering costs that can be significant and (2) investors are usually looking for a particularly strong track record or brand, which can be hard to illustrate with a diverse studio slate (something that both Pixar and DreamWorks Animation achieved within the niche of computer graphics based animated films).

Off-Balance Sheet Financing

A mechanism similar to equity financing, in that funds may be raised from a diffuse pool of investors, is a limited partnership. This structure differs, however, in that as opposed to raising equity capital it is referred to as off-balance sheet financing. The first and most famous examples were the Disney backed Silver Screen Limited Partnership offerings in the 1980s.

In 1985 Disney, through broker E. F. Hutton & Company, offered 400,000 limited partnership interests for a maximum offering of $200,000,000. The prospectus, under the use of proceeds section, listed the following in Table 3.1 (under the maximum offering scenario):

Table 3.1 Disney Prospectus

	Amount	Percent
Source of funds		
Gross offering proceeds:	$200,000,000	100%
Use of funds		
Public offering expenses:		
Selling commissions:	$17,000,000	8.5%
Offering expenses	$3,500,000	1.75%
Operations:		
Film financing	$179,500,000	89.75%
Total use of funds	$200,000,000	100%

The prospectus footnoted the film financing line as follows:

Funds available for financing films will be loaned pursuant to the Loan Agreement and invested in the Joint Venture to pay film costs which include direct film cost, overhead payable to Disney and to the Partnership for the benefit of the Managing Partner and a contingency reserve. Disney and the Managing Partner will receive overhead of 13.5% and 4% respectively, of the Budgeted Film Cost (excluding overhead) of each Joint Venture Film and 3.75% and 1% (which is included in the loan amount), respectively, of the direct production costs (plus interest) of the Completed Films ...

(Note: The summary reflects the initial offering of $100M and 200,000 units, which was then amended two months later to double the offering.)

It is an interesting exercise to read through these summary terms, which define distribution fees, require Disney's Buena Vista distribution arm to fund minimum marketing expenditures in releasing each film and allocate revenue disbursement. One item that is both obvious and not obvious (because it is not highlighted) is that the investment is cross-collateralized, given that the unit investments apply to the slate of films rather than to an individual film. As previously noted, this would be difficult to achieve in other instances, but because "Disney" is perceived as a brand and the offering limits the budget range and nature of the pictures, using revenues from multiple films to pay out a single investment can work.

Studios Leveraging Hedge Fund and Private Equity Investments

Hedge funds—loosely regulated investment vehicles for wealthy and institutional investors often requiring a minimum investment of $1M or more—flush with cash started cozying up to financing opportunities that covered a slate of studio pictures. Beyond simply seeking new investment outlets, another factor potentially driving the new studio–hedge fund (and private equity) partnerships was the quickly changing technology landscape. As release windows started moving, and iPods, DVRs, and the Internet ushered in a new era of digital downloading and access, investors familiar with technology plays were oddly more comfortable investing in the same landscape that was making the control-it-all studios less comfortable with their distribution roots and forecasts. Both were players in high stakes games and it was hardly a surprise they should ultimately team up.

85

To the extent studios were already acting like VCs, why shouldn't they play by the same rules as professional VCs and take in private equity groups in a syndicate as partners?

Table 3.2 lists a few deals announced by various studios and hedge funds in 2005 and 2006 during the height of this new trend. (Note: A number of these funds are not classic "hedge funds" but rather specialized funds combining elements of equity, junior debt with a stated return and equity kicker, and bank debt lines.)

Unlike more typical studio pacts that saw large independents like Revolution and Spyglass (at Sony), Village Roadshow (Warner Bros.), and New Regency (at Fox) take creative and production control and even certain distribution rights alongside investments, the most attractive part about these deals was that it was all about money.

Universal's Prexy-COO Rick Finkelstein noted to *Variety*: "You retain worldwide distribution, you retain complete creative control, you've got a financial partner and you're allowed to take a distribution fee. The economics are quite attractive."[9] Echoing this sentiment, Paramount's CFO Mark Badagliacca stated: "We like it because it's a slate deal without giving up any rights."[10]

So how do these deals work economically? Although each has its nuances, in the simplest scenario a studio and fund would each share production costs 50/50. In parallel, the studio and fund would similarly share profits 50/50. The issue then became how are "profits" defined. In this instance all revenues (except potentially certain ancillaries) would be accounted for — namely 100% of video revenues as opposed to a 20% royalty — and apply in the gross revenue line. In terms of expenses, the studio would usually take a reduced distribution fee (10–15% as opposed to 25–30%). Also, the studio would often fund print and advertising (P&A) costs and recoup those first, together with its distribution fee, out of gross revenues.

Table 3.3 is a simple example taking the United States and international box office numbers from *Batman Begins* (box office from www.boxofficemojo.com).

If the fund put in $75M (50% of estimated production costs) and received $21.5M, that would be a 28.6% ROI; if they also had to fund 50% of the P&A, however, then the total investment would jump to $127.5M and their return would drop to 16.8% (still high). (Note: These returns do not include leverage effects, where true equity returns would be higher assuming a mix of equity and debt.) On this logic, the investment would make sense. However, a couple of key items need to be factored in. First, the above is probably a rosy picture, for it assumes no gross players, no interest, etc. Factoring in

Table 3.2 Studio–Hedge Fund Deals 2005–2006

Studio	Hedge Fund Partner	Invested Amount	Sample Titles Included
Warner Bros.	Legendary Pictures	$600 M (upped to $1B)	*Batman Begins, Superman Returns, Batman—The Dark Knight, Where the Wild Things Are* (initially 5 years/25 pictures, expanded to 7 years and up to 45 pictures)
	Virtual Pictures	$528M	6 pictures including *Poseidon, V for Vendetta, The Good German*
	Alcon Entertainment	$500M+	15 films (*The Sisterhood of the Traveling Pants 2*)
Sony	Gun Hill Road	$400–600M	11 pictures across two funds
	Relativity Media	($300M)	
Universal	Gun Hill Road	$200M	Funding 50% of 7 pictures including *Doom, Nanny McPhee, The Inside Man, The Fast and the Furious: Tokyo Drift, The Kingdom*
Fox	Dune Capital	$325M	Across 28 pictures
Disney	Kingdom Fund		
Paramount	Melrose Fund	20% of budget	Across 25 films including *War of the Worlds, Mean Girls*

Sources: *Variety* "Funds Pop for Pic" 1/20/06; *Variety Int'l Weekly* 1/23–29/06; *Variety*, "Warner's Men in Tights" 2/23/06; *Variety* 5/16/06; "Even More Legendary," *Hollywood Reporter* 6/26–7/2/07; "As Others Shun Hollywood, FedEx Founder Bets on Movies," *International Herald Tribune* 7/22/08 regarding Alcon.

Table 3.3 *Batman Begins* ROI Example

United States box office	$205M	
International box office	$166M	
Total box office	$371M	
Rentals	$185M	Assume ~50% theatrical box office
Video	$180M	Assume ~$18 net wholesale × 10 M units worldwide
Net video	$100M	Assume ~55% margin
Television	$65M	
Total revenue	$350M	Rentals + net video + TV
Prod. costs	−$150M	$75 M returned to hedge fund (if pre P&A)
P&A	−$105M	Assume ~70% production cost
Distribution fee	−$52M	Assume ~15% revenues
Profit	$43M	Revenues — costs (P&A + production + distribution fee)
Hedge fund	$21.5M	Assume 50% share

these costs/expenses the profit probably dips to single digits (for a detailed discussion of profit calculation, see Chapter 10). Second, this assumes all the revenues come in up front. In fact, certain TV revenues will come in years downstream, and factoring in the time value of money the return per year becomes a much smaller amount. Finally, this is one picture, and this hit needs to cover losses on other films: if the return is not more than 20% on a hit then arguably it is going to be difficult to show a return across the portfolio.

Accordingly, the *Wall Street Journal* quipped in an article titled "Defying the Odds, Hedge Funds Bet Billions on Movies": "Yet in a business where the conventional wisdom says that 10% of a studio's films are responsible for 100% of its profits, even a passel of Harvard Business School graduates may not be immune to the pitfalls faced by nearly every investor to have hit the intersection of Hollywood and Vine."[11] The *Wall Street Journal's* article continued to highlight the limited return on investment, and cash flow issues previously described:

The problem is that under the terms of most co-financing deals, the new investors are often the last in line to get paid. Once exhibitors take their half of ticket sales, many studios take a distribution fee of 10–15% of what's left from the box office. Then, the movie's production and marketing costs are paid back, and any A-list actors or directors pocket their shares. After that, the revenue-sharing process begins and it continues for the next five or more years as revenue flows in from DVD sales, pay-cable showings, and toy or other merchandise sales.[12]

To Include or not to Include Tentpoles in the Slate — Do Limited Slates, and the Relatively Small Size of all Slates, Doom Fund Investments?

The studios are obviously quite savvy in the deals they choose, and frequently withhold their perceived best assets from financings that would require a material sharing of upside. It is therefore not surprising that hoped for tentpoles like *The Chronicles of Narnia* and *Pirates of the Caribbean* series were withheld by Disney from a 2005 co-financing deal, and that Sony excluded *Spider-Man 3*, the James Bond title *Casino Royale*, and *The Da Vinci Code* from its Gun Hill Road deal.[13] (Note: As in most financings there is more than meets the eye, and it is possible that the Regal Entertainment backing of Narnia and MGM control over James Bond could have forced an "exclusion" because neither of these stakeholders would likely want a further dividing of the pie.) In fact, what is surprising is not the exclusion of major franchise pictures from sharing, but the very fact that certain major tentpoles such as Batman and Superman (though the franchises had both waned, and the studios were hoping for a comeback) were included in the first place. Their inclusion is what arguably started to attract the most attention in the space.

One could have predicted at the outset, based on simple economic patterns, that this cycle would have to come full circle; namely, hits pay for misses (the above quoted 10% rule), and excluding some of the more likely hits from an overall slate dooms the success of a fund. It took less than one year for the inevitable cycle to start reaching an early maturity.

Poseidon, which reportedly cost $150–160M to produce, grossed only $22.2M in its opening weekend, leading to the questioning of Virtual Studio's strategy and a *Variety* headline "Sea Change at H'Wood Newbie: 'Poseidon' Capsizes Fund."[14] Other funds started to fare similarly, with Legendary Pictures (Warners deal) backed *Lady in the Water* (M. Night Shyamalan) and *Ant Bully* (Tom Hanks backed) underperforming. Quickly hedge funds were on the defensive, reminding investors about the underlying portfolio strategy.[15]

But how long would it take for rational economics to right the *Poseidon* tainted ship? This was not a mutual fund with hundreds of stocks diversifying a risk portfolio; even the largest of the funds was small with no more than 20–25 pictures in the mix. Nevertheless, the first arguments were focused on differentiating one pool from the next, rather than to address the fact that all the pools were too small to provide a true hedge against risk. Investors, no doubt trying to defend their strategy, first argued that one film did not undermine a portfolio strategy, and then as large films in the portfolio started to underperform distinguished their pools from others by challenging the scope of the slate. *Variety* noted: "Wall streeters said Virtual may be more exposed than the other funds by co-financing such a small slate."[16]

Because excluding some of the most likely hits by definition increased the risk profile, it was therefore not surprising that funds started to reconsider the composition of portfolios, with the organizer of the Universal and Sony deals with Gun Hill Road going on record that new studio deals would involve a studio's full slate of pictures.[17] No longer would it be so easy for studios to create off-balance sheet financing of $100M+ pictures while excluding other key titles.

Of course, a big hit will change all perception, for the amount of money a single film can generate may justify an entire slate investment. Legendary's share in *Batman — The Dark Knight*, which became the #2 box office film of all time surpassing half a billion in the United States (compare to previous *Batman Begins* example) could earn it upwards of $250M over time (and much more if they participate in certain ancillary revenues such as merchandising). Note that the increase in return is more than a linear relationship, because after a certain point additional revenues are not matched by additional costs (i.e., the production and print and initial advertising costs are fixed, so imagine the above *Batman Begins* example but simply double the revenue lines). It is because a single hit, which may represent less than 5% of the total portfolio (based on number of films) can potentially recoup 50% or more of an entire fund's risk that investors tend to ignore the relatively small pool size. Based on statistics, a sample size of twenty may not be large enough to ensure consistent deviations and therefore tempered risk, but one has to remember that these are not random samples and placing bets with proven producers should positively skew results, as long as all titles are included. A studio will rarely go zero for ten, but as discussed previously taking some of the best picks out of the mix may change the equation from a predictable statistical spread to more luck-based metrics.

90

Independent Financing

Independent financing is a catchall term that refers to a myriad of financing schemes, and is generally distinguished from the above discussion concerning funds because funds invest across a slate, and much "independent financing" applies on a per project basis. The common thread is that (1) money is sought to actually pay for production, requiring that cash is advanced before the project starts and (2) that the source of funding is, at least in part, from a party other than the distributor. This occurs in two very simple cases: when the producer cannot obtain the studio's commitment to fund production, or when the producer does not want to take the studio's money because it can keep something that the studio would have demanded. The "what it keeps" can range from creative control to a larger share of the pie (by bringing money to the table) to retaining specified rights. (Note: While some of the following discussion can apply equally to television (e.g., pre-sales), the bulk of independent financing and the overview below applies in the context of funding films.)

Most cases of independent financing are because the producer needs money to make or complete its project. Although there are no bright line categories, the following are typical methods of financing:

- Foreign pre-sales
- Ancillary advances
- Negative pick-ups
- Bank credit lines
- Angels

Although some of these mechanisms, such as pre-sales, are the tools of structuring co-productions, I discuss the nature of co-productions separately below and here focus on some of the line item issues of how the underlying rights are divided and treated.

Foreign Pre-sales

Foreign pre-sales are either full or partial sales of specified rights in a particular territory. For example, it may mean theatrical rights only or theatrical + video + TV rights in a territory. These sales can be structured either as percentages of the budget or in fixed dollar terms. Moreover, the deals may be structured on a quitclaim basis (outright

Table 3.4 Hypothetical TV Show Finances

Network/Pre-sale Partner	Territory and Rights	Pre-sold as % of Budget	$ Pre-sold
Pan-European broadcaster	Europe cable	15	52,500
French network	France	25	87,500
German network	Germany	10	35,000
UK network	UK	5	17,500
Italian network	Italy	5	17,500
			$210,000

sale of rights in perpetuity) or on the basis of an advance, where the producer shares in an upside after the licensee distributor recoups its investment per a negotiated formula. Table 3.4 is a hypothetical example for an animated television show budgeted at $350,000.

In the above example, if Producer A could obtain this level of commitment, it would have 60% of its budget secured while still having the balance of the world (United States, Asia, Latin America) available. Depending on the deal structure, the broadcasters may commit to a percentage of budget, rather than a set license fee, which can be advantageous if the budget increases; in fact, in theory only, is it possible to sell more than 100% and be in profits before production.

A wrinkle on the above is that not all contributed amounts fall into the same category. Some broadcasters/partners may put in their amount as a straight license fee, others may make contributions contingent on it being a co-production (requiring a certain amount of localized production/elements and control), and yet others may allocate their contribution between a license fee and an equity investment. To take this example further, the French amount may require a French co-production, where the government backed CNC actually contributes an amount and the French broadcaster contributes the balance as its license fee. In this instance, the French network may not demand an equity investment, and may simply acquire broadcast rights since its investment/cost has already been subsidized. The German amount may or may not include an equity component. If the broadcaster demands equity, it could be 50/50, for example, where $17,500 of the $35,000 would be considered an equity investment; namely they would hold a 5% equity stake in the profits. Finally, one partner such as the Pan-European Broadcaster may require ancillary rights, or a stake in ancillary rights, as opposed to a stake in the whole. If they were granted European merchandising rights and a fee, then Producer A may only have a secondary income stream from merchandising.

There is no obvious outcome, with a continuum of stakeholding moving up and down depending on the percent of ownership, percent of budget covered, and range of rights retained/granted by the producer. The final deal may cover enough of the budget to move forward, grant third parties 40–50% of the overall equity in defined revenues, and grant others a different percentage of merchandising or video. The end game is obviously to cover the production budget and retain as much of an equity stake as possible.

Ancillary Advances

I touched on ancillary advances above in pre-sales, but it is important to differentiate between primary and ancillary rights granted. Table 3.4 was predicated on licensing the television broadcast rights to a television show. By ancillary, I mean other downstream revenues such as from merchandising or video. Because these downstream revenues are dependent on the success of the primary revenue source (e.g., there will likely not be merchandising on an original TV property until it is a hit), these amounts are speculative. Accordingly, these are harder advances to obtain, and will usually be discounted given the uncertain value.

93

Negative Pickups

A negative pickup is a deal structure where the distributor guarantees the producer that it will distribute the finished picture and reimburse the producer for agreed negative costs (i.e., production costs), subject to the picture conforming to terms detailed in the negative pickup agreement. With distribution and reimbursement of production costs secured, the producer will then borrow money from a third-party lender using the reimbursement contract as collateral.

The advantage to the distributor is cash flow and the elimination of risk: nothing is paid until the picture is completed to the satisfaction of stipulated contract terms. The advantage to the producer is a greater measure of independence — the terms of the negative pickup agreement will often impose less creative control than if the studio distributor were directly overseeing production — and the elimination of certain financing charges such as studio interest. (These charges may not be market rate, and may continue to accrue until recoupment, which is set back to the extent distribution fees are taken out first leaving less cash available to recoup production costs.)

Under a negative pickup structure, the distributor would have approval over all material elements of production. Such approval rights may include approval over the budget, production schedule, the script, all above-the-line talent (i.e., principal cast, director, writer, producer), and contingent compensation granted (e.g., net or gross profit participations). In addition to approval of the creative and financing elements, the agreement will grant the distributor the right to approve delivery specifications. Such specifications will include, for example, that the picture will have a running time of not less than X and not more than Y, and that it will have a rating not more restrictive than ("R").

In both the negative pickup structure, and in any structure involving loans from a third party, securing a completion bond will likely be required. A completion bond is a contract with a designated completion bond company that can ultimately take over production and complete the film in the event of a producer default. These companies engage reputable producers, and will monitor the cash flow and progress of production against specified milestones. Of course, all parties will do whatever they can to avoid takeover, but in the draconian eventuality that a producer is failing to deliver these companies will step in and manage the balance of production. Completion bonds can be quite expensive and are calculated on a percentage of the budget, usually in the range of a few percent. Examples of what may contractually trigger a takeover might include:

- Over Budget: If the picture is materially over budget (e.g., if final estimated direct costs are estimated to exceed the budgeted costs by X, excluding costs of overhead, interest, and the completion bond fee)
- Over Schedule: If the picture is more than X weeks behind schedule
- Default: In the event of a material default

Third-party Credit — Banks, Angels, and a Mix of Private Equity

Bank Credit Lines

If a producer has a sufficient track record and consistent volume of production, a direct bank credit line may be able to be secured. This will often take the form of a revolving credit facility, and depending on the structure may cross-collateralize revenues from pictures to secure the overall facility. The economic advantage to a bank line is that it is all about money. The bank will only be concerned with the financial securitization and recoupment of its loaned sums and will not want to retain rights. Accordingly, this is an advantageous structure to retain the copyright, foreign and ancillary rights, and therefore upside in a property.

It is also possible to structure a bank line as so-called gap financing, where only a percentage of the budget is needed. This is a typical scenario where pre-sales and advances against ancillary revenues (such as a merchandising advance from a toy company) cover a significant amount of the production budget, and the bank line covers the bridge or gap to fund 100% of the costs. In this instance, the bank line will almost always come in first recoupment position, which gives the lenders comfort. In essence, they can look to 100% of the revenues to cover 20% of the budget lowering the risk. Nevertheless, films are inherently risky and obtaining a bank loan, even if for limited gap financing, is not easy; moreover, the documentation and legal fees can be quite considerable, constituting another expense to be built into the budget.

Mini-majors and Credit Facilities

Similar to a bank line of credit, producers, directors, and independent studios with a sufficient track record can raise enough money to create a so-called "mini-studio." This was the case when Joe Roth, former production head at Fox and then Disney, launched Revolution Studios. Combining a variety of distribution output deals, including theatrical distribution via Sony, Revolution raised over $1B for film production before a single picture was made. Similarly, when Harvey and Bob Weinstein left Miramax (the company they had founded and sold to Disney) they were able to launch a mini-studio with their new The Weinstein Company — a proposition that was only possible with the combination of distribution deals and significant third-party financing.

To an extent, this is an independent's dream, and it is common to see a mixture of distribution deals and bank credit facilities funding production (set in place with the security of the distribution arrangements). Another prominent example was Merrill Lynch's half-billion dollar backing of Marvel Entertainment, the comic book company whose characters include Spiderman and X-Men. (Note: The line between this type of deal and the previously discussed private equity/ hedge fund backed slate financings can be fuzzy; I have separated

Marvel here because it is an example of an independent brand raising financing, as opposed to a deal directly leveraging studio distribution.) In May 2006, Merrill took out a full page ad in the *International Herald Tribune* boasting:

Marvel Entertainment knew that by creating their own film studio they could profit directly from their legendary comic book characters rather than licensing the rights. But they lacked the production facility to achieve their vision. That is, until they talked to Merrill Lynch. We structured a transaction hailed as the "best Hollywood has ever seen," using Marvel's intellectual property as equity to raise $525 million—enough to bankroll up to 10 feature films. So now Marvel has full creative control over these characters. Not to mention their own destiny. This is just one example of how Merrill Lynch delivers exceptional financial solutions for exceptional clients.[18]

Of course, the "mother of all studio financings" was the 1995 creation of DreamWorks SKG. A studio, promising to be on the scale of a major not just a mini-major, was launched from scratch by combining the track record of legendary producers and directors (Steven Spielberg, Jeffrey Katzenberg, David Geffen) and backing by an enormous investor with Paul Allen (Microsoft co-founder) reportedly investing $500 million. Its initial credit facility was replaced by a $1.5B financing deal in 2002:

DreamWorks announces new financing
Los Angeles—DreamWorks LLC today announced that it has closed two major financing transactions totaling $1.5 billion. The new financing consists of a $1 billion film securitization— the first of its kind in the film industry—as well as a $500 million revolving credit facility. Together, these financings replace the Company's existing financing arrangements at a substantially lower cost of capital and extends the Company's access to debt capital until at least October 2007.
... The securitization uses a unique structure that finances expected film revenue cash receipts from DreamWorks' library of existing films, as well as from future live action releases. According to the terms of the securitization, funds are advanced

after a film has been released in the domestic theatrical market for several weeks, at which point the film's revenue stream over a multi-year period is highly predictable. In part, this predictability allowed the transaction to gain investment grade status from the two leading rating agencies ...[19]

Individual Producers/Directors Jump on the Private Equity Bandwagon

Finally, a trend also emerged where private equity funds partnered with former studio heads, as opposed to the studios themselves. Chris McGurk (former MGM Vice Chairman), Tom Pollock (former Universal Pictures Chairman), and Rob Friedman (former Paramount Vice Chairman) were all backed by fund money to capitalize respective film ventures. To a degree, these funds and mini-slates were filling a void in the independent market, with DreamWorks scaling back and The Weinstein Company still ramping up and not impacting the market as its founders had in the heyday of Miramax. The *International Herald Tribune* reported that McGurk's studio, Overture Films, would make 10 films/year in the $25M budget range, and that Pollock (together with director Ivan Reitman) obtained financing from investors, including Merrill Lynch, to produce a comparable slate of 10 pictures over five years.[20] (Note: Again, the line can be fuzzy, as arguably Overture can be classified as a mini-major, leveraging sister company distribution, such as Starz/Encore (pay TV) and Anchor Bay (video), for output deals; moreover, it is a strategic asset under the broader Liberty Media umbrella.)

97

Essentially, this new wave of financing was backing (until the 2008 global financial crisis put a halt to producer slate financings) a wave of independent filmmaking, with smaller budgeted pictures targeting, in some cases, more niche audiences.

Angel Investors

Similar to a venture capital structure, the film business tends to attract wealthy individuals that want to invest in pictures. These types of deals vary widely, but there seem to be a couple of consistent themes. First, the investor while wanting a return has a secondary objective of passion/fun/ego and will accordingly take a producing or executive producer credit; of course, this is not unfair in that much of the role of an executive producer can be putting together financing. Second, the investor is usually contributing a sizeable amount of the budget. These individuals are high stakes players, investing likely for high risk high reward rather than just as a gap financier. In fact, there is often a personal passion for the project and the angel investor may be putting in money because, simply, he wants to make the film.

A high-profile example of an angel financed film is *Polar Express*. Steve Bing, heir to a real estate fortune who turned to entertainment, partnered with Warner Bros. to back the Bob Zemekis (*Back to the Future, Forrest Gump, Who Framed Roger Rabbit?*) directed animated holiday film *Polar Express* starring Tom Hanks. The film was considered risky given its $165M budget (with some reports speculating it was more than $200M) and pioneering motion-capture animation technique (to give a unique look and range to animating human characters). Warner Bros. hedged its risk by partnering with Bing as *Business Week* reported: "And even folks at Warner Bros. are said to be thrilled that multimillionaire Steve Bing, who aspires to be a big-time producer, has put $80 million into the film. He's also covering half the $50 million or more in marketing expenses, according to a source with knowledge of the deal. Says the source: 'If it tanks, it won't leave Warner with that much of a hole [thanks to Bing].'"[21]

Sometimes the lines between an angel and a fund can blur, as seems to be the case with Alcon Entertainment. FedEx founder and CEO Frederick Smith teamed with Alcon founders to launch *My Dog Skip* (initially headed to DVD), and then went on to become an equity partner in a multi-picture financing deal, reportedly worth $550 M, with Warner Bros.[22] There are countless similar stories given the allure of Hollywood — most of them are simply less high profile and outside the public eye.

Rent a Distributor: When a Producer Rises to Studio-like Clout

The rent-a-distributor model is rarely used and limited to producers with enough of a checkbook and a track record they can pay for production costs and bargain for reduced distribution fees.

The most famous example of this model is Lucasfilm's deal with 20th Century Fox for the three Star Wars prequels, Episodes I, II, and III in the Star Wars saga. Due to the success of the original Star Wars trilogy, George Lucas had the financing and leverage to pay for the three prequels himself. Fox was reputedly investing no direct production costs, receiving a negotiated fee for distributing the Star Wars films.[23] This arrangement of only earning fees without taking any risk, while the producer in essence utilizes the studio's distribution operations (e.g., theatrical, video) and maintains the upside for having financed production, is often unfairly characterized as risk-free to the studio. By unfairly characterized, I mean that this premise tends to ignore the opportunity costs; Fox took on the responsibility and management of releasing these films, which was significant because they were destined to become the event titles of their respective years and require appropriate associated management and overhead time.

Presumably, the only reason a studio would agree to take on this level of time commitment is if (1) it was important to have a relationship with the talent and/or property and (2) if it believed even with no or minimal upside ownership stake it could earn significant distribution fees. This latter point underscores that the films in question need to be of mega box office stature, which leads to the corollary benefit of the studio leveraging one of the most desired films in its portfolio. While packaging is theoretically illegal under anti-trust laws prohibiting tying arrangements, if studio X comes to a client with a slate of pictures and one of those pictures is a must have picture, the wheels are greased for the other releases. All of these elements were satisfied: Fox had been the home/distributor of the original Star Wars films, clearly wanted to maintain a relationship with George Lucas, believed each film had the potential to generate hundreds of millions of dollars from which it could generate significant fees, and was ensured of multiple tentpole releases anchoring its summer slate over a number of years (from which it could directly or indirectly leverage other films).

The reason a producer would want this type of deal is to maintain the upside and keep control over the property both creatively and economically. Talking about the arrangement, *Business Week* noted of Lucas's control of the prequels: "He retains the rights to dictate marketing, distribution, and just about everything else about how they'll be seen in theaters."[24] The deal was the envy of every producer that could afford to bankroll his production, and before Disney acquired Pixar the distribution deal being negotiated was publicly referred to as a "Lucas type distribution deal" where Pixar would pay Disney a modest fee and retain the upside profit.

Applying the above test, Disney was in a similar position with Pixar as Fox was with Lucasfilm: Disney wanted to continue its collaboration with Pixar (one of the most successful in studio history), believed it would earn significant fees from distribution (even with a significantly discounted distribution fee), and with the track record of past Pixar films knew it would have a series of must have hits that would help leverage its other films and businesses. The one significant difference, however, was that while Fox and Lucasfilm had been successful partners, Fox was not a brand inextricably tied with Lucasfilm. In the case of Disney–Pixar, the fact that Disney is a consumer brand heralded as synonymous with successful animation and that Pixar for years had been upstaging them and could have become a competitor was clearly a factor. One could argue that the deal took on overtones beyond pure current economics, and that more than a distribution relationship was needed to restore Disney to its glory and market leadership in the animation space. To the extent that Disney may not have been willing to take a sliver of the pie on a successful animated film as opposed to holding the full upside (including character/franchise rights to cycle through theme parks and other vertically integrated divisions) simply tipped the scales in favor of a purchase.

Finally, even with all the clout in the world, a producer still needs the product distributed and cannot afford the massive overhead of a worldwide theatrical and video distribution team. Despite whatever Hollywood hugging one may witness, this is a relationship driven by necessity not love. It is this remaining underlying tension that fuels the passion for new distribution mediums, now enabled by digital technology, and holds the ace card of a producer bypassing the studio distribution system and going directly to the consumer. It is only the theatrical/video/TV infrastructure, marketing expertise and clout, and associated overhead costs that pose obstacles and require a partnership between production and distribution. What those who want to bypass the traditional studio system and distribute direct often fail to recognize is that the studios are quite good at what they do. Studios have become adept at efficiently creating brands overnight and repeating this feat on a regular basis. The infrastructure is not something to be dismissed lightly, for it is to the success of a film what an efficient supply pipeline is to a manufacturing endeavor; moreover, as discussed in Chapter 1, the efficiency is created by scale and cannot be repeated easily, if at all, on a one-off basis.

Reduced Distribution Fee Key to the Deal

While the relative advantages detailed above are all important, it is key to remember that the heart of a pure distribution arrangement is the producer's ability to lock in a below market distribution fee. For this to work economically for both parties, it needs to be primarily a financially driven relationship and not a competitive one.

While market rate fees can be 30% and higher, a rent-a-distributor deal where the producer is providing all the financing can drive down fees to single digit levels. DreamWorks Animation, in its SEC filing, noted that it has an 8% distribution fee with DreamWorks studio.[25]

While this could be perceived as a sweetheart deal between affiliated entities, it apparently set a benchmark for Steven Spielberg. When DreamWorks announced its split from Paramount in October 2008, backed by a reported $1.3B in financing from India's Reliance Communications and debt raised by J.P. Morgan,[26] it lined up a distribution deal with Universal, the studio where Spielberg made *Jaws* and began his career. Commenting on the deal, the *New York Times* noted: "Under the terms of the seven-year deal, Universal will distribute up to six films a year, according to a statement by the studio and the film executives. Universal will receive an 8 percent distribution fee, according to a person briefed on the negotiations."[27] Shortly after this deal was announced, however, the Universal relationship fell apart and DreamWorks instead teamed with Disney, where the studio announced it would release 30 films over 5 years under its Touchstone Pictures label. Evidencing the difficult climate of raising financing at the time (even for Spielberg, the ultimate luminary in Hollywood), as well as the sensitivity of how low studios were willing to reduce their distribution fees, the *New York Times* now reported that DreamWorks would instead be paying a 10% distribution fee: "The percentage is more onerous than the company had expected at Universal."[28]

101

Funding Ensures Tapping into 100% of Revenue Streams

As briefly discussed above, one of the principal advantages to funding all or a percentage of costs is that it tends to eliminate "Hollywood accounting" (see Chapter 10) and allows the backers to look to all revenue streams for recoupment and profits. Net profits definitions and participations are structured to define only a certain pot of revenues, such as video only being accounted for at a royalty percentage rate, rather than 100% of revenues. By partnering with a studio, a co-financier, if smart, stands in the same shoes as the studio; namely, they will recoup out of the same revenue streams and at the same time.

Television: How and Why Does It Differ?

To understand television financing, it is important to grasp that there are several micro-markets that are fundamentally different in their economics. While all TV is focused on ratings and attracting eyeballs, cable, network, pay TV, and syndication all behave a bit differently. The following is a short overview with the details of TV economics discussed in Chapter 6.

Network, Cable, and Pay TV Financing

Network

Network television is the most ratings sensitive of all TV, for historically 100% of the revenues from a broadcast show are generated from advertising dollars tied to ratings. This creates cutthroat competition for eyeballs, and fractions of a percent of a ratings point can make or break shows. Network primetime shows are the most expensive to produce with budgets in the millions of dollars; network license fees rarely cover the budget, but can exceed 50% of the budget. Accordingly, a TV production is usually faced with a healthy deficit. It would not be uncommon for a production budget for a primetime one hour drama to be over $2 M, and if there were 10 episodes ordered and the license fee covered half the budget the production would be in the red $10 M or more (and if a full "season" of 22 episodes are ordered this will more than double). The only way to recover this deficit is from off-network revenues, including DVD sales, international broadcast licenses, syndication (see Chapter 6 for more detail), and new online revenue streams (see Chapter 7).

It is because of this high risk, and the fact that few shows make it to syndication to recoup, that network shows are generally produced by parties with deep pockets — the studios and networks. The strategy is much like that of films: diversify production, hits pay for misses, and the vast majority of profits come from select properties that are breakout hits.

Cable

Cable is interesting because it is a hybrid. Cable networks earn money from two sources: advertising and carriage fees. Advertising works exactly like network, with inventory sold in the open market and dependent on ratings. The advantage cable has is that, in addition to advertising revenues, the networks are paid by cable operators to be carried on their system. In years past some stations had to pay the

102

cable operators to be carried, but currently the economics have flipped and almost all cable networks with material national reach are paid by the carriers. The issue is the amount of the fee, which can vary dramatically.

The basic economics are that the cable system will negotiate a per subscriber fee, which is then paid on a per month basis. If a network, for example, is carried in 50 million homes and is paid an average of $0.10/subscriber/month, then it would receive $60M/year. Another network with similar reach, demanding $0.50/subscriber, would reap $300M/year ($25M ×12 months). Because many major networks with national carriage now approach closer to 85M homes, the numbers can be staggering. At the $0.50 level this translates into over half a billion dollars on an annual basis. On the flip side, the cable carrier then offers consumers a "basic pay package," which bundles channels and takes the aggregate cable fees paid by consumers and reallocates the pool to acquire access to the various channels in the cable bundle. If a particular channel is in greater demand, such as ESPN, then it will have a higher per subscriber fee than a channel that is less critical to the average basic pay subscriber.

The fees paid by the cable operators ultimately allow cable stations to be a bit less ratings sensitive and to make larger episode commitments. The one element the cable stations generally do not have, however, is the upside of syndication. This is because cable itself grew up as an aftermarket, and tends to be the home for shows after network. Network shows go to cable or syndication, but there are few if any examples of shows moving upstream from cable to network. As more and more cable stations venture into original programming to differentiate themselves, there may be a secondary market that evolves for the best of these shows (a clear opportunity for online); until that time, the economics of cable rest on advertising + allocated carriage fees + DVD sales + international sales.

103

Pay TV

Pay TV differs the most dramatically; instead of advertising dollars and ratings, these "networks" are directly dependent on subscriber fees. To a degree, this insulates the networks from direct ratings pressure. This fact, coupled with greater creative freedom due to different regulatory restrictions (being outside of "free TV" standards and practices), allows a range of programming that cannot be shown on cable or network and has led to innovative hits based on violent or sexual themes, such as *The Sopranos* or *Sex and the City*. How many episodes a pay network wants to commission is simply an exercise in allocating a relatively fixed/known programming budget created out of its subscriber funded revenue stream.

As for subscriber funding, the economics are an extension of the cable per subscriber fees detailed above. In the case of cable channels, the per sub fees are generally in the cents/sub, as a portion of the fee consumers pay for cable is allocated by the carrier among the various networks. In contrast, the carriers can afford dollars/sub for pay stations since they pass along the cost to subscribers who pay a specific upcharge for access to the pay network. Basically, consumers can opt in and out of whether to subscribe to HBO, Starz, and Showtime, and the numbers of consumers that opt in and what they are willing to pay for the channel has a direct correlation on the channel's funding and programming budget.

What is interesting is that pay TV did not historically seek or depend on an aftermarket. With the new trend of certain shows "sanitized" for basic cable, plus the boon in DVD sales from TV season box sets, pay TV hits seem to have the best of all worlds: high subscriber fees, minimal ratings pressure, international sales, DVD sales, and secondary runs on cable.

Deficit and Risk Continuum

Logically, based on the revenue sources coming into cable, network, and pay TV programming, the risk continuum is fairly simple (see Figure 3.1):

Most Guaranteed Financing	Middle Ground	Least Secure Financing
←		→
Pay TV	**Basic Cable**	**Free TV/Network**

Figure 3.1

Pay TV broadcasters know their budgets, and if a show runs a deficit it is because the cost/episode is greater than the allocation the service has given the show; this may happen if there is an expectation of downstream revenues, and a conscious decision to run an up-front deficit simply to sustain a high production budget. In the basic cable scenario, ratings and advertising are still a material component, and because of the lack of aftermarket syndication opportunities shows need to pay for themselves up front. A deficit may be sustainable under the theory that a critically acclaimed show raises the basic cable network's profile, and thus ultimately its per subscriber carriage fee. This is a reasonable assumption when targeting more niche audiences, but an assumption with limited elasticity given the supplementary need of advertising revenues based on ratings performance. Network show financing carries by far the highest risk, as all revenue is dependent on performance and advertising dollars tied to ratings.

TV and Online's Relatively Lower Risk Profile

Television programs are less risky to finance than film for several key reasons. First, the up-front investment is simply not as high, as TV episodes are in the low millions of dollars rather than the average $70 M cost (pre P&A) of the average MPAA studio film. Second, the marketing costs of launching a show are materially lower; although there can be significant PR and off-air promotion costs, a significant part of achieving audience awareness is on-air promotion. Even if house ads are considered opportunity costs, the number is small next to the amount overall media spends to launch a major movie. Third, networks create pilots and test shows before launching series — while movies may be tested with audiences and tweaked, there is no pilot stage and a movie release is akin to all bets on the pilot. Fourth, TV series rarely receive full episode commitments, with broadcasters waiting to order more "product" until they see how the show is performing. Finally, in the case of cable and pay TV there are built-in revenue streams, creating a cushion; this is in contrast to a movie, where literally no one can show up.

Online

Financing online programming ratchets down the risk yet another level. Compared to television, budgets are a fraction, which is due both to the fact that programming is shorter — often literally produced in shorts — and the cost per minute of production is significantly less. While the cost per minute differential may narrow as efforts are made to attract TV-level talent, the shorter format will continue to provide an advantage: seven minutes will always cost less than twenty-two minutes of similar content (although, it is possible on a cost-per-minute basis it could become more expensive, given there are less minutes to amortize and series costs tend to be front-loaded). Accordingly, the sampling nature of the Internet will enable producers to create shorter pilots, which means that online production will indefinitely remain lower risk versus film and television provided that upsides materialize. One could argue that today the risks are higher because the revenue side remains immature and there are few proven models/examples of profitability regardless of how low production costs may be. This is why the business is launched predominantly with VC-type backing, and why we have not seen the development of similar financing structures as in other media.

I asked the CFO of ABC, Jim Hedges, how he viewed the landscape and whether we would see online financing mechanisms start to mimic those found in TV and other traditional media, and he advised:

We're at the beginning of real change in how consumers view television content. And the change is significant and will provide great new opportunities for media companies.

Historically, viewers consumed television content on the big three networks when it was programmed by a network executive. There were no other options. If you missed your favorite show Thursday at 9pm on ABC, you had to wait for the repeat or you just missed it.

Today, consumers are programming their own "networks" by using the many options available to them, including watching it "live" on the network, watching it on their DVR, their computer via the Internet, by downloading a purchased episode from iTunes, or on their mobile device. In the very near future, Video on Demand will also be another option available, and there will be others that follow. They can also buy the DVD of the season's episodes shortly after the season ends.

All of these new platforms provide the opportunity for viewers to consume the shows they love when they choose to, wherever they are—all with the potential to increase viewing. Historically, fans of hit TV shows only watched six episodes on average. If that average increases with all of these new opportunities to view, then media companies can monetize the additional viewing.

Some of the new platforms also have the added benefit (yet to be realized) of being able to target advertising to specific demographic and psychographic breaks, in large part because we'll be able to know something about that consumer, either by tracking where they go online or by asking them who they are. This should result in more efficient return on investment for advertisers, as well as higher ad rates for media companies.

In terms of financing, I believe the traditional methods will remain as viable options for big media companies. For online productions, I think it will be split into several buckets of financing: big media companies will finance online productions in a similar way to productions created for the linear television platforms, and may use online as a new development ground for TV shows; small production companies will develop and produce online content in a non-union environment, funded by venture capital and other traditional sources; user generated content will continue to grow as the price of entry continues to drop, although it appears to be difficult to monetize this content in the near term.

VC Analogy

All of these factors combine to make financing TV a much lower risk proposition than movies. Networks still function in a private equity-type role, financing a slate of projects where hits pay for misses. The fundamental economics of attracting consumer dollars is similar: performance translates into ticket sales with movies and to ratings and/or consumer demand for the channel in TV. Also, the number of movies a studio will release and the TV shows a broadcaster will back are in the same order of magnitude (ones and tens, not hundreds or thousands of different properties per year). Therefore, acting as a VC, educated bets will be placed on a relatively small sampling of projects, with up-front investment significant and an expectation that the majority of projects may fail or lose money. The hits, however, can have staggering ROIs in the hundreds of millions of dollars. Shouldn't broadcasters therefore be classified as a specialized form of VC or private equity investor financing a variety of projects it helps nurture but not directly produce/manage?

To the extent this analogy is accurate, then it is also fair to query why a range of financing mechanisms have not evolved in TV similar to film. In short, there are no obvious answers. It may be that broadcasters have sufficient financing and that there is no need to cede the windfall syndication/longtail profits on hits (having learned their lesson from the days of fin/syn regulations where producers earned more than the broadcasters; see Chapter 6). Also, it may be that timing plays a significant role (the return on TV is less immediate given the need to build up a library of episodes to syndicate over several years), that opportunities are limited by the absence of slate deals (networks pick up shows one by one), or that staged pickups coupled with guaranteed license fees apportion risk into manageable buckets.

The Wrinkles of Co-production

Co-productions, as described earlier as in the case of *Titanic*, are structures designed either to share financial risk or to bring together financial and creative parties in a form of joint venture. Co-productions are challenging because they usually involve a partner by necessity rather than choice: if you don't need to hedge the financial risk or could acquire the creative yourself, then a co-production should not be considered. Some of the most successful co-productions are partnerships between arch competitors who come together simply out of fear or necessity.

I will divide co-productions, other than instances of co-productions between two major studios to hedge risk, into three principal groupings:

- Case A: A party invests in a production in return for an equity stake
- Case B: A party invests in a production in return for distribution rights
- Case C: When there is creative collaboration between parties on a production

Case A: A Party Invests in Production in Return for an Equity Stake

The simplest scenario to understand is a 50:50 co-production, where both parties fund a production equally and profits are also shared equally (and paid at the same time). Even in a 50/50 split, however, if both parties bring different assets or expertise, it is likely that underlying rights may be divided by contract such that only defined elements are actually split 50/50. For example, it is possible to allocate copyright ownership, backend participations, and defined exploitation rights in a different ratio even if both parties funded 50/50 and the goal is to roughly equalize net profits from aggregate revenue streams. Accordingly, a 50/50 funded deal could vest copyright 100%

in one party, or vest a lesser percentage of the profits in one party if that party were compensated in other ways such as having exclusive distribution rights in a category and keeping 100% of a corresponding distribution fee. I have been involved in deals, as yet another iteration, where one party funded virtually 100% of the production costs, the parties shared copyright 50/50 (actually an awkward construct pursuant to copyright law), and the backend revenues were split in a complicated formula.

The core principle, though, is usually a sharing of up-front costs and therefore risk in return for some ownership stake. The tricky part is ownership, which can mean anything from ownership of the underlying intellectual property, to rights to exploit various distribution rights, to an income stream driven off of a contractual definition of specified revenues/profits. Because each of these categories is then divisible into a myriad of options, the permutations can be diverse and complicated — nice fodder for entertainment lawyers and analysts alike.

Case B: A Party Invests in a Production in Return for Distribution Rights

It is not uncommon for a deal in which one party acquires select distribution rights to be characterized as a co-production, especially when the value of such distribution rights is considered a significant part of the overall financing. Accordingly, a significant pre-sale or rights acquisition deal can rise to the level of a co-production when the acquiring party advances or otherwise guarantees a significant percentage of the budget in return for the acquired rights. This is especially true when principal rights are acquired for a region. For example, if Producer A is producing a television show and Distributor B acquires rights to distribute or directly broadcast the show throughout Europe, then Distributor B may be informally or formally referred to as a co-production partner.

The collateral impact is that downstream subdistributors may also then consider themselves co-producers, especially if the show has status attached to it, even though Producer A would neither have a direct relationship with the subdistributors nor consider them co-producers (but merely licensees). This may occur, for example, where a European-wide distributor licenses a show to a local network, and that network portrays itself on flyers and other literature as a co-producer. Because in this case a co-producer does not actually mean anything, it is akin to a status ranking where the broadcasting station wants to confer status or significance to its role. It would be highly unusual for this to happen in a simple license, but if they did commit and advance money early in a partnership with the broader European-wide distributor there is at least an argument.

The underlying reason for speaking about this type of scenario in co-production terms is that Distributor B has taken a significant risk, committing early and up front to the show and playing a material role in the financing of the production budget. Depending upon the exact percentage, and the relationship between the parties, the distributor may also have some creative input to ensure the end product works in its territory.

What is ultimately interesting in this scenario is that a third party, by committing to buy a property before it is finished (or in cases, before production even commences), can be treated as a partner even if they neither acquire any rights to the underlying intellectual property (i.e., copyright) nor any backend interest in the property. The entire investment and relationship is bounded by acquiring territory specific rights with revenues limited solely to such rights.

Case C: When There is Creative and/or Production Collaboration between Parties with Respect to a Production

This is a common scenario when parties pool different skill sets. A good example of this would involve outsourcing physical production, or certain elements of physical production. This is the typical pattern in animation, where an American studio, again for simplicity called here Producer A, commissions/develops and oversees scripts and storyboards, and then sends the packet to an overseas studio in Asia to produce the actual cel (and now more frequently CG) animation. This pattern is dictated by economic efficiencies and realities. A United States network, for example, may be more inclined to buy a show if it is written by local talent it is comfortable with and helmed by a director it knows; however, there may be acceptance or even lack of interest where the ultimate physical production occurs. In contrast, the overseas studio may have little or no development expertise or reputation, but instead can offer lower production costs due to labor rate differentials or local government tax incentives. By teaming up, the co-production arrangement maximizes its opportunity to license the show to a United States network while lowering the production costs.

The above scenario could easily be structured as simple work for hire, or outsourcing. However, if financing is desired, the overseas studio may contribute toward the budget either with direct cash or discounts to labor rates; namely investing sweat equity for a stake. Accordingly, if the Overseas Studio B wants to retain an equity interest, wants to retain local or regional distribution rights, or needs to retain certain rights to qualify for subsidies or tax credits, then the deal could be structured as a co-production. Moreover, if it is perceived that each party will have a better chance of striking a good local license for broadcast of the property, splitting the distribution rights so that Producer A and Overseas Studio B handle their local markets, a co-production becomes natural.

Hybrid and Example

It is possible to combine one or all of these options into a variety of hybrids. For example, Producer A could own the underlying copyright and IP 100%, but still team up with a partner with specialized production expertise and related distribution connections; Partner B, for its part, may have significant creative rights, retain an equity interest in the revenue stream of the production, invest directly or indirectly (e.g., discounted production fees), and also keep select distribution rights. This crosses over all categories above: there is creative collaboration, there is an equity investment in the project, and certain distribution rights are acquired. One can easily see this scenario in the context of a publisher, for example, that owns a famous book but wants a partner to produce a series for TV and help distribute it to networks.

111

The following is an illustrative example. Publisher A owns a book about a Green Tiger that has a moderate following. Distributor B based in Europe loves the book and wants to finance a low budget movie, believing it will be a great kids' video property. The budget is $4M, but Distributor B can only afford an investment of $3M. Publisher A has an affiliated animation division, and both parties believe they will be compatible partners to creatively produce and distribute the movie.

There is a shortfall of $1M in the overall budget, but 15% of this ($600,000) is for customary producer's fees and another $400,000 is from a 20% overhead markup on $2M of below-the-line production costs. Publisher A realizes that if they forego any margin and markup and produce literally at cost they can get by with the $3M cash and make the movie. They decide to do this, but only as long as they share the copyright and have a deal that gives them the appropriate upside for their investment.

The co-production deal may therefore be struck as follows:

- Publisher A and Distributor B share copyright 50/50 (or retained 100% by A)
- Distributor B has worldwide distribution rights for a fee of 25%
- Publisher A invests $1M in foregone markups (so called sweat equity)
- Distributor B invests $3M in cash
- The parties agree to share profits based on the ratio of investment (75/25)
- Publisher A has a backend creative percentage for the rights (X% of Net)

If $10 M in revenues is received, what is the split of the pot? Let us assume there are $2M in other costs (marketing, etc., beyond the production costs) and the $10M is net after taking out the 25% distribution fee off the top.

> $10M revenue – $6M costs
> (A gets its $1M, and B its $3M + $2M marketing costs) =
> $4M net revenues
> (Publisher A would keep $1M, and Distributor B $3M)

In the above example, the split would change to 67.5/32.5 if there were a creative participation of 10%. Publisher A would then take $400,000 from the net revenues, leaving the parties to split the balance of $3.6M 75/25; publisher A's share would be $400,000 + $900,000 (25% of $3.6M), which represents 32.5% of the $4M net revenues. This formula would then become more complicated if the parties split up distribution, such that one party held Europe and the other party the rest of the world. In such an instance there could be recoupment out of the revenues of their income streams, with shared upside in overages; if one party has recouped before the other, the sums over recoupment may go to recoup the unrecouped party until everyone has had their initial investment returned.

I could go on and on with further wrinkles, making this needlessly complex. The point is that when two parties share rights and underlying financing, the arrangement can range from very simple to formulas that in the end only the participation accountants may fully understand how to apply. The formulas become inherently complex when there is an actual or perceived inequality of either money invested or rights owned. Up front, some of the key hurdles to overcome include:

- Should a party have an equity investment equal to the percentage of the budget they funded, or is there a dilution formula applied from the beginning because one party's non-cash contribution needs to be valued? This is the case when one of the parties contributes the property/intangible creative elements for which they need to be compensated. Accordingly, if one party puts in 60% of the money, and the other 40%, that 100% may only recoup against 90% if the creative partner is separately granted 10% as inalienable compensation for the creative.
- Should a party be entitled to dollar for dollar weighted value for foregone margin, such as reducing or eliminating a producer fee? The project could take a year or more to make, and the producer fee would have been the profit margin — it may seem easy to say that was not real money, but the company may have foregone profitable work to invest in this project for which it earned nothing.
- What happens when one party recoups before another, if the rights have been divided up? Is recoupment cross-collateralized so that both parties get the benefit of the other's rights for recoupment, and then the splits adjust later or is each party dependent on its own rights to recoup its own investment?
- Who owns/controls the property — does one party by virtue of a greater investment have say over future exploitation/derivative productions?

The sharing of creative production on the one hand and financing/distribution on the other is always complicated. Look what happened to Disney/Pixar, and that was a relatively straightforward arrangement where who did what in terms of financing, distribution, and production was very clear. Few people talk about *Finding Nemo* as a co-production, but in certain structural terms the deal could easily be characterized that way. Financing was shared 50/50, but because copyright was not shared in the same way it was often simply characterized as a distribution relationship in the press.

Online's Relatively Low Co-Production Quotient

There are few examples of co-productions in the online context because creative tends to be home-grown, costs are relatively low, and

113

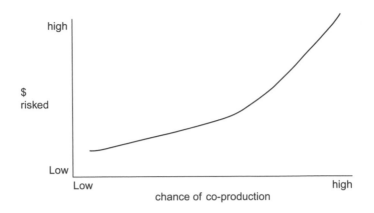

Figure 3.2

a key driver is the ability to produce and distribute independently. Because of the current immaturity of the revenue side, however, as more producers strive to deliver higher quality online content (thus driving up costs) capital risked will increase and co-productions will inevitably emerge. Said another way, the more online original production comes to look like TV, the more likely similar co-production structures will develop. In fact, because the chance of success should not dramatically increase with an increase in budget (assuming "nobody knows"), one can posit a proportionate relationship between the increase of production costs and the chance of forming co-productions (see Figure 3.2).

Government Backed Co-Productions: International Schemes and State Tax Subsidies

International Foreign governments often provide tax incentives to bolster local production. These take all sorts of forms, and can be implemented at a national or regional level.

In certain cases, the local government or fund will literally pay for a percentage of the total budget. Australia is one of the more aggressive regimes promoting local filming, and it is estimated that roughly 12% of the budget of *Superman Returns* was saved by local tax schemes/breaks.[29] France's CNC sponsors a variety of schemes to assist the French film industry, with layers of incentives permeating production and sometimes tied to local quotas. In the animation area, for example, French animation studios have a distinct cost advantage over American competitors, as between increased fees from local broadcasters for qualifying local production plus CNC subsidies it is common to cover over one-third of a production's budget through incentive-based schemes. Europe in particular has a flourishing co-production tradition, in part from the 1992 European Convention on Cinematic Co-Production which sanctions productions that cross borders within the EU to partake of subsidies offered by all participating EU countries.[30] Canada also has a particularly robust incentive system tied to an intricate system of tax credits, in part driven by its small domestic market when compared to the United States.

It is impossible to summarize all the worldwide programs, but there seems to be a rhythm of different countries luring production and then pulling back, with production moving around the globe seeking the best deals of the day. Germany, which had been very active with film tax funds in the 1990s, is now less aggressive. Recently Singapore, via its Media Development Authority and Economic Development Board, has focused on providing incentives for local Asian production (and as a disclaimer, I have personally been involved in a couple of significant deals in Singapore over the last few years linked to government-backed initiatives, including assisting Singapore and Europe based 6-6-8 in sourcing United States based TV and film projects for Asian filming, and helping establish a local hub for Lucasfilm Animation).

Abuse of Systems and Credits   Cinar, an animation studio that was publicly listed and known globally for such hits as *Babar* and *Arthur*, provides an example of how tax incentives and subsidies become so integral to production costs that people will bend the rules to comply. One of the tenets of many international schemes, including in France and Canada, is the tying of tax credits to hiring local talent; namely, the government is allocating money to stimulate local work, and imposes specific quotas that must be met as a quid pro quo for qualifying for the tax packages or other subsidies. These are often applied on a "points system" where the production must have a certain number of local points: engaging a Canadian director is worth X points, Canadian writers Y points and so on. Depending on the scheme, it becomes difficult to secure enough qualifying points without the majority of key talent being local. Cinar admitted wrongly claiming tax credits listing writers as Canadian when in fact the scripts were written by American writers — this and other improprieties then came to light during an investigation that led to the firing of the founders, tax fraud claims, and the delisting of the company from Nasdaq. The moral is simple: follow the rules, especially when taking government money.

United States Based Schemes   Just like foreign governments have established tax and other schemes to stimulate local production, various states have implemented programs to attract filming. I am always asking people "why are you filming in Oregon, Michigan, etc." only to catch myself when realizing it has little to do with the physical location and everything to do with the cross section of the environment working and local incentive programs.

The amounts granted can be extraordinary because most schemes are tied to percentages, which means as budgets go up, so does the taxpayers' commitment. Controversy followed Brad Pitt's movie *The Curious Case of Benjamin Button* (Paramount and Warner Bros.) when it created local tax credit obligations of over $27M as the film's budget climbed to a reported $167M.[31] (Note: The criticisms of Benjamin Button may fall into the "can't win" category, as part of the goal was to create local jobs in the post Hurricane Katrina economy.) Most states offer credits tied to production cost rebates for amounts spent in-state, typically ranging from 15 to 25%. Louisiana's program, however, initially offered credits tied to the entire budget, and therefore captured costs, including some costs relating to stars, that may have been incurred outside the state; this has now been changed and credits are tied to in-state production spending.[32]

The justification for such credits is creating local work and jobs. However, some argue that low cost production will migrate, that taxpayers will wise up to funding other people's productions, and that the employment created is short-lived. Regardless of the spin, the essence of the programs is that state taxpayer money is being used to fund production, and it is a difficult calculation to assess whether the local stimulus generates more money than is spent. The *New York Times* summarized:

> Some, like Michigan, simply refund a percentage of expenditures to the producers. Others, like Louisiana's, issue a tax credit that can reduce the taxes a producer pays or be sold to someone else. Either way, the state gives up revenue that otherwise would be collected to put money in the producer's pockets … critics have sharply challenged the notion that state subsidies for the film business can ever buy more than momentary glitter.[33]

States that are able to create a steady stream of production no doubt create local jobs; the challenge is not trying to match each new aggressive scheme to keep those jobs, as someone globally

116

will inevitably offer a better deal in an attempt to steal production away.

Online Impact

- Online production has created a wave of venture capital money funding niche channels.
- Risks associated with producing original online content, which is still an experimental market, should theoretically create co-production structures to help defray that risk (despite lower production costs); for a variety of reasons this has not yet evolved, but as budgets increase and more original premium content is produced online, co-production arrangements mimicking TV are likely to grow.
- The lower cost of online content may come to threaten traditional financing mechanisms.
- Oddly, the online and digital world has had less impact on film and TV financing than in distribution and revenue areas.
- Traditional financing schemes are not being applied to online production because despite the by-title risk in film and TV, distribution revenue streams for traditional media are relatively "bankable" whereas a dependable Internet revenue model has not evolved to support related financing.

117

CHAPTER 4

Theatrical Distribution

Unlike the market for traditional packaged goods where the goal is often to sustain and grow a household brand over time, the film and television business operates by media blitz to try and create new brands overnight. A movie can become a brand unto itself, and what business other than the film business strives to create a new brand over a weekend? The time, money, and effort expended to create public awareness of a film in its opening weekend is staggering, and has become the front edge of criticism by artists who bemoan the subjugation of art to the beast of box office grosses.

Because a major studio film frequently needs to recoup better than $100M between production and marketing costs — with the average cost of a studio film ~$70M and the average marketing costs ~$35M[1] — openings are critically important. One of the most interesting developments of the maturation of the distribution market is that the more important the revenue streams outside of box office have become, the more important the value placed on the box office. In other businesses, the thesis would be that as traditional outlets were overtaken by new channels of distribution, one might see the original outlets dwindle in importance and in cases be phased out entirely. Not so in the film world.

With the growth of other markets, and the potential for combined revenues from TV, video, merchandising, and new media sources to surpass revenues from movie theaters, the bellwether of box office has grown in importance. The reason is twofold, and relatively simple. First, the success of the box office continues to be an accurate barometer for the success in subsequent release markets. Second, the media frenzy surrounding theatrical release drives awareness that is amortized over the life cycle of the product and drives consumption months and even years later.

In terms of the influence of the Web and digital technologies on the theatrical market, while there are clearly major changes in exhibition and production systems (e.g., HD cameras and digital cinema), perhaps the most significant impact the digital revolution is having on theatrical exhibition is the way movies are marketed. Budgets for online marketing are growing, virtually every movie has its own Web site, and marketing executives are trying to generate "buzz" by pushing out trailers and other information to sites like YouTube. Additionally, review sites such as rottentomatos.com aggregate critics' opinions and reduce nationwide diverse reactions into a single, homogenized scorecard: What percent of reviews are positive or negative? The ability to broadly market via leading Web sites while narrowly targeting demographics via niche sites and seeding blogs is revolutionizing movie marketing—ask anyone under twenty-five today whether they check out a film first on the Web or look at a newspaper and they are likely to sneer that you even posed the question. Although I could delve into these influences here, I simply want to highlight the impact and instead address most of these factors in Chapter 9.

119

Theatrical Release as a Loss Leader

Basic Definitions and the Uneasy Tension between Distribution and Production

Theatrical release simply means the exhibition of a film in movie theaters where revenue is derived from members of the public buying tickets. The so-called gate, or the revenues derived from ticket sales, is what is referred to as "box office." The amount of money that the distributor keeps from the box office receipts is called "film rentals."

Box office can sometimes lead to misleading numbers when preparing macro statistics on industry growth and trends because box office captures only a cumulative number. There are a myriad of ticket prices and discounts reflecting regional and local differences and accommodations for seniors and kids. Basically, the box office is an excellent measuring stick and the ultimate source of revenue, but it does not provide marketing data on who the consumers were or even how many of them attended. Box office over a period may have gone up, but that could mean that attendance was down while average ticket prices were up. Because of this ambiguity, some countries choose to measure trends by "admittance;" namely how many people attended (i.e., tickets bought). This is customary in France, where the value of certain downstream rights is pegged to attendance rather than revenue figures.

Theatrical release is the first trigger among film windows, and because a film can be re-released the most common trigger is the "initial theatrical release." How long a film stays in movie theaters is a factor of the film's performance, and studios negotiate picture-specific deals with each theater into which a film is booked. Depending upon clout and stature, the distributor (e.g., the studio's theatrical distribution arm) may be able to negotiate for guarantee or hold weeks, securing a set minimum period of time the film will be in release; guaranteed minimum weeks are obviously risky propositions for both sides, because if a film flops the theater will want to drop it quickly and show something new, and the distributor will be reluctant to spend marketing dollars for fear of throwing good money after bad.

In extreme cases, the driving force may be neither of the negotiating parties, but the film's director or producer who secured a release commitment from the distributing studio. Lack of trust inevitably fuels the relationship, because producers and directors who have put years of work into a project want as many guarantees as possible that their film will have the best possible chance to succeed. Cries of "they didn't know how to handle the film" and other excuses are rife in Hollywood in part because a project shifts 180 degrees in responsibility from delivery to release. During production, the director and producer are kings and in almost total control over hundreds of people and millions of dollars. Once the film is delivered the distributor is in near total control. An often uneasy partnership is borne and in failure it is easy to point a finger at the other party.

Distributors may be burdened with certain expectations, politics, and commitments, but basically function to make tough on-the-spot business calls. Also, as suppliers, and factoring in their need to maintain good relationships with exhibitors, it does not behoove a distributor to keep a movie in theaters longer than makes sense. The relationship factor is then weighed together with opportunity costs (when the distributor could be substituting a more profitable picture) and the fact that the distributor is spending real money each day a film is in major release in marketing dollars to support cross-media campaigns focused on TV, radio, and print advertising.

120

The Theatrical Release Challenge — Locomotive for Awareness While Profits Remain Downstream

The other wrinkle is that weekly box office numbers aside, there may be a marketing justification to keep a film in theaters. Because film rentals will rarely recoup a film's investment, the theatrical release can be seen as a loss leader to create awareness of the property for downstream video, TV, and other rights. In fact, looking at the ultimates for the film (i.e., lifetime projections of all revenue sources), most distributors are reconciled to losing money through this stage of exploitation. Accordingly, the distributor is not running a straightforward breakeven analysis in trying to decide whether to keep a film in theaters versus pulling it (balancing opportunity cost vs. continuing marketing costs); this calculation is coupled with a more complex marketing analysis taking into account consumer impressions, market awareness, and impact on providing the bang to fuel subsequent exploitation.

Ultimately, those in charge of distribution are almost always in an awkward position — they have virtually no input in the creative product, and yet are responsible for opening the film (in tandem with the marketing department) and literally charting its destiny. A distributor must make a good picture great, and somehow find a way on "a dog" to pull enough box office out quickly to recoup some investment before the public sours; moreover, it needs to achieve this within a context of not really knowing what the reaction will be (given the "nobody knows" quandary of experience goods).

Hedging Bets and Profiling Release Patterns

The film *Titanic* provides another good example in this context, as it posed a dilemma for the distributor and studio having to make high stakes calls without the benefit of knowing how the audience would react. The reviews before opening were dicey, and the picture was well known in the Hollywood community to be suffering from budget problems. In fact, rumor had it that Fox was so nervous about the budget that it was desperate to sell off rights and reduce its potential downside, which it ultimately did with Paramount (see Chapter 3).

Selling off the upside and mitigating its potential downside turned out to be Paramount's gain, as the reviews were wrong and the picture became the all time box office champ. More than a box office champ, the film also defied the odds and literally played throughout the summer, staying on the charts for almost a whole year, ending up at

121

$1.8 B in worldwide box office ($600M United States, $1.2B international).[2] When a film continues playing like this, beyond a typical pattern where most films would see a decline, it is referred to in industry lingo as "it's got legs."

In trying to select the right strategy a distributor needs to profile its film and match the pattern of release to the nature of the film. This is really the ambit of marketing, which again is discussed in detail in Chapter 9. Briefly, however, for a picture where word of mouth is important, the film may only be opened in select venues for buzz to build. Assuming success, the picture then expands locations as its reputation grows. This was the strategy for Clint Eastwood's best picture Oscar (2005) film *Million Dollar Baby*. Warner Bros. believed they had a strong picture, even one that might be Oscar caliber, but the women's boxing theme and euthanasia twist needed nurturing to attract broad audiences. This strategy of building buzz before widening the release is also sometimes used when a film may be perceived as an art or period piece (e.g., some of the earlier Miramax pictures, such as Merchant Ivory productions) as well as when a picture is perceived to appeal to more of an intellectual crowd. Woody Allen films would fall into this latter category, and tend to open in big cities, including his hometown and frequent film backdrop Manhattan, before broadening after hopefully generating buzz and critical acclaim.

The more typical strategy is to open a picture wide, taking as much box office up front as possible when consumers are enticed into attending through the large up-front marketing campaign creating awareness.

History and Market Evolution

Consent Decrees, Block Booking, and Blind Bidding

The current exhibition environment has come full circle from 50+ years ago when most of the major studios owned theaters and vertically integrated the production–distribution–exhibition chain by preferentially selling to their own theaters. This included Paramount, MGM, Twentieth Century-Fox, Warner Bros., and RKO. As a result of complaints by independents, the Department of Justice sued these five studios alleging anti-competitive behavior and won a landmark case. In 1948, the *Supreme Court in US. v. Paramount et al.* forced these defendant studios to sign a consent decree and divest themselves of theater ownership, while retaining distribution and production.

In addition to forcing divestiture, the consent decree reached beyond the theater owner defendants and brought the remaining major studios (Columbia, Universal, United Artists) within its ambit regarding certain booking practices. At that time, studios routinely engaged in what is referred to as "block booking" where the license of one picture was tied to the license of other films; in the extreme case, a producer/studio would pre-sell its entire slate of films for a year to a certain theater or theater chain. One tenet of anti-trust law (at least at the time of the case) is that you cannot "tie" products, where a party uses the economic leverage of one product to force a buyer to also buy a second unrelated product that it does not want.

The justice department naturally saw block booking as anti-competitive and outlawed the practice as part of the consent decree. Going forward, distributors were forced to sell films picture by picture, and theater by theater with all theaters having a right to bid and compete to exhibit a film.

Another practice that was prohibited by the consent decree was "blind bidding." Blind bidding is just as it sounds: a distributor would make a theater owner bid on a film and agree to terms without the benefit of seeing the movie first. This was a particularly onerous practice given the inherent challenges of handicapping creative goods. The decree proscribed this practice, and the new law mandated that all films needed to be screened before being sold or put out to bid.

123

Multiplexes and Bankruptcies of Major Chains

A number of factors led to a spate of bankruptcies of several major chains following boom years in the 1990s. Probably the biggest contributor was the simple fact that screens grew at a pace that far outstripped the rise in movie attendance. According to the National Association of Theater Owners (NATO), in the period from 1988 through 2000 the number of screens in the United States rose to ~37,000 from ~23,000, representing a 61% increase, while theater admissions only rose only about 36%. The trend then leveled out, with screens flattening out and coming down only slightly from a 1999 peak to 36,000+ as of 2004.[3,4]

This growth was spurred by the phenomenon of multiplexes, which could leverage common infrastructure (concessions, ticket sales, ushers) across multiple screens, and vary theater size allowing them to match capacity to demand. This was a compelling economic proposition, but the 8 to 10-screen expansion seemed tempered compared to the next iteration of megaplexes. AMC, which originated the multiplex from a modest two-theater experiment, started the mega-plex trend in 1994 building a 24-theater complex in Dallas. The megaplexes included now common features such as coffee bars, stadium seating, and video arcades, and soon everyone followed.[5] The total number of theaters ultimately contracted, as exhibitors abandoned leases and consolidated screens into larger multi-screen venues; according to NATO, the number of locations actually contracted from 7,151 to 5,629 from 1995 to 2004.[6] The contraction, though, was not enough to counter the larger issue of a massive increase in screens, high operating costs from new megaplexes, and smaller percentage increases in ticket sales and price of tickets.

The net result was too many empty seats and too much overhead; a formula that led to the bankruptcy over time of most of the major chains such as Loews Cineplex Entertainment, Carmike Cinemas, United Artists, General Cinema, and Regal Cinemas.[7] In a sense, the economics of stadium theater venues are … like stadiums. Most of the time capacity is empty—some estimate that theaters operate in the range of 10–15% capacity (meaning most seats are empty most of the time)—and the key is maximizing consumption during peak full capacity events (i.e., hits). This pattern means greater pressure than ever on turning over screens, as operators want something fresh to drive the audience, unable to afford to wait for a middling performer.

124

The Digital Divide and Digital Cinema
The Growth of Digital Cinema
The promise of digital cinema (D-cinema) has been around for years, but despite all the hype as of Christmas 2008 there was reportedly only 1,000+ screens out of the 35,000+ screen universe in the United States equipped for digital projection. With the studios banding together and setting standards in 2005 under the Digital Cinema Initiative consortium, and the theater owners through NATO then building on the agreement and agreeing to specifications, the landscape was set for quicker adoption than has been realized. (Note: As discussed in the next section, new 3-D production has finally helped accelerate adoption, and the numbers look to more than double in 2009.)

Benefits of D-Cinema
D-cinema refers to the process of exhibiting a movie in a theater by digital projection rather than via a film print. The incentives are multifold.

First, most believe that once economies of scale are reached that D-cinema will dramatically reduce the cost of distribution, with the cost of a D-cinema delivery a fraction of the cost of striking and shipping prints. Second, a digital copy does not degrade like a film print, in theory offering a perfect copy with pristine picture and sound each time; in layman's terms, "no scratches." Third, because of the costs, prints are often "bicycled" such that the first run prints from larger cities and multiplexes will move to smaller towns after a few weeks. These locations are known as "second run" and their customers are forced to wait for new releases; eliminating print costs would expand distribution and bring films to these locations sooner. [8]Finally, installation of D-cinema allows a digital infrastructure that can convert cinemas into multi-purpose venues capable of special event programming including 3D- film and live event simulcasting (e.g., sports events, concerts).

Systems and Standards

D-cinema requires four elements that did not exist historically: a digital projector, a server holding the movie on a file, a digital master, and a delivery mechanism to transfer a copy of the film onto the server (Figure 4.1). Over time the costs will come down, but significant up-front investment is required from all sides. The exhibitors need to install projectors and servers (which collectively make up a digital projection system), while the distributors need to create D-cinema masters and settle on a delivery mechanism to clone the master and upload a copy to the in-cinema server.

All of this is made more complicated by different manufacturers making servers and projectors based on different standards. A major breakthrough in this free-for-all, aimed at avoiding format wars threatening to derail implementation just as interest was growing, came in 2005 and 2006. As previously noted, the major studios banded together to form a consortium for setting standards called the Digital Cinema Initiative, and in July 2005 it released its first set of specifications. Not to be outdone, the exhibitors through their own trade organization (NATO) released their own Digital Cinema System

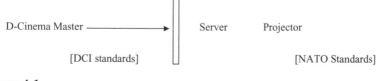

Figure 4.1

Requirement Guidelines. The specifications were designed to harmonize standards, establish a common threshold pixel standard, and address security concerns. (Note: This process was not dissimilar to the studios banding together in the early days of DVD to establish compression standards.) Despite this progress, equipment manufacturers and others are still lobbying for resolution standards with the de facto leader being JPEG 2000 ("2K") and some pushing for 4K projectors. An interesting question arises as to whether at some point improved resolution is actually a negative: some believed that the 4K resolution might be too high, creating an almost artificial, hyper-real, and defect-visible level.

Adoption

George Lucas and Lucasfilm helped pioneer D-cinema by shooting *Star Wars: Episode II — Attack of the Clones* digitally and releasing the film on 60+ digital screens in North America (2002). Much like Lucas had pushed sound presentation with his THX technology and business, D-cinema offered the potential of consistent picture quality. Given the lack of uniform standards, infrastructure, and others to come on board quickly, by the time Episode III came out three years later (May 2005) the amount of digital screens available had not appreciably increased. International growth has been faster, spurred by emerging theatrical markets (e.g., China) that could leapfrog to digital bypassing the costs of converting legacy systems.

Beyond cost, though, significant market confusion and lack of integrated systems is a continuing problem. Every year at one of the major theatrical trade shows there seems to be a major announcement, followed by relatively slow change. At Christmas 2005 Carmike Cinemas (third largest chain) announced that it struck a deal with Christie/AIX to install 2,300 D-cinema projection systems.[9] Roughly three years later a grander plan was announced by Digital Cinema Implementation Partners (AMC, Cinemark, and Regal), and several of the studios (Disney, Universal, Fox, Paramount, Lionsgate) announced a nearly $1B investment plan to convert more than 15,000 theaters to digital projection.[10]

In summary, the long technical road to adoption moved for years at glacial speed. What economics could speed adoption?

Costs and Virtual Print Costs

Although digital cinema raises piracy concerns, the main obstacle to adoption is the cost of installing systems. *Time* magazine, in its annual (2006) "What's Next" issue interviewed George Lucas for an article titled "Can This Man Save the Movies? (Again?)"[11] and succinctly attributed the delay to theater owners: "... When they hear the word digital, they reach for digitalis. Already feeling the hit for the 13% slump in moviegoing over the past three years, they aren't eager to spend the more than $3 billion or so that it would cost to convert approximately 36,000 film projectors to digital."

To solve the problem, George Lucas posed an interesting solution to speed adoption and amortize the theater owner's costs:

It costs about $1,200 for a film print and about $200 for a digital print. So what you do is charge the distributor the same $1,200 they would ordinarily be charged, and $1,000 of it goes into a pot that eventually pays for all the projectors and everything. In about five years you would reconvert the entire industry.[12]

Ultimately, with costs reputedly $100,000 (or more) to convert a theater, someone will have to foot the bill and a form of partnership is likely. The notion of virtual print fees to help the transition began catching on — where a studio pays a fee per screen roughly equal to the cost of a physical print — to defray the infrastructure costs and became part of these early distributor–exhibitor pacts.

I asked Tom Quinn, Senior Director of Worldwide Distribution for Lucasfilm, who has helped manage multiple digital releases with different studio partners, and has had a catbird's seat to watch the evolution of D-cinema, why given all the above factors he thought adoption which had been heralded for so many years has not materialized. He advised:

The promise of D-C cinema is undeniable from a long term cost savings point of view for both studios and production companies. The challenges have been who will pay for it and whose technology will be used. As a comparison to what we witnessed in the home video industry first with VHS vs. Beta and more recently Blue Ray vs. HD-DVD the issues are much more complex. Exhibitors don't really believe D-Cinema will drive more ticket sales, and unless there is an impact on a game changing scale as moving, for example, from cassette to DVD or black and white to color film motivating the consumer they

127

don't feel they should be the ones bearing the costs of converting cinemas. Added to this is a system that has been virtually the same for 100 years and continues to work well— the "don't fix what isn't broken" mentality is hard for the studios to overcome. This is especially true given the high upfront costs of conversion and the fact shifting technology could be outdated soon after multi-component systems including servers, projectors, etc. are installed.

Theaters on the Ropes — 3-D and Needing a New Hook

Against this backdrop of increasing piracy, potentially declining box office (as vicissitudes change the outlook every year or two), and increased competition from other media sources (including the Internet and downloadable devices), there is a frequent chorus of calls to save the movies. Talking about the business almost as if it were a dinosaur, articles and experts often cite reasons for moviegoing (aside from quality arguments) ranging from "movies are produced for the big screen experience" to movies are a social experience. The point is executives were becoming defensive and people, in particular theater owners, were concerned. What will bring people into the theaters in record numbers when consumers have a 50" LCD TV screen with high definition content and theatrical-like surround sound? Even studio heads acknowledge the high costs to a family to go to the movies versus renting a DVD (babysitter + four tickets + parking + food = $100 vs. DVD rental at less than $5). Although the deep 2008/2009 recession seemed to reverse the trend, as going to the movies proved an escape from economic gloom (as had happened historically), all of the foregoing challenges remain and no doubt the theaters will need to continue to provide an enhanced and differentiating experience to the moviegoer.

D-cinema, and in particular 3-D, was heralded as offering just this value-added experience. Beyond all the historical good reasons to go to the movies, and the quality upgrade of digital cinema, 3-D was marketed as something new—one could claim it was back to the future time, 3-D glasses and all. The argument was the glasses were better this time. Moreover, 3-D was perceived as enough of a differentiator to raise ticket prices, to as high as $25, which would both offset the higher production costs of 3-D plus help theaters defray the costs of digital conversion. In practice, the premium charged for

128

3-D tickets is about $2–4 more than for traditional 2-D, with Regal, for example, adding $3.50–4.00 for its venues that exhibited *Monsters vs. Aliens* (March, 2009).[13]

A group of prominent directors including Peter Jackson, George Lucas, Robert Zemekis, James Cameron, and Robert Rodriguez all spoke out in favor of 3-D and the theatrical experience. Some even started developing 3-D projects or converting prior films into 3-D, waiting to avail themselves of the new technological possibilities. Here was something that could not be matched in the living room. By 2007 James Cameron announced all his future films would be 3-D (his first non-documentary movie directed since *Titanic* is the 3-D picture *Avatar*), and Bob Zemekis seemed to be following suit. Disney, which announced that all its future animated and Pixar films would be released in both 2-D and 3-D, has even tried to co-opt the medium in its marketing by branding new releases as in "Disney Digital 3-D." For the first time significant numbers of 3-D films are being produced (e.g., Warner's *Journey to the Center of the Earth 3D*, Fox's *Avatar*, Lionsgate's *My Bloody Valentine 3D*, DreamWorks Animation's *Monsters vs. Aliens*), but the danger is that production is well ahead of digital screen conversion, leaving distributors in a quandary and forcing the dual exhibition of the pictures intended exclusively for 3-D in standard version simply to obtain enough screens for a wide release.[14] DreamWorks Animation, betting big on 3-D and having converted its pipeline to 3-D productions, was able to expand 3-D screen counts to 2,000 for its March 2009 release of *Monsters vs. Aliens*, making it the broadest new 3-D release while still falling well short of stated goals for a majority of screens exhibiting the film to be 3-D.[15]

More important, no one is taking the overall threat to theaters from the living room lightly. It was only a few years before that many of the US chains went under or flirted with bankruptcy and it was asking a lot for a newly re-constituted group of chains, that were just getting back on their feet, to take significant infrastructure risks.

Distributor–Exhibitor Splits/Deals

The following discussion analyzes how money that comes into a theater from customers is split between the exhibitor (theater) and distributor (studio). Figure 4.2 illustrates the theatrical distribution chain, but if one looks past the moving parts the key element in terms

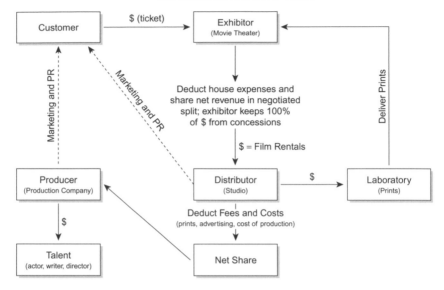

Theatrical Distribution Chain

Figure 4.2

of theatrical revenues and returns is the simple link between the cinema and booking studio:

Components of Film Rental

The amount of money that the studio/distributor keeps from the box office is all important, because this is ultimately the "at the source revenue." The industry rule of thumb is that the studio keeps roughly 50% of the cumulative box office: But how do you get there? Almost all exhibition deals are based around the following concepts:

- House Nut: The theater's overhead costs, including rent, maintenance, utilities, labor costs, equipment, insurance, etc.
- Film Rental: Distributor's share of the gross box office receipts
- Runs: Lingo for how many theaters a film is booked in (but can also denote the first run of a picture)
- Guaranteed Weeks: How many weeks a theater commits to a film
- Zones: The level of exclusivity in the market is defined by competitive versus non-competitive zones

90/10 Minimum Guarantee Deals

The 90/10 deal used to be the standard, but is now used in a minority of instances. Nevertheless, they are still found and are instructive in terms of how the concept of house nuts are applied and impact film rental calculations. When a distributor has screened a film for the major exhibitors, and is ready to offer them the picture, the booking negotiation will usually address the following elements:

- Playing time is the number of committed weeks (sometimes in two-week increments)
- Percentage split of box office, after deduction of specified house nut
- Minimum percentage/floor for distributor from box office, by week

Accordingly, a deal could look like the following:

- Playing time: 8 weeks (at high end)
- 90%/10% over $5,000 house expenses with the following minimums:
  - Week 1: 60%
  - Week 2: 55%
  - Week 3: 50%
  - Weeks 4–5: 45%
  - Weeks 6–8: 35%

Let us assume that the film brings in $40,000 in box office in week one compared to another film with the same deal bringing in $10,000. How are the splits calculated?

Film One:

$$\begin{array}{r} \$40,000 \\ -5,000 \\ \hline \$35,000 \\ \$31,500 \ @ \ 90\% \\ \$3,500 \ @ \ 10\% \end{array}$$

Minimum floor calculation: 60% * $40,000 = $24,000
Since $31,500 > $24,000, the distributor keeps $31,500
Exhibitor keeps $8,500 ($3,500 + $5,000)

Film Two:

$$
\begin{array}{r}
\$10,000 \\
-5,000 \\
\hline
\$\ 5,000 \\
\end{array}
$$

4,500 @ 90%
$ 500 @ 10%

Minimum floor calculation: 60% * $10,000 = $6,000
Since $6,000 > $4,500 the distributor would keep $6,000
Exhibitor keeps $4,000 ($10,000 − $6,000), and loses money

Years ago, revenue guarantees would sometimes be applied against the splits, such that in addition to minimum floors there would be minimum guarantees. Not only is this practice gone, but true holdovers are a bit of an anachronism; a holdover clause used to trigger an automatic extension for another week (often on a rolling basis) in the event the box office for the picture exceeded a stipulated threshold in the prior week. Today, however, holdovers are dictated by pure economics, and as discussed later a non-performing title will likely be "kicked out" regardless of contractual provisions to the contrary.

Aggregates: Alternative to 90/10 Deals with House Nut

An aggregate deal is one in which the distributor and exhibitor negotiate a fixed split of the gross box office receipts and do not apply/deduct a house nut. The economic incentives behind this deal largely include doing away with calculating the house nut (by ensuring the exhibitor will not earn less than its nut) and simplifying the accounting; the logic is that if after all the line item calculations the distributor knows it is likely to keep 50%, why not just agree to 50%? There is, of course, a risk that money could be left on the table, but the bet is that within a narrow band revenues will even out over time. If the spread were 10% this would not work, but if the parties through experience know the spread may only vary a couple of percent on a certain type of picture, then the risk may be considered nominal. Perhaps the best way to illustrate this is with an example.

If an exhibitor plays a major film that is likely to sell out regularly over the first week or two, it does not mind paying out on the 90/10

132

split — its nut is covered, and the seats are filled with patrons buying candy and popcorn. At any point that the minimum floor is triggered, however, the distributor is eating into the exhibitor's house nut. Accordingly, the exhibitor has to ask itself would I prefer to book the film where I may not keep my full nut, or should I book a different film where I keep my full nut? This may sound like a simultaneous equation, in that there should be no difference if both movies initially perform well. However, there is a difference with major pictures that may take multiple screens, and where the nut applied may vary per screen. By applying a fixed split the exhibitor is theoretically assured that its revenues will not fall below its nut.

Splits may then be negotiated in a number of ways. If the exhibitor has the leverage, then the rental percentage will be lower. Additionally, one can imagine cases making the calculation extremely complicated, such as in creating a scale of aggregates in which the flat splits change over weeks, stepping down similarly to the previous minimum floor 90/10 deal. In this instance negotiations could trade off up front versus downstream percentages. If the distributor achieves a slightly better deal up front, then it will likely give something up on the backend, somewhat evening out the equation. At this point, though, one has to question whether there is any efficiency or incentive to move to an aggregate.

Having come full circle, if all that happens is the net dollars are somewhat evened out, why bother? Again, the simple answer that no one will admit to but probably strikes close to the heart is ease of administration: a flat deal is easier to calculate and administer. Another reason could be that to book multiple screens in a multiplex (and stick the exhibitor with the potential opportunity cost of booking incremental screens that may yield better economics with another film), the distributor may want to offer an incentive. That incentive is the aggregate, which on the surface is calculated in a way that would otherwise somewhat match the expected return of a firm term deal, yet by its formula ensures in theory that the exhibitor does not risk a split below its house nut. The distributor forfeits incremental revenue equal to the delta between the aggregate split and any higher amount it may have earned on a different deal, but theoretically makes up the difference by expanding its release with the additional screens. (Note: The notion of additional screens expanding the pie is a theoretical statement, for it assumes both that (1) the box office is actually generated which may not happen, and (2) it fails to take account the incremental print costs of playing that additional screen.)

133

Firm Terms vs. Settlement

Despite contractual sliding scales (90/10 deals with minimums), the reality of the theatrical box office is that distributors and exhibitors have a symbiotic relationship and will often move off the letter of the contract. The contract with a sliding scale is sometimes referred to as "firm terms," because there is a clear formula used for calculating film rentals from the box office gross. In contrast, "settlement" is just like it sounds: at the end of a picture's run the parties will sit down to evaluate performance and agree on a percentage. If this smells like a scene from a movie with people haggling in a back office, that is not too far from what can happen. The theatrical distribution business harkens back to days of arm wrestling and handshakes, and in many cases it devolves to relationships and hard nose negotiations.

Because distributors have a slate of films, the negotiations need to stay within the bounds of precedents and customary practices. Again, the parties need each other and it is to neither side's long-term advantage to fleece the other. Whether horse trading numbers of screens, or holding over a print longer than the pure economics of that particular film may justify based on that isolated film's performance, there are lots of moving parts and chits to accumulate. When a studio promises a producer it can open a film to a certain breadth, or keep the film playing long enough to reach a certain total, it may need to do some juggling to achieve that goal. By splitting up the pie via settlement, there is obviously more flexibility; unfortunately, there is also more mystery. Ultimately, settlement can only influence results at the margins, because if the results strayed too far from firm terms then one title would benefit at the expense of another and the system would break.

Four-Wall Structure

To "four wall" a movie means to literally rent the venue. In this scenario, the studio distributor will agree to a weekly rental amount and then keep 100% of the box office. This is the one scenario where film rentals are equal to box office. (Note: Given the extraordinary costs, in theory, any accounting should either allow the deduction of some form of house nut from the gross revenues or else allow a true flow through of the costs.)

A four-wall deal is unusual, but still occurs. It can come up in a case where the distributor wants a unique venue and this is the only way to ensure its film will be played and will not be dropped early. Another situation when a four-wall deal may make sense is when parties cannot agree to floors and splits; if a distributor was unwilling to accept the terms countered by an exhibitor, and the splits were too low, it might roll the dice to take on the house nut and keep the full gross. In theory, this situation is most likely to arise with a unique venue, possibly with a single screen that has a high operating cost.

Release Strategy and Timing

There are no hard and fast rules regarding releases, but the following are a few of the critical factors taken into account.

Factors in When to Release

Day and Date

Films used to release in the United States and then open internationally weeks and even months later. Much of the delay was due to practical limitations: it would take time to complete the foreign versions (dubs and subtitles) and publicity tours were much easier to orchestrate in a staggered fashion.

With the globalization of the world, instant access from the Internet, and growing threats from piracy, more and more event films are being released simultaneously around the world — in film parlance, a "day-and-date" release. A day-and-date release allows for focused publicity, and affords international territories to capture the momentum rather than release a film when core fans are aware they are seeing the picture downstream. Moreover, for very large titles it allows the release to become eventized. The largest contributing factor though is the ability to defeat piracy, an issue that many obsess over given the potential for instant and global copies on the Internet.

Competition

All studios scrutinize the competitive landscape, as the cleaner window and the less competition the better. Competition can be segmented into a number of categories.

First, there is competition from other product being released by the same studio/distributor. This is obviously the easiest category to address, and while studios will downplay this issue (under the rationalization that if they were not competing against their own film they would still be competing against something) there is obviously no reason to tax bandwidth and potentially compete against yourself.

135

The second category is direct competition within a targeted demographic or genre. For example, if a major Disney animated movie is releasing, it probably makes better sense to pick a different time frame and not try to divide the animation audience; of course, given the cutthroat competition there have been conscious attempts to directly release against a similar film in attempt to crush the competition and sustain an upper hand in the market. Additionally, competitive titles may afford an opportunity to counter-program, and a niche or differently targeted film may be able to provide an alternative to certain demographics and in instances of box office dominated by tentpoles may even be able to draft off the overall box office uplift. Finally, there is generic competition — a big enough film that may monopolize the box office. This is especially true in cases of sequels, and often distributors will steer clear of event films such as the next Spiderman; if enough people move away, then opportunities arise to counter-program to targeted demographics.

Outside Factors (Events of National Attention)

Outside factors play a very important role; films are not simply competing against other films but also for consumer dollars against other media. It is generally believed that certain events of national importance will siphon off attention and can impact box office. Such events may include national political elections and major international sporting events including the Olympics and World Cup. These are all planned events that can be factored when planning release dates; however, in an increasingly connected and seemingly unpredictable world, news events including wars and terrorist attacks can also create reasons for last minute juggling.

While the potential influence on diverting attention from the film is real, another key concern is the increased difficulty of marketing a property against these juggernauts of public attention. For example, media will be harder and more expensive to place at the peak of an election cycle. Accordingly, there can be a double hit: releasing a film in the window of an event of national importance will likely make it more expensive to reach desired awareness levels and even if awareness targets are hit there is a risk that consumers will opt to spend their time and money on the national event that only occurs once every few years.

Acceleration of Revenues

Today, all focus seems to be on opening weekends, with distributors then modeling an ultimate box office based on an extrapolation from the initial week(s) and assumed declines. Historically films could play for months and it was not unusual for a blockbuster hit to play through and even beyond a season such as the summer. As the number of films made and released grew, competition grew with it. There are a number of interrelated factors that evolved, all feeding on each other, which accelerated this process and led to the compressed revenue cycle of a film taking in a higher and higher percentage of its overall revenue in the first 2–3 weeks of release.

First, people started to focus on opening weekends and records, putting pressure on openings. Marketing dollars were therefore allocated to open a film as large as possible — even if a film's box office had a sharper week-to-week decline at the beginning than it may have had with a debut on fewer screens. The initial larger box office could make up for this drop and theoretically push the cumulative total higher than an otherwise narrower release would have yielded.

Second, with more and more films the spacing between major movies shrank. Competitive windows have narrowed, and studios now look to all 52 weeks of the year to find the best competitive free window in which to release; moreover, the jockeying is all critical. Go out against the wrong film and you could be done in the first week, as it is extraordinarily rare that a film that is opened wide and does not perform to expectations then gains in a subsequent week. The system is designed not to let this happen, as a new movie is always on its heels, and if a film does not perform someone else will take its screens. The exhibition business is ruthless and all about filling seats, not second chances.

Accordingly, distributors are looking to maximize shorter and shorter runs: what am I likely to open up against, what am I coming after, and what is coming after me. Each of these factors can dramatically influence the film's performance, and while there might have been months or at least a month between major titles, with the volume and budgets in current Hollywood this is now measured in weeks. A film that has two or three relatively clear weeks is now blessed, and as late as the mid-1990s this was hard to fathom.

The net result of the acceleration of revenue not only puts inordinate pressures on distributors and content owners, but has a disproportionate negative impact on theater owners. As described previously regarding rentals and weekly minimums, the longer a film plays the more the split shifts to favor the theater owner; accordingly, theater owners are losing more of their upsides because they lock into revenue schemes where the upside is in downstream weeks that at worst no longer exist and at best have lower box office revenues to split. In discussing the plight of theaters, Forbes noted: "But the fact that films 'play off' and leave theaters faster is poison to the owners. It means that even if overall box office is constant or increasing, owners can be earning much less revenue. One *Titanic*, which didn't open particularly well, but played for weeks, is worth more to theater owners than five successful films, each of which earns one-fifth as much."[16]

Exacerbating these pressures are key holiday weekends and the built-in expectations of sequels (which often gravitate to these dates as a safe haven given the usually high budgets). Opening in holiday periods when people have more free time to go to the movies has become a cultural tradition. Memorial Day weekend, Fourth of July, November (to play into Thanksgiving), and Christmas have become prime real estate. If a studio has a picture they view as a sure thing they will leak out that date early and try and stake out that turf. Although the track record vindicates this strategy, because competition tends to cluster around these dates it may not be the best strategy; to wit, *Batman — The Dark Knight* opened in mid-July 2008 and went on to become the second highest grossing theatrical title of all time. Finally, what often is not talked about but can be the most influential factor is superstition. If a film (or director) has had good luck with a date, the studio may want to stick with that timing. I have seen many cases where a date seemed odd relative to the foregoing logical factors only to realize it was the "director's date" or that when the original film launched (in the case of plotting a release date for a sequel).

The Online Factor

Pressure from Review Sites

It is harder to open a movie with "word of mouth" in a world when slow buzz from the watercooler conversation is replaced by instant access to national reviews by a site like rottentomatos.com. Before a movie opens potential viewers are privy to whether a majority of critics liked it or not, and if someone wants an opinion from a more trusted source they are apt to check out opinions on their favorite blogs. This is just another factor compressing time lines. The immediacy and breadth of information makes it hard to hide a bomb, while providing an extra impetus to crash the gates if people are raving.

Online Release

One alternative is to release a film online, either simultaneously with theatrical or as an alternative. In November 2007 director Ed Burns decided to release his $4M movie *Purple Violets* on iTunes. Commenting that there was "not enough money to market the film, not a wide-enough release to even make a dent in the movie going public's consciousness," he pioneered releasing the film via iTunes, reportedly the first time a feature film was debuted on Apple's download service.[17]

Although Apple has had success with offering shorts, launching with the library of Pixar shorts, the model of launching a film online rather than theatrically has to date proven risky. The theory is that the online world provides instant access everywhere, and enough of a stampede to watch online would justify cannibalizing theatrical revenues. However, with 35,000 screens in the country and most of the population within a short drive of a theater, is a bit easier access really a compelling enticement? There are obvious consumer experience differences between seeing a movie online versus in-theater, plus serious economic hurdles including (1) theaters' willingness to boycott films that go online and do not grant an exclusive theatrical window, (2) the risk of further impact on the DVD market (on *Purple Violet* "video distributors had offered lower-than-expected advance payments for the films DVD right out of fear that its availability on iTunes would cannibalize home-video sales"[18]), and (3) the fact that online marketing has not yet been proven successful as the sole vehicle to market a film (though given the ability to demographically target with more efficient buys, someone is apt to take this risk and perhaps demonstrate a tipping point).

Records Aren't What They Used to Be — Dissecting Opening Weekends

An interesting fact about holidays and openings is that the record book is now more of a microscopic statistical analysis with lots of people holding bits of records, the accounting segmented to spread the glory. There are now records for biggest one day (which I am proud to have been part of when *Star Wars Episode III* opened to just over $50M, only to see the record fall to *Batman* in 2008), but even that record has previously been split into biggest Thursday opening versus biggest Friday versus biggest Saturday, with Saturday generally the biggest day for a film opening. *Star Wars* leveled out the equation (at least for a while — all records are eventually broken) when its Thursday was bigger than any prior Saturday, but it was only a matter of time before new boundaries were set.

Much more complicated is the notion of the weekend box office. As noted earlier, weekends are customarily calculated as the Friday–Sunday box office. However, holidays skew the mix and can be four or six days. What is the period when July 4th falls on a Wednesday? This naturally leads to debates over the "highest weekend," highest four-day weekend, highest holiday weekend, and highest four-day holiday weekend. Beyond holiday, there is the issue of studios opening so-called event films earlier. This helps build buzz for the film leading into the weekend, as well as having the corollary impact of expanding the weekend box office: what a film has grossed by Sunday night. And we are not yet done!

A further wrinkle occurs with sneaks and screenings. Sometimes a film will have a very limited release earlier in the week to build some awareness. This was the pattern with Russell Crowe's *Cinderella Man* released on Friday June 3, 2005. The film actually hit some theaters in major markets for a special sneak the prior Sunday. While it is clear that this gross should not be counted in the following weekend, the line becomes blurred when a film opens mid-week. Opening on a Thursday is now relatively common, and the Thursday numbers may or may not be included in the weekend. The studio will position the higher number as the weekend (taking it as a "four-day"), but the trades are likely to split that out and report the three- and four-day numbers (since there are different records, and presumably it makes things more interesting).

The final issue has to do with midnight or late night screenings that occur with huge event films. If you want to get picky, where does the 12:01 or 11:59 showing fit, and should these be separate or aggregated into the day or weekend? The only clear answer is that it all goes into the weekly gross and ultimate gross. I have not actually counted the permutations, but you should get the picture. To outsiders it may seem a bit petty, like the multiple boxing crowns. Within the industry, however, it is like chum to a shark.

This would not be so important if it were not for the press and financial market expectations. The press will jump on box office and hit the ground running on Monday morning. Studio stock prices can rise and fall on these stories, as was the case when DreamWorks Animation released *Madagascar* on Memorial Day weekend 2005. The film's performance was closely scrutinized, as it was the first release following the company's IPO, and analysts were watching carefully to gauge whether *Shrek* was a phenomenon, or whether the studio could repeat with blockbuster after blockbuster like Pixar. (Note: To be fair, there was further pressure in that just several days before

DreamWorks announced adjustments to its video numbers for *Shrek2*.)

Against this backdrop, when *Madagascar* opened to $61M, which is by anyone's standards a huge number, it was still not up to hyped expectations: "Shares of DreamWorks Animation hit a new low Tuesday, dropping more than 9% as some on Wall Street deemed as uninspiring the domestic haul of $61 million that 'Madagascar' garnered in its first four days at the box office and Lehman Bros. downgraded the stock."[19,20]

Studio Estimates

What is a bit mysterious is how that $61M is calculated. It seems difficult, if not impossible, to have final weekend numbers on Sunday (for the press to write about the weekend) without the benefit of Sunday's full figures. The studios accordingly have to estimate box office; however, the studios have been doing this so long and know their clients (theaters) so well, that they can extrapolate a market number with a fairly reliable measure of precision. Although the potential for gamesmanship exists, there are built-in incentives to keep reporting as accurate as possible; the studios want to avoid having to report that they overestimated and take down a number.

What does all this have in common? The big opening, which puts pressure on the splits and dogfights for screens and locations, also brings us back to the aggregate concept.

Table 4.1 is a hybrid example: assuming $100,000 in box office in week one, a decline of 50% to $50,000 in week 2, a further decline to $30,000 and $25,000 in weeks 3 and 4, a decline to $10,000 and $7,500 in the next two weeks, and two more weeks at $5,000 and $3,000.

Table 4.1   Box Office Revenue

	Box Office
2 weeks @60	$(.60 \times \$100,000) + (.60 \times \$50,000) = \$90,000$
2 weeks @50	$(.50 \times \$30,000) + (.50 \times \$25,000) = \$27,500$
2 weeks @40	$(.40 \times \$10,000) + (.40 \times \$7,500) = \$7,000$
balance @30	$(.30 \times \$5,000) + (.30 \times \$3,000) = \$2,400$
	Total Rentals = $126,900

Theatrical Booking

Locations, Types of Runs, Length of Runs, Frenzy of Booking

While other facets of the distribution business, in particular pay TV and video, have changed dramatically over time, the theatrical booking business maintains much of its decades old practices. This is a business of having to turn over thousands of screens and theaters every week, steeped in relationships at both head office and local booking office levels. There is almost the feeling of a never ending poker game: cards are shuffled and dealt every week, some cards are traded in, and when final bets are placed everyone is waiting to see who has the high hand on the weekend.

Zones and Types of Theaters

Theater bookings in the United States follow relatively standard patterns. The entire country's theater count is broken down into regions, cities, and districts, all falling under the management of the domestic theatrical distribution arm of a studio. This is typically managed in a regional structure, where a head office will manage multiple geographic regions such as the South, West, etc. Each region will in turn have a regional manager with an army of booking agents underneath them.

By having this level of management, the theatrical distribution arm will literally have a direct relationship with every single theater in the country, which totals around 4,000+ locations with 35,000+ screens.

In large urban areas where there are multiple cinemas within relatively close physical proximity, the theaters may be districted into zones or regions. These are not formal/legal classifications, but rather informal designations tacitly acknowledged by the individual theaters (or chains). If you are booking a film in a Regal cinema on Main Street it may be accepted that you do not then book your film in the theater across the street at AMC's multiplex, thus granting the theater a measure of exclusivity over its competitor. With the advent of multiplexes, and in particular the growth of large multiplexes, the level of jockeying has shrunk over time.

While focus is on multiplexes and optimizing top theaters (note: true top performing theaters are often referred to in industry parlance as "guns" or "gun theaters"), there are a couple of other categories that come into play. For example, drive-ins always want top pictures, especially in summer months, and threshold decisions need to be made whether drive-ins will be single or double bills (as they tend to book double features), and whether the film will play day and date with multiplexes or move over to drive-ins at a later date. There are many "second run" theaters, often located in smaller towns, where prints will be bicycled over to the local cinema after it has had its multiplex/wide launch. Accordingly, along with economic splits, zones, and lengths of runs (see next section), theatrical booking departments also have to deal with the placement patterns of first run versus second run versus specialty (e.g. drive-ins) venues.

Booking: A Last Minute Frenzy

When it gets down to a week or so before a film opens, it is a literal free-for-all. In a matter of days a film can go from zero bookings to 3,000+ theaters and 7,000+ screens. During this booking time it is all out war with distributors giving theaters terms including the splits, the number of weeks, etc. In busy times such as between Thanksgiving and Christmas and in the summer (especially Memorial Day through July 4th) every weekend is precious and competition for locations and screens is extreme.

Even though distributors cannot book a theater until the exhibitors have seen the movie (as a result of the prohibition on blind bidding), it is fully impractical to wait until two weeks before a movie release to structure a game plan for booking thousands of venues. Long before the screenings take place, the distribution team will look at the population of theaters and competitive landscape of films and plot a strategy for locations and screens. Because this is done on a weekly basis, the parties are aware of each other's general tactics and preferences, and relationships have evolved. Accordingly, if Disney is about to release a Pixar film, or Fox has a large action/star-driven vehicle, they will have a strong educated guess which theaters they are likely to target and be able to book in downtown Chicago. Much attention is obviously focused on securing prime venues. Not all theaters are equal, and every distributor wants to lock up its top "gun" site.

It is almost like Las Vegas, because there can be a feeding frenzy and yet it is all about placing bets — nobody knows how any particular film will actually perform. That is where exhibitor conventions (e.g., ShowWest) are so important. They sell to the theaters and make them believe before selling to the consumers. The theater proposition is much simpler than the consumer: no matter what anyone tells you, the theater owners are often single-mindedly focused on traffic. How many people will a film drive to the venue to buy popcorn is the bottom line. Forget about art, reviews, or actors. It is a business.

143

As an example, put yourself in the place of a theater owner with a screen in downtown Chicago. If you are offered a film starring Robert Redford at an X% aggregate, such as 55% with second week at 50%, would you take that film versus a new CG animated film from a leading producer with two 50s? And what if you also had another film with a 90/10 with a sliding scale of guarantees/minimums? What would you choose and what are the variables you would take into account?

Adding to the craziness of bookings are so-called exception markets and theaters, where rent costs of a prime venue are so high that theaters may be treated on a different economic basis. There is endless jockeying and side exception deals to manage, where the incentive is actually to strike fair deals for both sides. While it is a cutthroat business, it is also a 52-week-per-year business where it does not behoove a distributor to force a deal that would cause a theater to lose money. There are many more misses than hits, and the distributor is likely to need a favor from an exhibition chain to open a movie that has poor reviews or otherwise looks in trouble.

144

Length of Runs

Another factor in booking is the length of the run. Arguably, this is the single most important factor other than the splits, and it influences the splits given that they are tiered over the run. The following are the typical engagements:

- 6- to 8-week deals (less common)
- 4-week deals
- 2-week deals

Much of whether a deal falls into one category or not defaults to custom and practice. Certain towns (or locations) may be profiled as "8-week towns" and this is the standard deal for a picture of a specific profile. These weeks denote a so-called minimum run period, and end up serving only as guidelines both on success and failure. If a picture is still performing well and yielding returns greater than competitive/alternative product, logically it should continue to hold screens and keep playing. In the out weeks, there will be a floor for splits for which the picture will not drop below regardless of how long it plays. As noted earlier, a film like *Titanic* that played for weeks and months on end, while a boon to the distributor, is an even greater prize for the exhibitor — seats continue to be filled, and all at splits (if a 90/10 deal) favoring the theater. On the flip side, if a film is not performing it may be kicked out early with the distributor "granting relief" (see the section Being Dropped).

Prints and Screen Counts

When booking theaters, distributors book both locations and then actual screens at those locations. To state the obvious, there are many more screens than locations, and for a major movie the ratio can be a multiple (e.g., 2:1). The number of locations/theaters is therefore the less interesting fact in terms of economics: the actual screens dictate both applicable house nuts/allowances as well as the number of physical prints needed.

Prints can be very expensive with an estimated average of ~$1,500/print for a major motion picture released widely through the studio system. Of course, there are many variables that may go into a negotiation with a lab, including the type of film stock used and the length of the film (prints are still literally priced by the yard and deals are quoted in dollars or cents per foot). This does not sound too bad, until you run the numbers and extrapolate out worldwide costs for mega-movies that have a broad release, such as a *Shrek* or *Spider-Man* sequel. It is a trade secret how many screens were booked for Shrek2 and Spider-man2, but let us assume there were upwards of 3,500 locations and take an average of 2 screens per location. That could yield 7,000+ screens. For the sake of simplicity, assume some backup prints would be made for key locations, and the total print run was 7,500. The 7,500 prints times $1,500/print is $11.25M. And this is just for the United States, and does not include all the pre-print mastering and quality assurance services that would be on top of this variable figure.

As earlier noted, historically films played longer and did not open as wide, which meant that prints could be reused; a film might open in a major city, and after it had played a while it would then move to a smaller town or location. The benefit to the distributor is there is no incremental cost. However, when a film opens very wide and a distributor tries to garner as much box office up front as possible, then the opportunities for reusing prints are reduced. Moreover, prints could be reformatted to be used internationally in same language territories, allowing the "bicycling" of assets worldwide and amortizing these sunk costs over more runs. With the move to event films and day-and-date releases these opportunities are also eliminated.

145

One net result of a major, wide, day-and-date release is to dramatically drive up the print costs — a factor that makes D-cinema, which can radically reduce these costs, attractive.

Per Screen Averages

Partly as a consequence of multiplexes and booking multiple prints at a single venue, the concept of per screen averages is often misunderstood and at best inconsistently applied or quoted. Trade journals and general industry lingo will often refer to per screen averages, but the use of "screen" is a misnomer. Per screen averages quoted in the trades and viewed for distribution decisions are actually per location averages.

It is not rocket science to compare competitive per screen averages, as common reporting systems will report gross box office dollars and pretty accurately estimate the number of locations played. The math is simply total box office/number of locations. As a rule of thumb, an average of $10,000 or higher is extremely good, and a picture starts to lose momentum as the number dwindles into the low thousands and even less.

Although analysis is not taken down to the per seat level, it is possible to back into the numbers and understand why this average is such a good barometer. Let us assume the following:

Assumptions:

- Average ticket price: $7.00
- Average theater size: 300 seats (probably high, but makes math easier)
- 5 showings per day
- One print per theater
- Standard 3-day weekend calculation

Potential Gross: $7 \times 300 = \$2,100 \times 5 = \$10,500$ per day

Per Weekend

The screen average can then be segmented by these periods. Because the lion's share of the weekly gross of a picture comes in on the weekend, this is the customary measurement for screen averages. The weekend is considered "three day," meaning Friday–Sunday.

$$3 \times \$10,500 = \$31,500 \text{ potential weekend gross}$$

A film that has a $10,000 weekend per screen average would indicate that fully one-third of all potential seats for all shows for the whole weekend were sold. At 5 showings/day that takes into account 15 showings, which means that on average all of the primetime showings would need to be nearly sold out (assuming roughly 5 to 6 are at peak hours) to achieve this number, or that they could be 75% sold out with a smattering of audience at non-primetime dates.

When you start to see per screen averages well above $10,000, both intuitively and empirically it means that people are coming to the movie at multiple times (day and evening). This is generally only achieved with a wide demographic.

Of course, these numbers can be deceptive. The variables discussed previously can dramatically skew the results (as can demographics, where a kids movie will have lower average ticket prices). For example, the number of prints on average per theater (i.e., screens) will have the most profound impact, with the number of showtimes per day having the next most. Of course, the more showings and the more prints typically indicate a major film, and should boost the per screen average. If a film opens very wide (large number of prints) and the per screen average is not high, you will be able immediately to conclude the release is in trouble. The problem is that there may not be much time to adjust especially if marketing expenditure has been frontloaded. Finally, the above assumes a flat ticket price, but children's prices and matinees also influence the maximum potential gross (as can the new trend of premium pricing for 3-D).

Interlocking

Interlocking is the practice of running two screens off a single projector/print. This practice is discouraged, and in most cases prohibited, by distributors. There are concerns about accounting, as splits and nuts are based on per screen deals and interlocking usually takes place for overflow demand rather than regular showtimes. There are also quality concerns given the very nature of interlocking. Ultimately, fear of being mistreated overrides the economic efficiency of saving a print. In a true crunch, however, it is fair to assume that a blind eye may be turned. The chance to have another full house and additional gross is likely to hold sway at the margin.

Decay Curves and Drop-Offs — Managing the Release

Once the film opens, it becomes part art and part science in terms of managing locations and screens. What everyone focuses on are the

147

week-to-week decays, in particular the decays from weekend to weekend. Regardless of how one defines the days of the opening weekend, for a decay curve you need a like-to-like comparison and a Friday–Sunday benchmark is used.

It is unfair to refer to these charts as simply "decays," because depending on the release strategy a film can actually increase from week to week. A picture that has a strategy of starting small and building an audience through reviews and word of mouth will expand locations. It may start at a hundred theaters in major markets, and then wait to release wider nationally. The dream scenario is to open wide and have virtually no falloff, or even an uptick. This rarely happens, but occurred with *Shrek* in 2001, where its second weekend was nearly identical to its opening weekend (3-day to 3-day, as one weekend was Memorial Day). This zero decay immediately indicated to DreamWorks that it had a major hit on its hand. The original *Shrek* grossed over $267M, becoming the top animated film of all time at the point (yet another way to slice a record).[21]

Most films, however, follow traditional decays, meaning there is a relatively predictable pattern of drop-offs. The industry rule of thumb is that if you open well (namely large!), a drop-off of ~50% in week 2 is anticipated. If the film drops significantly more, such as 60–70%, then one initially assumes that the marketing worked to drive people into the opening, but that the film may not have been well received — either word of mouth or reviews or competition took the wind out of its sails, and once this happens it is virtually impossible to recover. (Note: Given competition and accelerated box office takes, a larger drop–off may not mean the film is in trouble, but simply in the case of a blockbuster or tentpole that the first week was so large it will represent a disproportionate share of the total. See discussion below regarding acceleration of box office.) If the decay is in the acceptable range or even less than expected (this is what every executive is hoping for), then the goal immediately becomes to keep the decay from week 2 to week 3 within the same range thereby keeping the momentum.

Depending on the percentage and the competition on the horizon, this is also when key marketing decisions are made. Do you run a hype or review advertisement ("Two thumbs up," "Best picture of the year according to ____, #1 at the box office... .)? There will usually be some marketing planned post release (called "sustain marketing"), but as films are becoming more and more frontloaded much sustain marketing spending, especially in weeks past the first 2–3 weeks, may be allocated literally on the spot during the week.

148

Trend of Accelerated Decays for Blockbusters

The bigger the film and the bigger the opening, the steeper the decay will likely be up front. On Star Wars episode III, for example, the Thursday–Sunday "opening weekend" was over $150M, with the following long weekend (Memorial Day) taking in $70M at the box office. The pure 3-day to 3-day, however, was $108M to $55M (49%), representing an acceptable 50% drop.[22]

This is a typical pattern for a blockbuster, but one then hopes for the decay curve to flatten out. Because the numbers are so large, and there are so many prints and showtimes playing, there will inevitably be a large fall. As weeks progress, however, and multiplexes are only playing one or two prints for normal showtimes, and locations consolidate, the decay curve will hopefully flatten and the weekly drops will not be as precipitous.

As noted earlier, in terms of prints and multiplexes, this is where it is important to distinguish between locations and prints, and in terms of prints to distinguish between sizes of auditoriums within a multiplex (see Move-Overs below). When a film opens particularly wide and one sees a print count in the range over 7,000, there are almost always multiple prints in one location. Continuing with Star Wars Episode III, on the weekend of June 2, 2005, for example, you could go to the movie listings and pull up a 16- or 20-plex, and notice that in counting up the actual number of films playing there it was only 9 or 10, and similarly in a theater half the size, namely an 8-plex, there were only 6 films playing. This is because event or would-be event films that were opened wide and had large demand played on multiple screens. One can assume that at the 8-plex playing only 6 films that both *Star Wars* and *Madagascar* had multiple screens (2 each); similarly in the 16-plex playing only 6 films, one of the films may have had as many as 4 or 5 screens at one point, and potentially more on opening weekend.

Move-Overs

There is yet another variable to consider in understanding the print placements — the size of theater. In a 20-plex, for example, theater sizes can range from several hundred seats to a couple of hundred seats or less. While not all theaters are equal, similarly not "all prints are equal" in terms of potential gross within the complex. Thus, when a print of a film opens in the largest screen, after it has run for a week or two, demand will likely wane and the auditorium will play to fewer people per showtime; in the extreme, which happens quite frequently, a print will move from playing to capacity to sparse crowds fairly quickly. Keeping the print in the theater may make sense to the distributor who wants the largest potential gross (I don't care if it's empty during the matinees and mid-week Joe, 'cause I want that gross on the primetimes …) in some scenarios. However, this will not make economic sense if the print/distributor is bearing the house nut; in fact, the print can lose money if the nut is significant.

The larger the auditorium, the larger the nut, so when demand wanes, the print "moves over" from a larger to a smaller screen. This has two benefits. First, as just noted, the smaller screen has a smaller house nut. Second, movie going is a social experience and most people prefer to have a full house rather than an empty house — it is inevitably the crowd reaction and the shared experience of hearing screams, cries, quick intake of air from being shocked, and even the occasional funny heckle that is part of the magic of the theater and makes seeing a movie in the theater fun. (Note: This also partially explains the preview and midnight screening crush of attendance, as it is just as likely that people want to see the film in an atmosphere charged with the same excitement they feel than that they have to see the film early. It is more the electricity and shared experience of the moment that likely drives most people than the bragging rights that they saw it a few hours or days ahead of someone else.) That social, collective experience simply cannot be replicated at home, no matter how nice a flat screen and home theater environment someone has created.

Move-overs thus have multiple benefits to both parties, for economically having full auditoriums is beneficial to both the distributor and exhibitor. Similarly, if a multiplex is playing a film on multiple screens, and the percentage of seats filled per screen/showtime starts to drop off, then a print will be dropped and the film shown on two screens rather than three, increasing the average capacity filled per showtime. Of course, the distributor wants to ensure that there are still sufficient playtimes for people to see the film, and it is the balancing of nearing capacity versus not turning away people (who may not return — carpe diem is the MO) that becomes the art of booking.

Finally, it is worth pointing out that all of these issues are tied to success. In the more typical pattern a film will play one screen per theater location, and hold on for dear life to stay as long as possible before becoming dropped.

Being Dropped

Inevitably, every film leaves the theater, and it is hopefully after several weeks rather than several days. The fight to hold screens can be vicious, and several factors influence a film's staying power. These key factors include:

- The weekly gross of the theater. What was the film's box office the prior week and weekend?
- The weekly gross of the film relative to the competitive titles playing in the same complex (i.e., other films in the theater, assuming it is a multiplex).
- The quantity of new films opening in the week, and the perceived strength/demand of the new product (e.g., is there an expected blockbuster opening that will command multiple screens in a multiplex).
- The number of screens in the complex.
- The number of weeks the film has been in the theater: Is it the first or second week, or is it now into multiple weeks being played?
- The terms: What is the rental percentage being asked by the distributor, and is there an applicable house nut?
- What are the contractual terms. Is there a minimum booking period?
- The quantity of competitive films in the marketplace that are "grossing" (are there several pictures holding over with strong to respectable grosses in addition to new films opening up).
- What other pictures does the studio have in release? All theaters want to keep each of the studios happy, and while there are no allocated slots it may be difficult for Studio A to keep multiple screens (when some are marginal performing pictures) at the expense of a rival studio securing a screen.
- Studio pressures/expectations driven by direct economics—achieving performance thresholds, which could be tied to economics, such as achieving a box office number that may trigger improved economics in a downstream revenue (e.g., pay TV output deals tiered to box office thresholds) and by indirect economics tied to relationships (e.g., fulfilling promises to the producer/director/actor—"are you fighting for my picture?")
- What investment does the studio have in the film? Not all pictures are equal in terms of the studio's financial stake, and while every studio will tell you that it is fighting for every cent on every film, it is natural to question whether there is a bit more fight in a film where the studio has a bigger stake.

151

These are the type of factors influencing the decisions. They comprise a unique mix by blending straightforward economics, cutthroat competition, allocations (within and without groups), politics, ego, and differing agendas. A studio is very conscious both of relationships and performance, but when counting relationships they are truly in the middle of two parties they need to please: the exhibitor and the producer. Although distributors have a tremendous amount of clout (without them you simply do not get into the screens/theaters), they are between a rock and a hard place. During a release they need to please the filmmaker who only cares about their movie and maximizing its results (at the expense of anyone else's film currently in release) and the theater chains who could care less about a particular film and only truly care about whether customers are filling the seats.

Tension arises because the factors weighed by the two sides (theater vs. distributor) are dissimilar. The distributor is weighing a nearly impossible matrix of agendas ranging from pleasing a star to recouping an investment to juggling multiple pictures within a slate to maintaining pole position relationship treatment with a particular exhibition chain of theaters. The exhibitor, however, has relative tunnel vision focused on attendance: they can remain emotionally neutral and have virtually no reason to care about the particular film, only focusing on whether people come and the theater is full (taking their split and raking in concession money).

Despite the potential for a dizzying complex matrix, the end result of what stays in a theater is rarely a complex balancing act. Instead, it is absolutely Darwinian, and the strongest pictures survive. After every weekend the distributor looks at a report of how its pictures performed and how they performed versus the competition. Box office information is freely available, and there is little argument as to relative standings. In an 8-plex theater, the local booker and theater are acutely aware of their ranking. If there are 8 screens, and Studio A has one picture that came in last (8th among 8), then that picture is going to get dropped in favor of a new picture coming into the market (or adding another good performer in the market that may not have been booked originally). The one exception to this rule is that by contract as well as industry practice virtually every major studio picture gets the benefit of the doubt for two weeks. If a studio is opening a movie with a major star or for a major director/producer, it will secure at least a two-week run and will be hard pressed to pull it before this minimum period.

The survival of the fittest mentality can be tempered by a few factors, such as the ability to move over. Because of the "not all screens are equal" factor, a film that is underperforming may still hold in a smaller auditorium because its gross remains strong enough to stay in the complex relative to competition. Moreover, all of the factors previously stated then can and do come into play at the margin. Most of the decisions are clear cut. If the gross in a complex is $1,200 for a week and all other films are $3,000 and above there is not much room for the distributor to argue; moreover, the smaller the complex the easier the decision. A single screen or complex with six or fewer screens can ill afford to carry its overhead without performing product — they need to attract bodies and cannot amortize across product. If a movie is not working they need to move on, and move on fast. However, with larger complexes, there is likely to be a range of performance and it is therefore easier to accommodate relationships. If you have a 16-plex and Disney or Universal needs a screen, is the exhibitor going to shut them out on a marginal picture when they have an every week of every year relationship? If the picture is truly a disaster, then maybe, but if the distributor is pleading then how much of a sacrifice is the 120 seat screen when there are 15 other screens booked with better (hopefully) performing titles?

At the margins studios may start splitting showtimes to stretch a picture's run. As the picture declines, it may play to specific demographics where splitting prints may make sense for a particular week: I'll play X in the matinees and Y in the evenings. This is a band-aid solution and rarely holds over into multiple weeks, but can make sense in the short term when there are tough calls. Essentially, this is a something is better than nothing mentality, and having capitulated half way you know your run is on a short rope. However, in the Darwinian world once you are out you are out and there are probably few to no incremental costs to staying in the extra week — the print is already there, and every incremental dollar of box office helps amortize that cost and climb toward profits.

Decay Curves and Predicting Box Office
There is a relatively predictable pattern to performance, and as discussed previously the name of the game is flattening out the decay curve so that the week-to-week drop-offs are as small as possible. All films have a decay because the nature of the business is to eventize a release, and marketing has to be somewhat if not fully frontloaded to create the awareness for people to attend. Word of mouth can

build a film that is opened small and then expands, but one can argue that this is merely a bell curve release pattern strategy and the decay starts being measured from the peak.

Accordingly, a decay curve is built from both expectations and by comparing drop-offs to comparable titles. By comparable, it may be that a film is compared to another title of similar genre with the same star (e.g., How does a Woody Allen movie or an Adam Sandler comedy decay?). If the film is part of a series or franchise, then the task can be easier: How will Harry Potter 3 compare to Harry Potter 2? Thus, a studio may build a model taking the best comparables it can find and look at the week-to-week decays of that film; namely, by what percentage did it drop week to week in weeks X to Y. The film being measured will have to have its own base, but once it has a starting point (opening week or two week data) then it is possible to plot its performance against like titles. Week to week you will measure whether you are above or below the imputed curve.

A challenge for marketing will be to keep the baseline up and keep stimulating the baseline with spikes of activity. The theory is that because a decay is inevitable, the higher the base the higher the net result. If you started from $10M versus $8M and were likely to decay the following week by 40% in either scenario, then the following week would be $6M versus $4.8M (an incremental $1.2M). Accordingly, if the prior week had been targeted at $8M and there was marketing activity/expenditure greenlit to boost box office achieving $10M, the net impact is hopefully much greater than the $2M; instead, it is the $2M + the gap in week 2 (incremental $1.2M), plus the incremental benefit in subsequent weeks.

This all assumes, however, that the decays are consistent (which is not the case) and that you can straightline the falloff tied to the higher base; in fact, no one really knows whether a program will truly raise the base in a trailing manner. Additionally, no one really knows whether the impact will be temporary and there will be a larger drop off the subsequent week where the decay is catching up to the prior equilibrium and tracking more closely to the film's "true demand" rather than the temporary demand that was stimulated.

Measuring the payoff or breakeven is therefore tricky, and the easiest benchmark is to look at the isolated period. Will the incremental costs spent this week be recouped from the lift this week in box office and resulting rental dollars? If the answer is yes, then this is a pretty good bet, for there is a payoff with the potential upside of having lifted the base and gaining the incremental value in subsequent weeks (i.e., gaining the $1.2M the next week).

Finally, it is worth noting that while the key decay curve to track is box office, it is also possible to track decays of both theater locations and prints. The final tools will therefore include a box office decay chart and a print and theater decay chart (Figure 4.3), which will include most of the following:

Week	Weekly Gross	Cumulative Week Gross	# of theaters	#of prints
Wk1				
Wk2				
Wk3				
Wk4				
Wk5				

Figure 4.3

Residual Impact of Theater Ownership

A final wrinkle in the mix is theater ownership. It is natural to assume that a theater owned by Warner Bros., for example, is likely to give preference to a Warner's title. Despite the breakup of vertical integration and the consent decree (see the section Consent Decrees, Block Booking, and Blind Booking), as anti-trust rules became relaxed in the 1980s under the Reagan administration, a number of studios began to acquire ownership interests in theaters again, in particular Warner Bros. and Paramount (Viacom). At the margin, this can influence a picture's placement, as issues of personal theater preference are likely to lose out to the pure economics of whether a rival studio-owned venue will afford you the best chance of a long run (especially if you know a competitive film from that rival studio is set to open in X weeks).

International Booking

The international market has grown to a point where it is common for a major studio release to have more locations booked internationally than domestically (though the numbers are relatively close); additionally, the international bookings may be more profitable on a per print average. I have not seen a direct study on this, but it is empirically true: if the print count is relatively even, and international box office is a greater percentage of the worldwide box office than domestic box office, then each international print (on average) must yield a greater return/box office gross.

The reason for this is largely due to the clustering of population in urban centers and cities versus the diffuse relatively rural and suburban population in the United States. It also suggests that there is international growth potential, although the shift in media and uptake of DVD and Internet is likely to encroach too quickly to let this theoretical experiment play out to its otherwise logical conclusion.

The international theatrical market has lagged behind the United States in a few areas, but that is now quickly changing. The US market, accommodating the vast suburban sprawl that has come to typify the dispersion of population, had a boom in the 1990s building multiplexes. While this trend was mirrored internationally, the phenomenon of 16- and 20-plexes did not grow at the same breathtaking pace. In retrospect this was good, for as earlier discussed virtually all the major US chains filed for or flirted with bankruptcy. Cinemas internationally reflect the local culture, and while there is an element of standardization and copying, there are many cinemas in Europe, for example, that maintain the character of great art houses.

One interesting trend is that digital cinema has taken off more quickly overseas than in the United States. To a degree this is a result of lag, for certain territories that are just now upgrading are skipping intermediate steps and installing D-cinema. This is especially true in Asia and in particular China. One has to be careful, however, in defining D-cinema as in the rush to enter the market a number of locations (at least initially) have been utilizing projectors below the 2K projector standard endorsed by most studios as a minimum resolution.

How a Property Travels

It is important to bear in mind that each film is unique, and the genre, star, and director can have profound influences on how the particular picture will fare in a particular territory. An American comedy may not travel well in one place, an action star may have disproportionate popularity in a certain country, and a franchise may for reasons obvious or inexplicable be relatively strong or weak versus its domestic market or even a neighboring territory. In some cases, the reason may be linked to a local star, and in others it may be that a scene takes place locally, some of the filming may have taken place locally, or the subject matter may strike a particular chord culturally. In many cases, however, it can simply be a mystery why a film works better in one country than another; this is the job of the marketing division, and the litany of excuses is longer than the list of why a film succeeds.

The animation industry is a particular curiosity. It became the trend with Pixar and then DreamWorks Animation and Blue Sky (*Ice Age*) to cast high-profile stars as voice talent. However, when Tom Hanks does not play the part in the German dub, nor Eddie Murphy in Spanish, then those actors truly do not ever appear in the film. The marketing hook and performance that was so pivotal to the domestic campaign (and arguably success) are simply non-existent. Somehow this does not impact performance to an extent that one would guess it should. Perhaps the clout of Hollywood and the brand expectations from these studios are able to overcome this hurdle, and people come and enjoy the film anyway, in a classic sense "not knowing what they missed." This may simply be a testament to the film's overall strength, or to the fact that when watching viewers focus on the character and do not necessarily associate the character with a particular individual/voice. In certain territories the voice-over actors tend to repeat, such that the person who dubs for Sean Connery or Pierce Brosnan in Germany tends to do so for all their films; in essence, a permanent stand in. This is the voice locally associated with the actor, and accepted. Because this is common practice for live-action dubs, it is all the easier for animation.

157

Europe
The largest European markets include the UK, France, Germany, Italy, and Spain (although Russia is close behind). The number of prints used for the markets is in the same order of magnitude for the UK, France, and Germany but this does not necessarily correlate to box office performance. The number of prints may often be the highest in Germany due to its dispersed metropolitan centers. Unlike the UK where a couple of cities such as London can dominate, Germany is more akin to the United States with many "states" and major cities (e.g., Berlin, Munich, Frankfurt, Hamburg, Cologne), and require a higher print count. For most US films, however, the UK box office will be larger than the German box office. France, despite the concentration of population in Paris with its rich film tradition, also tends to have high print counts, frequently exceeding the UK. Print counts may be from highest to lowest Germany, France, and the UK, while the box office could be exactly the opposite: highest to lowest UK, France, Germany.

This potentially inverse relationship between bookings/prints and box office revenues simply highlights some of the challenges in managing and maximizing contribution from international territories.

Asia/Pacific

The biggest markets in this region are a bit more straightforward. The largest market for major films is usually Japan, followed next by Australia and then South Korea. Unlike the situation in Europe, the number of prints tracks revenues, with the higher print count representing the larger market and corresponding higher box office.

Latin America

By far the largest markets in the region are Mexico and Brazil, with Mexico dominating both in terms of box office and prints.

Concessions

The unwritten rule of the industry is that "the theater keeps the popcorn." For decades producers, distributors, and everyone else in the food chain of profits has tried, without success, to add concessions into the revenue base derived from theatrical exhibition. The so-called popcorn, however, is considered sacrosanct and is reserved entirely for the exhibitor. As discussed previously and in Chapter 10, the revenue base upon which participations and profits are calculated includes only the distributor's cut from ticket sales (i.e., film rentals as previously discussed). The theater owner's cut from the box office and the concessions are a vital part of the macroeconomic picture, but these revenues are excluded even from the baseline of calculations.

Online Impact

- The online and digital world is profoundly influencing the release strategy and timing of theatrical distribution: piracy concerns, exacerbated by file sharing services and the potential for ubiquitous initial instant access to a film, are driving studios to release films "day and date" worldwide.
- Sites that aggregate nationwide critics' reviews, such as rottentomatos.com, are providing summary scorecards,

theoretically hampering the ability to open a movie slowly and build word of mouth; the nature of cumulative and instant scorecards further accelerates marketing time lines and puts additional pressures on box office openings.

- The online world affords a new, and still relatively untested, premiere release window, tantalizing some who could create sufficient demand to bypass the historical system and test online pay-per-view models.
- Digital cinema can deliver pristine quality and in the long run lower cost distribution, but its adoption has been slowed by multiple factors including the initial high costs of installation and fragmented market of different suppliers for the required elements (projector, server, masters).
- See also Chapter 9 for impact on marketing in the theatrical market.

159

CHAPTER 5

The Home Video Business

The ability to watch a movie or TV show at home on a videocassette or DVD has had a profound impact on the economics of the motion picture and television business. Not only has the video market altered the consumer's consumption pattern of watching movies, but it has also changed the underlying financial modeling of whether a movie, and in cases TV shows, are made in the first place. Despite the rapid and wide market penetration of new technologies such as DVDs, it is a testament to the cultural impact of videocassettes that the studios, at least colloquially, still refer to their divisions as Home Video. In fact, the word "video" in this context has become a misnomer, a catchall of sorts that conceptually captures the varied devices that have evolved allowing consumers to watch films on their television or over a computer.

In terms of profitability, the video market has provided a boon to studios' bottom lines. While the profitability on a new movie is generally measured in a single life cycle (e.g., theatrical, video, television, ancillary and new media revenue streams), the video market has added the magic of reincarnation by inducing consumers to keep buying the same product again and again with each new technological upgrade. The net result is that home video revenues have come to represent about half of studios' total film revenue (see Figure 5.1).[1]

Beyond capturing the biggest slice of the revenue pie and exploiting the churn factor, the studios have managed to keep a larger share of the video revenues, typically paying participations based on a royalty percentage rather than accounting for the gross sums, which in turn makes video distribution uniquely profitable.

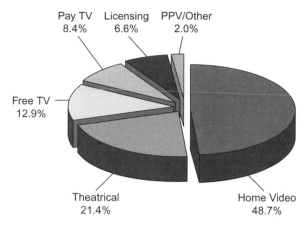

Studio Revenue Breakdown, 2007

Pay TV 8.4%
Licensing 6.6%
PPV/Other 2.0%
Free TV 12.9%
Theatrical 21.4%
Home Video 48.7%

Figure 5.1   © 2009 SNL Kagan, a division of SNL Financial LC. All rights reserved.

The evolution of the home video business is not over, and in this chapter I will review the genesis and growth of this ~$25B market segment,[2] explore the radical changes that have taken place at retail distribution since the early 1990s, and discuss the underlying P&L models of how the business works and why videocassette/DVD distribution returns some of the highest margins in the distribution life cycle chain. I will also review how this ancillary revenue source has spawned profitable original production (i.e., made for video), discuss marketing nuances driving home video consumption, outline some of the profound technical changes that have been catalysts for a re-invention of the category, and explore the impact that video release patterns/windows and piracy have had on the other parts of the business.

161

Finally, although new technology applications including downloads and video-on-demand (VOD) access are inextricably tied to the future of the video market, I focus on these growing markets in Chapter 7 and Chapter 8, and focus here on the traditional video market. Nevertheless, I will touch on aspects such as the intersection of electronic sell through (i.e., downloads to own) and the implications of infinite shelf space and depth of copy compared to physical retail sales.

In summary, this chapter will explain how and why the video/DVD business has emerged to drive the largest positive cash flow of any studio division while at the same time providing the safety net for studios to make certain pictures at all. With this level of vested interest in the business, it is not surprising that studios and networks alike are schizophrenic regarding download and other new technology platforms that are expanding video's reach while threatening to replace what has evolved into a pillar of the studio distribution (and financing) infrastructure.

Compelling Value Proposition

To grasp the value-for-money proposition inherent in marketing a videocassette of a hit movie, simply pause to think about one of your favorite recent films. That movie probably took over five years (and likely many more) to move from concept to release in theaters; over that period hundreds if not thousands of people were involved in the production and release of the movie. On the financial side alone, and assuming the film is a major studio picture, it probably had an investment risk, including costs of producing, marketing, and releasing the film of over $100M. Wrap those years of hard work, incalculable passion and creativity, and dollars together and what do you have? You, the consumer, can take home a product that cost the studio over $100M and years of work for about $20 and often less; better yet, you can rent the movie for about three bucks ($3).

Whether renting or buying, the product is also perfectly tailored to the freedoms made possible via innovations in the consumer electronics industry: you can watch it when you want and where you want. This pitch is not often made overtly, but at a subliminal level. When advertisements say "own it today" or "bring it home today" they are saying you can own for $20 what it took us over $100M to make, and you can watch it over and over for free and watch at your leisure. You do not have to go back very far when the concept of an average citizen owning a movie and watching it at home was beyond the grasp of reasonable expectations.

What other products can compete with the value of a video? Perhaps a record or CD of a concert, capturing the moment, are somewhat equivalent. If you had asked the people starting up studio video divisions, many of whom migrated from the record side, whether they would be happy to be as large as the record companies, they would have thought you were crazy. Certainly it was not within upstart business plans that the revenues could come to surpass the music industry. It is not a stretch to state that video recorders and videos, and the improved technical iterations spawned including most prominently the DVD, are the most important product invention to hit Hollywood since television.

How did video turn into big business? Where is the business headed, and why has it become the lifeblood of studio profitability?

History and Growth of the Video Business

Early Roots: Format Wars and Seminal Legal Wrangling

The first consumer-targeted video cassette recorders were marketed in the 1970s when Sony introduced the Betamax VCR. The introduction of the VCR faced the same chicken and egg dilemma that now seems commonplace with every new technology targeted at consumers' consumption of entertainment: Was there a match between the hardware and software base? When Sony's system was introduced, there was essentially neither software nor hardware available, much like the problem facing the launch of the DVD industry 20 years later in the mid-1990s.

To overcome such a hurdle, at least one party needs to take an enormous risk. In the case of the DVD it was Warner Bros. leading the charge (see later discussion in the section entitled Early Stages of the DVD: Piracy Concerns, Parallel Imports and the Warners Factor), but the true early pioneer of the business was Sony in the days of the Betamax introduction. Interestingly, and disproving the first mover advantage, despite building the market (and to many having a superior format/product) Sony did not emerge as the leader.

Sony's visionary idea was that consumers would pay to be freed from television's broadcast schedule (sound familiar today?): the Betamax VCR would allow them to watch programs when they wanted, not as dictated by the network's broadcast schedule. The VCR was not originally positioned as a playback device for movies. Sony's CEO, Akio Morita, said at the time "People do not have to read a book when it's delivered ... Why should they have to see a TV program when it's delivered?"[2a] Accordingly, Sony marketed the Betamax VCR hardware player, which utilized a proprietary tape generically called the Beta format. Its marketing campaign echoed Morita's theme, pitching the player as a machine allowing consumers to "time-shift": consumers could record television programs and view them later at a more convenient time.

Whether history is repeating itself or technology advances enabling services like Hulu are finally realizing Morita's original vision, it is clear we are now on the threshold of totally taking the programming out of the broadcast scheduler's hands. As alluded to in Chapter 6 and further discussed in Chapter 7, not only have DVRs made recording easier, but we can now envision future iterations where TV is consumed in a playlist fashion, where viewers through VOD or other access select the programs they want to watch and then consume them according to their own programming schedule (which may be optimized or random).

Returning to the roots of the business, two factors greatly contributed to the explosive growth of the VCR market. First, and a point not often cited (and I will admit somewhat subject to challenge), the advent of the VCR was in the same general period as the emergence of cable TV. Not only was the notion of time shifting attractive, but it was even more attractive in an environment of blossoming program choices. For decades US consumers were limited in programming choices to the three major broadcast networks plus a handful of local UHF stations; with cable TV came an explosion of choice.

Second, and more important, the ability to rent movies from video stores caught on like wildfire — the concept of building a library of tapes and renting tapes out for a price no more than a movie ticket proved revolutionary. Independent stores, which quickly gained the industry nickname "mom and pops," led the growth and proliferated throughout neighborhoods. It was an ideal small business, preying on pent-up demand and taking advantage of modest start-up costs (including the need for limited space); further, video rental was a cash business that built a loyal customer base virtually on its own via a regular supply of new product.

As great as this seemed for Sony and the new breed of video rental entrepreneurs, the whole notion of video rental seemed a looming disaster for the Hollywood studios who produced the films. The studios saw the VCR as a means of copyright infringement. The underlying economic fear was that individuals would copy movies and TV shows (and keep them for a home library), which would undermine the market to exhibit the programs on television. Universal's president, Sidney Sheinberg, upon seeing the Betamax time-shifting campaign, and fearing the loss of revenues that could lead from unauthorized copying of Universal's product, sued Sony for copyright infringement.

The resulting case, which was initially brought in 1976 and ultimately decided by the Supreme Court in 1984, was a landmark lawsuit that paved the way for DVDs and arguably saved the studio system.

164

The Betamax Decision: Universal v. Sony

The ultimate finding in what has come to be known as the "Sony Betamax" case is that time shifting via home copying for non-commercial purposes was permitted (in legal jargon, a fair use and non-infringing of copyright; for a further discussion of copyright see Chapter 2). Before the Supreme Court reached this verdict, *Sony Corp. v. Universal City Studios*[3] went through a litany of phases with each side supported by name-brand media allies. Universal was joined by Disney, who saw similar infringement of its copyrights and potential loss of television broadcast revenues. Sony was supported by the sports leagues, including commissioners of the national football, basketball, baseball, and hockey leagues; these leagues believed that VCRs were a benefit to live events, allowing fans/consumers to see games they would have otherwise missed. Another important Sony supporter was the Corporation for Public Broadcasting, believing that it was a good thing for children to be able to see educational programming and that VCRs promoted this end; further, it was endorsed by Fred Rogers, the star/producer of the classic preschool show *Mister Rogers' Neighborhood*.

In the end, after an eight-year legal odyssey, the Supreme Court reasoned that a significant number of copyright owners would not object to their content being time-shifted, that there was insufficient proof the ability to time-shift would undermine the value copyright holders would receive from licensing their content to TV (which proved to be true as license fees increased over the following years), and therefore the Betamax was capable of "substantial non-infringing uses." Interestingly, the Supreme Court, in an almost prescient statement recognizing that new technological advances — advances like the Internet and file sharing of which it could not have been aware — would force it to consider the broader issues in the future:

… One may search the Copyright Act in vain for any sign that the elected representatives of the millions of people who watch television every day have made it unlawful to copy a program for later viewing at home, or have enacted a flat prohibition against the sale of machines that make such copying possible.

It may well be that Congress will take a fresh look at this new technology, just as it so often has examined other innovations in the past. But it is not our job to apply laws that have not yet been written. Applying the copyright statute, as it now reads, to the facts as they have been developed in this case, the judgment of the Court of Appeals must be reversed.

It was a close decision (5–4), and whether or not one agrees with the logic (or cynically believes that the court needed to craft a political opinion, allowing the flourishing video business to continue), the video business was officially sanctioned. By 1986, just a couple of years after the landmark Sony decision, combined video rental and sales revenues ($4.38B) exceeded the theatrical box office ($3.78B) for the first time. By 1988 rental revenues alone ($5.15B) exceeded the theatrical box office ($4.46B).[4]

Among the ironies of the case is how the party most vested in the case (Sony) ended up losing the battle for consumer dollars, and how the plaintiff (Universal) came to be bought by one of the hardware manufacturers that benefited from the verdict. Matsushita, the parent of the Panasonic brand, and sister company to JVC (together with non-affiliated Hitachi), developed and marketed the rival VHS format which was incompatible with the Sony Betamax player. It was the VHS format that took hold and by the mid-1980s dominated. Video retailers did not want to stock alternate formats, and as VHS players became more dominant more VHS titles were stocked and the spiral grew until Sony's Beta format was doomed. Within a few years of the *Sony v. Universal* decision Sony threw in the towel and started manufacturing VHS players. Perhaps adding injury to insult, only a few years later the format war winner Matsushita bought MCA/Universal in an acquisition touting the merger of hardware and software.

The Sony–Betamax case continues to mark an important turning point for the distribution of content onto in-home hardware, as well as serving as a precedent for the current age of digital age cases such as Napster and Grokster (see Chapter 2).

The Early Retail Environment: The Rental Video Store

When videocassettes were new, and market penetration of VHS recorders was growing in the 1980s, the video business was almost entirely a rental business. By rental, I mean conventional rental stores such as Blockbuster Video or Hollywood Video.

At first, when the rental market was exploding, it was dominated by neighborhood video stores. The economics were relatively simple. The video store would buy units of movies from the studio distributor, and then rent the cassettes out to customers. The store would perform a simple breakeven analysis of how many times a particular unit would need to be rented to turn a profit. There were some add ons to mimic movie environment, such as selling popcorn or candy to take home with your movie. Marketing was relatively unsophisticated, led by film posters supplied by the studio distributors to advertise the hit and coming films.

As the business grew, chains formed and eventually dominated. At first, it was actually an acceptable retail strategy to be out of stock. If a store did not have enough units of a title, people would rent something else and come back for the other film; disappointment was a fundamental and accepted marketing strategy. This allowed the store to profit on two fronts: retailers could keep inventory down, not making risky decisions of possibly overbuying on a title, while virtually assured of repeat customer business.

For a period, consumers seemed to accept the delay as part of life, and would happily rent a movie other than the one they had come in for. The out of luck, but somehow not entirely dissatisfied, customer would come back for the film they really wanted when (1) the store called to let them know the title was back in stock (if they had placed their name on the reserve list), (2) at a somewhat random later date in the hope that they would be lucky and a copy would be available, or (3) at an even later date when they felt demand must have waned and they would have a really good chance that the title would be available to rent.

Amazingly, this lottery style mentality to renting did not dissuade consumers, and to some degree it helped fuel the growth and diversity of content offered by video retailers. Video stores recognized this phenomenon and were pleased for customers to rent a second or third choice title; as previously noted, this virtually guaranteed repeat business when the consumer returned the title they rented, but had not really wanted, and came back to rent the film they had come for in the first place. As a business model, this was almost too good to be true. Whenever one can make this type of statement, though, change is afoot. With the maturity of the business impatience grew and consumers no longer accepted dissatisfaction as the rule.

Over time rental stores became more competitive and needed to develop more traditional marketing campaigns to ensure customer loyalty. All types of schemes were implemented, from "rent 10 videos get one rental free" loyalty programs, to store clubs that came with discounts, privileges, and mailings. More sophisticated chains divided customers into complex marketing matrixes, looking at who were frequent renters, casual renters, deadbeat clients, etc., and devising targeted campaigns to increase rental frequency and store loyalty. As the chains grew, they also started to advertise directly, advising customers "Come to Blockbuster and rent … ," growing their business with an injection of direct marketing dollars plus cooperative marketing spends set out in their agreements with the product suppliers. As in any other product category, choice, growth, and competition added complexity, and rentals started to have price differentiation. Examples of offers included: buy 2 get one for free deals, keep the title for the same price for the weekend, and rent new titles at full price for one night while offering older titles for the same or lesser costs to keep for three or five days.

Finally, as a tangible example of the market maturing and retailers acknowledging that disappointing customers was not the best long-term strategy, marketing schemes shifted 180 degrees to implement guarantees that new titles would be in stock (and if not the rental would be free). When a new title came out, there would often be pent-up demand similar to that which creates lines at movie theaters. To the "I'll wait to see it on video crowd" that had socially developed in response to the growth of the industry, the video release date was like a premiere. New titles, which a few years earlier would be gulped up the moment they hit shelves and be out of stock, would now be available in large quantities.

This marketing shift also had a direct economic consequence on competition. To satisfy demand, a store needed to have key new titles in sufficient quantity which required a larger up-front investment. Whereas 10 or 15 copies may have been fine before, 10 times that number would now be required. An average retail price, which at the time when rental was king in the 1980s and early 1990s, was ~$70–$100, could change the inventory investment for one title from $700–$1000 to over $10,000. Volume discounts may have allowed some lower average pricing, but the elasticity was not great and the net effect was pressure squeezing the smaller, so-called "mom and pop" accounts. Not surprising, this timing coincided with increased clout from major chains such as Blockbuster and Hollywood Video, which had begun expanding and gobbling up smaller outlets to become independent market forces. Between 1987–1989 Blockbuster grew from a 19-store chain to over 1,000 outlets, and in 1988 with just over 500 stores became the country's top video retailer with revenues of $200M; growth did not slow down, and through further expansion and acquisitions the chain grew another 50% to 1,500 by 1991 before finally being acquired in a merger with Viacom in 1994.[5] The market was vibrant enough that with enough stores chains could go public, and rival video chains Hollywood Video and Movie Gallery both completed public offerings in the early 1990s.

And change was just beginning. The dominance of the rental store was about to give way to the sell through market, with rental revenue sharing becoming an intermediate solution to lower priced units in a still vibrant rental market.

Transition from Rental to Videos for Purchase: Retail Expands to Accommodate Two Distinct Markets for Video/DVD Consumption

During the growth of the rental video market, a new pattern was slowly emerging that would ultimately overwhelm rental sales and even threaten to eliminate the rental store completely: direct sales of videos to consumers. In trade lingo, this became "rental vs. sell through." Again, the rental store seems to be facing extinction, combating the dual forces of downloads for purchase — "electronic sell through" — and VOD access for rentals (both forces are discussed in more detail in Chapters 7 and 8, and serve as fodder for analysts who forecast new technology applications leading to the demise of historical markets).

The challenge in this earlier battle for survival was not played out as a public drama, as sell through was not initially perceived as a threat to rental's dominance. In fact, conventional wisdom questioned whether consumers would want to purchase a videocassette when it had become so easy and relatively inexpensive to rent a film. One threshold issue was would people really want to watch a particular movie more than once — the general consensus was no. Those customers who were passionate about a particular movie might rent it a few times, but for the rental store, which had invested substantial sums per copy of a title, there was every incentive to entice these fans back to re-rent the title.

For the video store, the game was all about amortization of inventory cost based on turn: How many times did an individual cassette/copy need to be rented to break even? Obviously, it was an attractive business model to turn a copy many times rather than sell it once. Simply, if a copy of a blockbuster cost the rental store $50, and the outlet charged $5 per rental, the store needed to rent that copy 10 times to recoup. Moreover, because each film is unique, inventory obsolescence only applied to the physical materials (e.g., how long could a cassette be rented before the tape quality degraded to an unacceptable level). A title that had paid for itself could sit on the

169

shelf as catalog inventory, providing pure profit for the indefinite future (subject to the number of copies originally stocked, as a store would obviously keep fewer copies in catalog than were acquired during the peak rental period of initial video release). In fact, one might say this was the first iteration of the "long tail" now so commonly discussed online. Accordingly, a hit title that needed 7 to 10 rental turns to recoup might have multiple future rental turns left, yielding more than a 100% return on investment on a per copy basis.

If a title was able to generate over 100% ROI, then the business model to sell that unit was initially far from compelling. Ultimately, the model comes down to the simple elements of units and pricing. At the early stages, the cost per cassette made it difficult to create a margin allowing for markups to challenge the relative earning power of a rental unit. Even at a substantial markdown, such as to $20 inventory cost, the retail pricing was quite high; moreover, there was a disincentive to lower pricing significantly when the rental business was thriving. A bigger obstacle, however, was simply the pattern of consumer consumption. The whole video market had exploded seemingly overnight, and people were used to renting, not buying. Something would have to fundamentally change to shift that pattern, including a dramatic lowering of inventory cost.

170

Not surprisingly, though, as in most consumer goods markets, prices inevitably started to come down. This was forced by pressure from large chains that demanded lower pricing for buying greater depth of inventory. More important than pressure from the rental stores, however, was the fairly rapid market shift from a predominantly rental business to a retail dominated industry. Just like renting had before, buying videos became a quickly adopted consumer behavior.

By the time the DVD market reached its peak in 2004–2006 (see the next section), and as evidenced by Table 5.1, the percentage of

Table 5.1 U.S. Retail Home Video Industry

		2000	2001	2002	2003	2004	2005	2006	2007	2008
Video Rental	($ bil.)	8.3	8.4	8.3	8.2	8.1	7.8	7.7	7.5	7.5
Video Sell-Through	($ bil.)	10.6	11.8	12.6	13.5	16.2	16.4	16.5	15.9	14.8
Total Video	($ bil.)	19.0	20.2	20.9	21.7	24.4	24.1	24.2	23.4	22.4

© 2009 SNL Kagan, a division of SNL Financial LC, estimates. All rights reserved.

sales for sell through had shifted to close to 70%, whereas only a few years before the split was nearly even.

Key Factors Driving Growth in the Sell Through Market

Among the key changes driving the growth of the sell through market were (1) the growing trend for consumers to collect videos, (2) the decline in pricing allowing consumers to purchase titles for the same amount of money (or at least not much more than) as a record/CD, (3) studio efforts to sell mass volumes of select hit titles, and (4) the growth of the kids video business initially led by Disney.

Examining these factors in a bit more detail, as the pattern of watching and renting videos matured, people started the habit of collecting titles. Although now accepted as commonplace, this was hardly an inevitable turn. Market research will tell that most purchased videos sit on the shelf: How often do you re-watch a movie that you have bought? For some favorites and classics, of course the answer may be yes, but once collecting transitions from buying your favorite film to a habit the answer will likely be different. And that is the key—becoming a habit—to seducing you to purchase titles that do not quite make your top five all-time list. As collecting became in vogue, studios started to mine their libraries and make older titles available, expanding the range of consumer choice. First there were books, then records, and now videos; in fact, the lingo that evolved was "video libraries." People started to buy videos, sometimes never even watch them, and keep them on the shelf as a new sort of trophy or archive.

171

And once a piece of media becomes a collectible, it becomes a gift, opening an entirely new marketing direction for sales. Studios, if nothing else, are brilliant marketing machines, and all video rights holders drove a truck through the opportunity to encourage sales as gifts. The fourth quarter is now the largest period for video sales (with the holidays an ideal time to launch gift sets and special editions), which is a far departure from the origins of the video rental business.

Second, and somewhat hand-in-hand, the market saw a reduction in pricing and corresponding upturn in sales of mass volumes of a title. By the early 1990s as the rental market was maturing and chains grew and consolidated, there was a rule of thumb that you could place 200,000 to 300,000 units of a key new title. For a title that was not a hit or one without a star driving sales, this number could be halved, while a big hit might sell twice this number of units. The key point is that there was limited elasticity of volume in rental.

Studios salivated at the notion of selling millions of units of a title, and on big hits it became commonplace to run breakeven comparisons to assess how many units would need to be sold at retail to justify a so-called sell through release (sales direct to consumer as opposed to rental). While sell through means direct sales to consumers, what it implicates at the distribution level is a whole new set of pricing and a dramatic expansion of retail outlets. The retail infrastructure for direct to consumer sales had to be built, and the expansion of outlets to mass merchants, drug stores, supermarkets, record stores, and independents took years to mature. In point of sale terms, this could mean going from low thousands of outlets at video rental to over 30,000 outlets for direct to consumer sales.

The challenges that came with the sell through market were the same as any other consumer product: inventory management, advertising, in-store merchandising, physical distribution, and order of magnitude issues in physical manufacture. This was a daunting, and at some level, risky challenge for an industry that was thriving on limited distribution to a finite group of key customers, and where inventory management (video rental was largely a no returns business) was a relatively minor issue.

So, putting aside the growing pains of becoming another consumer product challenging soap for advertising time and store shelf space, the nuts and bolts question became what was the multiple needed to sell at sell through versus a rental release. An important and to the studios somewhat comforting element in the matrix was that rental was still important. On any title significant enough to justify a sell through release there was a built-in sale to all video stores. The studio could still sell its few hundred thousand units into the channel; it would simply earn a significantly lower margin, charging a wholesale price of $15–20+ as opposed to the highly profitable $50–70+ rental price. For a period, and for many years following in several international markets, there was even the ability to price differentiate. The supplier (i.e., studio) would charge a higher price for rental units sold to video stores, and create a separate lower suggested retail price (SRP) for mass market sell through buyers.

The analysis was then a straightforward breakeven equation taking into account the sales uplift needed from a lower priced good to surpass the revenue and contribution margin of the higher priced–lower volume rental units (with variable manufacturing and marketing costs factored in on the expense side). As a rule of thumb, it

Table 5.2 Disney Animated Releases by Year

Year (theater)	Title
1989	*The Little Mermaid*
1991	*Beauty and the Beast*
1992	*Aladdin*
1994	*Lion King*
1995	*Toy Story*
1996	*The Hunchback of Notre Dame*
1997	*Hercules*
1998	*Mulan*
1999	*Tarzan, Toy Story 2*

turned out that a title needed to sell a roughly 4:1 or 5:1 ratio to justify a sell through release.

The ultimate accelerant for the sell through market were kids videos, in particular the emergence of Disney as a dominating force via its video division Buena Vista Home Entertainment. Earlier I pointed out the issue of whether people would watch a video repeatedly, the one area where this was clearly true was with children. Simply, kids would watch the same video over and over and over. It does not take brain surgery to recognize as a parent that buying a cassette for $20 that your kids will watch seemingly a hundred times is a good investment. To the parent that can gain an hour or more of near guaranteed peace and quiet, the value of the purchase is worth infinitely more than the cost. Hardly a babysitter could trump the satisfaction of a Disney video, and the combination of a babysitter and a Disney classic was as good a bet as there was out there.

Disney quickly recognized the goldmine that laid before it and the timing not so coincidentally dovetailed with the reinvigoration of its animated film business. With hit after hit, commencing with *Beauty and the Beast* in 1991 and *Aladdin* in 1992 (see Table 5.2), Disney was validating a new market and spinning box office gold both in theaters and then again on video — a classic example of repeat consumption as a key factor in maximizing value. Then in 1995 *Lion King* literally broke out of the box, reportedly selling a staggering 30 million units,[6] with reputedly 20 million units in its initial release window. The notion of 20 million units of a title had been seemingly unimaginable previously, and once the pattern of high volumes proved repeatable there was no stopping. It continued for more than a decade with *Finding Nemo* selling 20 million combined DVD and VHS units in its first two weeks of sales in November 2003, including 8 million on its first day of release for a record beating the prior *Spider-Man* tally.[7] Everyone tried to jump on the bandwagon, but during the 1990s growth spurt Disney seemed to have a lock on printing money between box office success of animated titles and the amazing upside that the video industry provided.

Year after year they continued to release a new hit, which became an instant classic given the numbers (though nothing again reached *Lion King* heights) and had strong enough brand awareness to spur made-for-video sequels (see later discussion, Beyond an Ancillary Market: Emergence of Made-for-Video Market).

The success of Disney videos catapulted the head of Disney's video division, Bill Mechanic, into executive stardom and in the mid-1990s he left Disney to become president of Twentieth Century Fox studios. In terms of animation, Mechanic never hit the peaks at Fox he experienced at Disney; acquiring Don Bluth studios and launching titles like *Anastasia* helped Fox enter the lucrative market, but failed to create a Disney-like brand engine from the genre. (Note: Fox eventually succeeded years later in building an animation brand via Blue Sky and its computer graphics hit franchise *Ice Age*).

The Emergence of and Transition to DVDs

The video market has been nothing short of a cash flow godsend to studios and producers. After the initial growth of rental and the consumer acceptance of the direct to retail sales model the market took off again. The next phase was the development of the digital video disc ("DVD" or in technical circles actually the Digital Versatile Disc).

Technology had advanced such that it was possible to make a leap in video quality similar to the transition the record industry had gone through years before in converting from cassettes to compact discs (CDs). The CD quickly replaced the cassette when Phillips invented the digital encoding technology; the marketing thrust, and inevitably the driver in quick adoption, was that (1) CDs were claimed to be indestructible (as opposed to cassettes, where the tape could get caught, jammed, or warped, permanently ruining the copy), (2) the sound quality emanating from digital encoding was a quantum leap forward from analog tape, and (3) CDs were smaller and therefore more portable than 12-inch vinyl records. While the random access convenience of just jumping from song to song on a CD was compelling (as opposed to fast forwarding or rewinding), the notion of having a portable, near perfect hiss-free and non-degradable crystal clear copy of music persuaded consumers. Sometimes with technology, there truly is a better product and CDs were a case in point.

I have digressed into the record business because the same forces were aligned against videocassettes. Different consortiums of motion picture studios, teamed with various consumer electronics manufac-turers (e.g., Toshiba, Matsushita), were pioneering DVD technology. They believed that the DVD offered the similar quantum leap from digital to analog quality that consumers had so overwhelmingly em-braced in the record industry when moving from cassettes to CDs. As in the early days of the videocassette, where format wars erupted between the Betamax and VHS format, similar format wars took place on the DVD battlefront. Matsushita, the Japanese consumer electron-ics company (Panasonic brand) that had pioneered the VHS format and acquired Universal Studios (only to later divest majority owner-ship in a sale to Seagrams) was supporting one standard, whereas Toshiba and Warners were supporting another.

An entire chapter could be written about this format war Volume II, but suffice it to say that given the investment, historical fallout from prior format disputes, and the potential market size the studios banded together to "adopt" a format. (Note: The acronym MPEG referenced regarding compression technology means The Moving Pictures Experts Group.)

How Does a DVD Work?

The underlying technology of DVDs is compression or the ability to take a huge amount of data and store it efficiently. Accordingly, there is a level of randomness since there is a direct relationship between the amount of data stored and the end quality; the more information, the better the resulting output quality. The inherent problem con-cerning compression for DVDs is that the amount of information that needs to be processed for a moving picture is staggering relative to an audio file. For a movie, each frame needs to be stored including all the elements ranging from backgrounds to characters to colors, shading, audio, etc.

The quantity of pixels that need to be reduced to digital 0s and 1s to compress a color film image was in fact too great to fit onto a disc, which was a driving technical hurdle preventing the invention of a disc or technology that could mimic a CD for film. The breakthrough came with the notion of looking at the differences between frames and only storing the differences; in this way, the amount of data that needed to be converted and stored was dramatically reduced. DVD compression actually "cheats" by omitting data. The compression digitizes and stores new elements, but in terms of going from frame to frame only differences need to be kept. This efficiency trick combined with massively greater storage/data capacity compared to a CD enabled compression of sufficient data to allow a typical film to fit on a single DVD disc.

Early Stages of the DVD: Piracy Concerns, Parallel Imports and the Warners Factor

At the Consumer Electronic Shows of the mid-1990s, gawkers and industry executives watching DVD demonstrations could intuitively grasp the leap in quality. DVD pictures were undoubtedly better, and the DVD offered the same type of ancillary upgrades to consumers that the CD had offered. Video tape often got stuck in machines, and DVDs eliminated those concerns and were marketed with an aura of discs being "ultimate" and "permanent" (no one was talking about scratches, of course). Another user-friendly element was the elimination of having to rewind a tape. Rewinding a tape at the end of a movie is a universal nuisance, and some video rental stores even charged penalties if tapes were returned unwound. With a DVD, when the movie ended you just hit a button—no rewinding, no hassle. As silly as it may sound, consumer market research regularly found the elimination of having to rewind as one of the most significant benefits of a DVD, which was statistically on par with the improved picture quality. Never overestimate the consumer!

A better mousetrap does not guarantee adoption, and in the case of the DVD adoption was further hampered by studios' reluctance to market and sell properties on the new format: virtually all major studio executives recognized the benefits of the DVD, but concerns over piracy and parallel imports were sufficient barriers to move slowly if at all.

The following was the cost-benefit matrix of the time:

Costs/Negatives:
- Expenses to encourage consumer adoption
- Need to manage duplicate inventories (video and DVD)
- Piracy — DVDs held the potential of people making perfect digital copies
- Parallel imports (see later discussion)

176

Benefits:

- Better quality and durability
- Favorable user-friendly features (e.g., no rewind)
- Smaller packaging needs
- Less expensive manufacturing costs, therefore higher margins
- Ability to turnover library/catalog product by selling new format

Despite the apparent edge to the benefits, the inherent nature of the DVD as a perfect digital copy created significant anxiety at the studios. Intellectual property is the lifeblood of the system, and while video piracy was always a key concern, that concern heightened with digital copies. If just one person were able to make copies from a DVD, then in theory a pirate could have access to a digital master and illegally distribute perfect copies into the marketplace. This had the potential of undermining franchises, new releases, and entire studio libraries. The risk was simply too high, and until sufficient security was implemented most studios held back DVD releases of new titles (another form of windowing).

Adding to the problem was a concern about parallel imports. While it is commonplace to theatrically release a major movie on the same date worldwide (day-and-date release, as discussed in Chapter 4), this was rare to non-existent back in the mid-1990s when DVDs were first introduced to the market. Parallel imports means buying goods in one territory and importing them into another. For example, if a movie were released in May in the United States it might be planned for a release in Europe or Asia at Christmas, the same time the DVD of the title would be coming out in the United States. There was nothing to prevent a retailer from buying quantities of the DVDs in the United States and importing them to the market where the movie was just releasing in the theaters, or worse in advance of the theatrical release. What would happen if consumers could view (or worse obtain) a perfect copy of the movie before it was even released in theaters? The potential of parallel imports had always existed, but like piracy the quality of digital copies heightened people's fears. The box office revenues in international territories were growing consistently, and the theatrical release was too important a driver of the entire studio system to risk.

A key strategy to combat this practice and enable the broader introduction of DVDs was the implementation of regional encoding. This was a process devised by the studios where DVD machines and related DVD software would only work within specific

177

territorial boundaries. For example, a chip would be placed in a machine telling it that it was a "European" encoded player, and this player would only play a disc encoded as European. If you put a disc from the United States (encoded as a United States disc) into a European player, the codes would not match and the disc would not play. The studios managed to gain acceptance from consumer electronics companies manufacturing players (likely helped by Matsushita's relationship with Universal and Sony's ownership of a Hollywood major) and all parties agreed to a worldwide map.

Interestingly, regional encoding is akin to a form of hardware-based digital rights management (DRM), and was instituted to restrict how and where a consumer could play back a copy. Conceptually, DRM systems enable the same type of restrictions, but further open up a panoply of options down to managing how many times a product may be played on a specific machine (or overall). Regional encoding is still enforced today, and software bought in one territory will not play on a machine manufactured and sold in a different region. For those wanting to defeat the system region-free players (which will play a disc regardless of which region it is encoded to) are available, but obviously for a premium price.

The net result of these fears, regarding piracy and the potential of undermining carefully orchestrated release windows, was that most studios were not releasing any titles on DVDs. Those studios that were entering the market were dabbling with older catalog titles where there was obviously no risk to current theatrical release. Sound familiar today? Again, history repeats itself and the adoption of downloads has been slowed by fears of pirating a perfect digital copy (just like the introduction of the DVD), and launching with catalog titles to mitigate the risk.

One exception to this reluctance to release a broad array of titles on DVD was Warner Bros. The president of Warner Home Video, Warren Lieberfarb, was among the earliest and most vocal proponents of DVD technology. Warners invested in a DVD authoring and replication facility, and simply believed that the DVD was such a superior technology that it was inevitable consumers would adopt the platform (not to mention the benefit of holding several related patents). For pioneering the technology, and championing its introduction against naysayers and those who wanted to delay launching, Warren Lieberfarb has been called "the father of DVD." Even within an incredibly competitive industry people acknowledge Warners' leadership position as the catalyst for the transition to DVD from video. Most people forget, or were oblivious to, the significant risks to protection and window management of vital intellectual property assets that stalled and almost prevented the introduction of DVDs.

Influence of Computers: Cross-Platform Use of DVDs Speeds Adoption

One significant factor in the acceleration of DVD penetration was the crossover between consumer electronics players and computers. DVDs had an exponential increase in storage capacity versus floppy discs as well as CDs. (Note: Currently a standard DVD holding a two-hour movie plus customary ancillary value-added materials (VAM) has roughly 9 GB of content, while Blu-ray boasts an increase to 50 GM.)[8]

As DVD drives slowly replaced other storage mediums on PCs, it was only a matter of time for convergence to take place. With a common software medium, consumers could store data, download pictures and music, and watch movies all with DVDs. Further, this convergence dovetailed with the increased penetration of laptop computers. It was now possible to bring a DVD of a movie on your laptop for a plane ride, jumping between spreadsheets and entertainment. Yet again history was repeating itself with integrated systems used to drive adoption — Sony included Blu-ray players with its next generation PlayStation 3 console system hoping the consumer electronics product (this time a games system rather than a PC) would help drive adoption.

Recordable DVDs and Perceived Threats from Copying and Downloading

Once it became clear that DVDs were the medium of the future and would replace VHS cassettes, the next obstacle was the ability to record. For the same reasons that slowed the introduction of the DVD, piracy and economic fears tied to the ability to make digital copies, a recordable feature was delayed in the marketplace. It was one thing to allow a DVD, but the dangers ultimately seemed manageable without the ability of the consumer to burn copies of movies. As an accommodation to the concerns of the studios the major consumer electronics manufacturers launched play-only DVD machines; when compared to the complexity of regional encoding, this was a relatively easy measure to assuage the software distributors.

Over time, however, pressures for recordable players overwhelmed this protectionist direction; moreover, the consumer electronics industry was not in a position to stop the computer manufacturers from deploying recordable drives. Memory and storage is the mantra of the personal computer industry, and computer manufacturers were inclined to encourage data storage rather than impede it. Whether music or digital camera/pictures, the new applications were growing at breakneck speed. It was unrealistic to expect that DVDs could record everything but visual entertainment software.

Giving the studios solace in terms of DVD burners becoming a standard accessory was the fact that movies are not easy to copy. The amount of data compressed is staggering, and it is cumbersome and complicated to copy a movie relative to a business file or music CD. Moreover, anti-copying mechanisms are encoded on films preventing the simple copying of a movie on DVD. The larger fear is the Internet, and while lengthy download times for movies (hours rather than minutes) seemed initially to pose a significant enough hurdle to give distributors comfort, technology again advanced and P-2-P file sharing exposed the underlying fear that had loomed with digital copies since the advent of DVDs.

180

At first, digital rights management systems (and the lure of new revenue streams) seemed to have progressed quickly enough to temper those fears and promise significant and ongoing roadblocks to the easy pirating of copies; however, it was this backdrop that caused the studios to take a strong stand in the Grokster case when the ability of P-2-P services demonstrated facility and scale for making pirate copies. This created the biggest challenge to the industry since the enabling *Sony v. Betamax* case roughly 20 years before. (Note: see Chapter 2 for discussion of file sharing, P-2-P downloading technology, and the Grokster case in terms of the relationship to piracy and digital downloading.)

Intermediate Formats: Laserdiscs and VCDs
Finally, it is worth mentioning that as in most areas of technology, there were intermediate steps between VHS and DVD adoption. Some may remember the Laserdisc, which was dominated by companies like Pioneer. Laserdiscs were about the size of an old phonographic record and had better clarity and durability than standard VHS tape; they were accordingly priced higher, and the early adopter videophiles built up collections of Laserdiscs. Laserdiscs were still, however, based on analog technology and were ultimately doomed with the advent of the digital age. Consumers that always wanted the best available

technology/presentation of the time built up collections, but the life of Laserdiscs was comparatively short and the penetration of the hardware players relatively limited when compared with the mass market adoption of both VHS tape and DVDs.

Similarly, in Asia, and in particular Southeast Asia, a market grew up for Video CDs (VCDs). These are CD size and look like DVDs, but simply have inferior compression and memory, and accordingly inferior picture quality. VCD distribution grew quickly in markets rife with piracy, and a consumer could usually find a low quality and unauthorized version of virtually all studio blockbusters on VCD in the local markets. Because penetration grew quickly it took some time for DVDs to supplant this market. However, with VCDs and Laserdiscs both intermediate and inferior products to DVDs, these formats began to quickly disappear and I am sure in a few years readers of this book will never have heard of them.

Revenue Sharing — Consequence of a Hybrid Market and Aid to DVD Adoption

Revenue sharing arrangements took off in the late 1990s. This was a scheme where the major studios gave the major video rental chains, such as Blockbuster and Hollywood Video, their titles on a consignment basis. Rather than charge $29–40 for a title, the studios deferred the up-front revenue in favor of a split of rental income. Although deals differed, it was reputed that a rule of thumb granted the studios 60% of the revenue from rental transactions; moreover, once a title had been past its peak release period excess inventory was sold in-store ($5–15 range), with the proceeds shared between the distributor and rental chain.

Some have theorized that the introduction of revenue sharing was a gambit to increase DVD penetration, as the studios encouraged the shift away from VHS (in fact, some former video division heads have alleged just this tactic).

Once DVD penetration had hit mass market levels prices started coming down for both players and new release titles and revenue sharing schemes waned. The *Hollywood Reporter* cited these factors and attributed the decline in revenue sharing to the increase of the consumer purchase market at the expense of the video rental store:

… Once DVD hardware market penetration reached about 50 million players in US households by 2002, WHV and other

181

major Hollywood studios began ratcheting down their rental revenue-sharing participation, while aggressively discounting the wholesale and retail price of movies on DVD. The new popularity of DVD combined with low-priced hit new releases and classic catalog product energized consumer spending on home videos, resulting in a national average household buy rate of 15 DVDs a year at an estimated price point of $19 or more each. That consumer action translated into triple-digit revenue gains at the studios. At the same time, the paradigm shift had reduced in-store foot traffic at video rental outlets nationwide, taking a huge bite out of gross consumer spending on movie rentals. ... [9]

Beyond an Ancillary Market: Emergence of the Made-for-Video Market

Direct-to-Video and Made-for-Video Markets

As video matured, and retail points of sale expanded, it became clear that there was an opportunity to release new/original product directly to the video consumer.

Paralleling the growth of the video market overall, the natural target base was the consumer buying the seemingly dizzying number of Disney videos. If it were possible to sell over 10 million copies of a movie such as *Lion King* or *Beauty and the Beast*, would the same consumer buy a branded property that was not released in the theaters and was instead an original property for the home video market? With the benefit of hindsight, clearly the answer is yes. The simplest and most successful path was to create sequel properties. Disney perfected this almost to an art, and empowered a specific division focused on producing spin-offs. Examples of "video sequels" or spin-offs during this video renaissance included:

- *Return of Jafar* (1994)
- *Aladdin and the King of Thieves* (1996)
- *Beauty and the Beast: The Enchanted Christmas* (1997)
- *Pocahontas II: Journey to a New World* (1998)
- *Lion King II: Simba's Pride* (1998)
- *Hercules: Zero to Hero* (1998)
- *The Little Mermaid II: Return to the Sea* (2000)

- *Lady and the Tramp II: Scamp's Adventure* (2001)
- *The Hunchback of Note Dame II* (2002)
- *Tarzan & Jane* (2002)
- *101 Dalmatians II: Patch's London Adventure* (2003)
- *The Jungle Book 2* (2003)
- *The Lion King 1.5* (2004)
- *Mulan II* (2005)
- *Tarzan II* (2005)
- *The Fox and the Hound 2* (2006)[10]

Fox jumped on the bandwagon with titles such as *Ferngully2*, as did Paramount leveraging well-known characters and brands, such as *Charlotte's Web*. Independents that had strong children's properties expanded their brand. A prime example was Lyric Studios franchise *Barney*; in addition to taking television episodes to video, live Barney concerts were perfect fare to release on DVD.

Perhaps the most successful example of a made-for-video property came from Universal Studios. Universal had theatrically released a film called *The Land Before Time*, executive produced by George Lucas and Steven Spielberg, to moderate success. Recognizing the inherent appeal of the characters, children's love of dinosaurs, and the franchise potential, Universal invested in video sequels. The Land Before Time franchise became so successful, and the potential for other made-for-videos was considered so high, that Universal created a new division called Universal Family and Home Entertainment. Headed by the former president of Universal's video division, Louis Feola, Universal produced a series of animated (e.g., *Balto 2*) and live action (e.g., *Beethoven 3, 4, 5, Slap Shot 2*) properties under this banner. (Note: more current made-for-video titles include *The Scorpion King 2*, and "American Pie Presents" sequels (*Band Camp, The Naked Mile, Beta House*), the latter of which are estimated to have sold 1–2 million copies each.)[11] The Land Before Time property spawned more than ten sequels, making it one of the most prolific and successful children's franchises in the marketplace.

183

DVD as a Fallback Release Outlet
"Made-for-video" titles are often confused with releases that may otherwise go direct to video. A title like *Land Before Time3* is made for debut in the video market, but with the expense of marketing and releasing a theatrical film studios soon realized that certain films that did not pan out as planned could go straight to video. This outlet has

developed into an important revenue stream given that there are many films made that never see the light of day in theaters or may have a very limited theatrical release to brand them theatricals (or otherwise qualify them for pricing tiers downstream delineated by output deals that have a theatrical release tier threshold). Interestingly, this has developed as a two-way street: there are also instances of film produced for the video market that come out well, and the studio may subsequently elect to release them theatrically. It is often hard to pinpoint these titles, however, for the distributor will likely be reticent to publicize that the title was originally intended for the video market for fear of souring the caché value.

Niche and Non-Studio Direct to Videos/Made for Videos

In addition to mainstream videos, the opportunity in the video marketplace led to numerous niche opportunities. One of the strongest sectors was health and fitness/exercise. Swimsuit and supermodels competed with the likes of Jane Fonda to release aerobic and other workout-related tapes.

Another burgeoning area was concert films. With the enhanced video and sound quality possible with DVDs, it became more attractive to sell a video from a concert tour or a specific performance to complement CD sales.

Finally, with the upside potential in the family/kids market it was only a matter of time before toy companies capitalized on their key brands and expanded into the video market. Lego produced Bionicles, and Fox announced a partnership with Hasbro to produce and release titles based on several of its popular brands. I could go on and on talking about documentaries, music videos, and a variety of other genres, but the point is that DVDs opened up a new market for virtually all forms of content production.

Next Generation DVDs: Blu-ray versus HD-DVD — Format War Redux

In 2006 two new competing high-definition DVD systems were introduced pitting rival Japanese consumer electronics manufacturers against each other (again). Blu-ray, developed by Sony, and HD-DVD, developed by Toshiba, were pitted against each other, offering high-definition images (1080) and a remarkable amount of storage capacity (25–50 GB). Different partners lined up behind each, with Microsoft in the HD-DVD camp and a greater number of Hollywood studios (e.g., Disney and Fox) initially jumping on the Blu-ray band-

184

wagon. Adoption was slow, however, as no parties wanted to be beholden to a format that might not win, the initial price points for players were high ($350+), and consumers were not convinced that the quality differential from standard DVDs warranted a pricey upgrade. Unlike earlier format wars, both sides tried to speed adoption by integrating the new players into other hardware: Sony including a Blu-ray player in each new PlayStation 3 game console, while Toshiba bundled its HD-DVD drives into notebook computers and Xbox 360 game systems.

It was a déjà vu scenario with full scale war between two major Japanese consumer electronics companies, billions of dollars potentially at stake, and the consumer caught in the middle waiting out the format winner. With both sides having sold ~1 million units by the end of 2007, there seemed no clear winner in sight, and headlines abounded. This one was seen in the *International Herald Tribune* on New Year's day 2008, just days before the annual mass gathering at the consumer electronics show in Las Vegas: "The Format Wars: Titans Stuck in a Stalemate — Despite Months of Tussling, No Clear Winner has Emerged in the Battle between Blue-ray and HD DVD."[12] I was even part of the prior lobbying efforts, with studio partners and other vested parties alike courting Lucasfilm for an endorsement. What do you do when you have different franchises with different studios, and you do not know who may distribute your next film or TV series?

Then suddenly everything changed and the battle was literally over. In February 2008 Warner Bros., the pioneer in traditional DVD, had been on the fence and then came out in favor of Blu-ray; within the same week or so Wal-Mart came out and announced it would no longer stock HD-DVDs or HD-DVD players. With the market share leader for DVD sales at retail and Warners both coming out in favor of Blu-ray, it shocked the market and Toshiba pulled out.[13] No doubt, there was growing fear that delay could doom the entire industry, and if all the studios did not start lining up behind a common format the danger existed that high definition would miss its window and be bypassed entirely by the growing download markets, akin to CDs being replaced by digital files.[14] In a sense, as typical with the introduction of new technology in the media, one battle had ended and another was just beginning.

Finally, one feature of Blu-ray puts it on a path to embrace the Internet. This feature creates certain interactivity that may be designed to ensure a place working within the new Internet world rather than having to simply compete against it. So-called Blu-ray live enables an interactive feature that allows viewers to simultaneously watch a film along with its director, seeing commentary and chat live while the movie is playing. Among the first tests of this component was an invitation to watch *Batman — The Dark Knight* along with its director, Christopher Nolan, and reportedly up to 100,000 people were supposed to be able to watch along together.

Product Diversification

In addition to the general video window of releasing a movie six months or so after theatrical release, it became economical to market other product at retail. Two major categories were exploited: catalog titles and television shows. As for catalog, every studio has a group of classics in its library, whether themed to stars (Betty Davis collection), awards (Oscar Winners), or simply so-called classics.

When releasing these films, the practice of having the producer or more often the director create a special edition (e.g., director's cut) evolved. This could entail releasing an extended version of the film or re-editing parts that may have been cut out for theatrical release (often dealing with time constraints that did not apply to home viewing). Additionally, in some instances special editions would "clean up" elements in the master given advanced technology (e.g., re-mastering, taking advantage of computer clean up or digital sound), and in other cases the creator may have even produced new elements and re-edited the films. When George Lucas released the original Star Wars movies (*Star Wars, The Empire Strikes Back, Return of the Jedi*) on DVD for the first time in 2004, all of these elements came into play: (1) all of the movies went through extensive clean up, utilizing a computer digital restoration facility; (2) all of the movies included re-mastering sound elements; (3) and a few new elements were introduced, utilizing special effects to alter select sequences.

Another growth area was releasing "seasons" of television series. This became popular, initially, with longstanding hits like *The Simpsons*, as well as fare that had developed a strong following on limited services such as pay TV but had not been exposed to a larger audience. HBO titles are a perfect example. Consumers that were aware of a show such as *The Sopranos* or *Sex and the City* but did not subscribe to HBO could rent entire seasons and watch them like a mini-series.

Soon, collections became the rule rather than the exception and full seasons of top TV shows could be found on shelves: *Alias* from ABC, *24* from Fox, and the complete Seinfeld. By Christmas 2004 box sets abounded at retail, so much so that video distributors and retailers for the first time started worrying about saturation and how far the market could expand. Collections, special editions, etc., are all further illustrations of Ulin's Rule — distribution maximizes revenues through repeat consumption opportunities, tied to differential pricing and timing.

Maturation of the DVD Market and Growing Complexity of Retail Marketing

The DVD/video supply chain, being tied to a physical consumer product, is far more complicated than the chain of licensing and delivery of movies and TV shows, respectively, to theaters and broadcasters. Figure 5.2 exhibits the key components of assimilating a variety of content into a product distributed in multiple SKUs and formats to outlets of fundamentally different character (rental vs. sale), and marketed to the customer by both the distributor and point-of-purchase retailer.

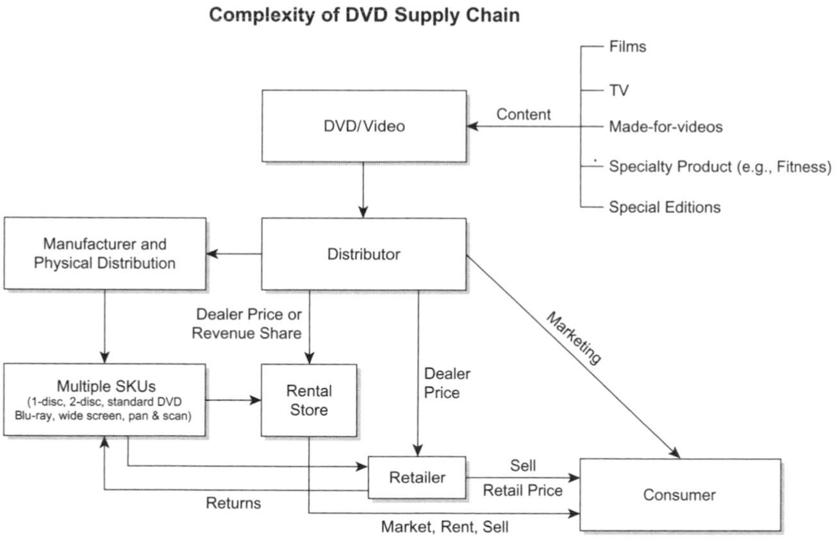

187

Complexity of DVD Supply Chain

Figure 5.2

Peaking of the DVD Curve and Compressed Sales Cycle

By the late 1990s it was clear that DVDs were the format of the future, and in the ensuing years penetration literally exploded. Growing from less than 10% in 1999, by the end of 2006 penetration exceeded 80% and had bypassed VCR penetration.[15] By 2003 annual DVD rental revenues exceeded VHS revenues,[16] and by 2005 the number of VHS units of a major title relative to DVD units was negligible. In fact, by 2005 many titles such as *Star Wars: Episode III Revenge of the Sith* were released only on DVD.

With the growth of DVD, the balance between rental and sell through started to shift dramatically toward sell through. The durability and quality of DVDs, together with the ability to include special features (see discussion regarding VAM), made them an ideal retail item as well as perfect gifts. All of a sudden it was not just Disney selling huge numbers of children's videos, but key titles from all studios were selling in the millions. And for children's properties, the numbers simply kept growing. *Shrek*, released in 2001, reportedly sold 2.5M units in its first three days[17] en route to selling upwards of 20–30 million units worldwide, as did Disney-Pixar's *Finding Nemo*.

Depending on whose statistics one believes, the DVD/video market peaked somewhere between 2004–2006, and by the end of 2005 it was evident that the market was entering into a phase of decline both on a by-title basis as well as overall. Given the size and importance of the home entertainment market in the media sector, this was mass market news, as *USA Today* highlighted: "For the first time in home video's nearly 30-year history, sales and rentals slipped in 2005 as slowing growth of DVDs couldn't overcome falling prices and a dying VHS market."[18]

While historically home video revenue from most blockbusters equaled or surpassed that of their box office take, the trend seemed to have peaked. Describing the drop in conversion rate — the ratio of video sales to theatrical — *Variety* reported that the theatrical gross exceeded the DVD revenues of films such as *Batman Begins* and *War of the Worlds* (e.g., *Batman Begins* video revenues $170M vs. $205M theatrical gross).[19] There has been a continuing decline in the DVD market ever since this peak.[20] 2008 appears to have been the worst year to date in terms of falloff, with DVD sales dipping 6.3% (versus '07), and the overall home entertainment market down 5.7%; driving this downward trend was a precipitous drop in new release volumes, estimated to be down close to 20%.[21] Illustrating the severity of the

188

Table 5.3   Top Five DVDs of 2003 and 2008[a]

Studio	Title	Date	Video Units
Buena Vista	*Finding Nemo*	2003	26,000
New Line	*Lord of the Rings: The Two Towers*	2003	21,050
Buena Vista	*Pirates of the Caribbean: Curse of the Black Pearl*	2003	19,450
Warner	*Matrix Reloaded*	2003	15,520
Universal	*Bruce Almighty*	2003	12,650
Warner	*Dark Knight*	2008	12,385
Paramount	*Iron Man*	2008	11,375
Fox	*Alvin and the Chipmunks*	2008	10,560
Warner	*I Am Legend*	2008	10,125
DreamWorks Animation	*Kung Fu Panda*	2008	9,750

Note: Units are projected lifetime shipments of the film on home video.
[a]© 2009 SNL Kagan, a division of SNL Financial LC, analysis of video and movie industry data and estimates. All rights reserved.

decline on a by-title basis. Table 5.3 lists the top selling DVDs for 2003 versus 2008 in the United States.

Given the overall importance of DVDs to the studio revenue base and ecosystem, this unexpected pace of decline is setting off alarm bells; whether or not the cause is ultimately attributed to the recessionary climate and the market stabilizes, the shift is putting even more emphasis on the future of electronic sell through and related new consumption patterns in the digital space.

Compressed Sales Cycle

The other factor impacting the market maturation was an increasingly compressed sales cycle. This has been accentuated by the flood of additional product trying to take advantage of DVD dollars. Whereas only a few years earlier shelf space competition was between different hit movies, the largest growth sector became TV product and box sets; with a glut of new and catalog TV releases together with made-for-DVD product, competition became fiercer, shelf space turned over more quickly, and sales cycles compressed. In a sense, the DVD retail cycle was beginning to mimic the box office, with revenues more frontloaded by the year, and films earning the majority of their video revenues within the first two weeks of release.[22] In fact, most studios acknowledge that the majority of sales on a title now come in this short period. The *Wall Street Journal* highlighted this shift: "Five years ago, a typical DVD release would rack up about one third of its total sales during the first week of release; the figure was even lower for animated movies, which tended to have longer legs. DVD sales would then steadily mount over weeks or months. But these days, DVD releases are generating a huge percentage of their total sales — typically over 50% and in some cases, up to 70% — in the first week."[23]

This trend developed outside the pressures of new media, making the issue of how to window downloads that much more complicated. The DVD cash cow was set for a reversal of fortune, and no studio wanted to accelerate that trend. Unless downloads could be proven to add incremental value, let alone not cannibalize DVD, there was little impetus to experiment with key new releases.

Expansion of Retail Mass Market Chains: Wal-Mart, Best Buy, Target, etc.

Routinely selling 5M+ copies of an A-title and on occassion over 10M copies of select hit children's/family titles could only occur with the expansion of retail distribution. Video rental stores jumped on the bandwagon as a point of sale for DVDs, but their bread and butter remained rental and the vast majority of sales took place at mass market retailers.

Because DVDs as a software entertainment commodity offered a unique product with each release (as does a CD or video game), both suppliers and retailers quickly realized the marketing opportunities. Not only could DVDs sell in record numbers, but DVDs could actually drive consumer traffic into stores. If the next Star Wars or Lord of the Rings movie were being released on DVD, customers would crash stores in droves. It was like Christmastime with each new major release.

Of course, nothing is that simple and greater sales and expectations were also driven by increased marketing. To sell several million copies of a title it is necessary to advertise the release, and advertising budgets for DVD releases multiplied several fold. Studio video divisions became expert at running sophisticated P&L models, trying to gauge the saturation threshold after which increased marketing spend would not yield additional positive contribution margin.

Increased marketing expenditure could ultimately only be justified with concomitant retail support. Accordingly, retailers went through a maturation period as well, with more shelf space dedicated to DVDs. In-store marketing campaigns grew in importance, with dedicated in-store display packs such as towers themed with images from the movie adding additional capacity during a title's initial release. Executing a compelling in-store campaign involves elements including:

- Posters
- Additional signage
- Stand-alone themed display towers
- Placement of stand-alone displays and regular shelf placement (e.g., on new release end caps vs. off the aisle placement)
- Employee education
- In-store trailers
- Dedicated retailer advertising
- Trade advertisements
- Store circulars in newspapers, etc.

To achieve this type of coordinated campaign at retail, several economic incentives evolved. Industry practice developed such that studios offered an allowance for both market development and co-operative spending. Typically, studios will allow retailers to spend a small percentage of the wholesale revenue against their marketing costs directly related to the title. Additionally, studios will allow another line-item for cooperative advertising expenditure. Where these lines are drawn is a bit fuzzy, with cooperative advertising a bit easier to track in that it is supposed to be allocated for actual advertising, whether print media, radio, or television. Cumulatively, a retailer may have a few percent of actual wholesale revenue to apply against its costs in advertising, marketing, and merchandising the title.

These sums are paid by the studio/video retailer, but in practice are administered as an allowance. The amounts calculated for marketing and co-op expenditures are deducted from the revenues otherwise due, yielding a net amount paid, thereby having a negligible cash flow effect. These are real costs, however, to the video distributor and are a key line-item element of the overall video marketing budget, just as direct advertising creation costs and costs of buying media (TV and radio advertising) are costs driving the P&L analysis and ultimate contribution margin.

Retailer Specific Implementation

Implementation of marketing programs is tailored at the retail level, typically tiered to the anticipated volume. In all markets, it is common to have a key account list, which will vary by studio and type of product (e.g., specialist account), but mainstream releases would

191

typically include the following retailers (excluding wholesalers): Amazon.com, Best Buy, Wal-Mart, Target, BJ's Wholesale Club, Borders, Circuit City (before bankruptcy), Costco, and Hollywood Video. Depending on the title and studio, a select few top accounts, such as Wal-Mat, Target, Best Buy, and Amazon, could easily account for over 60% of the total volume.

For the top volume accounts, and on certain key new release titles, it may make sense to customize programs. Types of programs can obviously vary widely, but examples of specialized focus may entail:

- Special product placement, such as guarantees of being positioned near the check-out register
- Unique creative campaigns for posters, or buttons for staff
- Rebate programs tied to individual purchases, such as point of sales rebates, or overall volumes
- Discounts tied to sale of other purchases
- Discounts tied to store gift cards
- Customized packaging
- Customized value-added offers (such as bundled merchandising, like an action figure)
- Special merchandisers, such as product towers
- Special placement in circulars or flyers
- Consumer prizes/sweepstakes

There is no limit to the creativity of a campaign.

Deals and programs will naturally depend on both the leverage of the title and market clout of the retailer. In many cases, it is the retailer with the premium shelf space as the interface to the consumer that can dictate terms. In fact, retailers with large traffic volume sometimes charge placement fees, such as to stock a video title in the end cap at the checkout lanes (e.g., charging a per unit fee, and in extreme cases even holding a mini-auction and granting the space to the highest bidder).

Loss-Leading Product and Fostering Consistent Consumer Pricing

Another product of leverage is loss-leading a product. For a big enough title, it is not unusual for a retailer to deeply discount the title for a limited period if it is likely the special price offer will bring customers into the store. Many of the top accounts obviously carry a wide range of product, and the likelihood of additional sales if they can attract a customer into the store is high enough that sacrificing margin on a video title pays off. In extreme cases the store is even willing to lose money on a title.

Although this sounds like a good deal to the video distributor (you can hear the video salesman gloating "they want my product so badly they're willing to lose money!"), the trick to successful sales is managing the overall market and one account can cause havoc. If a particular retailer dramatically undercuts its competitors, such that traffic is truly taken away from its competitors, then for the distributor the increased volume at that one chain better make up the difference. Otherwise, the distributor will be looking at lots of disgruntled customers who may want to return the product or may not be as accommodating on their next title or campaign. Remember, the wholesale pricing will have been relatively consistent, so a sale from store X is relatively fungible to a sale from store Y, and success is driven by making retail sales successful across the entire channel. No distributor wants to spend millions of dollars on an overall advertising campaign to support retail only to have one or two retailers undermine the overall effectiveness.

It is illegal to set onward retail pricing, and once a video is sold the buyer who bought in order to re-sell is free to set its price (first sale doctrine, anti-trust, price fixing); accordingly, a video distributor cannot prevent a specific retail account from pricing as they choose. A retailer could elect to give the DVD away for free, regardless of the price it paid for the unit to the distributor. If they want to lose money, that's their prerogative.

There is one accepted practice, however, that buffers this risk: establish minimum advertised price (MAP). A distributor is not obligated to financially support the retail marketing campaign, and there are certain quid pro quos established for committing to cooperative advertising and market development fund dollars. To be eligible for MAP contributions, a distributor may dictate that the retailer may not advertise the product for a price below $X. With this arrangement, the video retailer ensures a relatively consistent price band, yet the retailer maintains flexibility for the ultimate on-shelf price.

When MAP policies are set, they are almost always limited in time such that on expiry the retailer is free to set and advertise pricing at will. In some cases, a distributor may strategically set MAP expiry to dovetail with a specific anticipated time of re-promotion or anticipated markdowns (especially if dealing with seasonal dates).

193

E-Tailers and Next Generation Retail

Beyond the growth of mass market retail, the video market has benefited from e-tailers such as amazon.com stocking new and catalog DVDs. The growth of online shopping has been a boon for video, as DVDs were a natural complement to book sales and Amazon has matured into a key customer for distributors. What is particularly helpful beyond actual sales is the predictive nature of online sites. E-tailers customarily take pre-orders for titles, and the relative volume of pre-orders can often be a good barometer of total retail sales.

Although e-tailers tend to thrive on margin, offering lower pricing given the absence of physical retail space, this is one area where the online stores struggle to be the low price leader. In an environment where mass market physical retailers will on occasion loss-lead product to drive profit, and where competition between physical retailers is cutthroat, it is challenging for an e-tailer to undercut offline retail. What they can do, however, is create further pricing pressure for their physical retail competitors, thereby offering customers competitive pricing coupled with convenience, pre-order reservations, and targeted recommendations.

194

Struggling Alternative Delivery Systems and the Success of Netflix

For years video distributors have been trying to improve the accessibility of renting programs. Video kiosks were once predicted to be the rage, with vending-type machines located in high traffic areas (e.g., lobby of large office buildings): customers would pay, get the DVD through a slot when it dropped out, and return it to the machine within a day or two. These never really caught on as hoped (but are still found selectively worldwide, including in supermarkets and in international territories where retail space is at a premium such as Japan), but what did grow dramatically was mail delivery via services such as Netflix.

Netflix combined the inventory management and ease of access of the Internet via old world fulfillment—the mail. A customer could scan a seeming infinite catalog of titles (online viewing is not constrained by physical retail shelf space) and then simply place an order. Fulfillment was then quite clever: order one or more, and every time you return a DVD you could select another one that would be shipped out to your home. The movies came in simple paper cases (without the bulky video box) with prepaid envelopes: just seal and return. Netflix grew dramatically from a 1998 launch with less than

1,000 titles to over 1 million subscribers by 2003 at which point it had delivered over 100 million DVDs (and by 2007 over 1 billion).[19] This was essentially a virtual video store and the only drawback was fulfillment delay. That lag did not turn out to be the obstacle some thought, perhaps due to the ability to order in volume, so it was possible to build an inventory at home and always have something ready to watch while you decided what to see next.

By 2006, Blockbuster was on the ropes and Netflix had passed the 4 million customer mark. Blockbuster and other traditional video retailers had to compete directly, and blockbuster.com launched a home delivery service, even going so far as to advertise the new option during the Super Bowl (February 2006).

A step beyond Netflix's customary service is utilizing the Internet to download movies via video-on-demand and watching via a virtual VCR. Beyond streaming to PCs Netflix has launched an on-demand service via a proprietary set-top box (Roku), translating several thousand titles from its catalog to instant access on the TV screen. With these new iterations, the virtual video store seems to have truly, and finally, arrived. (Note: For more discussion of this VOD application and for a discussion of downloads as electronic sell through impacting the DVD retail market see Chapters 7 and 8.)

Window Movements

There is no doubt that given the importance of DVD revenues there has been pressure to tinker with the window. In analyzing the tug of war between competing media, *Business Week* summarized:

> To capture that DVD gold, Hollywood has for years made its flicks available to TV viewers only through a carefully structured system of "windows." DVD retailers waited six months after the theater premiere; cable's and satellite's video-on-demand (VOD) got the film 90 days after that, and HBO and other pay-TV services six months following VOD. But the windows have been slowly closing, and studios now ship DVDs to market sooner than ever before—on average, in 137 days (vs. 200 days in 1998), according to DVD Release Report ...[25]

While this may sound dramatic, I would argue that the shrinking of the window has been merely iterative; in fact, and perhaps not surprisingly, given the continued importance of both the theatrical and video markets, the window for video release, while accelerating a bit, has stayed relatively static for over a decade. Window protection is so important for theatrical releases that the cinema chains exert extreme pressure, and will even in extreme cases boycott studios that test closing the gap by accelerating a DVD release date too close to the theatrical release.[26] The movie cinema trade association NATO (National Association of Theater Owners) goes so far as to track the window/gap studio-by-studio, down to average days post release and "announcement" dates. Table 5.4 is a schedule of the video release window by year as reported by NATO:

Table 5.4   Average Video Release Window

Year	Average Video Release Window
1998	5 months, 22 days
1999	5 months, 18 days
2000	5 months, 16 days
2001	5 months, 12 days
2002	5 months, 8 days
2003	4 months, 27 days
2004	4 months, 20 days
2005	4 months, 18 days
2006	4 months, 11 days
2007	4 months, 19 days
2008	4 months, 10 days

NATO memo, December 12, 2008, Re: Average Video Announcement and Video Release Windows (as of 12/10/2008).

While there is significant experimentation with download/electronic sell through and VOD windows (as discussed in Chapter 7), the DVD window seems to remain a relatively stable fulcrum around which manifestations of physical and electronic video sales and rentals are trying to balance.

I asked Mike Dunn, president of Twentieth Century Fox Home Entertainment, what he thought about the video window relative to new media pressures, and he confirmed DVD's continued central role while highlighting the value added benefits that Blue-ray and online interactivity bring to the overall market:

Windows remain critical to the efficient delivery of content across an ever increasing array of platforms and device options for the consumer. That said, new businesses such as online and cable VOD present content owners with more options to deliver high value content soon after the theatrical window.

But the value of the online delivery channels, while growing significantly in percentage terms, remains a fairly small portion of the overall entertainment pie, and it will be many years before enough consumers use online channels as their primary means of accessing studio content to replace the physical medium. Blu-ray represents the easiest way for consumers to access the highest definition content, but online channels can be used to supplement physical media by allowing consumers to augment their disc experience with value added content accessed via online streaming or downloading.

Inventory Management and Impact on Pricing and Profits

Returns and Stock Management

Probably the biggest single issue impacting the release of a title into the sell through market is managing inventory. Rental units are generally firm sales, and when a rental chain decides it is overstocked or inventory has reached obsolescence it can either destroy the units or sell them. Sell through units/DVDs are, however, no different than any other consumer product and excess stock is most often subject to return.

There are multiple steps in inventory management, and I will briefly touch on the life cycle sequence in which they occur: (1) initial shipments, (2) replenishment, (3) returns, (4) price reductions and price protection, and (5) catalog management.

Initial Shipment

This is by far the most important step, because miscalculations on initial placement will plague the title's performance all the way downstream. It is debatable whether it is worse to over-ship or under-ship, but if demand outstrips supply and a title has been under-shipped there are really only a couple of issues to address.

First, the obvious consequence is lost sales, and opportunity costs are always the hardest element to accurately forecast. If the under-shipment is recognized early, by utilizing an efficient supply chain (see later discussion) it is still feasible to capitalize on demand. However, because marketing campaigns are designed to create intense demand on release, absent a honed and tightly managed supply chain it is obviously difficult to reach fully substitutional sales outside the window of coordinated advertising and retail marketing/focus.

Second, the distributor needs to confirm how feasible it is to quickly replenish inventory and mitigate lost sales. In the mid to late 1990s this would have been difficult, but as the market has matured so has the replication and distribution system. Today, single plants may be able to produce a million discs a day and deliver them nationwide to out-of-stock retailers within the week—full replenishment may not be possible literally overnight, but it is feasible in a matter of days. Again, days count when dealing with a coordinated marketing campaign; the consequences of being out of stock and replenishing late include (1) losing retail placement position, (2) losing retail focus, (3) selling against a new competitive title, and (4) missing key sales days such as weekends or seasonal specific dates.

If, in contrast, the initial shipment has glutted the market and it turns out the distributor has materially over-shipped, there is likely to be pressure to take returns. This leads to complex management challenges, including price protection decisions, as discussed later. Moreover, overstating revenues and having to reverse out earnings due to returns is a serious problem and (as also discussed later) has been responsible for significant downturns in the stock prices of companies who miss their targets.

Replenishment, Fulfillment, and Logistics

The sophistication of the market largely dictates how replenishment works. In the United States, the video arms of the studios and supply chains of the replicators and distributors are models of efficiency. On a major release, a studio has visibility into its large direct customers to the extent that it can check sales periodically during the day. The inventory and sell through numbers are constantly updated, and it is possible to see how a title is progressing on release early in the week and top up SKUs as necessary for the weekend. Replicators able to churn out hundreds of thousands of units a day (if not more) then further decide how many units to build at which stage of production, balancing finished goods inventory versus elements needed for a quick turnaround on the assembly line.

As the sell through business matured, the duplicators recognized that they could fulfill additional distribution functions. Not only could they make the physical good, but they could handle the logistics of sorting SKUs, packing the product, and shipping the product.

This step is frequently referred to as "pick, pack, and ship," and involves the logistics of everything in the chain from completion of the physical good to delivering the good to the retailer. It may seem simple here, but the process of sorting inventory for delivery to retailers is a mechanized art.

The management of the backroom logistics does not stop there, however. The replicator has now taken on the task of processing returns, repurposing stock, invoicing the client/retailer, processing related credits, and even handling some collections. Basically, the entire chain from manufacturing to delivery to payment can be outsourced, leaving the intellectual property owner to focus on delivering and marketing the product, and setting customer specific terms.

The less sophisticated the retail market, the harder it is to replenish efficiently — the replicators have the systems, but without the retail systems to report offtake efficiently, the distributor is left to place all its product up front. Otherwise, the distributor risks out of stocks without the ability to replenish; this is not a viable option when the product has a short shelf life, driven by a burst of frontloaded advertising to drive consumers to purchase in a relatively short window. As discussed previously, the decay curves for video sales are becoming steeper with an ever increasing percentage of total sales on a unit in the first couple of weeks of release. Again, this correlates to increased competition and the fight for shelf space with most displays rotating out on a regular weekly or bi-weekly basis and restocked with the "new title of the week."

No matter how efficient the supply chain and replenishment logistics, there is no guarantee of sales and always a risk of over- or under-stocks. While the risk is not nearly of the scale as on the theatrical release (as theatrical results convert the product from a nobody knows experience good to a property that can be more accurately forecast for subsequent market sales — conversion rates), significant risks, even if more bounded, still exist. Because of the marketing profile, the trend has been to over supply to ensure against out of stocks as well as secure optimum store display. While every distributor knows they need to ship in more than 1 million units to sell through 1 million, the art is to narrow the gap as much as possible without jeopardizing sales — the greater the efficiency in this stock management, the greater the margins and profits.

Returns
Historically, distributors have negotiated returns provisions with retailers that tend to be account specific. A customary provision, for

example, may be that an account is allowed a returns provision of 20%. It is also possible to negotiate for zero returns (a "firm sale") or allow a retailer 100% returns. A 100% returns allowance usually occurs when either a retailer has enough clout to insist on this flexibility, or the retailer has agreed to take extra units and aggressively market the title. Regardless of what is negotiated, it is important to keep in perspective that these provisions may change after the fact — a retailer that has agreed to 20% returns and finds that the title significantly underperforms is likely to ask for relief and return a much higher percentage. If this is a key customer and the distributor has another title coming out the following month it wants to push, it may not be so easy in practice to rigidly enforce the hard 20% number. The success of a title ultimately depends both on the distributor and retailer market, and both parties need to juggle short-term performance versus long-term relationships. This is where friction arises with producers, as someone involved with a specific title will not accept the sacrifice of their title's performance to accommodate client relationships that seemingly bear no direct impact on their film's video revenues.

200

Return Reserve

For accounting purposes, returns caps allow the distributor to take return reserve provisions; namely, in accounting for sales, a provision will be taken for returns based upon the contractual return allowance or a permitted reserve. When accounting for sales, there is always a gap and several elements need to be reconciled: what has been shipped into the retail channel, what units have actually sold through to date (bought by a consumer as opposed to bought by the store), what number of units are likely to remain at retail for future/continuing sales, and what number of units are likely to be returned.

Returns impact participation statements (see Chapter 10) and need to be looked at in terms of how returns are treated between the distributor and retailer, and how returns are accounted for between the distributor and the producer/participant. There may be separate deals, and this may not (though often is) be strictly a pass through relationship. One can theoretically imagine a producer with sufficient leverage inserting a returns cap in its deals to protect against a distributor favoring a retail customer or making a decision based on retail relationships as opposed to strictly on the title.

There may also be contractual provisions regarding the timing of returns and reserves. In addition to or unrelated to a returns allowance percentage, the parties could strike a deal prohibiting returns for a period of time (e.g., no returns for 90 days or 6 months); this has the advantage of keeping the product on shelf, and may allow for increased sales over a different or incremental selling season that would not take place without the protection (shelf space otherwise ceded to a competitive title).

On the participant side, there may be a push to stipulate that returns allowances may only be taken for a limited period of time and then released; it is customary to negotiate periods during which returns reserves need to be liquidated. Because the reserves are allowed, the distributor will naturally take advantage of potential returns and keep the money (in anticipation of returned units); however, these returns may never materialize, and all the while the money is held and not paid over to the producer. This practice, which is equivalent to the concept of "float" in other industries, means that the negotiated reporting and liquidation periods can be quite significant.

Spotlight on DreamWorks Animation and Pixar in 2005

The issue of returns was highlighted in 2005 when both Pixar and DreamWorks Animation were hit with returns on, respectively, *The Incredibles* and *Shrek2*.

The tempest was set off by DreamWorks statements and filings. In January 2005 DreamWorks Animation stated that it had sold 37 million units of *Shrek2* worldwide. However, in March the studio reported that it had only sold 33.7 million units and that it expected the title to continue with a strong performance and sell over 40 million by the end of the first quarter. When the day of reckoning came in May, DreamWorks Animation reported that it had only sold 35 million units (not 40 million), and admitted that the rate of sales that propelled the title to the top video seller of 2004 did not keep pace into 2005.

The reporting caused DreamWorks Animation's stock to fall 12% on the disappointing earnings, and the entire issue of returns and slowing down of the video market started making headlines. The *Wall Street Journal* reported: "In just its second quarter since becoming a public company, DreamWorks fell short of earnings forecasts by 25% and its stock tumbled as Wall Street wondered why the mistake wasn't disclosed sooner."[27]

Beyond the hit in stock price and negative publicity, the misjudgment on sales and returns even led to lawsuits, which in turn made headlines:

"Shrek 2 DVDs Subject of Lawsuit. Shareholders sue DreamWorks alleging misleading projections. … A proposed class-action lawsuit, filed in federal court in Los Angeles today, seeks unspecified damages from DreamWorks Animation for allegedly misleading stockholders about prospects for sales of *Shrek 2* DVDs."[27a]

In the wake of this news, Pixar warned that it would have larger than expected returns on *The Incredibles*; on June 30, 2005, Pixar cut its earnings per share estimate for the second quarter from 15 to 10 cents citing slower than expected sales. The issue became prominent enough that even the SEC started to examine the reporting process for each of these studios. Ultimately, the SEC's local arm investigating DreamWorks recommended that no enforcement action be taken, and *Variety* reported: "While the SEC itself still has to make a formal decision, recommendation makes it very likely that DWA will escape government sanction for failing to warn investors, before first-quarter earnings were announced last year, that returns on the "Shrek 2" DVD were running much higher than anticipated …"[28]

While the issue of returns seemed like a revelation to the press and some investors, the difficulty of managing inventory levels and balancing returns was nothing new to industry insiders. What had changed were two factors. First, as earlier discussed, there was a slowing down of sales in the industry, and within 2005 the market seemed to have hit its by-title ceiling; the overall market was still healthy, but with title saturation and withering competition the market appeared to be retrenching on the high end of sales. This was a trend that had been predicted, but the reality came quicker than anticipated and started to send shock waves through the market.[29] Secondly, with a microscope on the industry, there was the ability in the case of both Pixar and DreamWorks Animation to see the impact on a specific title. This transparency was rare, for studios would otherwise report numbers on a consolidated basis, and to outsiders it was impossible to glean the numbers or even trends on the basis of a single title.

With *The Incredibles* and *Shrek2* there was no way to hide the line item performance.

Format and SKU Variables

An important variable in managing inventory and returns is also managing product SKUs. It many cases a video or DVD release will be split into pan and scan and widescreen versions. Typically, a traditional box-shaped TV screen plays a 4:3 aspect ratio, which is referred to as pan and scan. In contrast, the horizontal aspect ratio of a wide screen, replicating the rectangular movie, is 16:9. The widescreen aspect ratio matches the way a movie has been shot and edited, capturing the full breadth of the scene. To create a pan and scan version, the filmmaker actually has to create and approve another version, because the picture cannot simply be squeezed into the other shape. Accordingly, a pan and scan version will often cut off images at the margins.

The advent of widescreen monitors and increased consumer market knowledge has led to an increase in widescreen versions. For years, pan and scan dominated as widescreen was limited to the "purist" consumer who wanted to see the picture as the director intended it/as seen on film so elements and scope are not compromised (and would put up with the black bars at the top and bottom of the screen). With the market maturation, plus increased consumer awareness of formats and the growth of rectangular flat screen monitors, the SKU balance started to equalize on "collector" type titles. By 2003–2004 certain titles were even selling a greater number of widescreen versions, a trend that had been predicted but until this point of intersection (DVD growth and alternate monitors) had not happened. With each year the proportion continues to shift in favor of widescreen.

Finally, in terms of SKUs, studios started to offer special "2 disc sets" of key titles, with one disc containing the film and the other disc filled with bonus material (or in video parlance value added material or "VAM"; see Chapter 9 for more discussion of VAM in the context of marketing). The extra material both justified a higher price point and had become a self-fulfilling expectation from the standpoint of consumer demand — once it was commonplace, it became an expected component. The net result of the bonus disc was the studio distributor had a choice whether to release one version including the bonus material, or two versions with the alternate SKU comprised of just the film disc. If two SKUs were released, this obviously complicated the release matrix: Would the physical packaging

203

change, would the artwork change to distinguish SKUs, would the price points vary, would the distribution points of sale change, etc.

Pricing, Price Reductions, and Price Protection

Pricing is not quite what it seems from customarily quoted numbers, and to understand the economics it is important to appreciate net pricing. The price charged by the retailer to the consumer is called the retail price. Because it is illegal to set an onward price, what is usually set is the SRP; MAP is a vehicle to influence the SRP, but ultimately there is market flexibility and neither the SRP nor MAP actually locks a retailer into a specific sales price. [(Note: When you hear about a store advertising as a low price leader, or matching in the market, it is important to discern between whether a specific store in the chain will alter pricing within the store to match a competitor, or whether the chain/store is actually advertising a specific price to the consumer. It is very different to claim you will match a price (where no figure is stated in the ad) and to actually advertise a specific price in newspapers and circulars.)]

The price that the distributor charges the retailer is often called the dealer price, which is the video term of art for wholesale price. As a rule of thumb, the wholesale price tends to be roughly 60% of the SRP. The wholesale price is basically fixed across the US market (in accordance with the Robinson-Patman Act); nevertheless, there can be marginal account differences in the wholesale price, as juggling can take place with marketing allowances (market development funds and cooperative advertising allowances) and tailored programs.

Like any consumer product, over time there are markdowns as new items enter the market. In the video sector, product is generally segmented into "new releases" and "catalog." When a product transitions from a new release to catalog, however, the price is not fixed, although generally product is re-categorized after its initial release cycle. The challenge of a distributor is to manage its library of titles, find ways to turn over its catalog titles, and maintain demand and premium pricing for the key titles in its library. Accordingly, segmenting the library becomes an important marketing proposition and to generate demand and interest titles are often themed or grouped (e.g., marketed as classics, award winners, part of director's collections).

In terms of life cycle management, studio distributors are always running models (and conducting market research) comparing units and corresponding contribution margins at differing pricing; for example, will dropping the price from $19.99 to $14.99 generate sufficient incremental sales to outweigh the lower per unit profit? Managing price is an art, not a science, and is influenced by factors such as the nature of the title, the competitive environment, retail pressures, inventory in the market, seasonality, life cycle promotional opportunities, and rebate programs.

On a typical release, it would be customary to release at a higher price (but a price that hopefully yields maximum net profit/contribution taking into account the matrix of pricing and volume), and then to reduce the price downstream; for example if a movie came out at Christmas, and the video came out in late spring the following year, the price may be reduced in the fourth quarter for a Christmas promotion. If competitive product pricing is lower there will be retail pressure to match, and subsequent price reductions will be implemented. All this activity may generate incremental sales, but there are two issues that need to be weighed. The first is that except in rare instances it is very difficult to raise a price—once it sinks to a certain level it is apt to stay there. Namely, once in the bargain bin, it will be very difficult for the distributor to sell more units into a retailer at a higher price. The second key issue is price protection.

What is Price Protection?

Price protection is money paid by a distributor to a retailer when the distributor drops its wholesale price and sells more units into the market at a price below what it charged the retailer for the retailer's previously purchased on-hand inventory. For example, if Studio X sold units into the market at a wholesale price of around $12, such that retailer Y generally priced the title at $19.99 to the consumer, and the Studio had a promotion where it wanted to sell in more units of the movie at $9 to drive a retail price of $14.99 it might have a price protection issue. The issue would arise because retailers would have current stock at the higher price, and would want to be equalized such that all stock had the same cost basis. To take in more units, it would insist that the studio pay or credit it back the difference between $9 and $12 on all units it had. This $3 difference is the price protection payment charged to the distributor.

205

The retailer holds the leverage here. If the studio does not equalize the stock, the retailer would likely have the option to return its unsold product for full credit.

Price protection generally only occurs on successful titles, for an inherent assumption is that there is an opportunity for a subsequent sell in of units.

Point of Sale Rebates

While price protection impacts the entire channel and effects a permanent pricing change, point of sale (POS) rebates are a mechanism to implement a temporary price roll back. A supplier may authorize a limited time price cut, either across the retail channel or with specific accounts, that is implemented at checkout. To create an incentive for the retailer to reduce the shelf price from $19.99 to $14.99 a supplier may offer a $5 POS rebate, which will be applied at the wholesale price level, with the expectation that the full discount will then be passed along to the consumer, lowering the shelf price as just described. The advantage to the supplier is that they only need to credit the stores for units actually sold rather than on the entire inventory. This is a strategy frequently used for promotional sales, or during key holiday periods where the seller is trying to move units during periods of heavy foot traffic, but where the seller does not want to implement a permanent price cut.

Moratorium

Another tool that a distributor can use both to manage inventory as well as pricing is to put a title on moratorium. This means simply that the title is no longer available for purchase. By limiting supply, this may help stabilize either pricing or inventory levels, as stores may be less likely to return product if they are unable to later reorder units. Additionally, putting a title on moratorium may stimulate sales: order now or else ... Disney has used this strategy very effectively on its animated classics, advertising that a title is available for a limited period only, helping to spike interest and demand. The product is then literally rested until another cycle or perhaps another special version is later released.

Putting a title on moratorium is especially useful in the instance of multiple SKUs. This may help send a message to retail that the current version of a title will not be replenished (staving off potential returns), and further limits supply to clean out the channel before a different version is released. One of the goals is to avoid market

206

confusion, so that the new version (e.g., a special edition) is the only widely available version, allowing focused marketing campaigns both at the retail and consumer level.

Price Erosion and Bargain Bins

One of the most difficult elements in managing a title or catalog is dealing with price erosion. As noted earlier, new titles can command a premium price, but once the initial sales cycle has passed the product is perceived as older and will often be re-priced in an effort to stimulate sales.

What counters price erosion is that unlike consumer goods which are fungible, every movie is a unique piece of software. There will only be one *Godfather* or *Titanic*, and pricing does not need to drop for that film to compete because there is another identical product coming into the market; instead, pricing may need to move for the consumer to view the title as competitive against other similar films. If a competitor has a classics line that under prices its rival studios, price sensitivity alone may influence the consumer's selection.

Managing consumer expectations is tricky, and as previously noted once there is a perception that pricing is at a certain level it can be difficult to move back up to a higher cost basis. Ultimately, pricing is based on brand and catalog management, and can be influenced by seasonality, new formats coming into play, inventory levels, and even corporate revenue pressures (e.g., dropping a price and stimulating sales can help achieve hitting an earnings target).

It is now common for certain retailers to sell older titles in "bargain bins," where consumers may buy DVDs for a couple of dollars. Even high-profile titles can be steeply discounted for promotions, as has been the case on Black Friday when some of the Harry Potter titles and the Lord of the Ring films could be found in the $5–6 range. This is a far cry from the former high priced rental market, and many video distributors bemoan the price erosion in the market. The discounting may be fine if volume is stimulated, but if volumes do not meet projections and the pricing becomes a consumer expectation, rather than a limited promotion, then the high margins the business has enjoyed could be in jeopardy.

Ultimately, there are no other Lord of the Ring movies by Peter Jackson, so how and when to move price and launch promotions is the realm of brand management that makes the video market so interesting. Again, even though all films fall into categories, all individual films remain unique, challenging video divisions to hit targets by simultaneously macro and micro managing its catalog of product.

International Variations

Most of the information discussed in this chapter applies equally to the international marketplace, but there are both obvious and subtle differences. It is beyond the scope of this book to delve into territory specific nuances, but I will try to highlight a few significant areas of difference.

Release Timing and Development of Market

Although video and DVD technology has been driven by European and Asian (in particular Japanese) consumer electronics companies, market growth and penetration has been driven by software and Hollywood pressures. The international video and DVD markets have usually lagged the United States in terms of maturation and retail sophistication.

In terms of retail and consumer patterns, the DVD market has generally mirrored the prior VHS sell through market. In territories such as France, for example, where there was a long sell through tradition and sophistication of key retailers such as the hypermarkets (Auchan, Carrefour) the DVD market is vibrant. Accordingly, key retailers such as the hypermarkets, or entertainment software chains such as Virgin Megastore or FNAC, tend to have the same challenges that exist in the North American market: how is the product merchandised, how is it displayed, what are the promotional campaigns, is the price point appropriate, etc.

Additionally, with sophisticated merchandising and placement usually comes quality reporting. The ability of the distributor to see through to actual consumer sales forces the development of state-of-the-art inventory management systems and distribution that allows quick store-level replenishment. Stock balancing can occur on a daily, and at minimum weekly basis, affording the distributor to respond to consumer demand while maintaining a greater level of flexibility in creating product.

The ability to tinker with stock balances, replenish inventory, and top up manufacturing is only possible with this level of reporting from retail, and the parallel ability of retail to handle changes rapidly. The type of systems that can report and consolidate by-title sales at store and chain levels on a daily basis, however, are only justifiable with certain threshold volumes; in essence, the entire supply side feeds on itself with volume driving sophistication, and fulfillment, merchandising, and manufacturing capabilities evolving with demand. The United States is such a large market with diverse and distant retail distribution requirements that it developed this level of maturity quickly. That process has lagged in many international markets, but has now caught up in sophistication across the territories one would expect (e.g., much of Western Europe, Australia).

Outside the pure supply chain, considerations such as competition and external factors in the local marketplace tend also to mimic the US market. Regarding external factors, video releases may be tied to natural key sales periods, such as national holidays and vacation periods. As for the impact of competition, all distributors similarly analyze the release schedule of competitive product and date ("street date") their releases to try and secure the optimal window for sales.

Any and all of these factors are reasons why a DVD may come out on a different date in different territories. Weighing against these factors, however, will be concerns about piracy and parallel imports: once a product is out in the worldwide marketplace there is a danger it may find its way to the local consumer before the product has been directly released in the country—an issue that is now exacerbated with Internet access, especially for English-language product.

Localization Challenges

The main challenge of international markets is the creation of language specific SKUs. Each DVD will need to be authored and compressed like the United States, but across the rest of the world there will be multiple SKUs covering both dubbed and subtitled versions.

In addition to language versions, marketing campaigns will be tailored to the specific market as will, in cases, the packaging. Whenever a creative campaign is changed, and especially when it is uniquely tailored to a specific territory, there is inherent delay. Additionally, depending upon contractual requirements, time may need to be allocated to obtain approvals from talent as well as for home office executives to coordinate their approvals with both international branches and the producer/production company that made the film. Hopefully these elements have been planned for (and lead times built into release schedules), but the potential for delays is obvious.

Pricing: Variable Pricing to Customers and Net Pricing

Pricing internationally can be a "free-for-all" relative to the US market where distributors set the same dealer price for all customers and do not differentiate price based on volume commitments. Instead, distributors have to manage the retail channel by other means including marketing commitment (co-op marketing and market development fund), returns policies, inventory placement, etc.

In contrast, in some European markets and specifically in highly price sensitive retail markets, the distributors may set different prices for different customers. Not only can the actual dealer price vary, but there may be different discount schemes applied to varying accounts with variable pricing at each stage of the chain: retail/shelf price, dealer price, net invoiced price.

Obviously the distributor needs to ensure a certain range to avoid chaos and resentment in the marketplace. This is usually achieved by applying larger discounts to key accounts, which in turn often break out based on relative volumes. While this may all sound simple in practice, think about having to account for net pricing at the retail chain specific level, rolling up to the market overall, and then equalizing pricing by backing out applicable VAT taxes and harmonizing exchange rates. The simple question "what's the price in the market" could easily have different answers.

Table 5.5 is an example:

210

Table 5.5   Pricing Table

	SRP	DLP	DLP as % of SRP	Discounts*	Rebate	Net Price	Shelf Price
Germany	€24.99	14.30		20%	5%	€11	€22.99
France	€24.99	20.50		25%	—	€15.40	€24.99**
UK	£24.99	17.00		20%	2%	£13.20	£15.99

*May be further subcategories, such as cash discounts and standard discounts.
**In France, it is a regulated market and the shelf price = SRP.

Within each market, the distributor needs to customize its terms with retailers, and will generally fix both the SRP and the DLP; however, the wholesale price/DLP may have significant discounts applied that can be sliced in a variety of ways. There may be standard discounts and rebates, which may be within a continuum (e.g., standard discounts within a band of 20–25%), or the formula may be quite complicated. Some markets may apply layers of discounts, applying at chain level and tied to variables such as cash payment/payment terms. Accordingly, historical relationships, retailer-level commitment to placement and marketing, trading terms, payment terms, volumes ordered, and return provisions all factor into the relationship matrix and ultimate per unit/per retailer pricing structure.

Another factor that is quickly impacting pricing patterns is the Internet. By cutting out the middleman certain e-tailers can effectively undercut traditional retail pricing. This puts pressure on margins, which comes back to the distributor in the form of physical retailers wanting additional discounts. In markets where differential dealer pricing based on volume commitments is legal, this can create enormous challenges in managing the market.

Video Economics and Why Video Revenues are Uniquely Profitable to Studios

The video business has emerged as a kind of hidden caryatid holding up the theatrical film business on the back of its retail sales. While there is a general awareness of the importance of the video revenue stream (~50% of the total revenue pie), what is less understood is that video is uniquely profitable for distributors and accordingly provides the studios with its most important source of positive cash flow.

Video Revenues

Video/DVD revenues have become so significant that they represent a critical if not the primary hedge strategy against the risk of making a film. There is an assumed floor for video units and even a movie with disappointing box office results can earn significant video revenue.

How video revenues are calculated depends upon one's participation deal. From a studio standpoint, the calculation is straightforward:

$$(\text{dealer price}) \times (\text{net units sold}) = \text{Video Gross Revenues}$$

However, video revenues as regards third parties are often calculated on a royalty basis. This is the case for most participations (see later cash flow discussion) as well as in licensee arrangements. In the case of a studio licensing video rights to a third party in a territory where they do not distribute directly, the third party licensee is likely to account and pay on a royalty/unit basis. (See the next section for further discussion on the basis and structuring of royalty payments.)

Video Royalty Theory and Influence on Cash Flow

When the VHS video business first launched videos were likened to an ancillary revenue stream such as soundtrack records. Following the record model, the conventional method of paying producers and artists was on a royalty theory: 20% of video revenues would be put into the general pot out of which profits would be paid. Seen generally as found money, this methodology was accepted and only later became the bane of artists who felt unfairly compensated from the windfall studios were making on video sales. This remains an undercurrent of guild-studio tensions in residual negotiations, where guilds are wary of leaving Internet and other new media revenues on the table and repeating the sins of video deals past (see Chapter 7 for further discussion).

This royalty theory and calculation is a fundamental element in the calculation of net profits (see Chapter 10). In a typical studio definition of net profits, video is accounted for only based upon the 20% royalty from video net revenues. The other 80% of revenues are simply kept by the video distributor, creating a significant stream of free cash flow.

Why Uniquely Profitable — At Least in Perception

Video divisions appear uniquely profitable for two simple reasons. First, pursuant to accounting for revenues on a royalty only, the vast majority of revenues are shielded from participations and kept captive for the distributor. Second, as an ancillary revenue the video division is not directly responsible for production costs; the division applies a gross margin calculation that in terms of content production generally only accounts for video transfer and mastering costs, as well as the creation of any bonus material. (Note: The studio accounting divisions will, however, keep track of all costs and revenues for creating film ultimates.)

Once fixed costs of mastering, authoring, and compressing material are recouped, video profits are based on the variable costs of manufacturing and selling through units.

Setting Royalty Rates

While true revenue sharing breaks down video economics based on line-item revenues and costs, many video deals are royalty based and do not go into this level of detail and accounting. In fact, many

212

royalty negotiations are simply haggling over a percentage or two, with the parties recognizing bands of historical rates or perhaps reverting to custom. However, there is grounded economic reasoning underlying rates, even if actual negotiations fail to delve into the detail. In theory, it is possible to deduct the assumed costs from wholesale revenue and arrive at an amount of profits available on a per unit basis. From this number, the parties can then negotiate a percentage split of profits; the percentage that the producer keeps could then be expressed instead as a royalty based on the wholesale number. For example:

Retail Cost	$24.99
Dealer Price	$14.99 (at about 60%)
Cost of Goods	$ 3.50 (estimate COGS)
Other Costs	$ 1.00
Marketing	$ 2.25 (assume 15%)
Profit remaining	$ 8.24 (about 55% gross margin)

From this available profit, the distributor and producer will share in an agreed proportion; in this example, at a 50/50 split the producer would keep $4.12 as its profit/contribution. Another way to arrive at this figure would be to ask what royalty rate on the dealer price would the producer need to receive the same profit? The answer is a royalty of about 27.5% (0.275 × 14.99 = $4.12). Similarly, if it were agreed that the producer should keep 60% of the profits, then the royalty rate would edge up to almost 33% [(0.60 × $8.24)/$14.99)]. What percentage each party keeps is the subject of negotiation and should reflect the relative values of what each is contributing. This is simpler in theory than practice when needing to weigh the relative value of content contribution versus distribution and perhaps financing.

While there can be many other factors in the negotiation, at minimum this is a credible way of examining how to split the pie. Moreover, even though this calculation is based on a myriad of assumptions, it has the end logic of simplicity. All the parties need to track is the wholesale price and the units sold in order to calculate, report, and pay a participation. This is infinitely simpler and less controversial than tracking all revenue and cost categories; moreover, it likely avoids auditing costs, which can multiply exponentially when adding on the complexity of multiple countries and currency conversions. (See Chapter 10, Section Online Accounting: Simple

Revenue Sharing and the Net Profits Divide for a discussion regarding Internet revenue sharing versus royalty accounting.)

Advances and Recoupment

Once a royalty rate is set, the other key item to agree on is an advance, if any. An advance will likely be due if the product is an acquisition. The amount of the advance will be a relatively simple calculation matching the expected unit sales times the revenue that will be due based on those sales—again this is an easier calculation if it is based on a royalty per unit. The variables will be the royalty rate and the unit assumptions and then what percentage of the total expected value should be covered by a minimum guarantee.

The next step is confirming out of which revenues the distributor will then recoup the guarantee paid. If it is a 50/50 costs off the top split of revenues deal, then it will take twice as long to recoup/reach overages than if the recoupment were out of 100% of revenues earned. This example, however, assumes a straight sharing without factoring in a fee. No distributor would likely agree to pay an advance, recoup the advance, and then start sharing profits without ever having taken a fee.

A further wrinkle on this is preventing a fee on a fee scenario (i.e., double dipping). The following is an example:

$300,000 advance and a 20% fee
20% fee on the advance = $60,000
20% fee with a $300,000 advance = $375 to recoup, for it takes $375,000 of gross to recoup the advance plus the fee
Advance
1 − fee = gross necessary to recoup plus fee
300/(1 − .20) = 375

Video P&L

Figure 5.3 is a hypothetical video P&L, which further exhibits the complexity of gauging the net profit amount and why royalties, being much easier to calculate and track, are instead frequently used. Additionally, below I describe in more detail several of the line-item cost categories.

Video Costs

Probably the best way to illustrate video costs is to walk through the costs at various stages of exploiting a new release DVD title. I will

REVENUE SIDE	Deescription	Sample	Assumptions
Gross Units			
Rental	actual number of units shipped into the rental store channel	100,000	
Sell Through	actual number units shipped into retail via direct accounts or wholesalers	900,000	
		1,000,000	
Gross Revenues			$19.99 Shelf from
Rental	simple formula of wholesale price multiplied by number of units		$26.99 SRP
Sell Through	simple formula of wholesale price multiplied by number of units		
		$16,000,000	$16/unit wholesale
Deductions from Gross			
Returns	returns either from defective units, or from accounts with returns rights	180,000	assume 20%
Rebates	POS rebate incentives, or overall adjustments to wholesale price		(of sell through #)
Price Protection	$ credited to lower COGs on unsold retail inventory, enabling price drop		
Net Units			
Rental	Units net of returns: units either sold through or not returned/returnable	100,000	
Sell Through	Units net of returns: units either sold through or not returned/returnable	720,000	
		820,000	
Net Revenue			assume ~60% SRP
Rental	Adjusted net wholesale price multiplied by net units		($16 wholesale price)
Sell Through	Adjusted net wholesale price multiplied by net units		
TOTAL		$13,120,000	DP x Net Units
	[note: another category could be revenue share]		
COST SIDE	[exclusive of creation of product and any value added material]		
Manufacturing Expenses			on gross units:
Mastering and Menus	Navigation interfaces and menus		
Replication/Duplication	physical cost of creating the DVD disc		
Packaging	the physical cost of labels, paper/sleeves		
Cases and assembly	the physical cost of the plastic box/case		
Misc. (returns, obsolesence)			
Distribution Expenses			
Assemble and sort ("Pick and pack")	supply chain cost of sorting and customizing units for delivery		
Shipping (freight)	physical cost of transport and delivery to customer		
Returns costs	cost of taking back and processing returns back into inventory		
Merchandising	rackjobber costs who manage in-store displays and placement		
Miscellaneous (customer admin)			
		$3,000,000	assume ~$3/unit
Marketing Expenses			On gross units
Trade Marketing	marketing to DVD/video accounts (e.g.Best Buy, Wal-Mart, Blockbuster)		
Advertsing (sales kits, etc.)	sales materials for the trade		
Point of Purchase (POP)	in store marketing elements, such as standees, counter pieces, posters		
Consumer Marketing			
Advertising (on and offline media)	TV, radio and online spots/banners (cost of creation and placement)		
Promotion and Publicity	Press junkets, PR costs, hard costs of talent/exec travel to promote		
Research costs	Cost of pricing studies, focus groups, etc.		
		$3,200,000	assume ~$3.20/unit
Sales Expenses			(20% of $16 DP)
Market Development Funds (MDF)	% of revenue allocation to aid retailer marketing and promotion efforts		
Co-op advertising	similar to MDF, but tied to actual media placement (e.g., a retailer ad)		
Trade Shows	allocated costs of attending trade shows: advance showing of product		
Miscellaneous (eg., mailers)			
		$960,000	assume 5-6% of GR
Total Net Expenses		$7,160,000	
Total Net Revenues		$13,120,000	
- Total Net Expenses		$7,160,000	
= Total Net Profit/Contribution Margin		$5,960,000	

Figure 5.3

break this into three sections: building and encoding the DVD material, manufacturing the DVD, and marketing and distributing the DVD. Paralleling the complexity of the DVD supply chain, the logistics of creating, manufacturing, and fulfilling DVD orders is a complicated process. The DVD is an inherently complex product and the physical plants are high-tech, secure, impressive facilities that rival the efficiency of any assembly line.

Building and Encoding DVD Material

The first stage consists of two parts: what material will physically appear on the DVD, and how will that material be converted to compressed digital form. Regarding the materials, it is important to recognize on the cost side that a DVD involves much more than simply transferring a film or TV show to the DVD. The value of the market and ability to tinker after the fact have created a consumer value proposition mandating that the DVD (for a major title) offers something extra. That something extra includes vast amounts of VAM as well as navigation. The entry point to a DVD is called the menu, and each major DVD has a uniquely produced menu and interface to enhance the experience. This is the interface screen that asks whether you want to watch widescreen or pan and scan (if the particular DVD gives you a choice), has a play button, and lists the other options that the particular DVD may give you. This can include traveling to all sorts of VAM, jumping to specific chapters, hearing director or talent commentary, or altering the presentation settings.

All of these choices are then integrated to a user-friendly environment that will thematically pull from the title. The page may be static, scrolling, or may have visual cut scenes that play and then dissolve into the static menu page. All of this obviously takes time and money, and depending on the budget and consumer expectations very significant sums can be spent creating additional material and the navigational interface through which the consumer can explore the hours of extra content. Because of these features the DVD has become an interactive product, allowing the viewer to customize its viewing experience and delve into extra features that can be much longer than the actual content around which this VAM is built. It is not unusual for a major two-hour film to come with four or more hours of so-called "bonus material."

Once all the elements are set (the title, the menus, and the bonus material), then all the material needs to be encoded. This step is called authoring and compression, which is technical lingo for transferring the material to the digital medium. There are specific authoring and compression houses who bid out product and create the masters from which the DVDs are then replicated. There has been a natural consolidation of video replicators and compression houses; in fact, some of the replicators have acquired authoring companies

216

thus allowing them to offer customers one-stop shopping through the production chain.

The cost of authoring and compression has come down over time with both improvements in technology and competition. One of the more significant costs comes from the international side, where different language masters require several different masters to be configured, authored, and compressed.

Manufacturing the DVD

Manufacturing costs are broken out into pennies– and pennies matter in a business with slim replication margins and unit volumes that can be in the several millions. Like any other good, the manufacturing costs are a roll-up of lots of sub costs, since every DVD is customized.

As a rule of thumb, usually half to more than half of the total costs come from the physical replication of the disc and the cost of the plastic DVD case (amaray case). What the actual disc costs are per unit will vary according to vendors and market conditions. Many studios have overall long-term deals with replicators. The vendors benefit from having secure capacity filled, and the studios benefit by incentives to lock up their business. If a distributor is able to bid out replication on the so-called spot market, they may or may not strike opportunistic deals. If the manufacturing is in the peak period where every studio is pumping out DVDs for the fourth quarter gift season, and capacity is constrained, then costs may go up. However, depending on the replicator, its particular flow of product from its studio deals may be up or down depending on the actual title performance (does the studio have three hit titles or three dogs) and pricing may fluctuate given the actual capacity expected. One thing is for certain: every studio wants secure capacity with the absolute lowest price, which virtually ensures a consistently competitive market.

217

The following are examples of the types of elements in the manufacturing process that go into assembling a finished goods price:

- Physical disc replication, which price may vary by the memory size of the DVD
- Price of the amaray case
- Costs to create/print menus, sleeves, and then insert the material into the case
- Spine labels
- Security tags (different retailers may require different tags/configurations)
- Booklet and disc insertion

- Shrink wrapping the finished product
- External stickers
- Bar codes
- Freight costs for delivery (if distribution bundled with manufacturing costs)

The above is the baseline, as the process can become more complicated for special gift SKUs, bundling product together (e.g., pack in toy), or special cases.

One great advantage of DVDs is that the physical replication costs are low when compared to making a VHS tape. The costs have come down dramatically over time, so not only are more DVD units of a title being sold, but the margins based on manufacturing alone are significantly up. The timing, product, and type of DVD (e.g., DVD 9 or 5) can all influence price. As noted previously, this is a negotiation of pennies, and it is the pennies that ultimately determine the margin and profitability of the DVD duplicator.

Electronic Sell Through Advantage

One compelling argument for downloads is the elimination of nearly all of the foregoing costs. Although limited costs, such as compression, remain, the cost reductions in delivery via electronic sell through drop directly to the bottom line. The issue is then whether the same product is being delivered and therefore whether pricing should be reduced. Often downloads are priced the same as physical copies, but with no physical costs and without VAM digital goods should cost less and yet yield the same or greater margins. As discussed in Chapter 7, given how new this area is, and until competition further develops, download services will likely continue to charge these premiums as they build market share and amortize backend infrastructure. However, over the long run the pricing relative to costs is not rational and we will see prices coming down including differentiated pricing based on the quality and volume of material.

Marketing and Distributing the DVD

(Note: The following is a summary overview of some key costs, but for a more complete discussion see Chapter 9.)

Marketing of DVDs entails two primary costs. The first is the consumer marketing and advertising campaign costs borne by the studio distributor. This entails the same types of categories as theatrical marketing, ranging from print ads to TV spots to online promotion. Beyond paid-for media, advertising costs (again like theatrical) also include posters, trailers, press/PR activity, and even junkets. As the upside for DVDs has grown, the marketing campaigns have become that much more complex—often planned months if not a year in advance of the release.

The other major cost category is trade marketing, given the importance of incentivizing retailers both to execute at point-of-purchase and to advertise themselves, utilizing DVD product to attract store traffic. As mentioned earlier, distributors will therefore offer market development fund and cooperative advertising allowances that the retailers may spend on in-store campaigns, circular advertising, and general promotions. These sums are variable and tied to a percentage of wholesale revenues: the more units bought, the more money available for promotion.

Sometimes with a significant enough title the retail campaign can also be stimulated with customized product or tie-ins. These can take the form of retailer exclusives, special product SKUs (e.g., double packs, packed in merchandise), and rebate programs. If programs are customized by the retailer, then a key customer such as Wal-Mart may be able to differentiate its offer and advertising, creating an incentive for the chain to advertise the product and perhaps feature the unique SKU in circulars. There is no limit to tie-ins, and with the release of the DVD for Star Wars Episode III Fox and Lucasfilm executed a unique program with Best Buy involving the Donald Trump television hit *The Apprentice*; the task for the contestants on the show was to build a display that would showcase Episode III and related product (Star Wars video game) at Best Buy stores, and then a version of the winning team's display would be utilized in select Best Buy retail outlets.

Finally, in very limited instances there may be the potential for promotional partners, akin to theatrical tie-ins. It is the bane of video marketing chiefs that despite the absolute size of video revenues, and the critical importance of DVD sales in the life cycle of any title, that such deals are the exception and not routine. DVD sales simply do not piggyback on marketing waves of theatrical release scale and are still largely viewed by consumer brands as ancillary.

The Future of Video

Technology is ever marching on and impacting the future of video; in fact, as quickly as DVDs appeared it is possible to imagine them becoming as extinct as video.

219

iPods and other digital storage devices demonstrate how DVDs could become supplanted with hardware capable of holding vast digital files. Imagine your library of DVDs all on one machine or storage box ... an iPod can hold your library of music CDs, your lifetime collection of photographs, and in the future your DVD collection. Conceptually, it is only a matter of storage, and already companies such as Amazon are building and offering so-called digital lockers (see Chapter 7).

What all of these options will do to the DVD world is a matter of speculation. People still love browsing book stores and there is an element of passion in collecting DVDs; however, it seems unlikely that the desire to collect boxes or a preference for physical artwork over thumbnails are strong enough forces to hold back the convenience (and arguably, inevitability) of digital copies. One countering force is retail pressure, as key chains will have every incentive to slow the shift and try to thwart the demise of a multi-billion dollar product line. Whether, or how long, the DVD can co-exist with the next generation of VOD and digital storage devices is ultimately up to the consumer, and as discussed in Chapter 7, it is not clear whether the entertainment pie will be expanded or could in fact contract.

I asked long-term industry veteran Louis Feola, president of Paramount's made-for-video division (Paramount Famous Productions) and former president of Universal Home Entertainment, how quickly he expected the full digital transition to take place:

The film and television industry has endured a century of new delivery systems that upon their introductions were predicted to displace prior points of distribution. It was the rarest of situations when that actually occurred quickly. Whether it be DVD or the new Blu-ray DVD system, the same is true when faced with competition from the Internet and digital delivery. The fact that the industry is creating additional content and crossing the widget with online activities will enhance their co-existence. No one can predict the future with absolute certainty, but in the short to midterm brick & mortar and electronic will co-exist.

Online Impact

- An entirely new category of "video distribution" has emerged in the form of downloads, with purchases via an iPod or other system now labeled as "electronic sell through."
- "E-tailers" like Amazon have developed a significant market share and are pioneering new ownership constructs, such as the ability to purchase content and maintain it in a remote digital locker; e-tailers are also putting pressure on retail pricing (given lower cost structure), as well as enabling new predictive release metrics via pre-order commitments.
- VOD services are threatening the existence of video rental, the sector that launched and once was the entire video business.
- Hybrid services such as Netflix, which combines online ordering with old world mail delivery, are adapting and introducing direct at-home VOD delivery applications converting large video rental businesses into a form of VOD; additionally, online outlets are enabling greater depth of available titles given the elimination of physical shelf space constraints
- Linked online applications enable interactivity, such as a Blue-ray feature allowing a "live" version, where you can watch a movie along with the director who is simultaneously commenting.
- Piracy concerns from file sharing are, similar to the theatrical market, leading to more front-loaded day-and-date releases and the compression of the video sales cycle.

221

CHAPTER 6

Television Distribution

The TV market is both a primary and secondary platform for content. Although TV is traditionally thought about in terms of TV series and other made-for-television productions, TV programming is a quilt that also relies heavily on other product. Accordingly, beyond analyzing first run programming, to understand the entire economic picture it is also important to review how television garners revenues for films and other intellectual properties that can be aired on television but were not originally produced for television broadcast.

This chapter focuses on traditional television, namely free television (commonly referred to as free over-the-air broadcast television) and cable/pay television. New technologies, such as cable video-on-demand (VOD) and Internet streaming and downloads, are blurring the lines of what has historically been categorized as "television," (see Figure 6.1) and this blurring and the emerging new media platforms for TV programming are only touched upon here and then discussed in greater detail in Chapter 7. It is worth noting up front, however, that the very nature of what we perceive as "TV" is changing so rapidly that by the end of this century's first decade the landscape will likely have completely transformed from what existed just a few years ago. Simply look at the new points of access that already exist (see Figure 6.2):

222

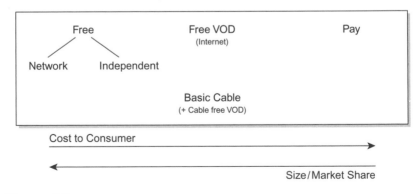

Types of Television

Figure 6.1

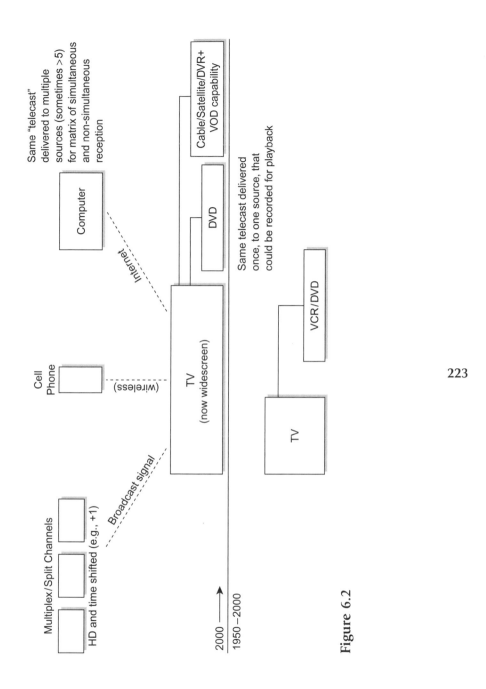

Figure 6.2

Against this backdrop, there are evident challenges including windowing as well as forecasting whether and how fast new media revenue streams will mature. I asked Gary Marenzi, President, MGM Worldwide Television, how he viewed this new landscape and how television distributors were adapting and tempering enthusiasm for new revenue streams versus the proven sources:

> We truly believe that digital/online enabled platforms will become a major source of revenue for us within the next five years, as the research about viewing habits shows that most people under the age of 30 are already utilizing their computers and mobile devices as their primary sources of video content. But while we welcome this growth from the digital/online areas, we need to also protect our traditional sources of revenue coming from "linear" television. We'll do this by adapting our windowing pattern to favor the medium that provides us with the most immediate financial reward and perhaps by even creating slightly different versions of each program for each medium. We'll also weigh the value of exclusive vs. non-exclusive licensing of our content across all media, as the key for us is to maintain the value of our programming for every potential audience.

224

Free Television (United States)

Free Television Market Segmentation

Free National Networks

The market is divided into terrestrial over-the-air national networks (NBC, CBS, ABC, and Fox) and cable or satellite delivered television stations. Networks are somewhat complicated entities, however, in that a network is really a grouping of local television stations that are either owned by or affiliated with the parent network company. The FCC regulates station ownership to protect against the concentration of media ownership within markets, a construct that may become moot as market shares continue to erode and access to media from online and other sources becomes ubiquitous. There are several regulations, but the critical ones governing television station ownership are:

- National TV Ownership Rule: prohibits an entity from owning television stations that would reach more than 39% of US television households.
- Local TV Multiple Ownership Rule: allows an entity to own two television stations in the same designated market area (DMA; as defined by Nielsen Media Research) provided threshold minimum of other stations in the market remain and at least one of the stations is not ranked among the four highest ranked stations in the DMA.
- Dual TV Ownership Rule: prohibits a merger between or among these four television networks: ABC, CBS, Fox, and NBC.[1]

Accordingly, the "big" networks are an aggregation of owned local TV broadcasters and affiliated stations, which cover all the major DMAs and reach nearly all the potential households in the United States (see Table 6.1).

The "network" only programs a certain amount of airtime for simulcast on a national basis, which generally includes the national news and a primetime schedule of three hours in the evening. In terms of original programming, this translates into around 22 hours/week (3 hours Monday–Saturday, 4 hours Sunday, excepting Fox which broadcasts an hour less in primetime). This is among the reasons why NBC's announcement at the end of 2008, amid the economic downturn, to eliminate original scripted programming in its 10:00 pm hour (EST/PST) was so dramatic (shifting a new Jay Leno talk show to its third primetime hour); this represents a shift of 5 hours out of 22, nearly a quarter reduction in original programming.

The affiliates are generally obligated to run the network programming during these hours, but for the balance of the schedule they have a measure of flexibility whether or not to take the network offered programming. The network actually markets and sells to its affiliates, trying to convince them to come on board for its slate. Economically there are strong incentives to stay consistent with programming: the local affiliates gain the benefit of the brand (e.g., ABC or NBC), and the more shows it programs from the parent the stronger and more consistent the brand. From the network's standpoint, it wants national coverage for its programming and will therefore incentivize the local stations to stay loyal to its slate.

Local Independent Stations
Alongside affiliate stations that make up a national network, there remain many local independent television stations. The recent

225

Table 6.1 Table of Broadcast Television Networks[1a]

Television Network	Founded	% of US Households Reached	# of Households Viewable	Type of Network	# of Full-power Affiliates	# of Low-power Affiliates & Transmitters
PBS	1969	≈99.00	≈105,579,120	Non-profit	349	≈342
ABC	1948	96.75	103,179,600	Commercial	229	≈266
NBC	1946	97.17	103,624,370	Commercial	226	≈338
CBS	1948	96.98	103,421,270	Commercial	215	≈299
Fox	1986	96.18	102,565,710	Commercial	203	≈202
The CW	September 18, 2006	96.18	102,565,710	Commercial	158+5 Cable-only stations	≈11

Excludes My Network TV.

disbanding of The WB and UPN (2006) for the new CW network freed up several local affiliates, creating a boon for the independent market, which for years had been in decline. In the 1980s and the early 1990s there was a plethora of strong independents, fueling off-network syndication opportunities, but the growth of networks such as UPN, WB, and Fox gobbled up the prime independents and relegated much syndication to an afterthought following cable options. It will be interesting to watch whether the freeing up of stations revives the moribund syndication market, or whether new grabs such as Fox's MyNetwork TV (launched 2006) aggregate the key remaining independents and relegate syndication to an ever smaller niche.

Cable Networks

There are currently over 200 cable stations in the United States, with top tiered channels bundled in "basic" carriage packages such that popular networks (e.g., Discovery Channel, ESPN, TNT, and USA) are provided in the overall fee charged to the consumer. This is distinguished from "premium cable," for which the consumer pays a direct incremental fee for access to specific premium channels such as HBO (so-called premium pay cable).

With the increased penetration of cable and satellite, many larger media companies have diversified programming by creating niche or specialized channels, and as in the broadcast space the independents have largely been consolidated. Examples of cable networks with national reach that are part of larger media groups include USA, Sci-fi, Bravo (under the GE/NBC affiliated family), Comedy Central, Nickelodeon, Noggin, Spike, MTV (under the MTV Networks/Viacom family), CNN, TBS, TNT, TMC (under the Warners family), Fox Sports, FX (under the Fox/NewsCorp family), and ESPN, The Disney Channel, ABC Family (under the Disney umbrella). A good resource for television programming issues and for identifying a complete list of networks is the publication *Broadcasting & Cable* (see broadcastandcable.com, which lists upwards of 250 channels/networks). Beyond the pattern of large media producers developing or acquiring cable outlets for their content, it may be a new trend to see pure play cable operators owning the cable networks carried over their pipe, in essence incubating their own viewers. Comcast, for example, is the parent to a variety of fledgling services including The Golf Channel, E! Entertainment, G4 (merged with the acquired Tech TV), and OLN (outdoor living network, re-branded Fine Living).

Free Video-on-Demand and Internet Access — What Does Free TV Mean?

It used to be that "TV was only TV," but with the advent of advertising supported Internet access, such as offered by Hulu, and cable free VOD (FVOD), the lines are blurring. In contracts, attorneys have to grapple with whether TV should be delineated by delivery mechanisms (e.g., analog, digital, free-over-the-air, terrestrial, satellite), and now dealmakers and attorneys alike need to categorize Internet streaming and other on-demand access. If a network such as NBC makes a show available for free Internet access on a non-NBC-branded site such as Hulu, or ABC makes a primetime show available via abc.com, or CBS makes its primetime series available for free viewing on cable free-on-demand, how should these be characterized?

As a consumer, you can access *The Office, Desperate Housewives,* or *CSI* for no additional charge and watch the same programming with the same or in most cases fewer commercials. Because the start time for access is in the viewer's control (and the site even perhaps embedded into a personalized page on a social networking Web site), it is a form of VOD; moreover, because this VOD is not transaction based (i.e., no direct fee to the viewer), but is advertising supported, it is coming to be known as advertising supported VOD (AVOD), a subset of FVOD. (Note: See Chapter 8 for more discussion on transactional VOD.) Whatever the label, free viewing at one's election is competitive with free viewing in accordance with a broadcaster's schedule.

Free TV is therefore becoming categorized not so much by where or how one watches, but whether the content is TV-branded and produced (so-called premium content). In the future, free TV will ultimately only mean programming broadcast on TV (or perhaps debuted or simultaneously launched on TV) in addition to being made available via other outlets, thus turning everything on its head. Today we think of the other markets as emerging and competitive to TV, but if and when content is everywhere then free TV will become the limiting not the defining factor, because unlike other platforms broadcasters have retail-like limited shelf space: just compare 22 hours of primetime versus an infinite range of choice on demand or via the Internet. The fact that a program at least was aired or launched on TV, or was produced for TV, may become the defining element of whether it falls within the notion of TV at all.

228

Distribution Patterns and Windows: The Decline of Ratings for Theatrical Feature Films on TV and Evolution of the Market

Historical Window Patterns and New Technology Influence on Runs

The market for feature films on TV has historically been very strong, and for years a key sales benchmark was a license to one of the major national networks. In the best of scenarios, the market even provides four successive TV windows, allowing for millions of dollars continually flowing in for well over a decade:

- 12–18 month window on pay television (e.g., HBO, Showtime, Starz)
- 3–4 year window on network TV (e.g., NBC, ABC, CBS, Fox)
- Multi-year window on cable TV
- Multi-year window in syndication

Assuming this historical pattern, a theatrical feature film will typically be licensed to a broadcast network for debut approximately three years after its theatrical release. This allows an exclusive period for the theatrical run, followed by the primary video window and a pay TV license (see schematic in Chapter 1). The so-called network window has generally been the most lucrative, as the networks simply had a larger reach and audience share and could therefore pay more with the larger advertising revenues earned. To the extent value is allocated over runs, the initial airing would command the greatest value because audience ratings usually show a decline with each successive airing. Accordingly, network licenses are customarily for relatively short periods and limited numbers of runs, such as for three or four runs over three or four years. Depending on the film, the first run, if not all of the runs, will usually be in primetime.

The Internet and digital technology are complicating even this relatively simple construct as the definition of a "run" (i.e., telecast) is transforming. If a broadcaster has a multiplex channel, such as NBC and NBC HD, are simulcasts on each only one run? What if there are time-delayed digital channels, such as is commonplace in Europe, where the entire channel is shifted an hour or two (e.g., ITV +1), thus expanding the hours programming is broadcast (program X is on at 9:00 pm on channel Y, and again at 10:00 pm on channel Y+1, with Y+1 the exact feed/programming as Y just shifted back an hour). Is

229

the +1 run considered part of the other run, or separate? And, finally, what about free streaming VOD repeats on the Internet, where a show may be available for a limited time (sometimes referred to as a "catch-up") after the TV broadcast, allowing viewers to see the show if they missed it live or did not record it? Are catch-up runs separate runs, or is a run the live broadcast plus a week's catch-up access?

Setting the evolving and boggling matrix of the definition of a run aside, in certain instances, with exceptional films, the license may specify exact airing windows such as around a holiday period or in a cross-promotional window if the movie is tied to a larger franchise. This was the case with Steven Spielberg's classic *ET*, where Sears sponsored the broadcasts and the film was licensed to play as a perennial on Thanksgiving. In the instance of a film series, such as James Bond, Star Wars, or Harry Potter, the license may be structured (or broadcasters may simply structure their schedules) so that airings take place around the promotional window for an upcoming new film in the franchise. Some believe that such an airing could detract from the theatrical release, but others ascribe to the theory that the TV broadcast helps cross-promote the film, and the film's marketing platform in turn helps cross-promote the TV broadcast.

230

Decline in Ratings for Films on TV

It is an acknowledged fact that ratings for films on TV have declined over time, and there are several factors frequently pointed to explaining the slide. Among these are the growth of DVD, the growth of other media options such as the Internet, fragmentation of the TV market with the growth of cable, waning tolerance for viewing films with commercial breaks, the ability to consume the film earlier via ancillary platforms such as VOD and PPV, the changing profile of network scheduling and programming (e.g., reality craze), and of course piracy.

It is no doubt also true that before the growth of the home video market TV had a more dominating impact: there was a large audience that had never seen the movie, and no matter how big a film was at the theater, the reach of tens of millions of eyeballs on TV inevitably dwarfed the numbers that had physically seen the movie in cinemas. With movies now selling on DVDs in the millions (and the expansion of other ancillary windows including VOD and PPV allowing earlier consumption), clearly prior exposure and time delay have contributed to the decline in ratings of films on TV. In the 1980s when a film played on television, this was its first and primary exposure after the movie theater; now, however, by the time a film is on free television years downstream from its theatrical release there have been innumerable opportunities to "consume" the movie on a variety of platforms.

Shared Windows, Shorter Network Licenses, and Clout of Cable

With the decline in network clout and the growth of cable channels, the traditional sequential TV windows are becoming more of an historical artifact. There are, of course, cases where films go to network and then cable and then syndication; however, it is now common for cable stations to buy-out network windows or to partner with networks on shared long-term windows with oscillating periods of exclusivity. The playing field is relatively level and cable stations like FX, USA/Sci-Fi, TBS/TNT, Spike, Bravo, and ABC Family can compete with and in cases are the frontrunners to the networks, even in cases where the networks may be an affiliated sister company. Because the licensors are trying to garner the best deal for their specific film or package, the best option may cut across different studio lines and strange bedfellows can emerge.

Ranges of fees are tightly guarded, but Table 6.2 outlines several high-profile deals over the last few years, and also illustrates how some films will share windows between cable and networks.

It is also worth highlighting that with the growing clout of cable, and especially in hybrid licenses where cable stations and networks may share runs, the licensed runs and period for networks are shrinking. Whereas it may have been typical to take three to four runs, scenarios now arise where a network may only take one or two runs.

Star Wars Example

I was personally involved in overseeing the licensing of the six *Star Wars* movies to TV. As of 2005, none of the films had aired on cable or syndication for several years, and Episode III, which was just launching in theaters, had obviously never been licensed to television. Given the unique nature of the saga, and knowing that there were no more sequel motion pictures planned for the future, it made sense to explore licensing all six films together. The highlight would be the television premiere of Episode III, supported with the first TV window for all of the films together. The final deal was made with Spike, a relatively new cable network under the ownership of MTV Networks/ Viacom, which catered to a male-skewing audience. Spike had rebranded itself as "the network for men," in contrast to women's branded networks such as Oxygen or Lifetime. The network had a variety of programming, but had been successful with franchise

231

Table 6.2 Movie Licensing Fees

Film	Network	License Fee	Term	Source	Windowing/Notes
Spider-Man	Fox and TNT/TBS	$60M			
Spider-Man 2	FBC and FX	$50M	10 years	HR 6/30/04 and Variety 6/29/04	Rumored carve outs for a second network window after first 3 years
Shrek	NBC	$30M		HR 6/30/04	
The Longest Yard	TBS/TNT and CBS	$27M	10 years	Variety 5/25/05	Windowed 5 years to TBS, then 1 year to CBS, then back to TBS multiple years, then back to CBS
Sahara	TBS/TNT and ABC	$10M	TNT 4 years, then ABC 1 year	Variety 5/25/05	
War of the Worlds	TNT and ABC	$25M	7+ years	Variety 8/26/06	5 years initially, split 3 to ABC, 2 to TNT, between first and second HBO pay window; then additional years on both ABC and TNT. Deal likely 7–10 yrs total
King Kong (P. Jackson)	TNT and ABC	$26.5M	8+ years	Variety 2/14/06	Noted $22M TNT first 6 mo. + 50 mo. post ABC; ABC $4.5M for 3 runs over 3 years following initial TNT exclusive window
Superman Returns	FX	$17–25M		Variety 1/11/06	FX bought out window pre film's release in June 2006
Hitch	TBS	$25M		Variety 1/30/07	
The Pursuit of Happyness	TNT and TBS	$25M+	6 years	Variety 1/30/07	$30M package including Open Season and The Holiday; The Holiday also sold to Lifetime for $1.5M for two 1-year windows, first one following year 3 on TBS

exploitation having been the home to the James Bond films. I cannot comment on the specifics of the deal, but it was significant, and *Variety* (without confirmation from either Lucasfilm or Spike) reported the package as being sold for $70M.[2]

I relate this story not as a travelogue of deals past, but as an example of how interesting the TV market can be. At the outset of this deal it probably would have been fair for analysts to speculate that the films would go to Fox, as historically movies of this stature would only debut on network; in fact Episodes I and II had debuted on Fox. Cable had grown to a point, however, and the market had changed substantially enough, that Episode III, the film with by far the biggest box office of 2005 ($380M US and $848M globally) and within the top ten box office films of all time (as of 2005 number 7 all time), was licensed to premiere on Spike.

There is no doubt this formerly network dominated business had experienced a seismic shift when Lord of the Rings premiered on TNT and Star Wars on Spike. This is also a sign of healthy competition as the big four networks and cable channels jockey for positioning and programming.

233

Economics and Pattern of Licensing Feature Films for TV Broadcast

Films were historically licensed in large packages. The size of packages could vary dramatically, from a few films to hundreds — a traditional studio package of films would often include 25+ films. A buyer would acquire all the titles for a "package price," with the titles having (usually) common numbers of runs and a common license period. There were always a couple of key lead titles, and buyers would be faced with the dilemma of potentially having to acquire a bunch of secondary titles simply to acquire the few titles they really wanted to program. With deals often going out several years, and with lots of airtime to fill up, this scheme satisfied buyers and sellers for years. The top pictures would be programmed in premiere slots, where premiums could be charged for commercial spots, and the other pictures could be used at off-peak times or even as filler. The art of valuing pictures within a multiple picture package lies somewhere between absolute logic and litigation.

Packages are still common, but as buyers have become more selective the number of pictures in those packages has shrunk, and the economics are more closely tied to true per picture valuations.

So, how do you value a license?

Runs and Term

The most critical elements are the number of runs and term. There are certain industry accepted benchmarks, and the jousting is then within these parameters. As noted previously for network television, licenses are usually for a small number or runs such as three or four. This is largely due to the fact, as earlier discussed, that the definition of "network" accounts for those hours that are programmed by the network as opposed to given back to the affiliates; this inherent limitation puts a cap on inventory and programming space. A second limitation is that films are long—with commercial breaks they take up a minimum of 2 hours of programming time, and can take up to 3-hour blocks. Completing the matrix is the fact of diminishing returns: ratings typically decline with subsequent broadcasts, echoing the general TV pattern of higher ratings for new episodes/programs than for repeats.

Add up the factors of (1) diminishing ratings with repeats + (2) limited inventory + (3) requirement of large chunks of prime programming inventory space and what you get is the need to space out broadcasts and cap runs. It does not really help to have the right to broadcast a film on network 10 times in 3 years because the network would never allocate that much space; the opportunity cost of foregoing a show that would likely draw higher ratings would force the network to omit runs. Moreover, for the licensor, if a film was played too frequently and the overexposure caused a severe dip in ratings then the future value would be diminished. Everyone would lose.

The result is a mutual desire to manage runs in a way that maximizes ratings and returns. As a rule of thumb, playing a film on network on average of more than once a year starts the downward spiral; accordingly, most network deals call for a couple of runs, and sometimes up to four, over a period of time that allows breathing room of on average at least a year between runs. A traditional network deal may therefore be structured as three or four runs over three or four years.

Cable licenses are more complicated, for there is more inventory space and the smaller audience share lends itself to more repeat viewings; cable, after all, grew up as a bastion for reruns and only in recent years have cable networks invested substantially in original programming to differentiate themselves. The pattern in cable is more dependent on the niche and individual station philosophy, and some stations will literally play programming to death. What is typical across all groups is that the average number of runs is substantially higher — it is not unusual to see film deals with 10 or more runs of a title per year. This allows the cable network great flexibility in programming, and enables customized blocks such as marathons, weeks focusing on subject matters, retrospectives, etc. The cable station is often branded as the "home of X," and for that to ring true it needs to appear enough to validate the identity. Airings once a year or so do not make sense, nor would there be (potentially) enough programming to fill up the schedule. As networks mature they often realize that they have the same vested interest in not overexposing a property and balance is ultimately struck.

It is important to note in this context that a run may not be what one expects of a single run; namely, before the layer of complexity created by Internet VOD or multiplexed channels, cable and pay TV required nuances on the notion of runs. A network run will be just as it sounds: a simultaneous broadcast aired by its network affiliates, run one time during the day. For cable, however, given the lower penetration and repeat programming as part of the landscape, runs may be defined similar to a pay television context with the use of exhibition days. An exhibition day is a 24-hour period (very specifically defined in a contract; for example, 12:00 am until 11:59 pm and then within the box defined as an exhibition day there may be multiple runs granted). Accordingly, the cable broadcaster may have the right to broadcast a title two or perhaps even three times within that single day. Often these runs are placed at unrelated times to fill up programming space, but in other instances there will be back-to-back runs (often marketed as an "encore" performance). The theory is that no viewer would watch the program twice in a day, and that the multiple start time schedule will not undermine the value: after all, there are only so many exhibition days allowed. So long as the number of exhibition days is within customary bounds, and likewise the number of runs permitted within each such exhibition day is standard, then this practice is generally accepted.

Setting License Fees

It is only after sorting out the runs and years that it can then make relative sense to value the corresponding license fee. That is why it is so difficult to make direct comparisons on TV deals: the playing field is not level. It is not like dealing with DVD units where there are bragging rights to absolute numbers (although this has its quirks, as discussed in Chapter 5, with performance influenced by pricing, returns, and inventory management) or the egalitarian barometer of box office. When you hear about a license value for a TV deal, it has to be put in context of how many runs, how many years, and was this a stand-alone or was an allocation of some sort involved. Moreover, in a world of relationships and horse trading, there may be political or timing elements that could further influence values.

Stripping out these other considerations, and looking purely at the underlying economics, the principles of valuing the license fee then becomes straightforward. The licensor will look to competitive product or historical licenses to set a range, and the licensee broadcaster will be running numbers on potential advertising revenues. The deal can thus be looked at on a macro level in terms of the gross fee, and then also be validated bottom up by analyzing on a per run basis (either straight-lining license fees per run or imputing a certain discount after a certain number of runs). At some level this can be over analyzed, because a buyer and seller will be negotiating here in a classic fashion trying to find common ground. Are you going to agree to $50,000 per run or not?

To gauge whether $50,000/run is fair value, if one side perceives there is too much of a gulf and they cannot agree on terms, then the negotiation may take on factors that apportion risk. This often takes two forms. First, a licensor may agree to a percentage of barter, such as a deal that is part cash and part barter. In this scenario a certain minimum guaranty is locked in for security, and the balance is tied to the ad sales. This is a cumbersome direction, for this requires being in the loop on the ad sales front as well as the determination and cost of potentially auditing the revenues. Another, and frankly easier path, may be tying overages or underages to ratings performance. If the fees are ultimately tied to a certain expectation level, then tying a bonus to over performing should protect both sides; the licensor will win by protecting an upside, and the broadcaster can easily afford the upside if they have earned a premium on the ad sales. Both of these scenarios significantly complicate a deal from a reporting, managing, and trust perspective.

Another method of valuation is simply to quote an industry-accepted range. On hit films it is sometimes quoted as a "rule of thumb" that the license fee should be in the range of 15% of domestic box office; however, this percentage cannot be relied upon as an accurate benchmark, and to the extent there is a benchmark range it tends to move over time. In the case of *Superman Returns*, *Variety* said of FX: "The network has agreed to pay Warner Bros. Domestic Cable about 12% of the eventual domestic gross, with a cap at between $17 million and $25 million, depending on the contract's length of term and on whether Warners finds another buyer to share the window with FX." In reporting the *War of the Worlds* deal *Variety* noted of the reputed $25M fee:

> That's a much lower stipend than the 15% of domestic box office, which used to be the benchmark for a successful theatrical-movie deal in the network window. But times have changed. Since "Worlds" has grossed more than $230M domestically, 15% would come to $34.5 million—an impossible figure for distributor DreamWorks to draw in a sluggish broadcast and cable marketplace for theatricals. ... Bowing to the new reality, distribs have put a cap on the total license fee, which can start as low as $22 million and rise to as high as $27 million a title, unless the buyer gets more runs and a longer exclusive license term.[3]

A final twist is licensing titles across channels within a larger group. If a particular film has crossover demographic appeal, together with a strong enough brand identity, then there may be a desire to play the title across multiple group affiliated networks. This obviously adds another wrinkle to the analysis and value for runs. Moreover, this is an area where analysis paralysis can loom, and from a macro point of view many will simply split this into network versus cable; namely, how many aggregated cable runs are required across various cable outlets. It may be that certain discounts are taken, or that certain outlets are either ignored (given limited reach) or excluded on grounds of fit (I do not want X on Y!). The primary impact of aggregating potential licensees is that the fee will usually increase given the greater exposure, and the time of the license will also be lengthened to allow for the title to be cycled through the different outlets without over saturating exposure both on a single outlet and across the group. While it was only the syndication market that traditionally had very long licenses, one may now see 10-year licenses in this context.

First Run TV Series

First run TV series tend to follow a regular cycle of development and launch tied to network seasons. Although the growth of cable, including powerful pay networks such as HBO, have altered this, and some networks have gone to a year-round launch calendar, most network shows debut in the fall and are committed to following screenings of pilots in the spring.

Pitch Season and Timing

Pitch season is traditionally in the fall. The new network season has launched and within a short span (and in many cases within the first two to three episodes) the broadcasters are already starting to evaluate which new shows will survive and whether to consider mid-season replacements.

After scheduling pitches ("pitch season") the networks will then decide which ideas to greenlight for a script, with the network's approval of the writer. The script will then be written later in the fourth quarter so the script would be ready to take to pilot in the new year. There is a brutal winnowing down of material, and only a small percentage of pitches are commissioned for scripts, and even a smaller percentage of scripts then are produced as pilots. The ratio can vary dramatically from company to company, with the economic incentive to maximize the percentage of pilots made from scripts commissioned. The Museum of Broadcasting once pegged the ratios as follows: "few scripts are commissioned, and fewer still lead to the production of a pilot—estimates suggest that out of 300 pitches, approximately 50 scripts are commissioned, and of those, only 6 to 10 lead to the production of a pilot."[4]

Pilots

Although expensive to produce, as discussed in Chapter 3, pilots are an efficient means to test a concept and evaluate a show before committing to a full series. To a degree this solves the problem faced by theatrical films, and inherent in experience goods, of having to complete the movie before it can be screened and tested; theoretically, a pilot dramatically decreases the risk on a per property basis because there is enough information to make an informed decision, yet the show is not so far along that it is too late to make changes.

Because pilots are the guinea pig of a series, experimenting with location, premise, cast, timing, etc., they tend to be significantly more expensive than later episodes. Once a show finds its rhythm, it should become more efficient to produce (but for escalating talent costs) as episodes are produced in volume and up-front costs of sets, costumes, and infrastructure can be amortized over the run of series. Although the amounts are now dated, the Museum of Broadcasting noted the following regarding costs and the risks at stake: "In the early 1990s the average cost for a half-hour pilot ranged from $500,000 to $700,000, and hour-long pilot programs cost as much as $2 million if a show had extensive effects."[5] Today, the cost of pilots is a multiple of those figures. In looking at the 2009–2010 pilot season, the *Hollywood Reporter*, noted that with the downturn in the economy the average cost of drama pilots had dropped to $5–5.5M from a high of $6–6.5M in 2008.[6]

Pickups and Screening for International Networks

The so-called network cycle continues in the second quarter of the new year as network executives tinker with and test pilots with focus groups. By spring, decisions need to be made and the networks elect which shows they will commission for their fall lineup. The timing is dictated by the "up-fronts" (see more detailed discussion later), where the networks put on a dog-and-pony show for advertisers, unveiling their primetime lineups and securing large up-front buys for the bulk of the season's airtime. Virtually as soon as the lineups are locked the networks host screenings for international buyers; the "LA Screenings" occur toward the end of May following the network up-fronts and comprise a week when international networks cycle through all the new offerings. The LA Screenings have evolved into a significant market given the growing importance of global license fees and the need for key broadcasters to launch series on a nearly simultaneous basis to avoid devaluation from piracy and potential early online glimpses.

Syndication Window and Barter

Syndication vs. Network Coverage and Timing

Syndication used to be the Holy Grail for TV: once a program reached a certain number of episodes, it could be sold into syndication for fees that can dwarf initial licensing revenues, turning a deficit into profits. The traditional magic number for syndication is 65 episodes. This allows a station to run a program five days per week ("stripping") for 13 weeks, corresponding to half of a network season (e.g., September–December); with repeats, this quantity provides adequate episodes to run a series daily throughout the entire broadcast year. Although this can still be true, the market has shifted dramatically from the 1980s and 1990s when syndication was king. This is due to a number of factors: the elimination of the Fin/Syn rules (see the section Impact of Elimination of Fin/Syn Rules and Growth of Cable for discussion), the growth of cable stations acquiring programming that used to be the staple of syndication, and the shrinking number of potential syndication buyers overall (by network groups such as Fox and the WB, now part of CW, aggregating stations and taking key independents off the market).

Before discussing these forces and the evolution of the market further, however, it is useful to clearly define syndication. Simply, syndication means licensing a program into the individual markets on a one-by-one basis. There are over 400 markets in the United States, and syndicators maintain dedicated sales forces to sell programming into individual stations. Table 6.3 illustrates the matrix of top ranked syndicated shows, coverage achieved, and their ratings:

Table 6.3   Ratings and Coverage of Syndicated Shows (2006)

Program	Stations/% coverage	Ratings — AA%
Wheel of Fortune	488/98	9.2
Oprah Winfrey	521/99	7.6
Jeopardy	464/98	7.2
Dr. Phil	523/99	5.6
Entertainment Tonight	484/99	5.6
Everybody Loves Raymond	432/99	5.6
Judge Judy	473/97	4.8
Seinfeld	408/99	4.7
CSI Miami	480/99	4.7
Friends	404/99	3.9

Variety, 12/18–24,2006; AA average refers to non-duplicated viewing for multiple airings of the same show.

240

As discussed earlier, stations are either owned, affiliated, or independent; even affiliated stations have programming flexibility and only take a certain percentage of programs from their affiliated parent groups, thus having residual program slots to acquire other programming offered by the network (such as branded late night shows or morning talk shows) or unaffiliated third parties. When all the network affiliates broadcast a program together it reaches 95%+ of the potential TV households, thus creating the unique convergence of saturation market coverage and simultaneous broadcast. This is a cumbersome way, in essence, to stay live.

In contrast, syndication is the broadcast of the same program over non-affiliated stations at times programmed by the individual stations. Accordingly, it is possible in syndication to achieve the same market coverage and the same amount of time on the air. The profound difference is in missing that intersection of simultaneous broadcasts with full market coverage. This pseudo-live nature of a network broadcast is what makes it so powerful: the network can reach an enormous number of people with the same programming at the same time. This cross section allows for targeted marketing and scheduling, which in turn allows for targeted advertising. Despite the explosion of new media options, there is still no better way to reach a population of over 250 million people. Broadcasters know that a certain percentage of X demographic will watch the nightly news at 6:00 pm versus Y demographic for a sitcom in primetime. And the game is all about that sole fact: how many eyeballs of which type (here young vs. old, male vs. female, kid vs. adult) will see the program.

Syndication, in contrast, is still about drawing eyeballs, but the task is much more challenging when the promotion is solely at a local level.

There is no absolute magic threshold for coverage, but there is a certain quantum of coverage that rises to the level of "significant." That benchmark is usually in the 70+% range. The composition of the coverage is often a hodgepodge of stations. It could mean an ABC affiliate in Denver and Dallas, a Fox affiliate in Los Angeles, and independent stations in Kansas City and Seattle. There are certain station groupings, such as the former "WB 100" that often license together, which can achieve a chunk of coverage in one deal.

Achieving a certain quantity threshold of coverage is critical for attracting advertisers, as many will not consider a program that does not hit an internal mandated coverage threshold (e.g., 80% of nationwide coverage). Beyond the absolute percentage, however, advertisers will look at both the quality of stations and the programming time. For a national buy, there will usually need to be a significant number of top stations in key markets. If, for example, there are no network affiliated stations carrying the program in the top ten markets (e.g., no network affiliates in LA, New York, Chicago …) then it is obviously a hard sell. Sometimes this can be overcome with a strong enough station grouping, such as a percentage of Fox or ABC affiliated stations.

Because the syndication quilt will not achieve simultaneous broadcasts, advertisers will also be keenly interested in the time slots. It

241

may be great to have a Chicago station, but if it is a CW station broadcasting a kids' show at 5:00 am then the value is clearly very different than had it been an ABC affiliate at 8:00 am. It is because of this particular challenge of trying to aggregate and secure advertising commitments across unaffiliated stations in less than full market coverage with non-synchronized broadcast times that anyone in this business needs a good advertising–sales team. The nature of the beast is such that it may be difficult or impossible to secure a national spot/ advertiser, and that advertising needs to be sold on a market by market, broadcast slot by broadcast slot basis. Because syndicators may air a program more than once a week, the matrix of total telecasts becomes quite complicated to manage.

Barter as a Solution to Fragmented Sales and Airings

Making this task of selling ads even harder is the speculative nature of viewership. Because of the fragmented placement, marketing can only be committed at the local level, and ratings are only meaningful within the discreet local market. Accordingly, what has emerged is a barter market.

The term barter syndication is often used in this context, and means a sharing of the advertising time. If a 22-minute program is shown in a 30-minute block, that may leave approximately 7 minutes of advertising space to sell (excluding time reserved for station promos). The licensor of the program may "own" all or part of this time, and is betting on the fact that he can sell the space for better terms than he would otherwise receive for licensing the program outright. This is also a mechanism for the station to hedge its bets and lower program acquisition cost. It may be better for a station to pay $1,000 rather than $3,000 for a program and cede some advertising time to lower its costs.

In this instance the station is obviously betting on a couple of factors. First, it is assuming that the value that the licensor will achieve from selling the advertising inventory is less than the discount the station has granted. Second, the station is assuming that there is residual value/benefit to having the programming; it draws viewers to the station generally in the time period, viewers are not going to a competitor, and viewers may stay tuned in for other programming because of coming in the first place.

There are even instances of full barter, where the station pays nothing and the licensor achieves any and all financial benefit from selling the space it retains. In this situation the station may reserve some spots and have a pure upside from selling inventory against no cost basis. Of course, there are always opportunity costs and the buyer needs to value whether another program would create greater ultimate value.

As a result of the complexity and difficulty of clearing markets, and then selling advertising across a scattered broadcast pattern, specialist distributors have evolved. Two of the powerhouses in this space are King World (now merged with CBS) and Tribune; additionally, given the scale companies will sometimes further partner with other specialists, as was the case of syndicating *South Park* where one company was responsible for market clearances and another for the ad sales.

Barter to the Extreme — Paying for Blocks of Airspace

The ultimate barter arrangement is the full auctioning off of airspace. This tends to occur in a couple of niche areas, such as certain children's programming.

One example was 4Kids Entertainment's arrangement with Fox. When Fox Family was sold to Disney, Fox opted to shutter its Saturday morning Fox Kids animation block and instead lease the space. It struck a deal with 4Kids, the company that represented the merchandise licensing rights to *Pokémon* (and certain non-Asian TV rights to both *Pokémon* and *Yu-Gi-Oh!*), where 4Kids paid Fox $25 million/year for the airtime; 4Kids then sold the commercial space within its half hour block and was betting that either its annual advertising revenue would exceed the $25M, or if it ran a deficit its merchandising sales would take it into profits. In essence, the company rented the commercial space, viewing the broadcasts as a giant commercial for the brand that would then drive non-TV revenue. Perhaps only in children's programming, where robust merchandising programs may be a primary goal, can a producer set a strategy to use the show itself as a loss-leader to drive ancillary revenues. (See Chapter 8 for additional discussion of this 4Kids–Fox deal.)

Infomercials is another area where one sees negative license fees and full purchase of airspace. Here a company is renting the airtime for a giant commercial. This presents even tougher economics than the 4Kids example, because an infomercial is not selling advertising against the airtime, and therefore needs to recoup 100% of the lease costs against product sales. At least in the 4Kids instance there is the goal for advertising to recoup the rental costs, with the deficit in the worst case merely a fraction of the overall lease costs. For this reason infomercials tend to air during inexpensive slots, because costs would become prohibitive during prime airtime.

243

First Run Syndication and Off-Network Syndication

First run syndication means programming produced for initial broadcast in the syndication market. These programs are often daily, unscripted shows such as talk or game shows (e.g., *Oprah Winfrey, Wheel of Fortune, Entertainment Tonight*). In the 1980s there was an upswing in the number of dramas that succeeded in syndication with spin-off Star Trek series (*Star Trek: The Next Generation* and *Star Trek: Deep Space Nine*) and *Baywatch* pacing the market. (Note: *Baywatch* was an interesting case because it aired initially on NBC and was cancelled, but then continued with new episodes in syndication.) The nature of first run syndication shows also leads to longevity not seen in other programming — two of the most successful syndicated shows have been *Wheel of Fortune* and *Jeopardy*, which both premiered in the early 1980s and have been running for roughly 25 years.

In contrast to first run syndication, off-network syndication refers to the playing of reruns of hit shows after they have finished their network runs (or in the case of multiple completed seasons for long running series). This captures the category of when shows such as *MASH, Seinfeld, The Simpsons*, and *Cosby* are syndicated to independent stations. As earlier noted, it is only the most successful of shows, those that reach more than 65 episodes and more frequently crest 100 episodes, that have the awareness and stature to succeed in this market. Achieving this status, however, is the ultimate mark of success and is where TV shows have their true upsides.

One of the most famous examples was *The Cosby Show*, which led the networks ratings race in the 1980s and in the 1986 network season had a record 34.9 rating on NBC (representing 63 million viewers at the time). *Time* magazine noted: "The show's success has created its own bonanza on the syndication market: Cosby Show reruns, currently being sold to local stations, have earned a record-smashing $600 million, and the total could eventually top $1 billion ..."[7] This is the Holy Grail of television, and the success of *Cosby* paved the way for its producer, the Carsey-Werner Company, to become one of the most successful independents in TV history: "Another hit show of the 1980s for Carsey-Werner was the *Cosby Show* spin-off *A Different World*, which aired on NBC beginning in 1987. The following season, 1988–1989, the company would accomplish the unprecedented feat of producing the year's three highest rated shows: *Cosby* at number one, followed by *Roseanne* and *A Different World*."[8]

(Note: As an interesting footnote, the wealth created here allowed Marcy Carsey to partner with Oprah Winfrey and Geraldine Leybourne (former Disney and Nickelodeon executive) to found the Oxygen network, and Tom Werner was part of the group that purchased controlling interest in the Boston Red Sox baseball team.)

Aftermarket sales continue to be the lifeblood of television success today, although the key difference is now that cable networks are competing with syndication for top programming. *The Sopranos* set a record with an estimated $2.5M/episode license fee from A&E for an exclusive run off of pay TV (HBO). A few other examples include: (1) *Sex and the City* to TBS for an estimated $700K,[9] (2) *The Office* to TBS + Fox owned and operated affiliates for $950K/episode ($650K/episode TBS),[10] and (3) *Law and Order—Criminal Intent* to USA/Bravo for just under $2M/episode.

Online's "Short Tail" versus "Long Tail" and Impact on Syndication

The ability via the Internet to monetize the long tail value of content through infinite shelf space sometimes leads people to assume that the long tail creates incremental revenue; however, that may only be true if there is no additional up-front exposure or what I will refer to as the "short tail." The increased access points for TV programming and the ability to easily see a show you missed via free Internet or cable VOD leads to such frontloaded exposure that downstream values are likely to drop. This is due to multiple factors, including fewer viewers who are watching a show for the first time in a long-tail window and less repeat consumption with greater access to more new programming in the short tail. Today, we are already seeing the impact on pricing and revenues, and there is a chance for the overall pie to shrink if the non-exclusive value of the short tail does not equal the prior exclusive value of the long tail. I asked long-term industry veteran and president of Fox TV International Marion Edwards about the new TV landscape and whether she saw the pie expanding from Hulu-type services or whether easy access is serving to undermine pricing for reruns. She noted:

There is no doubt that the world of "free on demand" viewing, whether accessed on a network branded website, HULU, or the soon to be launched cable delivered free on demand channels, is having a major impact on the traditional revenue streams associated with the distribution business. The obvious upside is that these services give the advertisers "unskippable" ads (which makes those ads more valuable), the networks have found a new way to allow viewers to "catch up" with shows they may have missed, and the viewers can watch programs when and where they choose. The distributor, however, has the challenge of trying to make the program seem fresh and unique in a world where it has become ubiquitous. We are already seeing the impact on the long-term value of TV programs in terms of re-license in the traditional after markets. How the overall economic model shakes out remains to be seen.

Impact of Elimination of Fin/Syn Rules and Growth of Cable

The huge off-network syndication revenues earned by producers such as Carsey-Warner were among the reasons that broadcast networks started to lobby against the elimination of the Financial Interest and Syndication Rules (Fin/Syn Rules). Summarizing the history, the Museum of Broadcast Communications notes:

The Federal Communications Commission (FCC) implemented the rules in 1970, attempting to increase programming diversity and limit the market control of the three broadcast television networks. The rules prohibited network participation in two related arenas: the financial interest of the television programs they aired beyond first-run exhibition, and the creation of in-house syndication arms, especially in the domestic market. Consent decrees executed by the Justice Department in 1977 solidified the rules, and limited the amount of primetime programming the networks could produce themselves.[11]

These rules were contested for years, with producers favoring Fin/Syn fighting the networks, and were eventually relaxed and then fully eliminated in 1995. One of the reasons for the elimination was a belief that media competition, including from the growth of the cable market, had weakened the networks' prior dominance and that therefore the protections were no longer needed. This was true, to a degree. The combined TV market share for ABC/CBS/NBC in the time of the rules promulgation in the 1970s bordered 90%, but 20 years later in the mid-1990s the share had dropped into the middle 60%. Nevertheless, the fear of vertical integration by major media groups and the difficulty for smaller producers to deficit finance series in the hope of hits that would pay for misses, remains a challenging reality for independent producers who want to keep the backend/upside in their productions. How easy do you think it is today for an independent producer to land a show on NBC and maintain ownership in the backend syndication revenues that could lead to the type of upside reaped by Carsey-Werner on *The Cosby Show*?

Virtually any producer will lament that the result of changes in the Fin/Syn rules has been to shift leverage to buyers/networks. I asked Ned Nalle, former president of Universal Worldwide Television and current executive producer of *Legend of the Seeker* for ABC Studios (along with Sam Raimi, director of the Spider-Man films), if he agreed with this trend. He noted:

Mergers and relaxation of financial interest regulations have led to market concentration. Putting aside whether the quality of the content has improved, deteriorated or stayed the same since the market contracted, it nevertheless means less competition among buyers for content. That means the leverage pendulum has moved decidedly over to the buyer, and away from the seller. It also seems to excuse that, absent more competitors breathing down his/her neck, a buyer can and will take more time to make a decision. The buyer will also exact more rights away from suppliers. It doesn't mean that worthy shows won't get ordered, and eventually on the air. But shows may be commissioned for financial interest reasons as much as creative or ratings merits.

Basic Economics of TV Series

The TV business has always been one of deficits; namely, the license fees for a show rarely cover the cost of production, and the resulting deficit is hopefully made up in off-network syndication sales or other revenue streams such as DVD. This holds as true today as when the Fin/Syn Rules were in force and Carsey-Warner was in its heyday. [Note: At that time it cost $500,000+ per episode to make a standard half-hour comedy, which would typically run at a deficit of $100,000 to $200,000.][12] The only difference today is that the gulf has grown, with the cost of production generally rising more than corresponding license fees. This is not surprising given the erosion of network market shares and in the increased competitive environment.

The macro picture is therefore similar to the motion picture business where hits pay for misses, and success is based on a portfolio strategy. The buffer that has sustained the TV business recently is the expansion of additional revenue streams. In the children's area, as described before in the 4Kids example, merchandising opportunities are sought after to recoup a deficit. With respect to live action, the growth of the DVD market for television series, now augmented by online and portable revenues such as downloads via the iPod, has created an additional buffer to projected deficits following initial broadcast license fees. The *New York Times*, in part quoting Twentieth-Century Fox Television co-president Dana Walden, analyzed how hit show *24* would likely not be made absent DVD revenues:

… the costs of producing a drama like "24" had become so prohibitive that it probably could not be made today without the DVD sales. Though the studio would not release exact figures, each of the series' 120 episodes has cost just under $2.5 million to make, for a total of about $300 million. Licensing fees from the Fox Network are not believed to have exceeded $1.3 million an episode, for a total of no more than about $156 million. The rights to broadcast the series internationally have probably been sold for $1 million or more an episode, for a total of at least $120 million. All told, that revenue—about $276 million—has not been sufficient to eliminate the deficit and provide a profit. DVD sales, however, have.

"The DVD opportunity on this series has enabled us to produce the show that is on the air," Ms. Walden said.[13]

Cable's Advantage and Move into Original Programming

The risk profile of a series is directly proportional to the number of likely revenue sources for recoupment. As discussed in Chapter 3, cable networks can theoretically take greater risks than the broadcast networks because they have a dual revenue stream from cable subscriber fees and advertising. The cable fees are guaranteed, and create a production funding pool insulating a particular series from the direct impact of advertising revenue; the subscriber fees are tied to the overall network and brand, such that a hit series can help drive brand value, but a one off failure will not change the underlying economics (other than of course the impact on advertising for that show). This is one reason that cable networks are starting to offer more and more original programming: a hit or group of hits can help increase the brand value of the network and differentiate it to a greater extent than reruns. Accordingly, a series on a cable network can now draw from (1) advertising dollars, (2) an allocation from cable subscriber fees paid to the network overall, (3) DVD revenues from box sets of seasons, and (4) emerging revenue streams such as VOD buys and iPod downloads. A network series benefits from all of these sources except for the cable subscriber fees; however, that element alone can be so significant that the cable network can afford to take different risks and accept a lower audience rating.

The success of original cable series, as opposed to original series in syndication (e.g., *Star Trek*) has only recently come into fashion. The ability for non-networks to produce hit original series was proven by HBO, with hits such as *Sex and the City* and *The Sopranos*. Soon, non-pay channels realized they could enter the market as well, and the following is a snapshot of a few of the shows evidencing the trend of cable networks to develop their own franchises (of course, this had long been the trend with kids channels such as Nickelodeon with *Jimmy Neutron*, etc.):

- USA: *Monk, Psych, Burn Notice*
- TNT: *The Closer, Saving Grace*
- F/X: *The Shield, Rescue Me, Nip/Tuck, Dirt*
- Sci-Fi: *Battlestar Galactica, Eureka*
- Lifetime: *Army Wives*
- A&E: *Dog the Bounty Hunter*
- Disney Channel: *Hannah Montana, Lizzie McGuire*

In some cases, the show's ratings have been extremely competitive, with TNT's *The Closer* scoring network primetime-like numbers in a few instances (especially with season premieres). From dabbling, cable networks started to gain confidence in their ability to launch original series and began to leverage two inherent competitive advantages. First, cable stations could counter-program and start seasons in periods when the networks showed reruns. F/X and TNT, respectively, ran seasons of *Rescue Me* and *The Closer* in the summer, enticing viewers who preferred new episodes to network reruns or replacements.

Second, because cable stations program a full day, as opposed to a network that has limited primetime hours and must share promotional time with affiliates, the cable networks can cross-promote new shows literally nonstop; further, because they may only have a couple of original series, the promotion can reach channel saturation, optimizing marketing support to help shows break through the clutter. Accordingly, the cable networks tend to program their originals in sequence, rather than as a lineup, thereby maximizing promotion and always having something new (e.g., F/X will plug its fall original during its summer original series).

The issue now may become whether the market can absorb all these shows. As the market has matured, it may be as Variety noted that everyone needs to run faster just to stay in place:

The one-time vast wasteland of cable networks filled with repeats and wrestling has been replaced by a world in which even networks as small as Sundance Channel are producing quality first-run fare. No longer a band of misfits, basic cable's top nets are spending more money on original fare and making more noise with marketing—yet they aren't seeing their numbers grow. They're having to do more just to maintain the status quo.[14]

Up-front Markets, Mechanics of Advertising Sales, and Ratings

Advertising is the lifeblood of free television, and networks essentially lease portions of their airtime to advertisers, charging rent based on ratings. Much like any other rental market, rates can be based on long- or short-term rates with discounts applied to prepayment or longer term security scenarios. To grasp the mechanics of the television advertising landscape, imagine you owned an apartment building where certain views commanded premium pricing (exchanging the notion of view for viewership), discounts were applied to someone leasing bulk space such as an entire floor, and each individual unit in the building was a unique property that commanded its own rental rate (yet still had some rational relationship to all the other units rented). In this analogy, the TV up-front markets would be akin to long-term rentals, the scatter market would equate to monthly or

250

weekly rentals, and ratings would be the cost-per-square-foot barometer for setting the rental rates.

Up-front Markets

There are a couple of times a year when networks pitch their new season lineups to advertisers, trying to secure commitments for shows before broadcasts. This obviously secures capital/commitments to underwrite production costs, the annual ritual of which has come to be known as the up-front markets.

The mechanism of the up-front markets is relatively straightforward. Broadcasters auction off their commercial space, referred to as "inventory," and receive guaranteed payments for the commercial space/spots. The buyers of spots obviously secure key placement for their products, as the up-front markets cover large commitments over long periods of time. Companies with a steady stream of advertising needs, such as auto companies or large packaged goods companies, will secure a range of spots that will then be allocated to specific products at a later date. Those companies buying large inventory and later allocating to clients tend to have products that need continuous marketing, and therefore do not need to have the first spot on *Desperate Housewives* on the week of November X. For this flexibility they buy in volume and gain both the benefit of guaranteed delivery as well as a certain discount.

251

It is in part this guaranteed, and to an extent, more flexible income stream that was put in jeopardy with the US auto company and broader 2008 economic crisis; without this revenue the networks cannot afford a basket of staple programming and risks, with the collateral impact hitting everything from the concept of primetime (NBC's decision to substitute Jay Leno for scripted fare in its third hour) to sports. And there is a lot at stake. The aggregate up-front markets in 2007, for example, secured over $15B for the broadcast and cable networks (respectively, $9B and $6.5B).[15]

The spots will be sold on a cost per thousand eyeballs basis (CPM). Spots can either be based on general ratings/viewership, or spots will be sold with a guarantee within a certain targeted demographic (e.g., certain rating in the 18- to 30-year-old demo). As noted previously, the seller has the benefit of secured sales and financing, and the buyer secures a certain number of guaranteed spots and eyeballs for their client base. The game is then in the pricing, with buyers trying to make efficient use of marketing dollars and the sellers/broadcasters trying to maximize the value of each second of commercial time.

Economically, what then happens is that the seller/broadcaster will guarantee a number of eyeballs with the guarantee used to drive the price as high as possible. The rub then comes when a show either under or over delivers. If it over delivers, then the buyer had a very efficient buy; it paid for X eyeballs and actually received a higher viewership than it bargained for. On the flip side, if a show under delivers, then the seller has to make good on its guarantee and compensate the buyer for the show underperforming. This practice is literally known as "make goods." The seller will allocate additional spots or other value to make up the difference. A good example of this market is likely the first season of *Survivor*. The show was a much bigger hit than anticipated, and those buyers who had space on the show benefited from the over delivery and had an efficient buy. The market then corrects in the next season/up-fronts, where expectations are adjusted and the broadcaster will increase the charge for the show, raising the CPM for the targeted rating.

One interesting economic factor in setting rates is that while the market corrects, it does not correct radically such that year to year the CPM value proportionately adjusts to the prior year's ratings. A network that has had a strong run over several years will command a premium in its CPM base value, whereas a network that has been struggling historically but has just come off a strong year may not be able to increase its rate to "current market" overnight.

Why the CPM pricing of advertising inventory does not correct to market and more quickly discount or grant goodwill based on recent performance is a lesson of relative leverage and limited players. The same scenario would not play out in the brutal maelstrom of the stock market. A key differentiator here is that a network is not going to discount its pricing more quickly than it has to, and will fight every step to avoid erosion, arguing that any recent correction is a temporary dip and its new lineup will place the channel back on top. The buyer is more likely to accept this because the pricing is in relative rather than absolute terms, and they will ultimately only pay the "true" value of delivery once make goods are applied (if applicable).

Scatter Market

The opposite side of the up-front market is the scatter market. The scatter market is just like it sounds: in this market companies can make specific buys for limited spots and placements. This market is needed when a buyer/advertiser has specific timing demands, such as the release of a product (for example the release of a film). If you want to advertise your product on a specific show on a specific night to either tie into a promotion or product launch, then you will likely be buying in the scatter market. The advantage the buyer gains is the specific timing and placement, but what they sacrifice is guaranteed delivery. The buy is at risk, and there will likely be no guaranteed make goods.

The process, art, and business of buying media is a complicated discipline, with millions of dollars at stake in increments of 15- and 30-second inventories. Perhaps the most cited example of advertising expenditure is the Super Bowl. Despite the claims of the demise of TV and new media impacting viewership, advertising on the Super Bowl continues to be vibrant, with fees charged per spot at the up-fronts and total advertising spending continuing to climb.

Understanding Traditional Ratings

Almost everyone uses Nielsen ratings as a barometer of the audience and demographics captured, and it is best to go to Nielsen Media for the relevant definitions. The Web site has an excellent glossary, and defines ratings, share, designated market areas, metered markets, etc. Nielsen explains the difference between a rating and share as follows:

253

- The terms rating and share are basic to the television industry. Both are expressed as percentages.
- Simply put, a rating tells how many people watched a particular TV program; it is the percent of households or persons within a universe (all TV households, or adults 18–49, for example) who are tuned to a particular program or daypart.
- A share expresses this same number of viewers as a percent of only the households or persons actually watching television during the program or daypart. Thus, a share is a percent of a constantly changing number — the number of homes or number of persons in a given demographic using television at that time. Shares can be useful as a gauge of competitive standing.[a]

Accordingly, if one looks at the entire US market (defined as the universe of TV households, which approximates 110 million homes), a ratings point would be 1% of this total, which means, as a rule of thumb, that a 1% rating translates into just over 1 million people/homes.[16]

[a]Copyrighted information of the Nielsen Company, licensed for use herein.

In Nielsen's glossary of media terms and acronyms, it further defines the metrics with specific formulas. Focusing again on the key measurements of ratings and share, Nielsen's formulas are as follows:

$$\text{Rating \% (average audience): Rating \%} = \frac{\text{Audience}}{\text{Universe Estimate}}$$

$$\text{Share (of Audience): Share} = \frac{\text{Rating}}{\text{HUT}}$$

$$\text{Households Using Television (HUT): HUT\%} = \frac{\text{\# HH With TV sets in use}}{\text{Total HH Universe Estimate}}[17]$$

In practice, ratings are dissected and used not only for an overall measurement but also targeted advertising buys. Clients will want a specific delivery with a defined demographic, such as adults 18–49 or males 25–49. The pricing of the buys is then formulated by indexing the value of a ratings point to the population reached on a per 1,000 impression basis. Nielsen defines these CPP and CPM measurements as follows:

$$\text{Cost per rating point (CPP): CPP} = \frac{\text{Average Unit Cost}}{\text{Rating \%}} \text{ or } \frac{\text{Total Sch Cost}}{\text{GRPs}}$$

$$\text{Cost per thousand (CPM): CPM} = \frac{\text{Media Cost} \times 1{,}000}{\text{Impressions}[18]}$$

DVRs and the Threat to Traditional Advertising

DVRs posed an immediate and profound threat to the traditional television broadcast model because consumers could fast forward through commercials. If viewers became accustomed to recording shows and zapping commercials, the value of advertising would be reduced and ultimately the entire ad-supported model of free TV could be undermined. Good statistics are shaky, but *Variety* noted "it's generally accepted that 35%–40% of people who watch programs played back on DVRs still sit through the ads."[19] Even if this is true, TiVo was likely smart not to enable a "skip" button; while it was

254

technically feasible it would have certainly encouraged the wrath of every free broadcaster.

As DVR penetration approaches mass market levels, it is creating new pressures, and as discussed previously it is altering the way ratings are reported and advertising purchased. Ironically, as TV programming is finding outlets on the Internet, one of the sales items for streaming content is that advertising can be embedded and not skipped. Thinking had come full circle: first there was the fear of the Internet siphoning away consumers from TV, then the fear of ad skipping undermining the entire broadcast infrastructure, and then the Internet perceived as a savior to broadcast because commercials could not be skipped if watching a show via your computer as opposed to your TV. The one sure outcome is that the traditional television advertising model is changing, and networks will need to find substitutional revenues as audience share declines from competing media options and advertising becomes more tenuous as more people can zap commercials.

I had an interesting conversation a few years ago with the founder of a technology company whose software enabled a TV-like interface via the Web. He mentioned that ad skipping was overrated: ask people if they ad-skipped and then ask if they had ever while fast forwarding stopped and rewound to watch something that caught their eye, and the percentage response was nearly identical. Why had the people stopped, rewound, and watched? Because the item was relevant. This simply created a need for better target marketing — something the Internet promised by feeding advertisements via customer-profiled databases (intelligent advertising serving), and a goal that TV advertising kept iteratively refining by slicing ratings into narrow demographic baskets.

A New Ratings Landscape: Live Plus Ratings and Ratings on Commercials

Suddenly, the ratings landscape was shifting as a result of factors including DVR viewing, and networks were insisting on moving beyond the historical measurements. The argument was simple: "live" ratings no longer accurately reflected how many people "watched" TV. (Note: I put watched in quotes because this was the argument just a couple of years ago, but going forward I believe the system will have to evolve even further to capture "consumed" via all outlets.)

After a tug of war in 2006 when advertisers succeeded in maintaining ratings based on traditional metrics of measuring the viewers who watched a program live (wanting to preserve this lower base as long as possible, arguably knowing they were only paying for live but recognizing a larger audience ultimately was captured), the advertisers and networks agreed to a new system that was introduced in the summer of 2007. Calling the pact on commercial ratings and DVR viewing "the biggest sea-change" in the TV ad business in two decades, *Variety* summarized:

Virtually all ad sales will be based on Nielsen Media Research's newly introduced commercial ratings—which measure the number of viewers who are watching ads, and not just the programs in which the ads air. ... As a quid pro quo, the advertising business had to acknowledge the existence of digital video recorders (DVRs). Most major advertisers will allow networks to measure their commercial ratings by adding in viewing via DVR that occurs up to three days after the initial telecast. (The new ad standard was quickly jargon-ized as "C3," or commercial ratings plus three.)[20]

The introduction of the new ratings system, providing the average ratings of a commercial within a program (and by corollary an indication of how many ads were skipped), was introduced just around the time of the 2007 up-fronts, delaying deals and creating unprecedented levels of uncertainty as parties were reluctant to commit big sums against a new and untested ratings system.

Despite the anxiety, most parties ultimately agreed to the new C3 system, as *Variety* highlighted: "NBC Universal last month cut a $1billion deal with Group M, the media buying arm of ad giant WPP, which included sales based on the C3 standard for the Peacock and for its cable sibs ... That deal more than any other set the precedent for the industry's broad acceptance of the C3 standard."[21] (Almost as a truism, *Advertising Age*, in a 2007 Upfront Study posed the question: What is the most significant new trend that has emerged during the 2007–2008 Upfront season? to the following groups: cable, broadcast, buyers, planners, clients. Every single category replied that it was the new ratings construct, and specifically the Live + 3 measurement.[22])

Live + Still a Limited Solution

While the new "Live +" system (see later) is an improvement because it more accurately gauges the total consumption of a program, advertisers that are focused on time-specific flights will want to discount or dismiss the added time, and accordingly will not want to pay the same rates. If I have a movie opening on Friday, and advertise on Wednesday, the value of a consumer seeing my advertisement the next week following the opening weekend (imagine Live + 7) is greatly if not fully diminished (especially if my ad was targeted to drive opening weekend box office).

The open issue is now reliability: "It's generally thought that 5% of auds leave during commercials, and that is built into the system of buying and selling. But what if the commercial ratings say differently? "Even a tenth of a ratings point equates to millions of dollars," noted NBC Universal's research president to *Variety*.[23]

Once the slippery slope is opened, broadcasters may find that they need to refine metrics even further. One direction would be to slice commercials more finely, measuring each commercial rather than tracking average commercial ratings. Many advertisers, however, are likely to go beyond ratings, realizing their statistics need to compete with the direct consumer information becoming commonplace online; conceptually, the advertiser wants the same type of tracking to measure the effectiveness of buys on and offline. One trend addressing this convergence is to track engagement; namely, tracking not simply whether a show is watched, but how much time is spent watching down to a per viewer level. While conceptually this may be a more valuable indicator, given the recent seismic shift, and the fact even online metrics are not yet valued based on duration, it is not likely this next iteration of valuation will be adopted in the near term.

Internet Intersection — Live + What?

As noted above, economic pressures are pushing for ratings and metrics to be more precisely calculated. This trend is no doubt accentuated by the gulf in online metrics versus TV ratings, where Nielsen ratings are based on statistical samples and averages, while the online advertising market has now become accustomed to exact by-individual costs-per-click and by-user impressions on the Web. There are, though, two different issues at play here.

First, there is the "what" should be captured, as in the argument that TV ratings should account not just for live watching, but also capture a viewer watching the program time-shifted via its DVR (hence the live + 3 rating). But what about all the other points of consumption evolving: Should this rating not also capture watching the show via Internet free VOD or on a mobile simulcast? The expansion of access points for consumption will inevitably cause a further shift in this metric to capture a total consumption number within a fixed period. To date, this has not been forced because with experimentation different ad constructs and values are being tested, such as trying fewer advertising minutes (*Wired* noted: "While broadcasters cram eight minutes of advertising into a half-hour show, Hulu sells only two"[24]) and increasing the CPM rate (value per ad) by not enabling ad skipping. (Note: Hulu is able to charge a premium, selling spots according to *Wired* for "two to three times the ad rate that the broadcast network commands."[25])

This leads into a second factor, namely dovetailing value and ratings systems: Is CPM for the Internet the same as CPM for a network advertising buy? (See also discussion in Chapter 3, Section titled Principal Methods of Financing Online Production.) Both are trying to track costs based on reach (CPM viewers). However, the TV ratings are based on statistical values, while the online ratings are theoretically based on direct, by-user clicks or impressions. Moreover, it is a dirty little secret that Internet metrics are not quite as precise as perceived, given that variables in Comscore ratings, impressions, and clicks can be significant (how many people audit the validity of a tracking beacon?). It will be interesting as these two systems, both based on different assumptions and data, yet trying ultimately to track the same information, continue to converge.

Pay Television

While there are some similarities to the free television market in pay television licenses, the underlying economics are significantly different. The market is dominated by a very small group of broadcasters, the inventory space has an elasticity component given multiplexing, and values are not fully dependent upon ratings.

The US market is dominated by three key players: HBO/Cinemax, Showtime/The Movie Channel, and Starz/Encore. HBO is by far the largest, with HBO greater than 20 million subscribers (excluding Cinemax). Because the economics of series was discussed previously, the focus now will be on film licenses and the macro economics of pay channel deals/programming.

Film Licenses and Windows

As discussed in Chapter 1 the film pay TV window is typically a year or so from theatrical release, and six to nine months following video release. This is heavily dependent on changing market conditions, and as pay services have grown and expanded channel offerings through multiplexing services, the windows have now become more complicated. Pay TV services are often granted second and even third windows, so that a couple of years or more of exclusivity are secured, punctuated over several years, where the first and most important window is 12 to 18 months long.

Pay TV license fees can run into the millions of dollars, and services recoup the costs by amortizing fees over high numbers of runs and directly charging consumers a monthly access fee. Because pay services are not ratings dependent, they are focused on two primary items for value: satisfying the current subscriber base and attracting new subscribers.

Subscriber satisfaction is an interesting issue. A service may feel it can pick and choose content, but there may be a built-in expectation from subscribers that they will have access to certain films or types of product. If a service markets itself as the top pay channel where "you'll get all the hits," it would not be delivering on its promise if it did not have the top three or four films of the summer. The value proposition is a bit different if focused on attracting new subscribers, and the challenge is whether the service is able to accurately correlate subscriber changes with the playing of specific programs.

259

Basis for License Fees; Calculation of Runs

License fees paid by pay TV services have almost always been based on a fee per subscriber basis. Accordingly, if the fee were $1/subscriber and there were 10 million subscribers, the license fee would be $10M. Carefully crafted legal language dictates how the subscribers are counted with choices ranging from at the time of contract, at the commencement of the license period, or as of the end of the period. It is also quite typical to calculate the average number of subscribers over a monthly period and then take the average of those averages over a specified period or aggregate the fees based on a per month calculation.

Because most pay services have grown over time (given the name of the game is acquisition and maintenance of paying subscribers), licenses often take this into account. One method is to take averages calculated over specified periods, and another is to simply impute a number. In a typical deal, the license fee may be specified as a certain minimum guarantee with overages due if subscribers increase past an agreed threshold. In the prior example, the licensee broadcaster may guarantee the licensee $10M, but also agree to pay $1/subscriber for every subscriber over 10 million. Because subscriber counts can go down, this can cut both ways; however, as licensors covet minimum guarantees it is less common to have reduction provisions. Similarly, pay TV licensees often refuse to grant a minimum guarantee tied to a current subscriber level, since this gives them no flexibility for a downturn. If instead the minimum guarantee is lower but overages apply, then everyone has hedged their bets and the fee should come out fairly.

Despite this logical pattern, as services grow there is a tendency to start moving away from the per subscriber formula to more fixed fees; namely, once maturity is reached, the risk of leaving money on the table is reduced and simplicity wins out.

Calculating Number of Runs — Complex Matrix from Multiplex Channels and Exhibition Days

The final important element of a pay TV license deal is understanding the implications of increasing runs by the notion of exhibition days and multiplex offerings. In pay TV agreements, an exhibition day usually is defined in a manner that allows multiple airings of the film within a 24-hour period (similar to the discussion on cable runs, but it was in fact pay TV that established the pattern now being copied). Similar to the cable example previously described, it would be typical to allow a couple of airings within a day. (Note: As discussed in Chapter 8, subscription VOD applications are now granting subscribers on-demand access to programs within the pay channel, a trend that obviates the need for exhibition days.) The theory behind exhibition days is that the structure affords the broadcaster greater programming flexibility, offering its customers more choice. For the licensor, because the viewings are confined to within the same day, it is more akin to time-shifting and as per custom has not raised issues of over-exposing the product.

In terms of exposure, an area that needs to be managed is runs on multiplexed channels. Multiplexing is simply the practice of successful services offering expanded channels. Sky in the UK, for example, offers a menu of channels such as Sky Movies 1, Sky Movies 2, and Sky Cinema. Each of these channels will have a slightly different flavor and programming skew, and each of these channels may have other affiliated channels. Language defining an exhibition day will therefore need to take account of the runs within a day and which channels those runs can be taken on. This sum can ultimately lead to a dizzying number of runs.

If we were to assume, for example, that 20 runs are allowed on a primary movie channel, as well as each multiplexed channel, and were further to assume that the total number of multiplexed channels allowed were capped at 5, then the total number of runs would be 240. This is calculated as 20 runs/channel × 6 potential channels × 2 runs per exhibition days.

Output Deals

Most of the above applies to the structure of a deal on a by-picture basis. However, most studio films are licensed via output deals. An output deal is exactly what it sounds like: a studio will license its entire output of product to a program service, thereby securing long-term and broad product distribution and revenues. The benefit for the supplier is a guaranteed exclusive supply of key product, thereby giving it a competitive advantage over a rival service.

Because these deals are difficult to negotiate and rely on averages (certain number of titles performing in different ranges over time), they tend to be for long periods. Fox, which has had a 25-year continuous relationship with HBO, re-upped its deal in 2007 for 10 years with guarantees of over $1B, as reported in *Variety*:

261

The money HBO pays Fox for a movie comes out of a formula heavily dependent on the domestic box office gross of the movie. But over the long term, HBO will pay an average of $6 million–$7million each for the titles in the output deal … HBO regards theatricals as the lifeblood of its multiplex channels and its on-demand service … Fully 70% of the schedule of HBO and its multiplexes consists of theatrical movies.[26]

Output deals are similar to free TV packages, only larger and with less choice. They work because pay services need to fill up a 24/7 schedule, catering to an audience that is constantly expecting something new, and to an extent different than they may have selected on their own. The great benefit of a dominant pay service is that it shows everything. Of course, subscribers expect and demand the key major releases; beyond the lead titles, however, the pay services offer exquisite variety. There are so many movies released every week that truly only a professional movie watcher could catch the complete variety of offerings. With the pay service that movie that you either did not want to pay for in the theater, or was not quite compelling enough to rent, or you were embarrassed to admit that you really wanted to see is offered up from your bed. I would argue that a pay service is close to the movie equivalent of your favorite radio station: you trust them to program the things you know you want to hear (see), but you are actually looking for the disc jockey (programmer) to introduce you to that new band (film) that you vaguely knew something about or may not have even heard of at all. Output deals put the catalog at the hands of the programmer. But, unlike the music analogy, you cannot flip to another channel if you do not like the schedule, because with content exclusivity it is the only channel.

Economics of Output Deals

In terms of economics, the key items in an output deal are length of term and fee. Because of the unique nature of the pay TV market, and the mutual advantages previously discussed, these deals are invariably for multiple years, and in some cases upwards of ten years. The service is incentivized by locking up a key supplier — again, giving it access to an enormous range of quality product while shutting out a competitor from product that may feature the hottest star of the moment or an award winning film. In addition to the aforementioned Fox deal, HBO has had several long-term deals, including with Universal, Warner Bros., New Line, and DreamWorks.[27] Each studio therefore has the security of knowing it has a constant income stream regardless of the performance fluctuation of its slate. When financing a picture, it is not an insignificant element that the studio can count on a secure sale.

All this would still not work if the economics did not balance similarly. In a typical structure, the pay service would have a baseline guarantee for films. The films may be designated within a band, such as an A, B, or C picture. Although these may be defined on strictly financial terms, such as by US box office gross, conceptually definitions can also include hybrid elements such as if a star or particular director is attached. In addition to a minimum, the studio will have an upside because fees will further be tied to financial performance. Different gradings will usually correspond to box office thresholds. If a picture achieves $50M box office that may trigger one fee, and if it is greater than $100M, it will trigger a different higher fee. The pay services are generally fine with this structure; they are simply indexing their exposure/cost to the value of the particular film. What they want to ensure is that there is some rational cap, and that on an amortized basis they are acquiring a certain overall volume for a certain bulk

262

price. This tends to work out, because the vicissitudes of the business ensure a range of hits and misses — to the extent that if someone has a string of hits, it may be more costly in the short term, but should help both parties in the long term. In terms of caps, the deals may set an artificial limit, such that a film can only earn so much. If the cap is $X for a film achieving $150M or more of domestic box office, for example, this will be fine for a film around that number, but will actually disadvantage a film that may achieve $250M. In theory, this is a risk the licensor takes (assuming a cap), and is one of the benefits that the pay service reaps: they get somewhat of a bargain (akin to an efficient up-front buy in TV) and are assured they are not gouged at the high end, and in return are pledging the security of taking volume regardless of overall performance.

Most output deals historically have incorporated escalating fees over time. This can be tied either explicitly to subscriber growth, ensuring that the per subscriber fee is maintained as the key element setting price, or in an imputed fashion over time. In theory, this is no different than a landlord having a rent inflation clause in a long-term lease, ensuring that the payments keep pace with market pricing. Accordingly, a ten-year contract is likely to include material escalators. This is one area where the pay services have been squeezed at times. If the assumptions are wrong, then pricing can rise significantly above what market pricing would have been absent the output deal. The service may have been forced to take the risk to secure the product, because the studio would not entertain such a long-term contract without the security of increasing fees. Given these dynamics, pay TV is one of the few areas where it is not uncommon to hear about deals being renegotiated (though still vehemently resisted).

To add further wrinkles, if you can think of a variable, it has probably come up. Some contracts will have what are called "gorilla clauses" allowing for special treatment of select films. Many deals will have carve outs, acknowledging that rights may be split in a way where the studio may reserve the right to exclude a picture. In virtually all deals there are notice periods; the studio has some measure of flexibility including a picture and must provide notice of inclusion by a specified date. To the extent there is some flexibility for inclusion, it may be tempered by volume commitments (so many A-titles/period), such that the true flexibility is at the margins.

Value of Individual Titles

The ultimate value paid is obviously a closely held secret. Because there is strong competition among three US services, however, it is fair to hypothesize that the value bears some relationship to the free TV window, which is longer but also comes later. *Variety*, in an article describing Starz's acquisition of 500 movies from Sony's library including *Spider-Man* and *Men in Black*, noted that for free TV "four-year-exclusive blockbuster titles in the first window can cost a network upwards of $20 million apiece." It then continues on the relative value of library titles to fill in pay TV slates, highlighting "… it's far cheaper. The typical non-exclusive library title will fetch in the neighborhood of $150,000."[28]

Another variable, in theory, should be some discount applied to the pay fee in an output deal, because unlike free TV it is a guaranteed sale. This is again, an important element in financing. Accordingly, if one believes the free TV value should be $20M, do the factors of (1) discounting for a guaranteed sale, (2) prior viewing in an earlier window, (3) smaller audience reach, and (4) a shorter overall window cumulatively increase or decrease the value relative to free TV? Many of the factors should net others out, creating a vibrant marketplace with license fees that can be in the high millions of dollars per title.

Revenue Model and Original Programming

264

As discussed in Chapter 3, pay Television networks derive revenues from the intersection of carriage fees and subscriber fees. Carriage fees are fees paid by cable or satellite operators for the right to carry the channel and subscriber fees are the ~$30/month that a subscriber pays to receive the channel; in macro terms, these numbers are aggregated by the cable provider, passing along a much larger fee to the channel ($/subscriber rather than cents/subscriber) given the direct consumer-funded per subscriber fees. Without delving into the P&L of a pay TV network, the economics are somewhat straightforward: simply multiply the number of subscribers by the average monthly fee for the gross revenue budget. At subscriber levels in the millions this quickly becomes a big number, and to the extent the service is able to maintain and grow its base there is a very secure continuous income stream. (Note: Let us assume $20/month × 10M subs; with these numbers the gross revenue approaches $2.5B over a year.)

Pay TV is therefore similar to cable in terms of the TV distribution chain, where consumer dollars flow to the cable operator, that in turn passes along the revenues to the pay TV network. This is somewhat akin to cable (where a percentage is passed through, but the network then directly receives advertising revenues), and fundamentally different than free TV where no consumer dollars are passed directly to the network. Figure 6.3 helps frame the value chain.

Television Distribution Chain

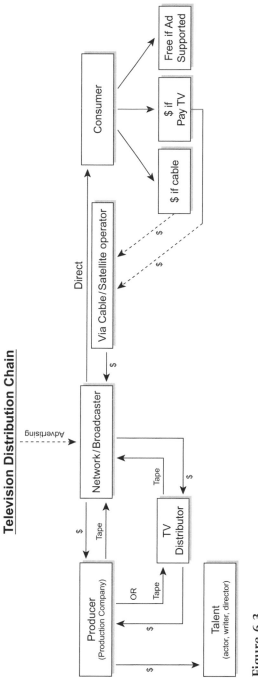

Figure 6.3

265

What has been interesting in the evolution of pay TV is that the operators have come to realize that its suite of programming optimizes subscriber satisfaction when combining access to films (traditional route) and supplementing movie fare with unique original programming. Because pay networks operate outside primetime network FCC standards and practices regulations, they seized the opportunity to create adult-oriented programming: the programs you always wanted to see but the subject matter was either too crude or risqué for network or cable boundaries. In fact, HBO's advertising slogan was "It's not television, it's HBO." And they're right: You cannot see sex which underlies *Sex in the City* (in its original/uncensored form), or graphic violence as seen in *The Sopranos*, or explicit gay lovers as seen in *Six Feet Under* on free or cable television. Consumers are drawn to these shows first and foremost because they are great entertainment. What consumers may not pause to think about is that they are also watching racy dramas or soaps on HBO because regulations prohibit elements that are central to these shows on non-pay TV.

HBO and other pay outlets have been very clever in taking strategic advantage of their positioning, insulated from competition (except by other pay networks) by law, to create original programming that you truly cannot see anywhere else. The other major pay services have not surprisingly jumped into the game following HBO's success: Showtime successfully launched *Weeds*, *The Tudors*, and *Californication* while Starz announced it was moving into the space as well (e.g., *Head Case*).

This strategy then has the knock-on benefit of being highly profitable in the DVD/video market. The very nature of the gloves-off shows makes programming more akin to mini-movies. Positioned as a hybrid between TV series and the freedom of expression found in movies, these shows have been highly successful in the DVD market. Although now counted for and built into financial plans, these revenues are to some extent found money, as releasing TV series on DVD is a relatively new phenomenon, and was not a cornerstone of the decision to diversify into original programming in the first place. When a series happens to also translate to syndication, as has been the case with *Sex and the City* in a cleaned up edited version for TBS, it is in theory all profit to the bottom line. As earlier noted, in 2006 *The Soprano's* hit a record $2.5M/episode in licensing second runs off HBO of the series on A&E. This is truly hitting the jackpot, and is revenue that cannot be expected from many other shows because

266

only shows achieving a certain level of success will be in demand for syndication/cable window, and also because not all pay TV original shows can be cleaned up for licensing into traditional free television.

The other key element of this programming is that it is somewhat ratings proof, because original series on pay TV are not dependent on the advertising market, the series are similarly not slaves to traditional ratings. It is often said that the best job in town is the head of production or programmer for a channel like HBO: high profile, good budgets, and minimal ratings pressure. Although this is obviously an exaggeration, it is truly within the network's prerogative how long to keep a show, because as long as subscribers are holding steady or growing there is no similar direct pressure on an individual show.

Deal Term Overview (Pay and Free TV)

Although license agreements will obviously be quite detailed, when stripping away many of the legal protections and basic information governing the parties, the fundamental economic structure boils down to a relatively short list of items. While many of these categories have been discussed before, it is useful to view them in a checklist form.

Licensed Channels

In a pay TV deal defining the range of primary and multiplex channels is critical. While focus may be on runs on a primary channel, there could be several additional multiplex channels (e.g., movie channel vs. action channel or other specialty theme). The multiplex options allow the broadcaster to amortize costs and increase the fees to the licensor; ratings are lower given limited coverage, but exposure may increase significantly. In some cases there will be formal trade-offs agreed, such that one broadcast on channel X may be substituted for one or more on channel Y.

A free TV deal will generally be to a specific identified channel, such as CBS; however, as technology allows multiplexed options such as high definition channels and even Internet carriage, the notion of a single channel actually existing as a branded channel that may appear in a basket of delivery and sub-branded channels will make this area ever more complex going forward.

Runs

As discussed earlier, pay TV has evolved in a more complex fashion, but with technical innovations allowing new possibilities with free TV, the concept of "runs" is fast becoming a more complicated issue. In pay TV deals definitions can become almost ridiculously complex: defining numbers of runs per primary channel, runs per multiplex channel, conversion ratios to exchange runs between channels, aggregate runs on each type of channel (e.g., no more than X on primary and Y on each multiplex), and aggregate runs across the range of channels (e.g., no more than X cumulative runs across all of the licensed channels, including primary channel X and multiplex channel Y–Z). When layering on top of this matrix the fact that runs will be linked to exhibition days, which will typically allows 2 runs/exhibition day, and that exhibition days are defined by time limitations (e.g., a 24-hour period commencing ...), calculating permitted runs and monitoring runs can become an exhausting and often unclear process. I have been involved in more than one situation where there were valid interpretation debates on permissible runs based on long-standing and seemingly clear definitions.

Term

The structure of a license period can be straightforward, such as a fixed number of years, or complicated if there are multiple windows; a layer of complexity can be added to either scenario when the periods are tied to pending triggers such as a specified number of months following yet-to-be-announced theatrical or video release dates. Additionally, beyond the actual window there will often be blackout periods and defined pre-promotional windows.

The above scenarios, even in the case of multiple windows, assume fixed terms with the variable being the start date; however, because rights are bounded by both time and runs, a license period can in theory expire on a fixed or variable date (the variable is the last permitted broadcast). Agreements may therefore often be structured to trigger the end of the term on the earlier of the expiry of the fixed term or the last permitted broadcast/run.

Calendaring software will keep track of this matrix, logging in the fixed date and accelerating availabilities to the extent runs are taken early, which is frequently the case, as licensees will not wait until the last day or even month of a term to exercise broadcast rights. All of this can become more difficult to track if there are multiple windows, which can be similarly triggered by fixed periods or variable dates if tied to the expiry of another right (e.g., following expiry of free broadcast window X). This in turn may be likewise triggered by fixed and variable dates.

Taken together, calendaring and monitoring rights availabilities is a complex task subject to errors. The simple question of "availability" can cause lawsuits and relationship issues, as licensees are paying premiums and basing deals on rights that will be compromised if windows are misstated; there is nothing worse than finding that two clients, competitive with each other, both have rights to the same product at the same time. This is a never-ending headache for studios and is an area that is taken for granted, but is fraught with danger if not micro-managed to perfection.

License Fee

This is again straightforward if the fee is flat. However, to the extent there are potential overages involved, or if this otherwise has a contingent element, this can be quite complex. An overage definition needs to account for the difference between the minimum guarantee, which may either be flat or based on cents/dollars times a minimum stipulated subscriber basis, and the ultimate fee due based on the actual number of subscribers times the agreed cents per sub-base. The actual definition can become almost unwieldy in that the "actual" number is often pegged to the average number of subscribers in a month. The result can be akin to a complex bank interest calculation statement with permutations of averages to refine the calculation.

269

Rights

The issues here can include:

- What is the territory? Is it physical or language bounded, or both?
- What languages are included? This may impact the definition of territory, such that rights may be both territorially and language bound (e.g., such as a grant of rights for "French Speaking Belgium"). Further, language can have three tiers: the original version of the film (e.g., English language), as well as dubbed versions or subtitled versions.
- What formats/cuts are allowed? For example, will there be one or multiple versions of the product, such as an original version versus an extended director's cut, or is the release in standard definition or high definition?
- Are the rights just free TV or pay TV, or are there variations such as subscription video-on-demand (SVOD)?

- Are there technical limitations, such as curtailing digital transmissions?
- Are there carriage/delivery restrictions, such as via cable and satellite?
- Are single or multiple feeds permitted? This issue can arise in a multiplex situation or in territories with remote locations where a relay may be required for coverage in secondary areas.

International Market

The international markets have historically lagged behind the US market in terms of maturation of both free and pay TV options, but that pattern is now changing.

History of Growth

Unlike the United States, many if not most international markets grew up with so-called state broadcasters. These were public as opposed to private channels that were either fully owned or controlled by the state, and accordingly funded by taxpayer money. Examples of channels are the BBC in the UK, ARD/ZDF in Germany, and RAI in Italy. In some of these cases funding is achieved through television license fees, where all citizens owning a television have to pay an annual TV license fee — a sort of tax. Even though I had been "in the business" for several years, I readily admit to the reality check of receiving my bill when I hooked up my television in London, and realized I was directly taxed to underwrite BBC programming. It is a common notion worldwide, but something of an anathema to Americans who have never experienced this system.

Not only did most countries have public broadcasters, but until the 1990s in many countries these were virtually the only broadcasters. As Americans were getting used to cable and an increasing number of channels, Europeans were just starting to auction off and authorize the first commercial licenses in the territories. In Spain, for example, the state network RTVE had dominated until the government allowed some of the first commercial licenses. The winners and resulting networks were free-to-air channels Antenne 3, which 10+ years later became a leader in exhibiting movies on free TV (such as the *Lord of the Rings* and *Harry Potter* films), and Telecinco (channel 5); additionally, Canal + Espagne was initially granted a monopoly in the pay television space. There were and still are regional broadcasters, but the virtual simultaneous launch of three new national commercial networks had an obviously profound impact on the marketplace.

In the early 1990s it was a renaissance for Hollywood Studios and networks, for rather than having a handful of buyers limited by public sector budgets, they all of a sudden had fierce competition from commercially sponsored national networks vying for viewership and profits. The pattern started in Western Europe, and then as the former Soviet bloc led to emerging democracies in Eastern Europe competition and new stations started to flourish there as well. Hungry for programming, stations signed up massive output deals with studios and networks. Suddenly the international TV divisions were no longer stepchildren with hundreds of millions of dollars of revenues (at minimum) per year at stake.

The pattern continues as democracy spreads and broadcast outlets are freed from state control. Currently one of the fastest growing markets is Russia. While piracy still plagues the video market, the theatrical and TV markets posted some of the most significant gains in the last few years; suddenly the studios were rushing in, converting the market from a licensee territory to a focused subsidiary operation.

271

International Free Television

The economics of international free television, on territory level basis, are not materially different than that of the domestic market.

License Deals

On the feature side, licenses tend to be for a fixed number of runs over a specified number of years. Also similar to the domestic model, license fees are fixed; on occasion deals can be indexed to performance, if licensed in an output deal type structure. Barter, however, is rarely applied for US product.

Finally, the pattern of packages that often typifies the US syndication market has been frequently applied in the international context. Whether a package is set as part of an output arrangement, or simply as a stand-alone package, the economic underpinnings are the same. The buyer/station obtains throughput from a key supplier, and the seller has a guaranteed income stream indexed to theatrical performance; as important, the seller has secure placement of its titles, ensuring that underperforming films still find a home. This is a critical fact when circling back to the key value of studios: they are financing and distribution machines, and if they cannot ensure a producer or director that they will maximize revenues and license their films into all markets then their role is severely compromised. (Note: Output deals apply more often to films than TV shows.)

The following 2007 deal between one of the two major German commercial networks, ProSiebenSat1, and Warner Bros., as described in the *Hollywood Reporter*, typifies this symbiotic relationship:

ProSiebenSat1. Group ... has inked a long-term output deal with Warner Bros. International Television Distribution for the free-TV rights to at least 30 films per year, the company announced Thursday. A ProSiebenSat.1 spokeswoman said the deal had a total worth 'in the low hundreds of millions' of euros and a term of "several years."[29]

High Margin

International television licensing is extremely high margin, as the two principal categories of costs are relatively small. The first, and largest, is the cost of a sales force to license product globally. This will often involve layers as follows:

- Head office: Management, marketing, and fulfillment
- Regional Office: Regional heads/coordinators, often for UK, Western Europe, Eastern Europe, Japan, Australasia, Latin America
- Local Offices: Virtually all studios have multiple local offices in Europe, an office in Australia, and an office in Latin America.

The personnel are fixed costs, and accordingly the business can be managed simply by overhead cost. This infrastructure is a defining element of studios as discussed in Chapter 1.

The other material cost is for delivery. International territories require different formats, such as PAL for Europe, as well as dubbed and subtitled tracks. While the licensee will often absorb some of these costs, it is not uncommon for the distributor to have to supply a foreign language master. On top of the physical master the licensee will need press kits, slides, marketing materials, and occasional special value features (e.g., customized intros or promotional pieces such as behind the scenes documentaries). The matrix of elements can become quite complicated, and additional personnel needs to coordinate the "trafficking" of elements (elements that need to be delivered in a time-sensitive matter given local broadcast dates).

Further, any dubbing or subtitling will be specifically defined and subject to quality control guidelines. Additionally, this becomes a significant economic issue as dubbing can be expensive and who owns the dubbed masters is a negotiated point. It is not uncommon for a local broadcaster to invest in dubs for a TV show and to hold the right to those dubs. Accordingly, a producer who later wants to release in video via another distributor may not own or even have access to dubs of its own shows and may have to negotiate license fees for dubs to its own programs (which costs in turn can influence whether the release is feasible). In terms of the macro picture, though, the key element of the foregoing costs is that they are one offs: a licensee will ultimately only require a single master. When comparing this to the video/DVD market or theatrical market, where variable costs for manufacturing units or creating prints run in the millions of dollars, the cost of delivery for TV is modest.

Repeatable
Unlike the theatrical market, where films are rarely re-released, television is a somewhat evergreen market. New titles are obviously licensed, but library sales can also be very significant to the extent that markets continue to mature and add new outlets such as secondary or tertiary channels that may be either cable or satellite delivered. The opportunities for continuing library sales lead to material revenues. Moreover, in cases of repeat licenses, element costs for delivery are either reduced or eliminated, leading to an almost 100% margin sale if overhead staff costs are not allocated out to the variable license.

273

It is a Big World
Probably the most significant factor in the international marketplace is the sheer size. As global markets have matured, it is possible to license product into more than 50 credible territories. Moreover, some of these have grown to the size that revenues as a percentage of the United States are high. Germany, France, Spain, UK, Italy, Japan, Australia, and select other territories can all yield licenses in the millions of dollars. Accordingly, it is not a stretch to target achieving cumulative international sales that total or exceed US sales. Of course, every market has its nuances. Add this truism to the fact that it is a relationship business and the value of maintaining a global sales force becomes evident.

Markets and Festivals
Most people think about Cannes when talking about film markets, but just as important, and perhaps more so in terms of money

generated, Cannes hosts the two biggest worldwide television markets. Run by the Reed Midem organization, MIPCOM takes place in October and MIP in April. Although each market has certain ancillary events that distinguish it from each other, such as MIPCOM Jr. focusing on kids programming just before MIPCOM in the fall, the markets are mirror images of each other affording a bi-annual marketplace for worldwide TV executives to gather.

These are remarkably efficient markets attended by virtually every major program supplier and broadcaster in the world. Most of the studios and networks have major booths, and newcomers and wannabes can make an instant global impression. Gone are the days of lavish parties and spending, but for those in the business the markets have become a must attend rite of season.

For a period there was a significant market in Monte Carlo in February, but with the US domestic market NATPE falling in the same time frame and becoming better attended by international buyers, there were just too many festivals. Certain executives felt obligated to go to from NATPE to Monte Carlo to MIP to the LA Screenings, and everyone admitted there was no compelling reason for this quantity.

274

Lack of Station Groups

One inefficiency in the international market is that there is a dearth of station groups that buy together across markets; in general, sales are made on a territory by territory basis. It would be attractive for a number of sellers to have "one-stop shopping" and license all of Europe or Western Europe in a single deal. A few companies have tried to aggregate station groups, such as CME, RTL, and SBS (now sold to a private equity consortium), but even in these instances many of the affiliated stations will acquire product independently. The reason is simple: countries have local sensibilities, and it is even more difficult to buy a program on the assumption it will work from Paris-to-Frankfurt-to-Barcelona than harmonizing a demographic audience from Sacramento to New Orleans. Even if demographics were aligned (e.g., targeting Gen X across affiliated stations), cultural nuances and differences make programming across borders extremely challenging.

Nevertheless, people will still try to aggregate station groups and more efficiently purchase content, and the recent purchase of ProSiebensat1 in Germany by the same groups (KKR and Permira) that bought SBS (originally a Scandinavian broadcaster that branched out in countries such as Belgium, Hungary, the Netherlands, and

Greece), has aims at competing with RTL as the only other potential pan-European broadcaster. The *International Herald Tribune* commented on this scale:

> The purchase of ProSiebenSat1, which operates five channels that draw 42 percent of all German TV advertising revenue, will bolster plans by KKR and Permira to create a competitor to RTL … Analysts said KKR and Permira were likely to combine the German broadcaster … with the Permira-owned SBS Broadcasting, a Luxembourg-based group of 16 radio stations, 19 free channels and 20 pay-TV channels.[30]

It remains to be seen whether this aggregation strategy will work given the inherent cross-border cultural barriers and the decline in advertising revenues tied to the 2008-2009 global recession.

International Pay Television and Need for Scale

The economics of international pay television networks and the structure of license deals largely mimic much of the discussion above regarding the United States. It is high margin based on few costs beyond acquisition expenses, most of which other costs are fixed rather than variable. License fees are tied to fixed sums per subscriber, with overages applied against minimum guarantees. Windows tend to mimic those of the United States, with pay television's window recently accelerating to nine months post video from an historical one year from video holdback (still mandated in France), and runs defined in terms of exhibition days. Buyers and sellers attend the same markets as free TV, with MIP and MIPCOM as the primary international festivals.

The major difference is that while the United States is cable dominated, many international services, such as BskyB in the UK, are predominately satellite delivered. Moreover, many of these services have been local pioneers, and the set top box is actually tied to the pay TV service rather than the local cable carrier. The incremental hardware cost has been a barrier to subscriber growth, but with the maturation of the market or free giveaways with signing up this is becoming less of a factor. What it does enable, however, is the networks to more efficiently capture new VOD revenue streams because they already have the technical infrastructure in place to offer the services without a third party controlling the intermediate pipe/

275

delivery mechanism. Additionally, international services have more quickly moved to digital delivery, again enabled by the satellite to home delivery, which builds in enabled capacity for interactivity — the staple of VOD and DVR functionality. (See Chapter 8 for a more complete discussion of VOD, SVOD, and the relationship to pay TV.)

Where the international services have faltered is the expectation of faster subscriber growth in the digital realm than has materialized. Many bets were placed several years ago (e.g., late 1990s), as was the case of Kirch guaranteeing $1B to Paramount (see the section Case Study: The Kirch Group), and subscriber growth never accelerating fast enough to recoup programming costs.

Monopolies and Need for Scale. Product Monopoly versus Broadcast Monopoly

The other limitation of international services is simply the size of local domestic markets. There is limited elasticity in revenues derived from subscriber bases — it is great and steady when reaching a certain threshold, but if the base remains too low there is no way to increase revenues. A hit does not bring higher advertising dollars, and if the program has been acquired from a third party it may only become more costly downstream without the benefit of upside from corresponding increased revenues. This inherent cap on revenue against this lack of a cap on expenses leads to the result that international pay services need scale to survive.

In nearly every major international market competition has not allowed networks to flourish, and in fact has almost crippled the stations. Cutthroat competition for Hollywood product and slowing subscriber growth, coupled with what I would argue is an inherent problem with scale when revenues cannot be increased in a linear way with programming success, has led to mergers in virtually every major market.

The push toward mergers has been fueled by infrastructure and programming costs plus the desire to aggregate content so that the service can offer the same range of titles that the consumer has become accustomed to at the video store. It is not uncommon to find monopolies in large territories, and for all practical purposes the key pay services in the UK, Germany, Spain, Italy, and South Africa have no material local competition. As of 2006 France joined this club with the merger of long-standing rivals TPS and Canal+ (though competition resurfaced in 2008 with the debut of FT-Orange's satellite pay services).[31] The result is an interesting dynamic: a monopoly negotiating with a monopoly. The only licensor with the rights to film X licensing with the only pay TV broadcaster. So, who has the leverage?

Interestingly, neither and both. The services assume that each studio must agree to certain parameters — if pricing is cut for one, it will be for all. Similarly, the studios all attempt to take a most favored nations approach, for heads will roll if one studio accepts a cut only to find out that its rival did not. The only out is dissimilar product and length of term. These negotiations can therefore resemble a sumo level wrestling match and can be drawn out over long stretches. Agreements are eventually reached, though, because both sides ultimately need each other. (Channels, even if a monopoly, still need content quantity and quality to attract and retain subscribers.) Fee escalators and pricing tied to bands of performance build in rational expectations and thresholds, and long-term output deals serve to provide mutual security both in terms of product flow and to an extent resource allocation avoiding frequent protracted negotiations.

The following countries started with multiple pay TV networks that have consolidated into virtual local monopolies (Table 6.4).

Table 6.4   International Pay TV Monopolies

Territory	Original Pay Services	Current Pay Services	Evolution
UK	British Satellite Broadcasting Sky	BskyB	Merger of prior 2
Spain	Canal + Espagne Sogecable	Digital+	Merger of prior 2
Germany	Premiere Teleclub (Switzerland)	Premiere	Merger
France	Canal+ TPS	Canal+	Merged in 2006
	Orange		New France Telecom service in 2008
Italy	Telepiu Sky	Sky Italia	Merger of prior 2
Japan	WOWOW Star Channel	Wowow	Still competition

This truly may be an example where a monopoly situation may benefit the consumer but not the supplier. Monopolies are never good for the program supplier, and usually lead to an increase in consumer pricing; however, as pay services are forced to compete against free services for viewer's time, as well as new media options, pricing has not increased dramatically. In fact, pricing has only so much elasticity against a universe with ever expanding media options, and has a direct relationship with subscriber stability and growth. Accordingly, pay TV monopolies have evolved as a result of requiring scale for local survival, while being capped on abusing monopoly status vis-à-vis consumers by having to compete against other television options.

Interestingly, and in a very different structure from free television, in several territories the Hollywood studios have banded together to co-own the local pay TV networks: creating scale from the supply side. This is true, for example, in Latin America where LAP TV is a partnership among Fox, Universal, Paramount, and MGM, and Australia where Showtime, the channel of the Premium Movie Partnership (PMP), is a joint venture among Sony, Fox, Universal, and Paramount. A partnership ensures a certain cap on programming costs, but similarly also caps the extreme upside. This is probably good over time for the studio owners, but potentially limiting to producers who are selling into an artificial market. Why would Universal approve a certain fee to a Paramount film whose producer is demanding higher fees, when Paramount is unlikely to approve a higher fee to a Universal film? What likely results is a sort of most favored nations output deal structure, aiding network profitability at the likely expense of an occasional individual film. (Note: I cannot prove this, but it is a logical assumption based on the structure.)

Again, It is a Big World

The flip side to the growth of pay services worldwide and the potential of millions of dollars for a single film is the infrastructure needed to sell into these multiple markets. As outlined in Chapter 1, pay television launched similarly to joint ventures in theatrical and video markets. UIP pay Television was a joint venture among MGM, Paramount, and Universal, literally mimicking the theatrical structure of UIP theatrical (and the video structure of CIC, although it was limited to Paramount and Universal). This venture enabled the studios to enter global markets with reduced overhead, and to offer a breadth of product that could literally launch a local network.

278

As the markets matured and revenues grew, the service was ultimately disbanded (after about 10 years). Today every studio has pay television divisions and sales forces that can be staffed relatively thinly with the merging of worldwide services; PPV and VOD are often tied to these groups, as so many of the services are spin-offs from and owned by their larger pay TV parents.

Trendsetters and Market Leaders
Much like HBO in the United States, select pay TV networks have become a fixture on the local landscape having a material impact on production and culture, and even growing into mini-studios. The two best examples are BSkyB in the UK and Canal+ in France. Two of the oldest global pay networks attained early scale with millions of subscribers, enabling them sufficient cash flow to diversify into other production; in fact, both grew successful enough that they are perceived as true competitors to the free networks.

Canal + grew so successful that it was the engine for Vivendi's acquisition of Universal Pictures (which combination ultimately proved unsuccessful, for a variety of reasons including exuberance of Internet expectations, with Vivendi selling off Universal to GE/NBC). At its peak, Canal+ had acquired multiple networks across the globe including:

- Canal + Spain
- Canal + France
- Canal + Poland
- Canal + Netherlands
- Canal + Scandinavia (Sweden, Norway, Denmark)
- Canal + Belgium (covering Benelux)
- Canal Horizons (French-speaking Africa)

For a period this created the potential of one-stop shopping for many suppliers, although it is likely many executives would have yielded that facility to lessen the leverage of Canal+ in continental Europe.

On a much smaller scale, I will never forget the discussion I once had with a fledgling pay service in Eastern Europe in the early 1990s. Because consumers in the former communist country had been cloistered from western entertainment, there was a voracious demand to watch new offerings. Pay services customarily cycle through movies on a multiple time/month basis (see discussion regarding runs), assuming that its audience will want to watch the new offering, and that with a repeating schedule they will ultimately find a convenient time to watch. In the case of this territory, everyone watched the show the first time it was on, and the only way to satisfy the customers would have been to build a huge inventory and only show new programs (defeating the economic model).

Co-Productions

The international market, unlike the United States, has a culture of co-productions. This stems in large part from the size of domestic markets and the need to aggregate markets to raise sufficient capital for projects. It is very common for multiple distributors or networks to fund percentages of a budget in return for local exclusivity plus a share of the overall profits.

As discussed in more detail in Chapter 3, a co-production is a much bandied term that can mean many things including (1) creative collaboration or a sharing of production versus distribution obligations; (2) co-financing, where more than one party invests in a production to share both risk and upside; (3) the sharing of distribution rights (e.g., a United States-European co-production may mean that the US investor acquires North American rights while the international party acquires European or all international rights (rights ex North America); or (5) certain pre-sales scenarios (e.g., if one party acquires rights to a product in advance of completion or production, thereby creating financing security enabling production, it may consider the risk it has taken as justifying its position as a co-producer rather than a buyer).

While co-productions can be compelling, they are complicated, often cumbersome to construct and administer, and involve compromise. Inherent in the structure is a sharing of responsibility, something that often undermines the creative process. Just like the concept of "final cut," every production needs a creative master; when production is run by committee, or when groups are trying to compromise to accommodate local cultural differences (let alone whims or power plays), the end result often suffers. The more parties, the more these problems are exacerbated. If three or four parties are all funding a production as co-producers, and each has an expectation of creative input and authority, it can be a recipe for disaster. For those needing the money this is a necessary evil. Many in Hollywood would never cede this level of control, and in fact the studio mantra tends to be keep all control and all rights. Hence, co-productions are generally an international financing mechanism, and a staple of international TV production.

Case Study: The Kirch Group

Most Americans have not heard of Leo Kirch, even though he is a media mogul on the scale of a Ted Turner or Rupert Murdoch (well, maybe a mini-Murdoch). Similarly, most Americans have not heard of KirchMedia or Betafilm, but the Kirch Gruppe's production reach spanned the globe and was behind the scenes of some of the more well-known shows — everything from the *Gone with the Wind* sequel *Scarlet*, to *Baywatch*, to *Star Trek* spin-off series (e.g., *Star Trek: The Next Generation*), to *JAG*, to co-producing/financing in Europe *The Young Indiana Jones Chronicles*.

What Leo Kirch achieved was total vertical integration in the German marketplace across TV stations, supply of TV product, and local production. At its height, the Kirch empire, worth billions of dollars, was akin to wrapping NBC, HBO, Disney merchandising, and the largest local production company under one umbrella.

On the network side, Kirch built and controlled two of the three largest national free television commercial broadcasters: Sat 1 and ProSieben. On the pay television side, the group built the dominant pay television network, which after a few iterations is now known as Premiere. What was remarkable about the Kirch empire is that Germany is highly decentralized and to gain national licenses it was necessary to gain buy-in from each of the autonomous regional areas. This was not wholly dissimilar to Fox aggregating enough local independent stations to form a national network. The difference in Germany is that when Kirch first built these networks there were no other comparable national commercial networks: they were in essence creating the first commercial competition to the public broadcasters.

To feed the programming needs of the stations, and grow them, Kirch virtually monopolized the supply of programming from the United States. Early on Kirch lobbied the US studios, even bringing the regional stations they were trying to aggregate, to meet people like Frank Wells at Disney (at the time co-head of Disney with Michael Eisner). Ultimately, they succeeded, and secured long-term output deals with all the major American studios. In a bold stroke, they created a duopoly. The only viable place for US studios to license their product for top value became Kirch. In turn, Kirch had a monopoly

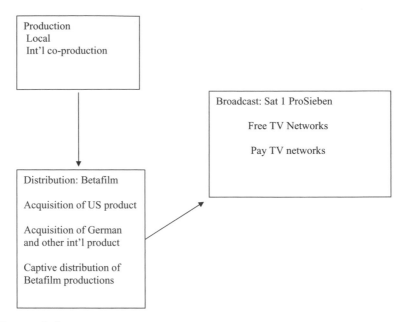

Figure 6.4

on the programming put on its controlled networks. The result was a vertically integrated media empire (Figure 6.4) that for a period controlled the television landscape in the country.

Over time, the Kirch group built up one of the world's greatest libraries and largest integrated media companies in the world. An online encyclopedia summarized that:

> By 1993, Kirch Gruppe had become the largest entertainment program provider for German-speaking countries, including Switzerland and Austria. The group was involved in all areas of the movie and TV entertainment business, such as production, synchronization, distribution, rights and licensing trade, movie and video rental, and merchandising. Besides owning about 15,000 movies and 50,000 hours of TV shows, Kirch's many production firms put out about 400 hours of new movies and TV programs per year.[32]

In addition to building a library of owned and licensed titles, the Kirch group built state of the art technical facilities to store and archive the vast product accumulated. The technical group and storage vault at BetaTechnik became world renown, and many international producers used the facility to store negatives, prints, and masters as well as to create foreign language versions. The BetaTechnik storage vault looks like a scene from a sci-fi movie with tall rows of film prints in a secure/clean climate-controlled room reaching stories high, and mechanical computerized robots able to pull and access individual elements. When US studios and leading producers wanted to archive treasured masters and prints, despite local options and promises of salt mines able to withstand nuclear strikes, many ultimately turned to Leo Kirch. If you want to find the old reels of a classic film, your best bet is not Hollywood but Munich.

Like so many entertainment company stories, however, the reign of Betafilm and Kirch ultimately came to an end. KirchMedia's bankruptcy was nothing short of spectacular with far reaching consequences across borders. The *Hollywood Reporter* chronicled: "KirchMedia's bankruptcy in April 2002 was the largest in German post World War II history. Before it fell, the company built by Bavarian mogul Leo Kirch had the largest library of films and TV rights outside the U.S. studios ... Observers estimate that when Kirch went belly up, the company's bad debts totaled euro 10 billion ($13 billion)."[33] The impact of the bankruptcy sent ripple effects through an incredible array of high-profile businesses and even governments:

- The banking world: HypoVereinsbank, Germany's second largest publicly traded bank, and Bayerishe Landesbank (owned 50% by the Bavarian government) combined had loaned Kirch well over $1B.
- Kirch had employed over 10,000 people.
- Kirch held the rights to Formula One racing, and some worried it could destabilize the entire sport.
- Kirch held the broadcast rights to the German soccer league (and the worldwide broadcast rights to the World Cup), and missed payments could have thrown the sport into turmoil.
- It became a political issue, in that the Bavarian premiere Edmund Stoiber was the opponent in 2002 to Chancellor Gerhard Shroeder's re-election; speaking of the Bayerishe Landesbank's $1.7B in outstanding loans, *Time* magazine quoted Shroeder as saying: "This is not an indication of economic competence but the opposite ..."[34]
- Kirch owned more than a one-third share in Germany's largest publisher, Axel Springer Verlag.

There are many reputed causes, but two facts were at minimum catalytic forces. First, in an effort to build a digital pay service Kirch tried to reproduce the strategy that had been so successful in free television: lock up rights. The difference was that by the late 1990s the international markets had matured, studios had grown more shrewd (and perhaps greedy), and the costs had ballooned. In 1996, for example, a 10-year deal with Paramount was announced for $1B.[35]Unfortunately, the field of dreams thinking did not lead to subscribers rushing to the service. Pay TV subscriptions did not come close to estimates and the service, as described by *Time*, was losing money fast: "Kirch managed to sign up 2.4 million subscribers; the breakeven point was 4 million. The company was losing more than $2 million a day and he borrowed heavily to keep it running."[36] Second, Kirch acquired the distribution rights to Formula 1, another investment reportedly in the billions. This acquisition was targeted in part to gain monopoly broadcasting control of the sport to drive viewers to its channels. A second, and more controversial theory, was that the group was also working to rescue EM.TV, a company that had a somewhat symbiotic relationship with the Kirch family of companies. Animation producer and distributor EM.TV was founded by a former Kirch executive, Thomas Haffa, and had a meteoric rise in value. Germany had never had a small market cap exchange like the NASDAQ in the United States, and in the heyday of the Internet had launched a new exchange, appropriately called the NeurMarkt. EM.TV was the star of the Neur Market, going public, as described by *Business Week*, on revenues of only about $15M and soon seeing its stock rise to into the multibillions:

284

... EM.TV & Merchandising, a Munich outfit that may well be Europe's hottest company. EM.TV had a tiny $15 million in annual sales when it went public in October, 1997. But over the past 10 months it has grown at an explosive rate as Haffa has spun deal after deal with the biggest players in the world of entertainment, from Walt Disney Co. to German media titan Leo Kirch. Its stock is up around 10,000%, to nearly $1,000, on Germany's growth stock exchange, the Neuer Markt (chart). The stock carries a price-earnings ratio of roughly 90; Merrill Lynch & Co. estimates the company will earn $38.3 million this year on sales of $117 million.[37]

Part of its success was directly tied to Kirch, as EM.TV formed a venture and programming block called "Junior" which gave EM.TV the exclusive rights to Kirch's entire 20,000 title library of animated titles; for its part, Kirch helped land programming on its stations, guaranteeing distribution for the titles. EM.TV then leveraged this base with the fortunate circumstance that few if any major German media companies had ever been available to the public for investment; the two local giants, Bertlesman and Kirch were both closely held private family companies.

EM.TV used its stock market value to go on an acquisition binge, first buying or acquiring investments in smaller animation studios, and then nabbing a big fish with the purchase of the Jim Henson Company. In a story on the cover of *Business Week* titled "The Cartoon King," Thomas Haffa boasted that they would rival Disney, and securing the prized Henson company was almost a metaphorical move to prove its ambition.[38] Several years before, after the death of Jim Henson, a pending acquisition of Henson by Disney fell apart in a public spat and now nearly a decade later the Germans had won the day. Of course, there was an enormous price: the reported sales price was $680M, a figure that many insiders considered a significant premium over other market offers.[38a] (Note: In an odd twist of fate, EM.TV ultimately sold Henson back to the Henson family, (for a fraction of what it paid, who then turned around and sold the company to Disney, completing an odyssey that had the Muppets initially and then again in the Disney family of brands.)

The next deal was the straw that broke the camel's back. EM.TV, which up to that point had been a company focused on children's programming and drew strength from its merchandising abilities, diversified to acquire controlling interest in the sport of Formula 1 racing. In October 2000, EM.TV came under fire for irregularities in the reporting of earnings tied to the Henson acquisition, and the stock price crashed 32% in two days and then shortly fell to less than one-third of its 52-week high.[39] Caught in a downward spiral, with insufficient cash flow to sustain operations, the company started selling assets. The big prize was Formula 1, which Haffa sold to Kirch. (Note: As another aside to the story, the German Nuer Markt, which had been based on NASDAQ, eventually went out of business; although I have not seen it written about, EM.TV had been a significant percentage of the market's overall capitalization (e.g., several percent), and the failure of EM started the spiral that led to the downfall of the whole market! Imagine a US bankruptcy that actually helped take down the whole stock market, and you can glean the enormity of the Kirch and EM.TV saga.)

The Formula 1 acquisition did not stem the tide of the digital pay services losses, however, and the collective weight of debt eventually put the once dominant company into bankruptcy. Perhaps in a move to gain scale as global media partners were growing and perhaps to raise capital given the slow subscriber growth (partially attributed to an expensive set top box digital decoder), Kirch started offering small stakes in his empire for the first time; Silvio Berlusconi's Mediaset in Italy, Rupert Murdoch's NewsCorp, and German publisher Axel Springer all took small shares or had put options. When Axel Springer exercised its put option worth $670 million, and then Murdoch followed, the company, as described by *Business Week*, collapsed:

> What went wrong? Everything, say industry execs and ex-Kirch employees. The set-top decoder cost $500, and Kirch stubbornly tried to pass the cost onto subscribers … Underlying pay TV's woes were the huge sums Kirch paid for rights to films and sporting events. His deals with foreign media companies obligated him to pay some $2.6 billion for films through 2006, West LB estimates. Vivendi is just one of the companies embroiled in litigation as it seeks to collect some $200 million from Kirch. Industry insiders believe he owes Paramount $100 million … Most important, Kirch had a 45-year history of borrowing big, betting big, and winning big. It was hard to imagine he would fail.[40]

(Note: At the time, Vivendi was the parent to Universal and Canal+.)

Within a few short years, both Kirch and EM.TV were reduced to shells of their former selves and the heyday of Germany as the key territory financing Hollywood television came to an abrupt end. The country, though, still remains one of the strongest TV markets. ProSiebenSat1, previously consolidated by Kirch (ProSieben had been founded by his son Thomas), was acquired by Israeli Power Rangers mogul and Fox Kids founder/co-owner Haim Saban. Saban, cash rich from the sale of Fox Family to Disney (since re-branded as ABC Family), cleverly bought during the tough days following the dual crashes of the Internet and Kirch, and in just a few years turned the network around and sold the group at the end of 2006 for more than $7.5B, a multiple of the purchase price.[41]

I have included this detailed background to illustrate a few salient points about the international television market. First, it is large. Once a stepchild of Hollywood, individual countries now have the scale to compete on a level playing field with the United States. Betafilm and Kirch produced and acquired quality programming in a quantity that rivaled any US group; in fact multiple groups. Second, the market dynamics are no different than those found in the United States. Fierce competition for programming and eyeballs on networks leads to enormous risk taking. Third, all Hollywood studios had deals with Kirch, gaining significant cash flow they could count on against production budgets. Fourth, the international TV market is a perfect example of the world economy. In the case of Kirch, a German company became a global media player that fueled and supported the cash flow of multiple Hollywood studios and producers. It acquired the TV rights to the second most watched sport in the world, and ultimately sold its leading network in bankruptcy to an Israeli born entrepreneur (Haim Saban) who made his fortune on kids and animated programming in the United States (having leveraged the fortune from *Mighty Morphing Power Rangers* into the building and sale of Fox Family). For Saban, his timing and navigation of the kids programming space outwitted EM.TV. In the end, somehow, most of the key children's assets, (the Muppets and Fox Family), ended up with Disney.

287

A New Landscape — Impact of DVRs, VOD, and Digital Television

In 2005 a sea change began to take shape in the television landscape. From the inception of television through the first few years of the new millennium the concept of television was relatively static. Viewers watched a monitor, and over time the quality of the monitor had improved as had the channel offerings. From black and white to color, then from standard definition to high definition, from analog to digital, from square 4:3 to theatrical 16:9 aspect ratios, and from stereo to home theater the viewing experience kept improving. Similarly, the quantity, and arguably the quality, of programming increased and improved from the big three networks, to tens of channels on cable, to hundreds of options via satellite. The range of programs available diversified exponentially. What fundamentally started to change in the beginning of the 21st century, however, was that the viewer could become the programmer. The world had evolved to a media mandate of "whatever you want when you want it and how you want it."

This change started with the Internet, and then the file sharing capabilities enabled by Napster in the music/audio world. It was only a matter of time before digital compression improved enough and bandwidth became cheap enough that the same trends and demands emerged in video media. While DVRs had already started to become popular and improved user-friendly VOD options were integrated into the TV remote via the customer's cable or satellite box, 2006 was the watershed year that ushered in an era of mass experimentation. Not only was VOD and DVR penetration growing quickly, but in a span of only a few months virtually all networks and broadcasters were seeking ways to make their television programming available via Internet access, downloadable portable devices, and mobile phones. When the right models hit (i.e., iTunes, Hulu), consumers adopted the new services/products with unprecedented speed.

Chapter 7 discusses the economics and emergence of these new distribution platforms in more detail, while the next section simply highlights some of the new options that were poised to change the television landscape overnight; what everyone was scrambling to assess was whether the changes doomed broadcast television, or if well managed, created yet another new ancillary revenue stream.

TiVo and DVRs

First, there was TiVo, a revolutionary technology that allowed the pausing of live television. The essence of TiVo was that the technology converted a television into an easy, better, and virtually idiot-proof VCR — but not just a VCR that recorded shows, a type of digital recorder that allowed viewers to manipulate television shows as if they were being played via a VCR. Soon the technology became more common, with cable companies such as Comcast offering bundled recorders with its service. The functionality initially enabled by the TiVo brand gave way in an OEM world to generic versions labeled digital video recorders (DVRs).

TiVo had the first mover advantage in terms of digital recording technology, and in addition to being able to pause live TV and record programs for playback with VCR functionality, the storage capacity enabled viewers to record a season of programs with the press of one button (record all episodes in the season of X). People that used TiVo became quickly addicted, but by 2005 the upstart Silicon Valley based company was facing fierce competition from cable providers offering copycat DVR services. In particular, large cable providers like Comcast aggressively marketed like services at competitive prices with the marketing advantage of upgrading a captive installed base of customers. (Note: Comcast and TiVo then struck a deal to offer customers TiVo, meaning specific TiVo interface features.) As earlier discussed, the adoption of DVRs and resulting change in viewing patterns had such a profound impact that it led to a fundamental change in measuring ratings (Live +).

The New TV Paradigm/VOD

Beyond the expanded access to programming enabled by free VOD (as discussed previously when asking the question: What is free TV?), we are at the tip of the iceberg in terms of VOD applications. There is no reason conceptually that once viewers become more accustomed to VOD applications that they will not demand more personalized scheduling options: we should expect the TV paradigm to shift again to one where the viewer can be the programmer.

If I were to download 30 programs and pay for them (or select a cue of programs from free VOD options), some from TBS, some from CBS, some movies that were only available currently on DVD/video, some content from the Web, and store them for viewing on my hard drive (or set top box or iPod or whatever), what would I call this compilation? Would it be my favorites? Would it be akin to a Netflix subscription where I paid to have 20 titles out at once for a fixed monthly subscription fee? Would it be akin to my having programmed my own mini-TV channel where I paid for the programming access? As technology puts more control in the consumer's hands, the boundaries defining TV become more blurred.

Despite the revolutionary pace and changes in the marketplace, there was still a missing element: convergence between the hardware that accessed and downloaded programming and the hardware that played it back. Again, this had to be temporary. There are several companies working on the interface between the computer and the TV. It is simply a matter of time before this divide is bridged and the television receiver truly becomes a "monitor" capable of accessing a myriad of signals and inputs, including uploading content from a PC, game platform, and the Internet. Apple had hoped it may have the "killer ap" with its introduction of iTV, but living room convergence continues to be more a promise than reality, with consumer electronics companies, TV manufacturers, computer companies, and game

289

consoles all vying to become the one-stop nerve center. (See Chapter 7 for a discussion of living room convergence.)

Digital Television Switchover

The switch to digital television has already started. The Netherlands turned off analog television broadcasts in December 2006, and most major countries around the world have government regulated switchover dates over the next several years; the EU has a 2012 target switchover date, and the US analog signals were switched off in 2009.[42]

In most instances, the switchover only impacts a minority of people, as signals received via cable or satellite boxes will automatically convert; it is the 10–15% of households that receive free channels via over-the-air signals that require a converter box. To understand what is happening with the digital transition, the FCC provides an excellent summary under its "FAQ's–Consumer Corner" section of its Digital Television Web site. The site notes the following regarding the question: "Why are we switching to DTV?"

... rather than being limited to providing one "analog" programming channel, a broadcaster will be able to provide a super sharp "high definition" (HDTV) program or multiple "standard definition" DTV programs simultaneously. Providing several program streams on one broadcast channel is called "multicasting." The number of programs a station can send on one digital channel depends on the level of picture detail ... DTV can provide interactive video and data services that are not possible with "analog" technology ...[43]

Online Impact

- What is "free TV" is a rapidly moving target, with the development of advertising supported AVOD services such as Hulu.
- Where you can watch TV is evolving quickly, with networks offering "catch-up" VOD access on their own branded Web sites.

- Technology is shifting advertising metrics — DVRs have changed ratings tracking to "Live +3," but how soon will we see Live + Hulu?
- Piracy and global access to debuts via English-language Web sites is creating pressure to launch shows "day-and-date" internationally with the United States.
- Second run repeat values, which historically drive long-term library values, are threatened because of wider, earlier repeat access from VOD applications (the pie may actually shrink and reduce ultimates if new revenues do not exceed resulting declines in syndication values).
- Multiplexing of channels is creating block-based time-shifting to add flexibility for viewer access (and quality flexibility with HD channels), enabling linear channels to compete more effectively in a more a la carte VOD world.
- In the new TV paradigm, we can imagine the viewer becoming the programmer, aggregating a type of "favorites" list from a variety of channels and sources and creating a personalized schedule.

291

Internet Distribution, Downloads, and On-demand Streaming— A New Paradigm

More content from this chapter is available on
www.businessofmediadistribution.com

The years 2006–2008 will be viewed historically as revolutionizing how consumers watched, accessed, and paid for video-based content. The explosion of video on the Web came about suddenly, fulfilling the promise of what many envisioned almost a decade earlier before the .com bust. Much of the change was enabled by technology, such as widely adopted DRM solutions, increased broadband penetration, and the advent of video-capable iPods and then iPhones. For the technology to take hold, however, other adoption accelerants as well as conducive legal and economic platforms were needed. All of these factors came together in a period of not much more than a year and pointed toward a radical shift in the landscape. The confluence of several factors, a number of which are discussed in the following sections, ushered in the digital revolution that threatens to upset and cannibalize traditional TV and video distribution:

- The Googleization of the world and proving the Web can be monetized
- The YouTube and Hulu generation, instant streaming, and the emergence of free video-on-demand (VOD)

- The introduction of the video iPod and then the iPhone
- Implementation of reliable, flexible digital rights management (DRM) technology
- Traditional distributors, not pirates, legally making the market
- Mass market adoption of high-speed Internet access (fixed and wireless), together with the adoption of common standards

Initially, the quick pace of change and related murky legal waters cast fear among traditional distributors that the lifeblood of their business may be snatched away before they could even respond (with some arguing via illegal means). The crisis in the music industry, which was first paralyzed by online piracy and then rescued in part by iTunes, was threatening to similarly upend visual media as peer-to-peer services enabled file sharing of movies. Long form video content, which previously had been thought to be somewhat immune given the inherent barriers of hour plus stories and correspondingly large file sizes (i.e., a film cannot be divided into independent consumptive elements, like a record can be split into songs) was suddenly vulnerable. Whether melodramatic or not, the fate of media was literally perceived to be in the balance—and to many it still is.[1]

Soon the impact spread to virtually every aspect of the business. In July 2007, the major networks came together to announce they wanted to abandon the historical system of residuals that had paid writers, directors, and actors reuse fees for rebroadcasts and served as a core tenet of the Writers Guild of America (WGA), Directors Guild of America (DGA), and Screen Actors Guild (SAG) collective bargaining agreements. At the center of the debate were payments for online use. One concern was whether unlicensed clips appearing on the Web were illegal (an issue spotlighted by Viacom's $1B lawsuit against YouTube), but now the underlying economic concern was being brought to the individual rather than the corporate level—content owners protecting their assets wanted to get paid for online broadcasts, and now the creators wanted to ensure they had their cut as well. All of these issues were symptomatic of a quickly changing landscape, with electronic access for downloading and streaming video content suddenly viable. Exacerbating the urgency for the studios to act and restore a sense of equilibrium was the fact that all this change was taking place on the heels of the decline and peril experienced by the music industry. There was a feeling that this stage of change was somehow fundamentally different than prior iterative technological advances (which despite previous fears had served to

293

expand total revenues); moreover, there was a realization that without action the historical safety nets could not be counted on to preserve current markets.

Because everyone was unsure whether online would be an ancillary market or instead be the whale that could swallow the whole, as well as where lines should be drawn concerning viral access, people were scared and tending to take absolutist positions. With no obvious solutions, unproven monetization, different metrics than traditionally employed, fear of piracy, conflict between protecting valuable windows versus leveraging the Web's consumer marketing reach, and unprecedented adoption rates (e.g., YouTube, Facebook), media conglomerates at once acknowledged the changes were real and struggled to craft solutions that would expand rather than shrink the revenue pie.

Grand Experiments and Revolutionary Changes in Consuming Video Content: Downloads and On-demand Access Coming of Age

Just as software drives hardware (content is king), compelling new user experiences (enabled by pioneering technology) tend to drive digital distribution channels, and there was a gold rush to develop platforms realizing the new on-demand, on-the-go paradigm. Apple (iPods), Hulu, and YouTube are among the companies that leveraged the serendipitous moment in time to launch the right site or product (e.g., YouTube offering free file hosting, together with a user-friendly interface for uploading and accessing content, at the same time users could easily download the flash video application for free). The online video revolution was unleashed and whether a new entrant (e.g., YouTube, Hulu) or market leader (e.g., Amazon, Netflix) all companies were experimenting with business models that could tap into but would not stifle the almost obsessive new consumer habits.

The Explosion of Video on the Web

By mid 2006, everyone was predicting a revolution in the world of video content and how programming would be consumed over the Internet as opposed to traditional television viewing. At the World Economic Forum in Davos, Switzerland, Bill Gates proclaimed: "I'm stunned how people aren't seeing that with TV, in five years from now, people will laugh at what we've had."[2] *Wired* magazine, in an article that also asked how a couple of students "make their way through the 5 billion-channel online universe to you," spoke of the changed dynamic in nothing short of revolutionary terms:

Online video has arrived ... Thanks to growing bandwidth, easy access to the means of production, and cheap storage, it's exploding all around us and becoming a very real, very different way to experience news and entertainment ... What's happening here isn't just TV online. Gone are the rigid 30- and 60-minute blocks; now the clip is it—be it 30 seconds or eight minutes, we're watching only the money shots. Gone is top-down broadcasting; instead, the network has been, well, networked, with thousands of creators and places to watch ... And gone, too, is the at-this-time, at-this-channel programming; now, we're not only time-shifting with DVRs, we're space-shifting as well, watching stuff on our laptops, iPods, and cell phones—even loading it back onto our TVs ... What's on? Whatever you want.[3]

295

By this point in time there was an explosion of experiments, with networks, studios, Internet companies, and start-ups trying to stake out sections of the new frontier. At the same time all of the following were taking shape:

- New points of access for video were emerging (Internet, phones, hand-held)
- New applications of offline revenue models were being adapted (e.g., VOD, advertising supported)
- Convergence between Internet access and the TV started to feel real
- DRM solutions were enabling both streaming and digital downloads
- Delivery solutions were evolving (e.g., streaming, peer-to-peer)

The variety of offerings tempting consumers—from portability to living room convergence, from rental to ownership, from free to paid-for content—was dizzying and confusing. Beyond YouTube, Table 7.1 is illustrative of some of the early entrants toward the beginning of the revolution in 2006.

Table 7.1 Early Entrants as of Q1, 2006

Consumer Device (Platform)	Product/ Service	Type of Content	Revenue Model (Launch)	Backers
PC/Internet	Google Video	Any and all video content	Pay per download	Google
PC/Internet	Amazon	(pending launch)	(pending launch)	Amazon
PC/Internet	Vongo	Starz movies	Subscription	Starz/Encore
PC/Internet	In2TV	Catalog TV shows (14,000 episodes)	Inserted advertisements	Warner Bros. + AOL
PC/Internet	MovieLink	Studio movies (e.g., Sony, Paramount, Universal, Warners)	Pay per download	Studio consortium
PC/Internet	CinemaNow	Studio films, TV shows	Subscription and VOD	Studio consortium
PC/Internet	My BBC Player	TV shows, BBC content	Free for 7 days (public service)	BBC
PC/Internet	Netflix	Movies, all video/DVD content	Subscription	Netflix
Hand-held	iPod	TV shows, shorts, music videos	Pay per download ($1.99)	Apple
Hand-held	PSP Portable	Sony films and TV shows	Pay per download	Sony
Game System	Xbox Live	Long form video content	Variable	

296

Device	Service	Content	Payment	Owner
Mobile phone	Vcast	Video clips, news, weather, "mobisodes" (e.g., 24 linked); CBC To Go	Subscription	Verizon
Mobile phone	MobiTV	Retransmits content: ABC News, Fox Sports, Discovery, music videos	Subscription	MobiTV (private)
Mobile phone	Mobile ESPN	ESPN content	Tiered subscription w/phone	ESPN/Disney
Set Top Box	Akimbo	Retransmits TV channels, such as BBC, National Geographic, Turner Classic Movies	Subscription and VOD	Warner Bros. Akimbo (private)
Set Top Box	CBS/Comcast	CBS content to Comcast subscribers	Pay per download ($0.99/episode)	CBS and Comcast
Set Top Box	NCB Universal	NBC content to Direct TV subscribers	Pay per download ($0.99/episode)	NBC-Universal and Direct TV
Set Top Box	Yahoo and TiVo	Yahoo! Media content	Bundled with TiVo	TiVo and Yahoo!

Web-based Video and VOD's Threat to Traditional Distribution Models and Outlets — Will the New Markets Be Additive or Substitutional?

As the market evolved, everyone was trying to ascertain whether new distribution channels were truly additive, or merely substitutional and therefore threatening to traditional outlets. Everyone seemingly agreed on one point: The online video market would be large, and by the summer of 2009 US Internet users were already viewing more than 13 billion videos/month.[4] Informa Telecoms & Media, a London-based research firm, predicted the market for online VOD would grow to $11.4B,[5] while Forrester Research estimated that it would quickly account for more than 10% of the total interactive marketing spend (see Figure 7.1):

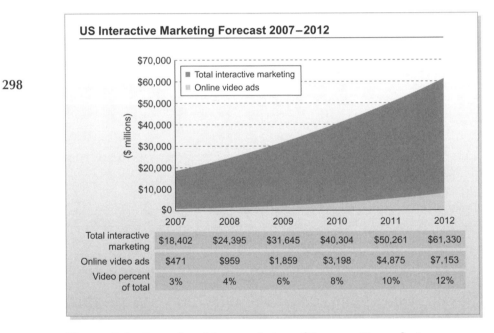

Figure 7.1 Reproduced by permission of Forrester Research, Inc.

No matter what hype, however, until the on-demand and download markets approach revenue levels of the video market, they still represent secondary revenue streams. As noted throughout this book the video/DVD market is too important to the overall economic equation to assume transactions will simply migrate until revenues are at least substitutional. Video-on-demand may be the video of the future, and advertising-supported VOD (AVOD; free VOD; FVOD) will be a critical element of TV going forward (see Hulu discussion), but the associated revenues from each remain a small fraction of the larger markets; moreover, it is not certain which markets will actually converge, nor whether different access methods will be complementary or whole segments will be eliminated. This is a critical issue given the Ulin's Rule factors outlined throughout: historically, licensing content through windows fostering exclusivity, repeat consumption, variable timing, and price points has optimized the pie. Because VOD can largely fulfill the consumer's appetite for access to all "when I want it, how I want, where I want it," there was a simultaneous attack on not just the concept of windows, but more fundamentally the elements of exclusivity and timing upon which windows are constructed.

Economically, one of the key factors underlying this jeopardy is straightforward: online trends toward non-exclusive access, and TV licensing in particular is premised on exclusive windows. The much hyped long tail of the Internet affords a broader platform for access to library titles than has ever existed before, but the long tail does not prove enhanced monetization of that content. The jury is out. Even if access to a program and consumption dramatically expands, that would still not ensure greater licensed revenues than could be achieved from competition over exclusive rights. The threat presented by online is that expanded access and consumption could for the first time actually shrink the pie if that expansion was enabled by free and non-exclusive access. If windows are not choreographed and controlled but content is instead subject to the free-for-all of the Web, then many fear the bar will be lowered. Moreover, lower distribution costs given the elimination of physical goods does not guarantee higher margins given the downward pricing pressures online.

299

In summary, the safety net that new technology would expand revenues — as had repeatedly happened, such as when video did not cannibalize TV as early pundits feared — was in jeopardy, and executives in various segments such as television were left with the challenge of inventing a new market and revenue models or else, as in television, watch their repeat licensing revenues fall in the face of earlier online access that did not make up for their losses. Within a couple of years, as discussed later in the context of Hulu, new markets and models did start emerging, giving hope that at least a balance could be restored. It is still too early to declare whether such new models will ultimately be additive. What is abundantly clear, though, is that consumers will demand multi-platform access, with repeat consumption in the future meaning consuming content via an iPhone, Xbox, PC, DVD, etc., in a pattern dictated more by convenience than a distributor-crafted linear sequence.

Download Services — Challenges to Adoption, Growth through Internet Leaders Not Pirates, and a Market Made by iPods

The promise of download services is tremendous, but factors influencing adoption are complex, with functionality and piracy among the key issues. As discussed in Chapter 5, permanent downloads are now categorized as electronic sell through (EST) and increasingly accepted as complementary to video retail sales.

Impact of Piracy on Limiting Adoption

Although many pundits forecasted downloads to be the fastest growing segment of the distribution pie, until 2006 the growth in this market had simply not materialized — at least not legally. While there are no fully reliable statistics on illegal downloads versus legal buys, most industry insiders would admit that legal watching is simply a fraction of overall Internet viewing. At first, there was a proliferation of illegal services, and the motion picture industry, like the music industry before, had to contend with how to convert people to pay for something they were quickly becoming accustomed to receiving for free. The biggest danger came from peer-to-peer services that could virally distribute thousands of copies of a film almost instantly.

The threat of piracy, and the impact of the new breed of peer-to-peer services, was dealt with in 2005 by the Supreme Court decision in *Metro-Goldwyn-Mayer vs. Grokster*; this case, discussed in Chapter 2 in the section Copyright in the Digital Age, was a turning point for how Internet piracy would be perceived and contained. For here, it is simply worth reiterating that the peer-to-peer file sharing services, such as Grokster, Kazaa, and BitTorrent, enabled individual users to efficiently share and download movies for free. There was enormous pressure, both at the government and industry level, to nip this in the bud and avoid a crisis similar to that experienced by the music industry prior to the white knight arrival of iPod and iPod look-a likes. Additionally, because the Web knows no geographic boundaries, it has become equally critical for foreign jurisdictions to act similarly. The Swedish court's 2009 jailing of individuals behind

300

Pirate Bay — a notorious site thumbing its nose at the notion of copyright protection — bolsters the trend fought for in Grokster.[6]

A key technological advance inherent to controlling piracy, as well as essential to managing the delivery of and access to content via the Internet, was the improvement in encryption systems. History is repeating itself, with the prior fear that DVDs provided perfect digital copies that could be pirated holding back the introduction of DVDs. This was overcome both by market forces and the perceived sense that DVDs were not so easy to copy. Now that DVD recorders are more prevalent, and the safeguards have proven to restrict rampant copying of films, the fear has dissipated not because there is a perfect preventative mechanism in place but because the market has grown so large that naysayers have been marginalized. It is amazing what short-term memory and large revenues can do to both theory and well-grounded concerns.

Now the same issues are surfacing with the Internet, and the same scenario is playing out. Licensors are anxious about their jewels being placed on someone's hard drive, and all the implications that go with that loss of control. Yes, the files are encrypted with the latest and greatest software to ensure that your copy is truly on the end of a digital yo-yo, with the distributing service able to pull the strings to cut off the copy, pull it back after a set amount of time, and virtually control its ability to be played and copied (despite the fact it is stored on your computer). All of this is both critically important in the short term and somewhat irrelevant in the long term. Just as with DVDs, once this market matures it will become impossible to exercise the micromanagement controls over individual copies that are now exercised. Users will be able to break loose of the shackles, but the hurdles will be hard enough, and legitimate use (hopefully) will become custom enough that most users will follow the rules and the percentage of those people violating the protocol will be containable. Once this level of maturity takes place, the violators of the platform will be relegated to the same basket as DVD pirates: a serious threat that needs to be managed, but not a category killer.

301

To DRM or Not to DRM

While DRM systems were responsible for giving studios comfort to release content in digital form, there are many that argue DRM is both contrary to the open nature of the Web and an inhibitor of adoption. Different hardware systems with different DRM technology create the potential for a whole new version of format wars. These are more complicated than the historical video market battles because there are multiple competing versions. The music industry struggled with DRM issues for years, and in January 2009 the record labels and Apple struck a new deal: the music industry abandoned its insistence on DRM and Apple agreed on flexible pricing (moving off the $0.99/song structure and allowing labels to differentiate pricing and charge premiums for new and/or hit songs).[7] Consumers were arguably ecstatic, as the knock on DRM had been the inability to move libraries from one system to another, thereby locking a consumer into its portable storage device and limiting flexibility in terms of download sites and devices (ironically, making portable media to a large degree non-portable).

The same dilemma faces the Hollywood studios over video content and, with DRM synonymous with copyright protection, simply allowing free access is not a favored solution regardless of the music industry's stance. One suggestion has been an industry registry, a kind of clearing house where consumers can register their device. Movies and TV shows downloaded from different registered sites could then be matched and played on any device similarly registered by a manufacturer.[8] If one believes in the historical trends, and compares the market adoption of downloads tied to DRM systems to the entry of DVDs, then it is likely that over time DRM controls will be relaxed and, whether via a registry or not, a more fluid and open system will mature.

302

Speed and Quality as Limitations to Adoption

A second limiting factor to download adoption has been the immaturity and slow speed of the delivery mechanism. Films and TV shows are dense graphic files, and the download speed is still quite slow. The total file for a film is in the range of 1 gigabyte of data, and yet even over a broadband connection the download time is closer to 1 megabyte/second. At over 90 minutes of content, the total download time of a film still averages over an hour, and for a long film can be closer to an hour and a half (e.g., a movie needs about 1 gigabyte of hard-drive space and can take less than an hour to download via a high speed Internet line[9]). The pure inconvenience of this lengthy download is a clear inhibiting factor, and the competitive advantage of peer-to-peer systems able to break content into scattered bits accelerating downloads is a key factor that stimulated pirate services; however, despite comparatively slow downloads the market is growing. It is clear that as download times decrease, and the population downloading content increases, this market is sure to accelerate its growth. Whether this distribution method will cannibalize other windows and become the dominant method of acquiring content, though, remains unclear.

How fast the growth of downloads accelerates depends not only on the foregoing factors, but also the speed by which the ultimate end monitor for viewing experiences converge. Currently, Internet downloads are stored on computer hard drives, and the resulting film watched over monitors or portable devices. While monitors have been steadily improving, the experience is still vastly inferior to watching over a good TV set (this is being enhanced rapidly with the growing market penetration of flat screen sets). Moreover, the sound quality of watching via a computer is arguably a worse experience relative to viewing over a home theater system than is the differential in visuals from the PC screen to the big living room set/monitor.

Limited Studio Attempts to Make the Market

Recognizing the potential of the market and the need to have legitimate platforms to counteract piracy, the studios launched their own Web-based download services. The largest was MovieLink, a service co-owned by the following consortium of studios: Sony, Universal, MGM, Paramount, and Warner. A competitive service, CinemaNow, also offered a range of studio product.

As for how these services work, the owners/licensors of the intellectual property will produce a master just as occurs for other replication; the difference is that instead of a glass master or internegative, the licensor will provide a compressed encoded master that the online distributor will then encrypt. The encryption is part of the sophisticated DRM system restricting how, where, when, and how often the content may be played. While pioneers in providing a legal option for movie downloading, neither of these services—both hampered by slow download speeds and starting up during the heyday of the peer-to-peer services that were eventually shut down by the Grokster decision—caught on and adoption remained limited. Whether the problem was functionality, piracy, pricing, or available content does not matter, as part of the early strategy was for the studios to simply show they were offering a legal alternative to pirate peer-to-peer sites. In the end, with the platform showing increased promise and piracy curtailed, MovieLink was acquired by Blockbuster in the summer of 2007 to provide its download solution.[10]

303

A Landscape Changed Virtually Overnight by iPods; Market Legitimized by Major Brands

The introduction of an iPod that could download and play video content in October 2005 revolutionized the market. Whether this can be called a "killer ap" is debatable, but what is not subject to debate is the phenomenal rate of market penetration and adoption. Although Apple did not break down statistics within the video category, or even what number of video-capable iPods were sold relative to all iPod purchases, it did confirm the following facts: (1) there were 1 million video downloads in the first month, (2) there were 8 million video downloads in the fourth quarter 2005 post launch, and (3) there were upwards of 4 million video downloads in the first month of 2006. By September 2006 the *Hollywood Reporter* quoted Steve Jobs boasting: "In less than one year we've grown from offering just five TV shows to offering over 220 TV shows, and we hope to do the same with movies … iTunes is selling over 1 million videos a week, and we hope to match this with movies in less than a year."[11] Despite the introduction of competitive players, including the Microsoft-compatible/ backed Zune, by the end of 2006 Apple had a phenomenal ~80% market share of the space.[12] The dominance continues, with iPods at mass market penetration levels, and NDP Group research pegging Apple's market share at greater than 70%, and key competitors such as Creative Labs and Microsoft each at less than 5%.[13]

This adoption rate is staggering when compared to the growth, for example, of Netflix, which was the most successful Internet-based method of acquiring video content to date before the iPod (though Netflix was not a download service, but a hybrid using Internet ordering like Amazon to then ship physical goods [rental DVDs] via the mail). Netflix took roughly 3 years to reach its first million subscribers, and another couple of years to reach 3 million (admittedly, not an apples to apples comparison given downloads vs. subscribers).[14] (Note: As discussed later, Netflix, which has delivered over 1 billion DVDs, is one of the most successful companies adapting to online permutations.)

Further, the iPod adoption rate was remarkable given the relatively limited amount of content available. While the iPod for music launched with a catalog of thousands of songs (and to the consumer, a catalog of content crossing the spectrum of virtually all labels, genres, and major artists), the iVideo application launched with a handful of TV shows, including ABC hits *Lost* and *Desperate Housewives*, and shorts from Pixar. (Note: It was this cooperation between Apple and Disney, with *Desperate Housewives* being the top property available to launch the iVideo application, that was among the factors turning the much played out saga of the Disney–Pixar distribution negotiations back onto a positive track, before ultimately quickly shifting direction and leading to the January 2006 announcement of the $7B+ acquisition of Pixar by Disney. Digital distribution was for real, Steve Jobs was perceived as the industry's guru, and in one stroke Disney regained its animation market preeminence as well as gained Jobs as a key shareholder and board member to help steer them into the digital future.)

Seeing the success of the iVideo, competitors quickly rushed to market. In January 2006 the following services either launched or were announced:

- Google launched Google Video, an Internet pay-per-download VOD service
- Amazon announced that it would launch a video download service (Unbox)
- Netflix announced that it was working on introducing a download service
- Starz/Encore (Disney, Columbia pay TV rights) announced a new Internet-based subscription service called Vongo (an acronym for video on the go)

These were not small players angling to join the space. This represented the market leader in Internet-based video rental (Netflix), the market leader in Internet consumer shopping including the top Internet site for DVD purchases (Amazon), and the top Internet search engine whose stock had just made it the most valuable Internet company in the world (Google). Of equal importance to who was entering the market was who was not. Unlike the music space, there were no Napsters emerging as viable leaders. While some peer-to-peer companies may have been dominating Internet traffic, the upstarts were wannabes; funded by venture capitalists, the technology was not dominating the models, and in fact the technology was fast becoming a commodity and playing second fiddle to the larger brands. Perhaps the seminal Grokster case plus the earlier focus of the studios and the Motion Picture Association of America (MPAA) to squelch illegal downloads (and head off the woes that beset the music industry) together created a safe environment for companies to jump in and focus on the legal business. The issues debated were not the illegality of downloads, but the economic models of subscription versus pay per buy, adoption rates, conversion rates, etc. Against this landscape the debate became (within a matter of less than six months) not would video downloads be viable, but who would compete with Apple for the market, how fast would it grow, and would an economic model develop to rival iPod's flat $1.99 pricing for any download?

305

Of course, this is a bit of an oversimplification, and the market still had significant growing pains. Among the key issues holding back the market were battery life of the players, and the ability to upload from the iPod to another monitor/TV; notwithstanding these technical limitations, the consumer at the time did not seem to care. There were scant complaints about battery life and about download times. And to the degree that portability or other issues had technical limitations, consumers assumed that one of the next versions would solve the issue. The key elements were that the product and technology were not perceived as intermediary, waiting for adoption of the next evolutionary product (as was the case of Laserdisc before DVD); rather, the download market and portable devices enabling the market were perceived as permanent, with upgrades expected akin to the PC market. Just like the next laptop would be faster, sleeker, etc., there was a built-in expectation that the next generation of downloads would be faster with more storage capacity … In a flash, the consumer adapted to the digital world, and did not even notice that content viewing was being thought of in computer expectations rather than TV or video terms.

Finally, it is important to mention the inherent limitation of the iVideo space — screen size. While the hand-held medium is acceptable for music videos and some TV shows, it is unlikely to be the screen of choice for long format productions such as movies. Accordingly, how and whether a large market emerges for films is still open, and may be delayed until the convergence of the PC and TV. One could easily imagine a download service that can store data and port it both to a hand-held platform as well as to a TV. In fact, this digital living room is what Microsoft began targeting with the introduction of its Xbox 360, and the target of Apple's iTV and Netflix's Roku box (see the section entitled Living Room Convergence — Truly Marrying the TV and Computer). One ultimate vision is of transportable digital media stored in remote digital lockers, such that you can access and move your library of content from wherever you are, as Amazon is pioneering via its Amazon Video-on-Demand service (see also the section entitled Digital Lockers and Remote Download Access). It should not matter if you are at home or at a vacation ski home to access the program you have bought and then simply upload it onto the local monitor.

Traditional Brick-and-Mortar Retailers Offering Competitive Online Solutions

Just after Thanksgiving, and in time for Christmas 2006, Wal-Mart introduced its own download service. This step was a strategic reaction to the perception that online sales were threatening the DVD market, and Wal-Mart needed a solution if the company was to maintain its market share for consumers buying movie videos for personal use. The guinea pig title was Warner's *Superman Returns*, as *Variety* summarized:

Deal allows Wal-Mart customers to download the film for use on portable devices for $1.95, computers for $2.95 or both for $3.95, in addition to the cost of the DVD, which retails in Wal-Mart stores for $14.87. The retailing behemoth, which accounts for 40% of DVD sales, said it hopes to expand the pricing model to other titles … Deal marks Wal-Mart's attempt to convert its enormous walk-in DVD customer base into download films.[15]

This launch and hodgepodge pricing was symptomatic of the confusion in the market — the pricing model was clunky compared to the simplicity of all songs for $0.99. What the retailers were doing was trying to add comparable value ("we have it too") as opposed to something revolutionary.

Clearly the studios were taking a cautious approach. Discussing the fine line between online adoption and maintaining a vibrant DVD business at retail Jeffrey Katzenberg, CEO of DreamWorks Animation and co-founder of DreamWorks SKG, was quoted in the *Wall Street Journal* as saying: "we must not undercut our bread and butter … The consumer decided when VHS was obsolete … Not the hardware manufacturers, not retail, not us."[16] The same article that quoted Katzenberg went on to describe the awkward position both Wal-Mart and studios found themselves in, and the retailer's reluctant entry into the digital market as highlighted by its dilemma with Disney: "After Disney announced a deal to provide television shows to Apple's video iPod, Wal-Mart threatened not to carry the DVD version of the hit Disney Channel movie *High School Musical*, according to people familiar with the situation. After talking it through, Wal-Mart ultimately relented and carried the DVD in its stores."[17]

Capability to offer downloads is one thing, but turning the new business to profitability is another. Wal-Mart was entering the same murky waters of its competitors, hedging its bets against the future. Like everyone else, they would have to wait and see whether the new revenue streams would be additive or substitutional for its traditional business. Wal-Mart, it seemed, quickly made up its mind: Not much more than a year after it struggled with Disney and launched digital distribution, Wal-Mart abandoned its experiment. The reasons for its abandonment are likely many fold, but one interesting point sometimes referenced is its DRM requirements were tied to playing content via Windows Media Player. This factor essentially precluded content from being watched on iPods, the hardware platform of choice for watching downloaded content.[18]

Digital Lockers and Remote Download Access

Recognizing that download times were an inhibiting factor given the large file sizes of video-based content, services started to experiment with ways to combine instant access (to complete with online streaming) and ownership. Amazon launched its Unbox digital video service in 2006, and followed up with an enhanced version of the service, Amazon Video on Demand, in 2008. The Amazon service offers a so-called digital locker to address the dual issues of file size (a handful of movies could eat up the hard-drive capacity of most computers) as well as the challenge of moving purchased content from computer to computer. The streaming component of the service does not require the maintenance of a video file locally on your computer or hand-held device; instead, it is streamed through the browser, and accessible anywhere through the digital locker labeled "My Video Library." While both downloads and streams are available from the "Your Video Library," the streaming version expands the reach of the service because the file resides remotely. This provides security and storage, meaning that you can consume your content from virtually any device, anywhere, anytime, and not worry about capacity; moreover, the streaming solution counters piracy problems because the content is streamed and no permanent file exists to share or copy. The download is still available to consumers in locations where Internet connectivity is not possible, such as while traveling in a car or plane.

I asked Josh Kramer, Principal, business development and content licensing, Amazon video on demand, how he viewed digital downloads today and where he saw Amazon and the market moving:

One of the challenges Amazon has taken on is to make the ownership proposition in the digital sphere as compelling, if not more so, than the value proposition offered today by DVD and Blu-ray disks. A DVD has the inherent advantages of being highly transportable, durable, high quality, and playable on just about any TV anywhere, due to ubiquity of the DVD player. What does digital add to the value proposition? One key element is instant content delivery—giving customers access to their video collection, on whatever screen is most convenient for them. One of the ways we are working to deliver on this promise is through our cloud-based digital locker ("Your Video Library"), which aims to "un-bind" content from a specific device, but instead associates the content with the customer himself, and the "domain" of screens to which he has access. The other side of the story is the viewing device itself. We're extending our reach into the living room by enabling customers to directly access their content from devices they already use. Our integration with TiVo, Roku, Panasonic and Sony bring us closer to that goal. The point is not to replace the DVD, but to maximize the value and flexibility of content ownership: we want to make it easy for the customer to buy a movie or a TV show, whether on shiny disk, or through a myriad of digital access points, and then make it easy for customers to enjoy their media whenever and wherever they want.

Economics — Macro Issues

This is an immature and emerging market, and it is fair to hypothesize that both the windows and deal structures will evolve over time. Currently, the number of downloads is small enough and the medium experimental enough that one does not often hear of guarantees. Perhaps this was to be expected when the historical main suppliers (e.g., MovieLink) owned the service; however, with the advent of video iPods the construct shifted. When and if a truly competitive environment emerges and the revenue on a per product basis is more real than merely potential, then the economics of this market will likely change. I can easily posit that players will begin to differentiate themselves via pricing, types of pricing mechanisms (e.g., pay per download vs. subscription), and willingness to carry content exclusively and pay guarantees. (Note: Although, to the extent online outlets are akin to retail locations, then non-exclusivity and no guarantees make continued sense.)

In the music space, suppliers that are jealous of the money Apple is making on its iPod hardware have long balked at the flat $0.99 price per song for download. Not surprisingly, as previously discussed, the parties are now instituting a measure of variable pricing. The same challenges are now heard regarding the flat $1.99 pricing per video download from Apple. It is in the long run irrational to pay the same fee for a five-minute Pixar short as for an hour-long episode of a hit primetime TV show. There will inevitably be pricing tiers here as well, taking into account how recent a show is (e.g., the MovieBeam differentiation of a title being available day and date with video as opposed to delayed a month or two), what genre/category it comes from (e.g., a short, TV show, music video, feature film), and whether the transaction is based on a rental or purchase model. Further, services will offer subscription rates to content (like pay TV services) as Vongo tried to pioneer and the consumer will therefore have the choice between à la carte pay per product options and subscriptions. Subscriptions will accordingly become more complicated, mimicking the pay TV or cable models where there will be tiers of content.

Of course, there have been attempts to differentiate offerings, but in many cases this simply seemed to lead to market confusion. In the instance of downloads, for example, which often omitted bonus features available with physical DVDs (e.g., deleted scenes), consumers could buy a DVD of a film at a physical retailer for less than some online services were charging: "They are giving the consumer less and charging more for it," said Warren Lieberfarb (former president of Warner Home Video) in a *New York Times* article on downloads, and continuing: "To me, this really stacks the deck against mass consumer adoption. The studios are caught between a rock and a hard place. If they don't make movies available electronically, piracy will get them. But they have to take care of their brick-and-mortar customers."[19]

Maybe the one fixed fee model that so quickly built the market via iPods will continue to take precedence. I would argue, however, that in the long run this is highly unlikely, again given the interplay of factors in Ulin's Rule. Differential pricing is one of the key factors driving maximization of content value over time; rational economics posits that the inequality of value per purchase, and the crossover of so many different types of content that are differentially priced and consumed in the non-digital retail space, should favor price differentiation in the online space.

Other factors influencing the pricing trends include loss-leading software to drive hardware: The download market has to be viewed in terms of related hardware sales. Apple can afford to price songs via what constitutes an arguably illogical price matrix because on the one hand the content is a bit of a loss-leader for driving hardware sales, and on the other hand simplified pricing is helping develop a market that otherwise was slipping away to piracy. However, once the related

310

hardware and software markets mature and competitors make inroads, there will inevitably be a shift toward greater price differentiation indexed to varied types of content. It is the current odd construct of a virtual monopoly on hardware by Apple coupled with the broadest content availability that distorts the overall market.

Another oddity is that one might expect guarantees to secure content in a scramble to establish positions in the fast growing download space. However, inclined to support market growth at the expense of piracy, and recognizing that initial revenues will at best be incremental, content owners are apt to view the EST distributor as a new kind of retailer. Instead of worrying about returns, the issue is allowable margin, with the calculus the wholesale markup (i.e., discount form SRP) converted from a retail dealer price to a distribution fee. Because the retailer and distributor are the same entity, the revenue splits (e.g., 70/30) are arguably artificially low given that 30% is an amalgam of the retailer margin and the distribution fee. Let us compare online margin with retail (Table 7.2; excluding cost of goods), and assume (1) in both cases the same distribution fee, and that (2) the customer price is lower online (which is the expectation given no packaging and incentive to purchase):

Table 7.2   Online versus Retail Margins

Video at Retailer	Electronic Sell Through
SRP $29.95	SRP $17.99 (assume ~10% < retail shelf)
Wholesale $18 (assume ~60% SRP)	Distribution Fee $5.40 (assume 30%)
Shelf Price <u>$20.00</u>	Content Owner $12.59 (assume 70%)
$2.00 Retailer profit Retailer Margin 11% (2/18) Distribution fee $5.40 (30%* 18) Net to owner $12.60 (18–5.40)	
$12.60 is the same:	Content owner keeps $12.60
	EST distributor foregoes 100% of retail margin, and takes this as a price discount to consumer If a "retail margin" were imputed on top of the distribution fee, such as 10%, then distributor would keep $1.80 + $5.40 = $7.20 @$7.20, the split would be 60/40

This is a hypothetical evidencing how both sides win and keep as much revenue as possible from retail, even when pricing is lower. The actual splits will likely evolve based on these and a variety of other inputs, including leverage, timing, volume, quality of content, etc. — all like the traditional market.

Finally, because there are fewer fixed costs, with cost of goods negligible relative to video manufacturing, managing inventory, and physical delivery to thousands of points of purchase, most revenues drop to the bottom line and margins are high for both sides. This is a further benefit and a fact that may explain the relative quick adoption of simple revenue sharing splits. EST services could therefore afford to drop the price even further and still yield the same net margin to content owners as traditional retail.

Download Revenue Model Wars I: Subscription versus Pay-Per-Download

This is a battleground for digital download models, and the issue of whether subscription or pay-per-download pricing drives more subscribers and revenues applies equally whether discussing mobile phones, hand-held devices, or Internet services. I have met people who feel passionate on both sides of the coin.

The quick market penetration of the iPod is strong evidence of the viability of the pay-per-download model; however, it grew up in an environment without other choices. One can equally argue that Netflix is evidence of the successful application of a subscription service (although, a rental one). The ultimate answer is less likely to turn on whether subscription or pay-per-download models are the best, but on customer interface, reliability, security, marketing, pricing, and range of content offered; as noted at the outset, user experience matters, and top experiences drive successful online distribution platforms. In theory, in a world where convenience and choice are the mantra, rival services with these opposing models (and compelling user experiences) will both be successful. Inherent in choice is the notion that a sizable consumer population will want the ease of one bill subscription, while another grouping will want the control feature of à la carte pay-per-download choice. In fact, this is exactly the point I will make next, and punctuated by a remark from Netflix: Just as retail sales, rental, and other media co-exist offline, there is no reason that a similar rental, purchase, free on-demand construct cannot similarly co-exist in the online arena.

A key limitation to certain subscription services, however, which focus on providing a programmed basket of content, is the diminishing returns to content providers, as an aggregation model is akin to cable. A mobile phone aggregator that charges by subscription only takes in a fixed amount of revenue regardless of the amount of content: revenues are subscribers times the monthly fixed fee ("monthly subscriber revenues"). If a subscriber pays $15 for a certain variety of content choice, by expanding that choice (e.g., doubling the number of available programs) the provider takes in no additional revenue. Accordingly, if there are 10 channels of content on a mobile phone, then the operator is paying those content holders out of monthly subscriber revenues. If the channels go up to 20, and the operator is still only taking in monthly subscriber revenues, then the amount available per content provider goes down (×/20 instead of ×/10).

The only way to counter this is to charge more as content choices go up, much like cable companies offer tiered subscriptions. The problem is that cable is limited to about 100 channels and the pricing tiers can match the relatively limited universe. In a download, digital environment content choices are limitless (long tail) and consumers are going to demand greater and greater choice and flexibility. However, there will be a natural ceiling for price increases; the tier charges will cap out while the demand for more content choices will continue to expand (Figure 7.2). This will inevitably be difficult for operators aggregating content and offering subscriptions to manage. Either they will squeeze the content providers—where top content driving subscriptions will still command a premium but the average provider will see pressure to accept less rather than more even with subscription volume

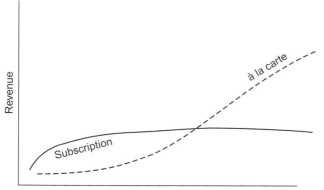

Figure 7.2

increasing—or they will have to limit content and segment offerings into genre silos (TV shows, sports, etc.). In contrast, pay-per-download services simply have to negotiate a split with the content provider.

Streaming — Fundamentals of Monetizing Internet Advertising

The mechanisms for monetizing advertising, and especially video content on the Internet, are all relatively new and seemingly evolving by the quarter. It is therefore important to have at least a basic understanding of the elements of the Internet advertising market, at least as it pertains to video content. Despite the growth of many Internet sites, it remains a challenge to convert traffic into revenues, and especially profits. Chapter 6 describes a number of trends in advertising, including the emergence of FVOD, including AVOD, as the online equivalent of TV (hence the phrase Internet TV); further discussion focuses on the nuts and bolts of the advertising market/metrics as opposed to the structure of the FVOD window.

Types of Internet Advertisements and Relative Value

Among the many types of online advertisements, the oldest and most common are banner ads, which are bought and programmed in standard pixel sizes. For example, there may be rectangles (e.g., the ubiquitous 300×250 unit) or a vertical box on the side of a page (a "skyscraper" ad). With the advent of video content there has been a corresponding growth of video advertising. It is assumed that just as with television, a video commercial will be more compelling than a static banner advertisement. Given the nature of the Internet, including the trend for content to be delivered in shorter segments, video ads often come in short increments such as 15 seconds (though there are certainly 30-second and longer spots as well). More important than length, though, is placement. Where such advertisements are placed may be more critical online than with respect to TV because of the shorter Internet attention span and tendency for users to move on quickly (taking the concept of channel surfing to a new level); accordingly, services are experimenting to try and ascertain what mix of pre-roll, interstitial, or post-roll advertising optimizes viewing and therefore monetization.

All of these factors can affect value. Advertising is priced on a CPM model (cost per thousand eyeballs), with CPM rate cards differentiated by type and placement of commercials. For banner advertisements CPMs are much lower (such as $1+ or less) than for video ads (which can command CPMs of several dollars, even more than $25), and because a viewer is more likely to watch an ad before a piece of video than stay and watch one afterwards, the rates tend to be higher for so-called pre-roll ads than post-roll ones. The highest CPMs are achieved with "relevancy" and advertising from behavioral networking sites that can serve targeted advertisements based upon knowledge of a user's preferences and interests. These networks will aggregate sites or otherwise gain access to users' preferences, and will interpolate that if you have visited an auto site recently then it may make sense to serve you a car related advertisement (even though this is being served to you on a non-auto related site). In a sense, these networks are taking an Amazon-type recommendation engine to the next extreme, matching what it knows about you not to what you may want to read next but rather by imposing advertisements on you to entice you to buy, read, visit, etc., something next.

The methodology of capturing engagement can also vary, with the historical valuation method linked to traffic. Traffic, however, can be differentiated by impressions and unique users. Advertising rates (such as banners) tied to impressions are a less exact measurement of a user's engagement than tracking what that user did, what exactly they watched, how long they watched, and whether their viewing then led to another activity (such as a related purchase, where conversion percentages are tracked). If what the user does (conversion ratio) is the critical value, such as in a search engine where people buying advertising care about users clicking through to their site via their advertisement (consuming or even making a purchase), then a cost-per-click model will likely be utilized. As the metrics improve and advertisers become more savvy, the media buys are being more closely crafted to pay out on actual results.

Exclusions: Frequency Caps and Out of Market Traffic

Among the notable changes (~2007) as the advertising market matured was the imposition of frequency caps. This means that if an advertisement (such as a banner) was served to a specific user who came to the site, then that impression was counted in the traffic to calculate the CPM and resultant payment; however, the frequency cap meant that the site could only count that user once or twice, for example, in a period of 24 hours. Accordingly, for a site dependent on repeat visits from a loyal base, it became harder to monetize because most and in some cases all repeat visits were excluded from the economic calculations.

Beyond frequency caps, the more advertisers can directly correlate traffic to specific demographics for their brand/product the more they

315

will seek to link payment obligations to specific delivery to a target user. Until recently international visitors were bundled into traffic numbers utilized for monetization purposes, but over the last couple of years it has become more accepted to exclude international numbers from the impressions counted. For some sites, by backing out international visitors (who are not impacted by an advertisement for a local product or event) and applying frequency caps the impact could seriously erode its monetizeable base.

Cost Side: Cost of Goods is Lower, but not Zero

All of the previous discussion deals with the revenue side of the advertising equation, but revenue splits are increasingly based on net advertising revenues. Because there are few physical costs, margins are extremely high; there are, nevertheless, some costs. First, ads need to be hosted and served to a site; this is invariably a third-party function given the need to cycle through ads and the nature of placing advertisements at Internet speed. One of the leaders in this space, DoubleClick, was purchased by Google, and like all competitors in this space charges a fee per advertisement served (usually a very low fee, but makes its money on volume). In addition to the costs of serving and hosting, it is not unusual for yet another third party to actually program and insert advertisements, as well as report metrics back to the advertisers. An advertising buy may guarantee a dollar commitment, but it will usually be based upon certain delivery of impressions; accordingly, this service will not only program the advertising, but report back to the advertiser whether the site playing the ad delivered the requisite impressions (and then may cycle out the ad once it has met targets). Similar to the hosting and serving company, the provider of this service will tend to charge a fixed fee (again, very low, with profits made on volume) per advertisement.

Available Inventory

The final element in the advertising matrix is inventory, and who is authorized to program what, and when. Everyone wants to "sell out" their available inventory of space at the highest CPM rates, but in practice just like other media (e.g., TV) there are higher and lower performing sections of sites — a fact exacerbated by many sites being hundreds of pages deep. A site owner's goal is to maximize sell out, and also maximize the value of key real estate. Key real estate may be the home page, and for video-based content may be the landing pages for the content, and the pages/areas surrounding the player through which the video is seen. To sort through this maze, a site's

316

ad/sales department will work to set up a waterfall of options, frequently contracting with multiple third-party advertising sales companies and networks. One party may have the right to sell video advertising inventory, and another banner advertisements. Similarly, one party may have the first right to sell a space, but it may then default to someone else if either inventory remains or they have not secured advertising for inventory X with minimum established CPM thresholds. At the bottom of the waterfall will be "network" or other advertising which carries a lower CPM, but can be placed to fill remaining inventory (often referred to as remnant inventory). If space still remains then the site may elect not to include advertising or to run "house ads" cross-promoting its products and services (and certain amounts of space may be reserved for house advertisements in premium sections for promotion in the same manner that TV networks run commercials to promote their own shows).

One of the key challenges for any site is trying to incorporate inventory space without turning off users. When I was managing starwars.com, this was an issue I always considered, and all mangers of visual-based sites to some degree struggle with striking a balance appropriate to their brand. Content Web sites range from a purist vision to Coney Island commercialization, and every site needs to find its right proportion. What a good designer can enable, though, is increased inventory in a non-intrusive way, with the dynamics of how many ads can be incorporated within prime real estate potentially the tipping point for profitability.

Table 7.3 summarizes the continuum of values and how the P&L works:

Table 7.3   Continuum of Values/P&L

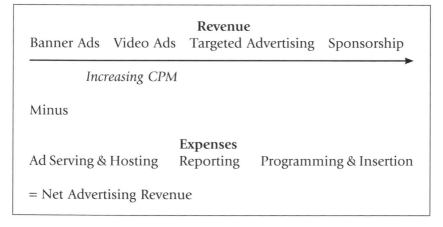

Bold International Experiments

Interestingly, some of the boldest experiments in terms of pricing are taking place in Europe, not the United States (see also Chapter 6). Interactive television services, such as Maxdome in Germany (linked with free TV station ProSiebenSat1) were starting to offer viewers the opportunity to see an episode early for an upcharge: If you do not want to be left with a cliffhanger, pay a couple of euros and you can see next week's episode early. Additionally, they offered a "season pass" where a viewer could pre-pay for early access throughout the season; to preserve demand for the regular broadcasts, however, consumers were not able to jump ahead more than one episode. This innovative approach to access (though admittedly a VOD application or a hybrid, and not a download model) was also catching on in the UK and France, with Britain's Channel 5 selling passes (£40) to download episodes of *CSI* before it hit television.[20]

The challenge with this model is economic—there may be incremental revenue, but this capacity undermines the "who shot JR" effect where a cliffhanger drives masses to watch a show that resolves the mystery. It should be a simple analysis to deduce what number of people need to subscribe to/buy the shows early to equal the value of what an exclusive premiere will yield with a rating of X. The difficulty in practice, though, is that both options are by their nature compelling, and both the buy rates and ratings are moving targets.

Internet Viewing and Immediacy of Content — Video on the Monitor and the YouTube Generation

The Emergence of YouTube and Its Acquisition by Google

At the same time that iPods were fueling the adoption of downloads, free streaming video services led by YouTube were experiencing exponential growth and consumer acceptance. The following is the growth curve for YouTube, exhibiting nearly unprecedented growth from start-up phase to over 80 million users per month in a 2- to 3-year period (Figure 7.3):

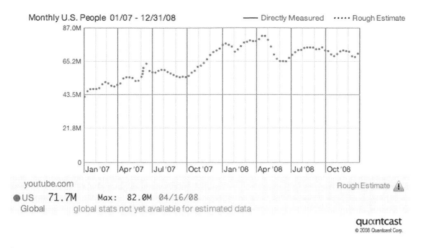

quantcast
© 2008 Quantcast Corp.

Figure 7.3

In fact, the growth was so rapid, and YouTube had catapulted so far ahead of its competitors, that it was acquired by Google for $1.65B in October 2006 — an enormous deal given that YouTube was reputedly losing money. The *Hollywood Reporter* quoted Ken August, principal at Deloitte Consulting, commenting on this dynamic: "It's a huge price for a company that isn't profitable … It's a reflection in general of the huge interest in video on the Internet."[21] In fact, the deal was reminiscent of the high-flying deals of the .com days before the first bubble burst in 2000, as the move was driven by traffic — where Google's own Google Video lagged behind — with the assumption that monetization would follow. In terms of relative size, at the time of the deal's announcement the same *Hollywood Reporter* article summarized: "Google Video accounted for 60 million streams and 7.5 million unique visitors in July, according to comScore data, a far cry from the 649 million streams and 30.5 million unique visitors that YouTube drew."[22]

Not only was this deal risky given the money paid for a company that was reputedly not yet profitable, but YouTube carried litigation risks. Certain videos on the site were from content companies that viewed the site as infringing its copyrights, and were requesting YouTube to "take down" the material. This remedy, in theory, would insulate YouTube from copyright infringement liability under the Digital Millennium Copyright Act. (Note: Timed as part of the deal, Google announced revenue sharing deals with major content owners, including CBS and Universal Music Group, where these copyright owners would supply content and sell advertising around the videos.[23])

319

With the advent of the YouTube acquisition, parties that were previously threatening to sue were now striking deals and finding ways to make money from revenue sharing of advertising around their content (see further YouTube discussion in the section User Generated Content). Nevertheless, Google was aware of the risks and it was rumored that a portion of the acquisition price was reserved to combat litigation claims. Moreover, not everyone and in particular none of the major studios fell in line, and in early 2007 Viacom demanded that 100,000 pieces of content be "taken down" from YouTube. According to the *New York Times*: "Google, which owns YouTube, has offered some studios as much as $100 million to reach agreements, but it has struck none so far."[24]

One of the reasons cited was that Google/YouTube had been promising the implementation of filtering technology. While significant progress had been made in so-called audio fingerprinting technology, which would compare music to catalogs of copyrighted songs and enable the automated identification of infringing material that could then be taken down, progress on implementing a video system was lagging. Tensions and stakes were extraordinarily high, and a Universal Music spokesman commented in the *International Herald Tribune* on companies' actions to prospectively cure the problem and ignore the past: "The copyright law doesn't give people the right to engage in the massive infringement of our content to build a thriving business and then, after the fact, avoid exposure by saying they will prospectively start to filter …"[25]

Although it was not clear whether YouTube would be weighed down by the type of copyright infringement problems that led to the demise of Grokster and other peer-to-peer sites, there was a significant difference in this context. Google/YouTube was not a pirate and pledged to clean things up. It was viewed as the type of player that could legitimize the market, much like Apple had done in the music space, and developing and implementing filtering technology was at minimum an effort to take a best practices approach. (Note: YouTube made good on this pledge, innovating filtering/flagging tools, and enabling content owners to control whether items were sanctioned for display.)

Viacom versus Google/YouTube

Perhaps it was inevitable given the high stakes of distribution, the Hollywood produced copyrighted programs appearing on YouTube, and Google's seemingly overnight leap to market leader that a nasty

320

fight would erupt. In March 2007, just months after Google's acquisition of YouTube, Viacom sued Google for $1B.

The amount itself was a statement, but the suit alleging "massive intentional copyright infringement" was a serious counter-punch to failed negotiations over the uploading of clips to YouTube from popular Viacom shows. Reuters reported: "Viacom contends that almost 160,000 unauthorized clips ... have been uploaded to YouTube's site and viewed more than 1.5 billion times. The decision to sue Google followed 'a great deal of unproductive negotiation,' the company said."[26]

Instantly the case was cast as battleground central for old versus new media; moreover, the suit promised to be the seminal case in the evolution of copyright law, following the Sony–Betamax case and *MGM vs. Grokster* (see also Chapter 2.) [Note: The principal arguments on each side are relatively straightforward. Viacom's thesis is that YouTube had knowledge of unlicensed copyrighted material posted on its site and is therefore liable for unauthorized display of Viacom shows (e.g., *The Daily Show* with John Stewart, *SpongeBob SquarePants*). Google, in contrast, points to the "safe harbor" provisions of the Digital Millennium Copyright Act; these provisions insulate Web site owners from liability for the copyrighted material uploaded by others to their site as long as they "take down" the material when put on notice.]

321

Common Platform — Behind the Scenes Accelerant

Not much seems to have been written about this factor, but simplicity and common platforms have been essential to the areas of explosive growth of accessing and viewing video content via the Web. The case of iPods is well documented in the download space, but what beyond the concept of YouTube led to the exponential growth of streaming video? Other companies, such as iFilm, had been around for years with similar aspirations, but were leapfrogged by YouTube. Why? Arguably, part of the answer was the compelling nature of YouTube coupled with both mass market high-speed adoption (whether by DSL or cable) and use of common browser-based players. In the Web 1.0 days there were "player wars" with Real Player, Windows Media Player, and Apple's QuickTime fighting to become the de facto standard. As video on the Web grew, spurred by YouTube's rise, Macromedia's Flash player seemed to gain dominance, with most users seamlessly adopting newer improved versions (e.g., Flash 7) to watch online video. Flash was becoming standard, and while companies routinely transcoded source material fewer were actively supporting multiple platforms.

Marketing Benefits: The Elephant in the Room

One of the oddities of the tug-of-war playing out in debates around what content users may permissibly upload is that while studio and network executives deride online sources that enable the playing of their content without permission, a large number of executives — and often from the same companies — advocate utilizing highly trafficked online sites for marketing. To the distribution boss a clip or episode played without permission is taking money away while to the marketing boss the exposure of content to tens of millions of people with a viral effect is driving awareness and interest. Harmonizing the positions, however, is far from simple, and to date no one has mastered this conundrum.

I turned again to former president of Universal Worldwide TV and producer of *The Legend of the Seeker* (ABC Studios) Ned Nalle and asked him how he viewed the marketing benefit compared to the risks:

322

The ubiquity of content via the Internet has an attribute: the free marketing. A debutante series can be viewed on the bus to work or school, at lunch, conveniently, and not just at home. While TV programmers may be horrified that they have lost exclusivity, the paradox for them is the Internet offers free word of mouth on series. Positive word of mouth on a show can drive previously unaware viewers to the channel in their community that showcases that show at a regularly scheduled time.

On the downside, as I write this, no producer is getting rich off Internet delivery of his series. Hard-working production union members have grown poorer striking for their share of hard-to-count Internet revenues. Advertisers have refused to pay network prices to reach viewers on-line, because Internet usage is not yet as reliably measured as TV watching. But broadband siphons viewers away from traditional broadcasters. As network exhibitors earn less to showcase content, they will want to spend less to acquire it. Aside from some mitigation in launching a new show and its brand, coping with the dilution of value brought about by broadband distribution will lead to some necessary innovation in the near term.

To survive, producers and distributors who survive will have learned the great lesson of the industrial age: "make it better, but cheaper."

Next Generation: Personalized Channels and Search

The YouTube phenomenon was taking place all over the world, and while some were emulating the model others were already assuming the basics and moving to the next level. Joost—the new baby of Niklas Zennstrom, who had first started the peer-to-peer file sharing service Kazaa (that was crippled by copyright infringement suits) and then the free Internet phone service Skype—allowed the seamless integration of infinite video channels with a peer-to-peer backbone and search functionality. Now you could truly be the programmer, creating personalized channels. Imagine your cable guide list, but you could select from literally any content producer or broadcaster in the world that would allow access. The interface allowed a simple way to coordinate and list data: here was your TV guide and Internet TV guide in one, with instant links to the content listed. Additionally, it would combine interactivity with the prior linear format, revolutionizing TV according to Zennstrom, as quoted in the *International Herald Tribune*: "… the television is becoming more difficult to distinguish from the computer screen, and yet there has been almost no real technical innovation in the television itself … On the simplest level, the History Channel should know that I prefer to watch ancient Greek history, but it should also allow me to interact and engage with others watching."[27]

While Joost's launch fell short of the initial hype, and the company adjusts to the ever changing environment (e.g., integrating its player into the Web rather than requiring a download), the service represents an example of the literal coming together of a global application to see and even interact with whatever you want, when you want it, organized in favorites lists of how you want it, with good quality and instant access. (Interestingly, also in 2007 Viacom made an investment in Joost, seemingly validating the promise of the Web for distribution even while it was suing YouTube.)

Video Search — The Missing Link

One of the missing ingredients in the evolving video-based landscape was an efficient and user-friendly method to search and harmonize where and when to find content. Search on the Web had been keyword based since inception, but now the notion of video search was

323

becoming important, as exemplified by the growth of companies like Blinkx. In a non-network scheduled world, simply finding what content was available, how it could be accessed, and when it would be available was a missing element.

Another example of a company tackling this issue is Veoh TV, a software application pioneered by Veoh Networks, an Internet start-up backed by heavy hitters such as former Disney CEO Michael Eisner. VeohTV's software functions similarly to Web browsers, and generates video playlists that the user can access and then directly link to and play onscreen. (Note: This is still an area rife with copyright concerns and debates.)

Search leader Google is also working on these areas, recognizing that voice and visual search are the next quantum leaps. Skeptics, and even Google, acknowledge the extreme technological challenges. Marissa Mayer, VP Search Product and User Experience and Google's guru in the area, tempered expectations in an interview with Charlie Rose, speculating that true vision search could be many years away.[28]

Revenue Model Wars II: Free TV Advertising Supported versus VOD

During this embryonic stage of Internet broadcasting, the US networks and anyone trying to broadcast on the Web were testing a variety of business models. The two most prevalent were free advertising supported and pay VOD access. CBS was one of the early entrants, offering rentals of programs such as *Survivor* for $0.99 on CBS.com. This was in contrast to the earlier, and albeit continuing debate, of subscription versus pay-per-view models (as discussed in the section Download Revenue Model Wars I).

In contrast, Disney, the company that had teamed up with Apple for the earliest video available on iPods, did not embrace purchased streams, and instead adopted a free advertiser supported model. Disney offered ABC programs on the Web, free for viewing at any time, the morning after they aired on TV.[29] Disney did plan to eventually offer a download to own option, and prior to launch was toying with differential pricing (a quasi pay TV model where shows without advertising would be priced at a premium).

Clearly everyone was experimenting and by 2007 CBS was mimicking the Disney model, offering its shows for free after network debuts on cable on-demand systems, while on the same systems NBC was charging a pay-for-viewing fee of $0.99. It was unclear at the time which model would win out, but the track record of the Internet has been "it's tough to compete with free" and it was entirely possible that a model could emerge where permanency was charged for and repeat broadcasts (via cable VOD, online on-demand, or on network Web sites) were free to the consumer and advertiser supported. Especially when the studio and network are unrelated, this division seems to strike a compromise granting each interested party a key ancillary stream. The 20th Century Fox produced and NBC broadcast comedy *My Name Is Earl* provided a good example, as summarized in *Variety*: "The network holds onto streaming rights—which is essentially an ad-supported business, much like on-air TV—while the studio retains electronic sell-through (a backend model similar to syndication and DVD) … 'They get to stream, we get to do electronic sell-through,'" said Fox's TV President Gary Newman.[30] The outcome was also certain to have implications for tracking ratings: already DVRs were creating new ratings rules (e.g., Live + 3, see Chapter 6), and this wrinkle added another level of complexity as advertisers groped for the new metrics to track brand impressions and engagement.

325

AVOD Takes Off — The Hulu Generation, Original Online Production

Hulu, a joint venture launched in Spring 2008 between NBC Universal and News Corp (Fox parent), successfully pioneered an AVOD model leveraging network content; namely, TV shows and other premium content were available for free streaming, with revenues earned through the sale of video ads. As discussed in Chapter 6, Hulu believes "less is more" and tends only to serve up a couple of video advertisements per 30-minute episode in contrast to nearly 8 minutes of advertising typically cut into a network commercial half hour. By restricting advertising and prohibiting ad skipping, the service can charge a premium per ad as well as offer a more compelling viewing experience.[31] Not only are there fewer ads, but a unique feature of Hulu is that tied to certain campaigns viewers can select among advertising options before the program rolls (e.g., electing to watch a longer pre-roll advertisement, such as two minutes before the program starts rather than have the show interrupted with a couple of shorter advertisements spaced interstitially).[32]

The structure and service was quickly a big hit, as only roughly 6 months after launch Hulu could boast providing 142 million streams to 12 million unique visitors making it, according to Nielsen Online, the "sixth-most-popular online video brand in the United States, surpassing online video networks operated by ESPN, CNN, MTV and Disney."[33,34] By spring 2009, roughly a year post launch, it had leap-frogged the competition to become, according to Nielsen Media Research, the number two most popular video streaming site behind only YouTube.[35] Further, comScore reported that Hulu's video views surpassed 332 million, and its unique users had nearly tripled to almost 35 million. (Note: Ranking it a bit lower relative to competition, placing it in both categories behind YouTube/Google, Fox Interactive Media, and Yahoo!.)[36]

The site had become so big, so quickly, that Disney bought into the venture (May 2009) to become an equal equity partner, adding its content from ABC.[37] The deal represented a significant strategy shift and potential game-changer in the space, as Disney altered its go-it-alone position of driving viewers to abc.com, while creating a near network monopoly (only CBS missing) to compete with the leading sites, such as YouTube, born of the online world.

Hulu's ultimate monetization challenge, which is a microcosm of the overall challenge of the Internet with content, will be to blend the value of equal streams over diffuse locations (see next section) and time versus the live effect of television. How much are 10 million viewings in "syndication" worth versus live?

Another unique feature of Hulu is that while the company promotes viewing at its Web site www.hulu.com, from day one it embraced distribution partnerships. One of the radical departures Hulu innovated from the get-go was providing embed codes enabling users to show its programming within their own sites and allowing the programming to virally circulate.[38] Hulu thereby enables third-party Web sites to embed its player into their sites. Not only are major players such as AOL, MSN, MySpace, and Yahoo! distribution partners, but Hulu had over 6,000 Web sites distribute its content while in the beta test phase. This is a radical departure for the network owners (Fox and NBC, and now also ABC), which thrive on driving viewers to a distinct location. The Hulu model casts the distribution net as wide as possible, with where and how Hulu is accessed as a second thought to offering a range of premium content free to viewers. Hulu is the quintessential example of convergence: while positioning itself as Internet TV it is a kind of hybrid that can be thought of as VOD, free TV, and Internet TV. It is not surprising that its window pattern is not obvious for unaffiliated content licensors, especially when Hulu offers no license fees/guarantees but rather a cut of advertising revenues generated via its diffuse distribution (making the model to the content owner more like syndicated television).

I asked David Barron, VP of Content Partnerships for Hulu, what he thought about the comparison to TV syndication and what Hulu was doing differently that was making it successful in monetizing the new space. He advised:

To compare what Hulu is doing to TV syndication, you first have to understand that TV syndication is just one of many windows in the lifespan of a piece of content. Traditional entertainment companies have always relied on windowing content, whether by platform, time, technology, territory, etc. Hulu is proving that there is another viable window of free-on-demand that can live alongside other distribution windows such as TV and electronic sell through. For current network programming, the on-demand period extends for some number of weeks post initial TV airing, thereby extending the period viewers can watch their favorite show. For library content, the new on-demand window allows people to discover programs that either haven't been available for a long time, or weren't available in their market, and therefore provides a new revenue stream for the content producer. Of course, these are all businesses in development, and therefore the rules are changing regularly.

In terms of how Hulu may be better exploiting this opportunity, including the long tail of library product, we create a great environment for people to enjoy long-form premium video, and whereas others have focused on user generated content or in cases quantity over setting a quality bar, Hulu recognizes that entertainment is impulse driven and we want to make it very easy to watch high quality premium content in an equally high quality environment.

With success inevitably comes competition, and in a move apparently targeted at diversifying its offerings, improving monetization, and challenging Hulu's leadership in the premium content space, in the spring of 2009 YouTube announced it was creating a new section devoted to Hollywood/professional content. YouTube struck deals with ABC for short videos and with Sony for both TV

327

shows and movies; both distribution deals also enhance the content supplier's own brand, and in the case of Sony will play via its crackle.com (its video streaming site, renamed from Grouper) player.[39] ABC's relationship with YouTube may have proven just a tease, however, as shortly thereafter it became (as noted previously) a partner in Hulu. Perhaps this was a signal of the new order, with the networks banding together for scale (see Joint Venture discussion in Chapter 1) to regain the turf online upstarts had grabbed. It will be interesting to watch this evolution, and whether a couple of dominant players remain (e.g., Hulu, YouTube) that compete for distribution of studio product in the streaming space in a manner paralleling the jockeying to secure rights as seen in the pay TV arena. Already YouTube announced deals with Lionsgate and Sony, and Hulu (beyond its partners' content) with MGM, Paramount, and Universal, indicating that the force of exclusivity (Ulin's Rule factor) is at play against the open nature of Web syndication when monetization is in the crosshairs.

Advertising Supported Streaming Video — Is there a Better Advertising Solution?

In the summer of 2007, when Google had basically folded Google Video into YouTube and was focusing entirely on a click-through based advertising model to provide free streaming video, Google introduced a new mechanism: a translucent ticker-type overlay on the bottom of the screen.[40] If a user ignored the overlay it would fade out, but if they clicked on the video it would pause for an advertisement (e.g., 15 seconds) to play. Advertisements are therefore enabled by the user, and would also only be coupled with those third parties who were YouTube content partners and licensed videos to YouTube. In terms of the metrics, the *International Herald Tribune* advised: "Google would charge advertisers $20 for every 1,000 times the ads were displayed. Its adoption of overlay ads for online video could turn the format into an industry standard, advertising executives said."[41]

The challenge here is building an entirely new advertising model to monetize content. This is a tall order when factoring in that advertisers need to accept the new pricing and metrics, and when it took years and mass market penetration of DVRs before traditional advertising metrics adopted the Live + 3 measure of capturing viewers. (See also Chapter 3, the section entitled Principal Methods of Financing Online Production for a discussion of the difficulty in simply equating online and offline purchase values/metrics.)

New Original Made-for-Online Productions

The new online video advertising market enables more original programming made for the Web, allowing producers to rely on more revenues than simply from integrated product placements. This, as discussed in Chapter 3 in the case of Bebo's *Kate Modern*, has proven a viable financing mechanism for shorter form content. Also, as discussed in Chapter 2 in the context of development, this is starting to attract top talent, such as Ed Zwick's foray into the space with *Quarterlife* and Rosario Dawson starring in the Web serial *Gemini Division*.

Accordingly, the number of players and variety is increasing. Disney's Stage 9, a dedicated made-for-the-Web production arm (which has since been folded back into the studio), launched the sitcom *Squeegees*, Sony is producing *Sofia's Diary* for Bebo, and *Big Brother* producer Endemol is producing an interactive reality show *The Gap Year* (also for Bebo). Alongside such majors, new media studios such as 60Frames, Worldwide Biggies (launched by former Viacom executive, Albie Hecht, who headed Nickelodeon programming and launched Spike), and Electric Farm Entertainment (producer of *Gemini Division*, and whose founders include former CBS Entertainment president and co-head of Sony Pictures Entertainment Jeff Sagansky, along with *Lizzie McGuire* producer Stan Rogow) are trying to match talent and programming to launch the next generation of online shows.[42,43] It is this growth of original online programming and fear of where that would lead that, in part, led to the stalemate in the SAG negotiations, where the union was holding out to ensure that residuals were due on all made-for-online original content (see later discussion).

Over time, it is inevitable that more, and better, online original content will be produced. Sites like Hulu may migrate viewing patterns of traditional media online, but currently this is simply a new window/medium for repurposing content; the analogy to pay TV is apt because whether or not consumers are paying, the service is aggregating studio/network content to watch after it has premiered elsewhere. This will work successfully for a while, but it is also likely that as with pay TV networks needing to add original content (e.g., *The Sopranos*, *Sex and the City*) to redefine brands and keep customers loyal, Hulu watchers will want new content as well. Will we soon see original content debuted by network partners on Hulu, and the network runs then being either a parallel or secondary window? As discussed in Chapter 6, the notion of "what is TV" is not easy to define as television morphs into a branding construct and may no longer be defined simply as a single platform.

Living Room Convergence — Truly Marrying the TV and Computer

Living Room Convergence: The Launch of Apple's iTV and Streaming DVD Rentals

It is a testament to the level of convergence that I was unsure whether to discuss iTV under market convergence versus the section regarding download threats to the DVD market. The ability to access video over the Internet and then watch it over your TV is the ultimate goal, and the premise of so-called living room convergence.

Apple's iTV may not have been the "killer ap" people wanted, but regardless of the reason (e.g., people did not want another box) it was only one among a number of hardware solutions trying to provide the bridge. In a sense, it had been tried before (remember Web TV?), and whether the bridge is a new box or a feature in an existing box, in the long-run there seems something a bit doomed about trying to create an interface to a television when the next generation of televisions can do it themselves (though innovative devices, bridging the Internet and TV and enabling customization will undoubtedly drive new markets before such devices become standard integrated TV features, and a monitor is the access point to all). One notable interface, though, where convergence is manifested today is via integrated games platforms such as Microsoft's Xbox Live Arcade (XBLA); these systems/environments enable both access to linear content and connectivity via XBLA to millions playing interactive games. The growth of the live platform (boasting more than 10 million members) and integrated ecosystem demonstrates a compelling application of living room convergence.

In terms of television, already new sets are being conceived and built with enabling chips, such as evidenced by a deal announced in the summer of 2008 between Amazon and Sony. The Amazon Video-On-Demand video store is being placed on new high-definition Sony Bravia televisions. The Amazon store will initially be available through a Sony Bravia Internet Video link, a separate piece of hardware that tries to compete with Apple's iTV to stream Web video directly to the Bravia TV. This is just the first step, and as the *New York Times* reported: "future Bravias are expected to have this capability embedded in the television, making it even easier to gain access to the full catalogue of past and present television shows and movies, over the Internet, using a television remote control."[44]

Another example of the same type of enabling of the virtual video store is Netflix's service that first allowed users to access and watch

330

movies and TV via their computers, which was then expanded to direct-to-TV applications. As initially launched, the consumer was offered instant electronic delivery, via streaming to the PC, of a rental DVD rather than having to wait for the DVD in the mail. The next iteration was a version announced in partnership with TiVo (Fall 2008) where the Netflix Watch Instantly streaming rental service would be included within TiVo's suite of offerings. The stated goal was for a consumer to order a movie from Netflix via the remote control, which would be streamed directly to the TiVo box/TV. In the spirit of covering every angle of living room convergence, Netflix was also closing deals to deliver streaming programs not only via TiVo, but also through independent set-top boxes much like the iTV box (Roku) and next generation game console systems (e.g., Xbox Live). Its Roku set-top box enables instant streaming of several thousand titles to a consumer's TV, with a remote and functionality mimicking DVD playback.[45] Regarding consoles, Netflix issued a joint press release with Microsoft proclaiming that over one million users had downloaded the Xbox Live application from Netflix in less than the first three months of the partnership, and that Xbox Live users had viewed over 1.5 billion minutes of TV and movie content.[46]

I asked Steve Swasey, Netflix's Vice President of Corporate Communications, how the company viewed all the experiments in the market, and whether in terms of streaming content to the living room there was space for multiple players and models or whether we would see more convergence. He noted:

Netflix is at the forefront of offering its customers the same type of services via online streaming and other applications that it has always provided—in terms of implementation we believe content is king, and our business model is grounded in offering convenience, selection and value in equal measure regardless of the delivery mechanism. It's clear to us that the consumer has a strong appetite not just for new releases, but for product in the "long tail"—this was clearly demonstrated to us on Oscar night (February 22, 2009) when 1.8 million DVDs were added to customers' queues encompassing over 45,000 different titles. With new technology, we are simply able to diversify access to the long tail (and new content) via a subscription rental model tied to streaming as well as physical DVD. We now offer access through a variety of platforms, including the Roku box, and the more hardware partners the easier it is for consumers to watch the content they want.

We believe the combined DVD and streaming subscription rental, enabled by the Roku box or through our other hardware partners, can live in a healthy way alongside other options, whether free video on demand services such as Hulu and YouTube, or pay per view access offered by Amazon or Apple. This is really no different than the brick and mortar world of rental video outlets, mass market sell through outlets and television all co-existing, and what we are seeing is a transition of these models from the physical to the online world. It doesn't matter whether you label our Internet streaming delivery as subscription rental or a type of subscription on demand service, because at essence it is the same model as DVD rental, providing great selection, ubiquitous content and convenience to the customer. However, the more we can expand that principle—again convenience, selection and value—the better, and the next step beyond access via physical set top boxes is to integrate our streaming feature directly into televisions. At CES we just announced partnerships with both LG and Vizio, whereby future TVs will embed the Netflix streaming application, and we expect to see this next generation product out within the year.

Rationalizing the Burst of Convergence

With so many moving parts, it is nearly impossible to clearly diagram this burst of convergence. Figure 7.4 is an attempt to capture the following key factors: (1) the market is largely driven by the online market leaders in related sectors, neither by pirates nor by traditional media distributors; (2) convergence is not business model dependent, as subscription, rental, and free delivery models are all being deployed; (3) TV remains the Holy Grail to many, as whatever the primary viewing platform online market sector leaders are looking for ways to leverage content delivery to the TV; and (4) technology is enabling the migration of traditional media markets (e.g., TV, sell through video, video rentals) into new online adapted versions of the traditional markets. (Note: For simplicity, I have omitted the further layer of delivery to TV via gaming systems.)

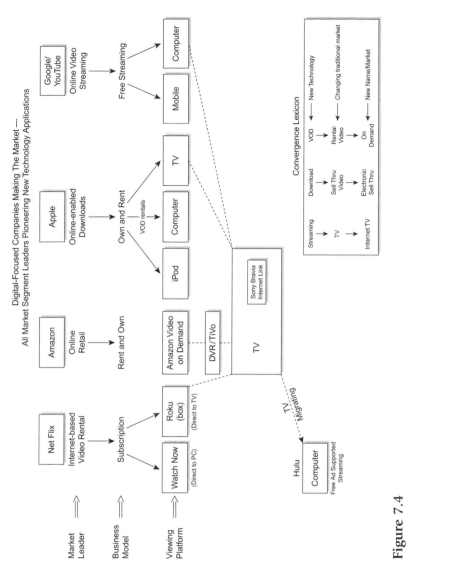

Digital-Focused Companies Making The Market —
All Market Segment Leaders Pioneering New Technology Applications

Convergence Lexicon

Streaming → TV → Internet TV

Download → Sell Thru Video → Electronic Sell Thru

VOD → Rental Video → On Demand

New Technology → Changing traditional market → New Name/Market

333

Figure 7.4

Impact on Residuals and the Changing Landscape: How Online and Download Revenues became the Focus of Hollywood Guild Negotiations and Strikes

The potential for rapid revenue growth from online streaming and downloadable transactions has become a critical topic in the overall compensation of talent. Members of Hollywood guilds remember conceding issues and participation in the early days of video, not recognizing what an important element those revenues would become for film and television properties. The fear of "never again" has driven entrenched bargaining positions, and served as the emotional lightning rod for negotiations between the WGA and SAG with the Alliance of Motion Picture & Television Producers (AMPTP). Essentially, even though online and downloadable revenues are minuscule today compared to sums generated via traditional outlets, actors, writers, and directors all want to protect themselves in the event these revenues grow — especially if they grow rapidly and start to cannibalize the monies that they have fought so hard to protect in past guild agreements.

To read about the issues in the press it is easy to think that everything is unfair, and residuals are the lifeblood of compensation. In fact, as discussed in Chapter 2 regarding the compensation of writers, it is important to recognize that residuals (and what is being fought over in guild new media negotiations) represent just one element of the overall compensation pie, and in many cases a relatively small fraction of the total compensation an individual will earn with respect to a particular project. While securing fair compensation for reuses and ensuring that new media exploitation does not undermine revenue streams previously fought for has obvious logic, this is arguably an area where emotion and perceptions of just compensation play disproportionately to the actual compensation at hand.

Does Abandoning the Historical Residual System Make Sense?

A new and dramatic twist emerged in July 2007 when the AMPTP, represented at a press conference by the heads of three networks — Warner Bros. Entertainment Chairman-CEO Barry Meyer, CBS Corp. Chairman-CEO Les Moonves, and Disney-ABC TV Group president

Anne Sweeney—publicly called for a complete overhaul of the almost 50-year-old system of residuals for writers, actors, and directors. While the WGA contract had been in the spotlight, with an October 31, 2007 expiry and pending threat of a strike, suddenly the AMPTP had upped the stakes by also simultaneously taking on SAG and the DGA. As *Variety* reported: "We're operating under terms and conditions that were formulated 50 years ago ... Barry Meyer explained on Wednesday. "We have to look at the models and allow our investment to be recaptured. And this is the time to do it because off all the new-media issues."[47] The Web was clearly at the heart of the debate, with the studio and networks initially rebuffing any attempt to extend residual-type payments to Web, download, and other new media exploitations.[48]

The AMPTP members had proposed a freeze in the current residual system for three years, during which period the parties would agree to a study to revamp the overall system. After the WGA promptly rejected the proposal, the study was pulled from the table and the negotiations degenerated into a dramatic and caustic stalemate.

As noted previously, the heart of the AMPTP's proposal was to scrap the old system that paid writers, directors, and actors "reuse" compensation when properties were replayed in ancillary media (i.e., free TV reruns, pay TV, home video); instead, creative contributors would be paid a percentage of profits. The producers, lamenting fixed payments when distribution and production costs may still leave projects in the red, argued they should recoup their investment before paying out residuals. Barry Meyer was again the spokesman, quoted in *Broadcast & Cable*:

335

The goal, Meyer said, is to find "a way to recoup the sizeable investment in movie and television programming before there is a sharing of profits with anybody. Why," he asked, "does the model work that says you have to reuse that product trying to recapture a loss? Why isn't (there) a model that says once the investment is recovered, maybe there should be a higher percentage paid of the profits? ... It is clear to us that those old models don't work anymore, that models based on reuse of programming before you've recouped your costs, or any semblance of costs have been recouped, don't work anymore. And we think that the study we're asking for has to look at that."[49]

Countering the AMPTP view, the guilds, deeply suspicious of so-called Hollywood accounting (see Chapter 10) outright rejected the notion that a profits-based system could be fair. SAG's president bluntly noted that they did not need a study to show that a sharing mechanism based on profit accounting "would be inaccurate, unreliable and unfair. Talent can't be asked to share the profit risk when creative artists have no control over what projects are made or how they are budgeted—particularly for promotion and advertising."[50]

Another wrinkle in the negotiations was suspicion that the AMPTP's stance was simply a negotiating ploy, posturing to change the whole so that an eventual compromise would be pinned on the lowest residual base rather than tied to a higher ancillary market. Residuals differ across markets, but the studios countered that in fact the producers were focused on the overall picture, and not staking out ground for the pyrrhic victory of linking payments to the lowest base (pay TV a lower residual based than free TV given relative market sizes). The studios were adamant that this was not gamesmanship, but rather about capturing revenues from all sources to recoup investments in production, and then sharing in the upside.[51] In the end, probably recognizing that scrapping residuals was too severe a change, the studios backed down a bit and the parties agreed to formulas in both streaming and EST contexts.

SAG — The Last Holdout

After the DGA and WGA settled their differences over the treatment on "new media" residuals and, respectively, agreed to new collective bargaining agreements (2007), SAG elected not to follow suit and was stalled in protracted negotiations with the AMPTP. In justifying its holdout, the SAG Web site noted under the heading "Why not just take the deal — other unions have?" that one cannot equate the working life of an actor to that of a director or writer.

Oddly, despite the difficulty in reaching an overall accord, both sides were in apparent agreement regarding a residual formula for the principal new media categories: (1) when a consumer pays to view a TV show or movie via a new media platform, including in the instance of downloads-to-own (EST) and (2) when a producer makes a TV show available via advertising supported streaming. SAG's Web site, under a Special Bulletin pertaining to the negotiations, advised that if a TV show "… were to be streamed on the Internet, it would have 24 free streaming days … Then, after the 24 days of streaming, they would have the right to exhibit the episode for two 26-week periods if they pay 3% of the applicable minimum for each 26-week period. In the case of a day performer who works one day, that comes to approximately $22 for each 26-week period …"[52] The calculations can become complex, as in the instance of EST, the SAG site additionally noted "the casts would share in 5.4% of 20% of the DGR (distributor's gross receipts) up to the first 50,000 units downloaded for features and up to the first 100,000 units downloaded for television programs."[53]

What created the stumbling block was covering productions made for new media. The parties were at loggerheads whether this should be subject to a union agreement in the first place, and whether programs created for the Internet should trigger residuals for downstream reruns on the net (e.g., should a show produced for abc.com be available later on abc.com or anywhere else on the Web, for unlimited access with no residuals ever due?). The SAG Web site, again under the Special Bulletin posted in the fall of 2008, summarized more than ten outstanding items, but started with the following two (Table 7.4)[54]:

337

Table 7.4   SAG versus AMPTP

Issue	AMPTP Proposal (6/30/08)	SAG Proposal
Union contract coverage in new media	If producer chooses, no original new media production costing less than $15,000 per minute would be covered by this contract's terms.	All new media productions made by AMPTP companies are covered by TV/theatrical contract, regardless of budget. We have proposed a tiered system, similar to our low budget feature contracts, which sets minimums per budget level.
Residuals in new media	No residuals for made for new media program reused on ad-supported new media, meaning the program would run forever and never pay residuals.	All new media productions should pay residuals, regardless of the exhibition platform. Residuals paid on all programs used in new media.

Accordingly, SAG argued the merits of new media on its face, plus preached the slippery slope that to cede residuals on new media would in essence be the beginning of the end of all residuals in all media.

Beyond Professional TV and Video — User Generated Content

User generated content (UGC) is at the heart of YouTube: content created by individuals and uploaded to the Web for anyone to see and potentially share. At first, the ease of uploading a video file was spurring growth, but quickly the ability to upload images and video from cell phones created a new level of access and potential. A generation of citizen reporters was enabled, and suddenly nothing was private. A recording of Saddam Hussein's hanging exemplified that there were now, in essence, no limits to what could be uploaded and accessed. The new gatekeeper was editorial and search, not content creation, access, or technology.

338

The challenge of UGC, as well as video content on the Web in general, has been how to monetize viewings. The advertising categories are there, whether banners or video advertisements, but the initial expectations of free coupled with concerns about juxtaposing brand advertising next to unfiltered and so-called unprofessional content, have slowed adoption such that monetization has not matured in pace with traffic. Nevertheless, companies are improving the match, led by YouTube, which as the market leader has the most at stake. I asked Kevin Yen, Director of Strategic Partnerships, YouTube, about the progress of the industry and YouTube, and he was very bullish:

YouTube's potential as a monetization platform is unparalleled, and we are in just the nascent stages. The fundamental factors that drive monetization are the number of playbacks and the money earned per playback. Many partners find that YouTube generates the most playbacks for them and that these views are steadily increasing due to our continued work refining search algorithms, site navigation, and partner tools. In terms of yield, YouTube has and continues to innovate many methods of converting views into dollars, including different ad formats, sales models, community engagement programs, and commerce transactions. Online video can be a great win-win-win for content owners, users, and advertisers. YouTube is committed to making this future a fast reality.

Power to Create Stars

In the context of UGC, I further asked Kevin Yen why the Internet had not yet led to the "discovery" of new celebrities. If one thinks about reach and frequency of a television network, YouTube's reach can be deemed as nearly on par with the 100M+ TV Household market, and arguably given video views certain demographics are consuming content at a similar or greater rate. Why then has no Jerry Seinfeld or Oprah Winfrey emerged from the Internet, and can those with success online ever hope to reap the financial windfall stars achieve in traditional TV? Kevin advised that given the infancy of the Internet we need to be patient, and as the medium matures and successes migrate into mass market culture, we will indeed see, and are already seeing signs of creating stars and those stars benefiting financially:

339

The power of YouTube to generate stars is real. Already, several musicians have been discovered on YouTube then signed to major labels, and creative talent on YouTube are receiving pitches nearing or even exceeding a million dollars. As marketing dollars continue to flow online and traditional media companies embrace the power of community-procured stars, this translation of YouTube celebrity into real-world financial gain will increase in frequency and intensity. Overall rising ad sell-through rates and individual talent deals, combined with concerted promotion that often accompanies both, can systemically trigger virtuous cycles that fuel fame and fortune to levels of success impressive by any measure.

Use Propelled By New Tools

New tools and types of content are starting to emerge and converge. First, companies started to offer simple editing systems, allowing users to make mini-movies, digitally editing and uploading with an ease that seemed unimaginable a few years earlier. Second, companies realized that with facile editing and unlimited content users could create "mash-ups" combining elements of their own content with third-party content. Yahoo! bought the editing system Jumpcut and technology start-up Eyespot signed deals with Lucasfilm (the relationship has since been discontinued) and the NBA. I could never have imagined a few years ago that I would run a site enabling mash-ups, and being pitched proposals to stimulate engagement by challenging users to create their favorite amputations from *Star Wars* scenes. Managers overseeing brands realized, that properly structured, they may be able to better engage their customers by offering their own material to be edited by fans, or even combined with fan material.

Additionally, an array of widgets, applications, and functionalities on social networking sites has become a phenomenon; the sandbox will continue to be expanded, as giving consumers new tools to interact with, modify, and personalize content is a trend just in its infancy. The great challenge for media content in a number of these contexts is artistic integrity, and we are seeing the evolution of boundaries in terms of how far a creator or owner (and the law) will allow individuals to manipulate their work. In instances fully open platforms have evolved, with Wikipedia as a prime example of encouraged modification and Creative Commons enabling open licenses and granting creators simple toggles such as "share alike" and "attribution" within a rules-based open framework for free content licensing.

Mobile Phone Applications

Beyond Internet download and streaming services, mobile telephony is regarded as the next great distribution platform.

A fundamental open question remains, however, as to whether this is a new market or whether the phone is simply another portal to the Internet. For example, why would a consumer need unique access to content through its mobile carrier versus gaining access to the same content via the Internet (which is accessible via its phone)? The answer, in part, is that mobile carriers are trying to carve out a piece of the pie and provide a unique offering, and in some cases partnering to co-brand portals and gateways. Moreover, in a world craving immediate access to content, the phone can be likened to a super remote control with its own video screen for instant gratification: with the press of a button you can access and program your home DVR, via a browser you can find content on the Web, and by a branded icon you can directly link to select programming.

340

The potential for this market is just being realized. According to Nielsen's Three Screen Report comparing television, Internet, and mobile viewing, as of the beginning of 2008 there were more than 90 million mobile subscribers who owned video-capable phones (representing 36% of all US mobile subscribers) and nearly 14 million people were paying for a mobile video plan (only a 6% penetration of mobile subscribers).[55]

The online supplemental material includes a general discussion of mobile phone applications and content, including:

- Types of content (e.g., customized for phones, repurposed from other media, created for mobile)
- General windows and economics
- International aspects of mobile phones and Internet distribution

341

Ancillary Revenues: Merchandising, Video Games, Hotels, Transactional Video-on-demand, Airlines, and Other Markets

More content from this chapter is available on
www.businessofmediadistribution.com

This chapter combines a bit of a hodgepodge of revenue streams, but that is because an intellectual property asset, by its divisible and malleable nature, lends itself to being exploited via endless permutations, associated with a dizzying array of physical products, and distributed by any platform capable of attracting eyeballs. Given this open ended sandbox to bring in additional dollars, in exceptional cases revenues from so-called ancillaries can become the proverbial tail wagging the dog, generating more money than the property in its original incarnation. Merchandising, a category that could mean a thousand different products (e.g., ranging from toys to games to apparel), is what one tends to associate with ancillary revenue. Notwithstanding the importance of merchandising in the film and television world, in the context of distribution, a series of ancillary streams have carved out additional niche windows for exploiting content. The most prominent of these include:

- Hotel/motel
- Pay per view
- Video-on-demand (VOD) (here in its transactional form rather than free)
- Airlines
- Non-theatrical

It would be fair also to add online into this mix, because many view online as just another ancillary. However, given the new applications enabled by online use and digital technology, I am treating online as a separate category, focusing on how it is impacting mainstream and ancillary revenue windows alike. In summary, that is the challenge of convergence: Are revenues from downloading a TV show to an iPod or streaming content to a computer ancillary revenues, or rather new kinds of digital exploitation changing the very character of traditional markets (electronic sell through supplanting DVD retail, and streaming content challenging the nature of what is TV)?

343

Merchandising

Merchandising revenues can be so significant that this ancillary market actually becomes the primary revenue stream targeted. Many animated properties originate from toys or with the intent of generating toy sales, with the producer sometimes viewing the cartoon (and in extreme cases, its telecast) as a marketing expense. The challenge is that merchandising revenues can be even more fickle than the film business, with toy vendors wary of the high risks even when dealing with name properties.[1] Basing toys on a movie runs a dual risk that the movie will work and then that the movie's performance can be converted into retail success with products based on the movie and its characters.

And yet, when a merchandising program takes off, it can be extremely big—in select cases even bigger than all other traditional media streams combined. I had the privilege of cross-promoting videos with Star Wars merchandise, the all time leader in merchandising sales from a film property, which the *Wall Street Journal* (quoting Lucasfilm) advised: "... topped $12 billion since its inception in 1977, about three times the world-wide box office for all six movies combined ... ."[2]

As Risky and Lucrative as the Film Business

What Properties Can Spawn Successful Merchandising Programs?

Most successful film or TV-based merchandising programs are built around either franchise properties or properties targeted at the kids/family demographic such as animated features. To the extent that a property crosses over to both categories, namely franchises and kids, then the potential is that much greater. This is why films based on comic books have become so hot, and why companies like Marvel have seen a resurgence in value. Even with this type of triangulation, nothing is a sure thing. Batman has been a success story, and more recently Spiderman has hit its stride, but product based on Superman has struggled by comparison.

Star Wars has been the industry's leading and enduring success story, somehow managing to strike a continuing chord with multi-generational fans and collectors. It is a legendary industry story how Lucasfilm was caught by surprise by the product demand back in the 1970s following the launch of the original film. Demand was so high that toy company Kenner shipped empty boxes with vouchers for product that would be shipped later. This story is instructive to illustrate (again) the similarity of vicissitudes to the film business; namely, the market is hit driven and no one can fully predict what will catch on and when. Accordingly, the business tends to segment into two major categories: established properties where the merchandise becomes part of a larger franchise management program, and newly released properties that launch with the hype of presumed success (e.g., a new Pixar film).

It then becomes the challenge of major product providers, such as toy companies, to place large up-front bets. The two largest US toy companies, Mattel and Hasbro, are heavily courted by every studio and network, because having a major toy program in place not only validates the expectations for an upcoming release but also provides cross-promotion via the brand marketing of the toy company. It is like joining a craps table, but now there are more people betting on the roll, with the energy and expectations feeding on each other; moreover, the drama is heightened by the fact that everyone gets only one roll (the film's opening box office, or a TV series initial airings).

The Difference with TV

In many ways, merchandising driven off of TV is a much better business. This is because with a continuing story it is possible to hold back and see how a property is performing before ramping up too far. It is not unusual to wait for the second season of a series before launching major product; the time delay allows programs to be built around what the merchandisers now know is a hit. Moreover, with TV there is the ability to keep the property in front of its consumers week after week. The combination of a more calculated risk and a longer tail should produce a healthier ROI, a fact further buttressed because TV production costs should be lower than film costs.

Among the great success stories in this space is *Power Rangers*, a series/franchise that became so strong that it (together with thousands of hours of other animated content controlled by Saban Entertainment) allowed producer Haim Saban to launch and co-own Fox Kids with NewsCorp; Saban then netted a huge personal payoff (in the billions) when he sold the kids cable network to Disney (which then re-branded the network ABC Family).[3] (See Chapter 7 for a discussion of how these profits were leveraged to make billions more with the purchase and sale of one of Germany's leading commercial TV networks.)

It is the hope of these types of returns that excites the executives at all channels focused on kids programming. At Nickelodeon, *SpongeBob SquarePants* sustained a successful merchandising program for years. Disney uses its Disney Channel airtime to keep key characters fresh, such as with a CG animated Mickey Mouse; moreover, it is also able to cross-promote items through its theme parks, networks, videos, etc., thus creating purchasing demand among each new generation of toddlers. A key recent Disney success story is in the teen demographic, led by its Disney Channel special *High School Musical*. This TV musical and its sequels (e.g., *High School Musical 2*), per *Variety*, "have sold nearly 15 million CDs, 50 million books, 4.8 million video games, and spawned stage shows, concerts and an ice tour. Disney expects to reap $2.7 Billion this year [2009] from "HSM" and "Hanna Montana" products."[4]

In contrast, name a successful TV or film merchandising program not aimed at kids. There are a few, such as around *The Simpsons* and *South Park*, but outside of these edgy shows where the merchandising leverages the cult appeal of the show, there are hardly any examples. Dramas, police shows, action movies, romantic comedies, sitcoms, and even niche genres like horror do not lend themselves to converting property interest to product purchases. Why? Arguably, it is all about time, focus, and independence. As people grow older and are more independent with their choices, with more influences competing for their attention, marketing messages are diluted and the desire to affiliate with a character or item becomes less compelling. Simply, think of a graph, where the Y axis is range of choice and influences, and the X axis is age. The older you get the more choices and the more exposure. In contrast, children watch hours of certain TV shows each week (if not a day) on kids channels, and a particular property is more integral to their lives.

Chicken and Egg: When Merchandise Drives TV

As outlined in Chapter 7, on occasion producers will pay for airspace and take on the risk of selling the commercial inventory to guarantee a broadcast slot. This risk tends to be limited to instances where there are strong ancillary revenues, such as built-in merchandising from an established brand, where the P&L is not simply based on advertising sales. A prime example was 4Kids Entertainment's deal with Fox (4Kids holding TV merchandising and broadcast rights to *Pokémon* and other hit animé titles).

According to 4Kids Entertainment's Annual report, "The Company, through a multi-year agreement with Fox, leases Fox's four hour Saturday morning children's programming block. The agreement, which commenced in September 2002, requires the Company to pay annual fees of $25,312 through 2006."[5] The Annual Report continued:

> The Company, through a multi-year agreement with Fox leases Fox's Saturday morning programming block from 8am to 12pm eastern/pacific time (7am to 11am central time). In January, 2005, the Company changed the name of the Saturday morning programming block from Fox Box to 4Kids TV. The Company provides substantially all programming content to be broadcast on 4Kids TV. 4Kids Ad Sales, Inc., a wholly-owned subsidiary of the Company, retains all of the revenue from its sale of network advertising time for the four-hour time period.[6]

Fox secured over $100M over four years without any risk, presumably on the assessment that it could not sell $25M of advertising/year in this space or otherwise net better than this amount after programming costs. The network's bet seemed to pay off based on the 4Kids report, which lists advertising media and broadcast revenues for

2002, 2003, and 2005, respectively, as $11.2M, $22.54M, and $24.1M. In addition to running a deficit on the airtime, 4Kids had programming costs to amortize. And yet, as the report further noted, the company's belief that TV exposure would drive other revenues tied to the already established franchise justified the risk: "The ability of the Company to further develop its merchandising, home video and music publishing revenue streams were significant components of its evaluation process which resulted in the decision to lease the 4Kids TV Saturday morning programming block."[7]

In the context of leveraging well-known brands with strong merchandising lines, the 4Kids Entertainment strategy of broadcasting new (and inexpensive to produce) series on network to drive awareness for ancillary revenue streams was a bold play. However, absent this context the notion of paying for production, receiving no license fee (and in fact having a negative license fee given the lower ad revenues versus the cost of the airtime), and betting the entire economics on ancillary revenues may carry worse odds than gambling.

Animé Mania and VIZ Media's Life Cycle Management (from Manga to TV to Toys and Beyond)

In the last decade there has been an explosion of animé-based properties including *Pokémon*, *Yu-Gi-Oh*, and *Dragon Ball*, hitting US television. Nintendo's *Pokémon* turned into a phenomenon, becoming such a figure of pop culture that it appeared on the cover of *Time* magazine and *The New Yorker*, and a gigantic Pikachu balloon floated through the Macy's Thanksgiving Parade.[8] As an aside, I remember meeting the woman in Tokyo who created the signature yellow pocket monster character Pikachu, and autographs were so in demand that she regularly kept stickers with her to sign. In terms of numbers, Pokémon sales figures were daunting: from over 1,000 licensed products it is estimated that global Pokémon merchandise sales exceeded $5B. And these numbers are from legitimate licenses — in 1999 Nintendo of America, the licensing agent for Pokémon, asked a New York court to crack down on pirates, alleging they were losing $725M per year from counterfeit goods.[9]

Most animé properties derive from manga, manga a form of Japanese comics (and animé literally meaning Japanese animation). Outside of its home market in Japan, animé tends simply to be equated with its distinctive design style (e.g., big-eyed characters, jagged edge hair). While most US consumers will recognize the manga/animé style, one needs to look specifically at the Japanese market, where kiosks sell new manga offerings inches thick by the week, to understand the roots.

Perhaps one of the best case studies of merchandise, and specifically animé-based properties, inextricably linked with TV production and distribution opportunities is VIZ Media. VIZ Media is a subsidiary of some of the most successful Japanese publishing companies, including the two largest manga publishers (Shogakukan, Inc. and Shueisha, Inc.) and merchandising company/agent Shogakukan Shueisha Productions (ShoPro), which has handled local Japanese merchandising rights to some of Hollywood's biggest licensing franchises (e.g., *The Simpsons*, *Rugrats*, *Star Wars*).

VIZ Media in its marketing brochure "Manga/Anime 201" discusses how properties are nurtured through the cycle and with *Dragon Ball* as an example notes:

Dragon Ball
↓
Weekly Shonen Jump (a manga magazine)
↓
Tankōban (paperback graphic novels)
↓
Animé TV series

The combined strength of its manga (graphic novel) properties, the growth of the animé market, and the continued popularity of animé on US TV and DVD led VIZ Media to create a dedicated ex-Asia company focused on maximizing their brands' exposure on an all rights basis (including TV broadcast, publishing, home video, licensing, consumer products and promotions, and now adding online distribution and feature film production). In essence, they have captured the value chain from the licensing of the intellectual property at the manga publishing stage to its broadened exposure via TV and the Internet and are capitalizing on consumer licensing activity tied throughout. A US network or studio, in contrast, creates vertical integration through the production–distribution chain and then hopes for upside on franchises through ancillary exploitation.

Even in the world of product merchandising leveraging traditional print-based comics, the online world is having an impact, which further may vary by demographic. Tonik Barber, VIZ Media's General Counsel advised:

Merchandise marketing activities based on animé properties largely should be geared to the target demographic and the media frequented by that demographic in order for the audience to get to know the brand and for the brand owner to best reach its consumer. In the case of animation geared to the 6–11 demographic, merchandise marketing tends to be more mom-friendly, mass-market and/or kid-centered. As a result, those marketing activities focus on key media (e.g., kids' cartoon TV hours and kid-directed online Web sites) as well as the key influencers of consumer choices for this group who are guided (especially in these times of limited discretionary income) by trusted sources (traditional TV ads, in-store promotions and discounts, and peer-directed activities). By contrast, merchandise marketing activities based on animé geared to an older demographic increasingly use the Internet and mobile platforms to provide interactive product options (e.g., DTO, DTR, streaming, interactive online gaming, viral marketing) to meet the ever-evolving needs of a media-savvy audience which attaches itself to aggregators with offerings that have a community element and/or meet targeted preference expectations.

349

E-commerce and Online Extensions

Although discussed in Chapter 9 regarding marketing, it is important to highlight in the context of merchandising the role the Internet plays. Virtually all films and major TV shows have dedicated Web sites, and within these Web sites users can often directly link to e-commerce applications to buy related merchandise. When I took over managing starwars.com I was pleasantly surprised to learn (and I guess I really should not have been surprised) that one of the thriving parts of starwars.com was the Star Wars shop. This store, like many other Internet boutiques, was able to include within its product mix special online exclusives; more targeted marketing, and the ability to offer limited quantities, will sometimes allow a diverse SKU of unique items that may not be viable in the hypercompetitive environment of retail shelf space.

In addition to enabling e-commerce merchandise applications (both for digital and physical product, including items available only via the Web), the Web has enabled the phenomenon of secondary markets. Everyone is familiar with stories of the value of old comic collections, and e-Bay has enabled a vibrant marketplace for collectors — in essence giving an entire new life to the collectibles market. While e-Bay is obviously a broader phenomenon, it is a boon to the world of merchandise.

Licensing Programs

What Is a Licensing Program?

A licensing program is based around trademarks affiliated with a movie or TV show, and creates a variety of product categories leveraging the brand and key characters. The categories are as diverse as one can imagine, and the following is just a sample list:

- Toys and games
- Apparel and accessories (including backpacks)
- Publishing (e.g., books, magazines, activity books)
- Interactive (e.g., computer games, platform games)
- Mobile (ringtones, wallpaper, etc.)
- Domestics (e.g., sheets, towels, bath and bath accessories)
- Housewares
- Social expression (including greeting cards, stationery, etc.)
- Sporting goods
- Food (including salty snacks, cereals, packaged goods, frozen, etc.)
- Gift and collectibles

350

Top brands can have literally hundreds of licensed properties, and the range of the program and how fine the categories are segmented depends on the property and philosophy of the licensor. The digital and online world is further expanding the possibilities, as movie sounds and music have been adapted for popular ringtones, and it is now possible to license avatars and digital accessories in a variety of environments.

Product merchandising, however, is an area where more is not always better, and the success of a program will depend on the commitment of the licensees and the licensor's ability to exercise controls both with licensees and with retail to ensure quality and a level playing field for product.

Retail Buy-in and Support

A licensing program does not stop with concluding licensing deals, because a successful campaign will also have the licensor working with key retail accounts and licensees to ensure placement and coordination at retail outlets. For example, large retailers like Wal-Mart, Target, and Toys R Us will stock a variety of products related to the brand, but will be dealing with separate and unrelated licensees with each pushing its product at the level of the department buyer. To the extent an event (e.g., movie launch) or brand warrants it, special standees and sections can be created pulling product from multiple departments, creating incremental retail placement, and highlighting the brand; moreover, if the retailer buys in and believes aggregating product will drive traffic, then the retailer is also more likely to promote and advertise the selection, either in circulars and/or with hard media using co-op advertising funds. When the last *Star Wars* movie was released, for example, the merchandising program was robust enough that Wal-Mart even participated in special "tent" events at select locations: What could be better than not having to leave the parking lot to fight with a light saber?

Any successful licensing program will therefore focus on retail specific programs. You know you have stepped into a licensing meeting when an executive is talking planograms and live on-shelf dates. Another reason retail engagement is so critical is that the very nature of product merchandising speaks franchises, and if there is oversupply of product or too many licensees, such that the retailers get hurt (as opposed to the product licensees), then a campaign is not only unsuccessful but the future is undermined. Some will take a "take the money and run" approach, focusing on guarantees, but a successfully managed campaign will spend as much time working retail engagement, placement, and metrics as the deals for the products themselves.

351

Quality Control and Timing

Licensing has a longer development/planning cycle than any of the traditional media categories (e.g., theatrical, video, and TV distribution), which often puts crazy pressure on divisions to lock in plans before the details of a project are even worked out. If cutting a trailer for a film is difficult because the movie is not yet done, then creating product for that movie takes the challenge one step further because decisions often need to be locked before the filming even starts.

Timing
Lead times of two years are not unusual, and anything short of 18 months may make developing product and getting it on shelf in time

impossible. This is simply the nature of product development — the entire supply side from designs, to materials, to molds, etc., takes time. Virtually everything is outsourced for manufacturing, which means location and subcontractor decisions are involved, plus product samples need to be made and approved. (Note: Product placements [which can sometimes be confused with merchandising], such as a special car being featured in a film, similarly need long lead times, as the integration has to occur before filming. See Chapter 9 for a discussion of product placements.)

Style Guides and Quality Approval

Before any product is made, the licensor will create a detailed style guide. This guide will include the logos and typefaces to be used (including a variety for different types of packaging and sizing), approved artwork for characters including in different poses and turnarounds (e.g., flat and dimensional), approved trademark and copyright notices, approved color palates, approved phrases, approved peripherals (such as weapons or vehicles from the property), approved size charts (relative scale of one character to another), etc. *KidScreen* magazine, describing how a style guide can differentiate a pitch and is at the heart of any consumer product program, referred to style guides as "doing overtime as a calling card, a presentation piece, a licensee manual and a brand road map all at once. So getting the right style guide is crucial to scoring a [merchandising] hit." It then continued to detail the elements of a guide: "Most guides start off with a general description of the film or TV show and then get into the nitty-gritty graphic components, including icons, logos, color guides (breaking out main, secondary and accent palettes), character and background art, prints, borders, patterns, phrases and text that can be used, fonts and sample product applications."[10]

The goal of the style guide is to create brand consistency. If over 100 products are made in varying media and mediums, the licensor needs to provide a blueprint around which specific items are then designed. In the case of Barbie, which has ~1,000 licensees working across 45 product categories, there is a template to rein in too divergent elements, but Mattel claims that while "you do need a few rules, because that's how a brand becomes clear and cohesive," they strive to work with licensees throughout the process and avoid steering the process through too narrow a creative tunnel.[11] The style guide then provides a working anchor for quality control, as sample designs and product must stay within the parameters outlined. To the extent the product is consistent, then the licensor's review for quality approval is infinitely easier.

This is one of those areas where I touch upon it in a paragraph or two, but the execution of the style guide and approval over designs and sample product are the lifeblood of the merchandising campaign. Failure to timely approve items or to properly inspect quality are the surest way to doom a program, and cannot be taken for granted. This becomes an economic consideration, because once deals are signed there is the temptation to assume "licensees know what they're doing," and relax. In fact, it is tempting to cut budgets around personnel to review product, especially as the numbers and categories grow. Almost all merchandising managers will testify that they have rarely seen cutting corners pay off, because there is nothing more competitive than the retail shelf, and consumers are always savvier than anticipated. This is why companies will invest significant funds up front in the creation of a style guide with the bill ranging from tens of thousands to well over one hundred thousand dollars.

Licensing Deals

I have waited until this point to describe key elements of licensing deals to punctuate the point made earlier that while signing up licensees is obviously critical, if a licensor puts full stock in that element at the expense of developing sophisticated plans for approvals, style guides, and retail management then at best license deals will not be optimized and at worst undermined.

Licensed Products and Property
"Licensed Product" is exactly as it sounds: the specific products being authorized, such as action figures, T-shirts, or key chains. The "Licensed Property," in contrast, refers to the underlying rights (e.g., trademarks) upon which the products may be based.

Licensed Rights — Exclusive versus Non-exclusive Rights to Licensed Properties
The license agreement will make it clear (hopefully) whether the licensor conveys either exclusive or non-exclusive rights to use the Licensed Property in connection with a defined category of Licensed Products (and to add further legal boundaries, of course during a limited term, and restricted to the defined territory). Because the license rights ultimately derive from the ability to use the licensor's

trademarks with products based on the underlying property, to the extent the licensor is allowing multiple products, then conceptually the license is non-exclusive; however, most licenses carve out a measure of category exclusivity, such as the exclusive right to make watches or trading cards. It is this niche level of exclusivity (whether a de facto practice adhered to on a relationship basis, or expressly granted) that allows franchises to spawn hundreds of licensed goods and obtain minimum guarantees against narrowly defined category exclusives.

Although most film-based licenses tend to be category exclusive, one can also find general market examples of non-exclusive product licenses. A prominent example is found in sports, where individual teams may permit a number of manufacturers to make a product such as multiple companies creating apparel using team logos (in which case one shirt may bear trademarks of Nike and Team X, and another shirt Team X plus Y).

Not only can the license be bounded by time, territory, product category, and exclusivity, but even by types of distribution outlets (e.g., novelty stores, grocery stores). This is somewhat akin to the video market where the market is differentiated into retail categories (such as rental and sell through), though ultimately much more complex because the segmentation adds the complexity of the character of the outlets rather than resting on the clearer dividing line of price and type of transaction (see Figure 8.1).

Economics: Minimum Guarantees/Advances

Minimum guarantees are important at two levels: first and foremost they ensure the licensor a revenue floor, and second they create incentives for the licensee to push the product to meet and hopefully exceed the guarantee. Licensing deals rarely stray from the concept of an advance against royalties, with these two items as the focal point of negotiations. This is not to trivialize other elements of the deal, or argue that when and how advances and royalties are paid is not critical, but it is important to recognize that at the heart of any licensing deal are relatively simple and direct economic terms. Unlike net profits from a film (see Chapter 10), Hollywood has not evolved arcane accounting standards around merchandising: at its guts are how many units are being sold, what are the royalties (and how are they calculated), and what amount if any will the licensee front against the royalties.

One wrinkle that can arise around minimum guarantees is that a licensor may want minimum royalty payments over defined periods

354

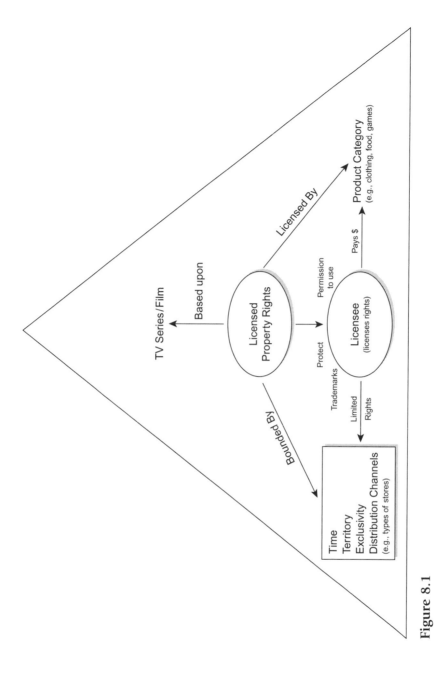

TV Series/Film

Based upon

Licensed Property Rights

Licensed By

Product Category
(e.g., clothing, food, games)

Permission to use

Pays $

Protect

Trademarks

Licensee
(licenses rights)

Bounded BY

Limited Rights

Time
Territory
Exclusivity
Distribution Channels
(e.g., types of stores)

355

Figure 8.1

such as on an annual basis. These thresholds are designed to ensure that licensees are continuing to market and push products; if certain sales targets are not met, this could trigger the right to terminate the license (or conversely, extend the license if they are met).

Licensors are dealing with brands that have inherent awareness and goodwill (here someone willing to pay money pursuant to a trademark license to associate a consumer product), and the ability to guarantee continued levels of sales and exposure can be as critical to brand management as the associated revenues. These types of licensors will not "take the money and run," but rather take the money and make the licensees keep running. This is fundamentally different from deals based on straight license fees (e.g., TV, assuming no ratings bonuses), in which initial marketing commitments may be established, but thereafter the broadcaster has flexibility. In the context of TV, broadcasters typically have the obligation to pay the license fee, but then assuming the fee is paid they do not actually have to broadcast the property. Merchandising deal structures are more like video, where product sales are dependent on shelf space, retail execution, and thousands of points of purchase; similarly, both are consumer products, upsides are generally tied to volume, and with a licensor's participation set as a per product royalty.

Royalties

Royalty calculations are generally straightforward, and are expressed as a percentage of sales. The challenge is in defining sales, and then specifying what if any adjustments or deductions are permitted. First, in terms of sales, the product can be sold at multiple levels, such as wholesale and then retail (with further wrinkles if a product may be purchased from an overseas manufacturing facility where the pricing is pre-shipment and wholesale mark-up). Much like the context for video sales/royalties, the only pot of money a licensor taps into is at the wholesale level. A licensee makes its product and sells it to a customer (e.g., a retailer), and any corresponding royalty needs to be based on the gross revenue derived at this level. This is nearly an exact parallel to royalties/revenue that are accounted for at the wholesale price with respect to video.

Once the "gross" pot is defined from which the royalty is calculated, the next concern is defining whether there are any adjustments to this gross; a concept that is sometimes made confusing by defining this gross amount as "net sales." There are multiple elements that may come into play to reduce the base from which royalties are calculated (e.g., Can a licensee apply trade and other discounts, such as cash discounts? Can a licensee have an allowance for free or promotion goods?). While it is standard to allow some deductions, as well as apply a cap on total deductions, much of the risk ends up transferred to the licensee. As noted earlier, the concepts of net and gross track common sense expectations and generally do not devolve into arcane accounting schemes.

Finally, it is worth touching on setting royalty rates. Unlike the video context, where there is a relatively clear economic logic to splits (see Chapter 5 for discussion of setting royalties to approximate cost of the top splits), royalty rates in the merchandising areas tend to be set on straightforward percentages without the parties trying to match a cost of the top split or other structure (likely because of the low cost of goods, the production of which has been outsourced to Asia decades before this became trendy in other businesses, and the opportunity costs of having to deal with this calculation on hundreds of different products). Of course, the notion of splits underlies the setting of any royalty, but the point is that there is less of a conscious mechanism here; rather the percentages tend to be within customary bands per product category.

It is a trade secret what those bands are, but suffice it to note that certain product categories may be in the very low single digits, while others can be a multiple of this range and command double digits. The *Los Angeles Times*, quoting a toy analyst, noted regarding the range: "The Studios license the rights to toy manufacturers and also receive royalties of 7% to 15% of the sales, said Chris Byrne, an independent toy analyst and contributing editor of Toy Wishes Magazine."[12] The *Hollywood Reporter*, in its survey article prior to the annual New York Toy Fair [2008], pegged the numbers a bit higher; estimating for top properties that licensors usually receive an advance guarantee in the $1M range, it references a group publisher from License Global magazine in citing that studio licensors receive a 10–15% royalty on wholesale (and that wholesale is roughly 50% of retail), and that for certain franchises like Pixar's *Toy Story* the percentages can be even higher.[13]

extent driven by thin margins) and very high off the top fees — a formula that means only a fraction of the wholesale revenues (and remember, this is a fraction of the often quoted retail sales) ends up paid to the producer/owner of the TV show or film upon which the product is based.

Premiums

Premiums are licensed product that are given away to consumers rather than sold. This may take the form of a figure included with a kids' meal at a fast food restaurant chain, and the issue for the licensor is on what basis is it paid: the consumer has not paid anything for the item of merchandise, and yet the licensor needs to be compensated. Economically, there are two theoretical routes for compensation. The first would be to allocate a portion of the sale, treating the premium as a bundled good and attributing a percentage of the purchase price to the premium. This, however, is not feasible for a variety of reasons: (1) the retailer (e.g., restaurant) is not going to allocate away from its core product; (2) the product is temporary in that the premiums are offered only during a short promotional window, which means that the same allocation would need to be offered for all product among competitors (e.g., Burger King is not going to give Warner Bros. a better deal in March for the product packed in a kids meal than they will give Universal the following month); and (3) there may be no wholesale price (as the retailer will sometimes directly commission and manufacture the item).

Given these complications, compensation, to the extent there is direct compensation at all and this is not viewed as marketing, may instead be based on the manufacturing price of the item. A royalty would then be calculated based on the production cost, which amounts to a nominal number per item. The licensor will agree to this small basis because the nature of premiums is promotional (and at some level it is only mutual leverage that keeps them from having to pay for this promotion), and at essence royalties on the product are an incremental upside and not the driver of the deal.

Role of Agents

Licensing at an elemental level is about sales, and every company has to make economic decisions balancing the cost/benefit of an in-house licensing department versus outsourcing the function. Even with a large in-house staff, however, some elements will still be outsourced to ensure global coverage (there is simply not enough consistent throughput for most companies to have dedicated staff in all major markets worldwide).

Most companies will therefore utilize either a master agent or a network of agents, managing this sales staff via commission structures. The agent will be responsible for sourcing deals, helping negotiate contracts, monitoring quality and performance levels of the licenses, and in some cases even overseeing collections. The licensor then has the decision of what level of autonomy to authorize, and to what degree it will delegate management functions either up front (deal terms/selecting licensees) or during management and maintenance (e.g., product approvals). The degree of work will dictate whether the agent receives only a commission tied to royalties, or has an additional retainer/higher fees for performing overhead functions.

In addition to agents scouring the market to set up product licenses, the business is now so big that Hollywood agencies separately represent toy companies and individual properties to try and set up tie-in movie and TV deals (e.g., William Morris representing Hasbro to turn games, such as Trivial Pursuit and Candy Land, into film and TV products tapping its talent roster).[14]

Toys as a Driver

Toys are the sweet spot of most merchandising programs, and a licensor leveraging a film property will usually first attempt to sign a master toy license. Such a toy license will cover a range of potential products, such as toy vehicles, action figures, and themed props (e.g., swords, guns, apparel). For perspective, it is important to understand the breadth of the market, not simply in overall licensing program terms but also in terms of diversity of toy revenue. For example, while action figures are undoubtedly a key driver, creating stimulus for kids role-playing and buying ancillary accessories and props, action figures make up only a part of the puzzle. In analyzing the correlation of toy sales to box office, the *LA Times* referenced research group NDP's estimate that in 2006 action figure sales accounted for "close to $1.25 billion of the $22.6 billion in overall toy revenue ..."[15]

Mega Deals: Star Wars and Spider-Man

The amount of money that can be made from toys can reach extraordinary heights, as evidenced by Hasbro's success with Transformers and its deal with Lucasfilm for Star Wars merchandise. Discussing an extension of its initial $590M agreement with Lucas Licensing (Lucasfilm's merchandising arm), Hasbro advised that in addition to a term extension the new agreement lowered "… the minimum payment guaranteed to the film producer George Lucas because of less-than-expected sales. The minimum payment was reduced by $85 million, to $505 million."[16]

Another example is Marvel, where Hasbro put up a $200M+ guarantee for toy and game rights across Marvel's properties, including Spider-Man, Fantastic Four, and X-Men for five years; Spider-Man was clearly the driver in the deal, as the *New York Times* reported the "license guarantees Marvel $205 million in royalty and service fee payments, of which $70 million and $35 million would be payable on the theatrical release of *Spider-Man 3* and *Spider-Man 4*, respectively."[17]

These types of guarantees and deals are clearly high stakes. In the case of Hasbro and Star Wars, to some degree the toy manufacturer bet the company, as in addition to paying huge guarantees Lucasfilm was granted $200 million in warrants for Hasbro common stock, which Hasbro had the right to repurchase.[18]

360

In recouping guarantees in this order of magnitude, one also has to keep in perspective that the dollars available are based on the wholesale amounts. As discussed previously, just like box office and film rentals, the relevant sums here to recoup advances are based on the net wholesale revenues, which extrapolate up to staggering sums needed at retail to break even. In analyzing the risks Hasbro was taking on its Marvel licensing deal covering Spider-Man sequels, one analyst that ultimately believed the deal would be profitable despite its cost was quoted by the *LA Times* as saying: "The company needs $1 billion in Marvel related sales over the next five years to make a profit on the license …"[19]

With this level of sales, it is not surprising that studios, networks, and producers controlling franchise rights are among the largest sellers of licensed merchandise, along with sports leagues and other major consumer brands (e.g., clothing, electronics, autos). A *USA Today* list (Table 8.1) of the top sales of licensed merchandise (referencing *License Global*) itemized 8 of the top 20 licensors coming from this media sector.[20,21]

Coming Full Circle: Toys Spawn Films Spawn Toys

In the ultimate example of coming full circle, the Hasbro toy brand Transformers spawned a movie, with the movie then serving as the

Table 8.1 Top Licensors

Rank	Company	2007 sales (in $M)	Brands
1	Disney Consumer Brands	26,000	Hannah Montana, High School Musical, Disney Princesses, Disney Fairies, Pixar's Cars, Chronicles of Narnia
3	Warner Bros Consumer Brands	6,000	Harry Potter and the Order of the Phoenix, The Dark Knight, Speed Racer, Where the Wild Things Are
5	Marvel Entertainment	5,500	Spider-Man, X-Men, Hulk, Iron Man, Fantastic Four, Avengers, Spider-Man and Friends
6	Nickelodeon and Viacom Consumer Products	5,500	Dora, Diego, The Backyardigans, Ni-Hao, Kai Lan, SpongeBob SquarePants, South Park, Neopets
15	HIT Entertainment	2,400	Thomas and Friends, Bob the Builder, Barney, Fifi and the Flowertots, Angelina Ballerina
18	Sony Pictures Consumer Products	2,000	Spider-Man movie, Ghostbusters, Surf's Up, Cloudy With a Chance of Meatballs
19	20th Century Fox Licensing. and Merchandising	1,750	The Simpsons, Halo, Ice Age, Family Guy, Alvin & the Chipmunks, Fox Sports, 24
20	Lucas Licensing	1,500	Star Wars, Indiana Jones

catalyst for a diversified product licensing program. The *Los Angeles Times* noted that Hasbro, confident of boosting its Transformers brand, had "signed deals with 230 licensees worldwide for T-shirts, bedding, cell phones and shoes."[22] This Transformers campaign turned into a huge success, with the initial film garnering more than $300M at the US box office (and more than $700M worldwide) and increasing Hasbro's sales of Transformer toys fivefold from $100 to $500M, proving synergy between merchandising and toys.[23] This tie-in was so successful that the company is aggressively trying to repeat this type of success: Hasbro is behind a G.I. Joe movie (Paramount 2009 release), is tied to both a Transformers TV series and a sequel movie, and struck a multi-picture deal with Universal to develop films related to brands including Monopoly (directed by Ridley Scott), Candy Land, and Battleship.[24]

Toys and the Internet — Growing Crossover with Avatars and Virtual Worlds

One would think, conceptually, that toys, dolls, and stuffed animals would be one category somewhat isolated from the impact of the Web. This is not the case, as toy companies and studios are finding ways to cross over categories, creating new interactive elements to established franchises and growing entirely new brands and worlds.

Mattel, which previously took Barbie from a doll to TV movies and direct-to-videos, launched Barbiegirls.com where kids can play with avatars, and unlock "VIP" content (by paying for them, or plugging in a Barbie MP3 player bought at retail, that unlocks characters when connected). Rival toy company Hasbro, built a virtual world to complement its Littlest Pet Shop, where each pet has a code in its collar that allows users to enter the site. Not to be outdone by the toy companies, Disney is experimenting with a couple of Web related toy lines including "Clickables," which is based on Disney fairies that enables kids to interact with a linked virtual world. Summarizing the trend at the 2008's annual toy conference, Toy Fair, the *Hollywood Reporter* noted: "The biggest trend industrywide at Toy Fair ... is the increasing number of toys being sold that connect to Internet play and, with the inputting of special codes found on the toys, unlock virtual worlds."[25] And when there is new value, everyone starts to jump on the bandwagon: one of the original success stories, Webkinz, had a value in 2008 estimated by some in the $2 billion range. Their Web site is kid friendly and simply states: Webkinz pets are lovable plush pets that each come with a unique Secret Code. With it, you enter Webkinz World where you care for your virtual pet, answer trivia, earn KinzCash, and play the best kids games on the net![26,27]

Whether or not an avatar, used in a virtual world, on a mobile phone (e.g., tied to instant messaging services), or in social networking sites (where the lines are being blurred for kids, such as in communities like Club Penguin), is a type of virtual ragdoll is up for debate. What is clear is that toy companies and entertainment brands are striving to find ways to expand their characters and worlds into the virtual space. Moreover, once this transition is made, the entire merchandising food chain starts anew in the virtual world, with opportunities for e-commerce (pay to dress up your character or buy them accessories), linked games, etc.

I asked Howard Roffman, president of Lucasfilm Licensing, who has overseen Star Wars branded merchandise for over 20 years, what he thought about the online world's impact and whether virtual merchandise would become as big as toys. He stated:

> The online world is definitely beginning to impact the world of merchandise licensing, and that impact is rapidly evolving; we are just seeing the beginning today. Online retailers can offer higher-end collectibles that would be challenging to sell through traditional retail, such as the very large and expensive building sets that are offered exclusively through LEGO's online "Shop At Home" outlet. Online also offers opportunities for customization and targeting discrete market segments that would not be practical through brick-and-mortar outlets. While it is hard to imagine purely "virtual" goods such as avatars and ring tones becoming as large a market as traditional toys and many other popular mass-market categories, the day is clearly coming when content-driven items such as video games and DVDs will be consumed primarily via the Internet, all but eclipsing traditional retail.

363

Extending the Franchise: Video Games, Books, etc.

Video games and books are somewhat unique within the merchandising realm, because as opposed to toys or T-shirts, video games and books are derivative properties that often branch a story in a different direction. While still grounded in a movie, or the core iconography or characters of a franchise, games and books allow the creative freedom to explore different tangents and backstories, extending the core franchise. Of course, certain games and books are merely direct translations of a property into another medium, such as a novelization of a film, but the bigger a franchise and the deeper the fan base the more options the rights holder has for creating new intellectual property grounded in but not directly parroting the underlying franchise.

The online supplemental material includes a discussion of film-based games in the context of the overall games market; further, to set the context this section addresses basic video game economics, including game development costs, platform history/dynamics (i.e., history of consoles), revenue splits, and pricing.

Additional Ancillary Revenue Streams: Books, Film Clips, Music, Live Stage, etc.

It is beyond the scope of this book to delve into the niche economics of each of these categories. What I want to point out is that depending on the property, any one of a number of categories could be fundamental either to the initial planning for a property, or the ultimate revenues downstream. There are countless films where music is an inherent element (e.g., *8 Mile* starring Eminem, *Mama Mia*), and expectations of music-related sales can be as important an element in the overall forecasting as the video expectations. In contrast, a musical is a classic ancillary capable of out-earning a related film, but would rarely (if ever) be conceived of at the time of a movie. Mel Brooks' Broadway musical *The Producers* (originally starring Matthew Broderick and Nathan Lane) likely earned a multiple of the return on the original film (starring Gene Wilder and Zero Mostel), yet it is highly unlikely these potential monies were factored into the calculus of whether the movie, made decades earlier, was to be made in the first place.

Surely, there was similarly no thought as to *Spamalot*, the 2005 Tony award winner for best Broadway musical, when Monty Python released *Life of Brian* in 1979. The endurance of the Monty Python franchise almost reads as a testament to the power of ancillary rights, as well as evidence of the Internet as the next great sandbox. The *International Herald Tribune* elaborated: "For decades, Eric Idle has made sure that the Monty Python name continued to grace books, DVDs, concert tours, a Broadway show, even ring tones and video games. And now, he is helping bring Monty Python to the Internet. Pythonline.com, a social network and digital playground, offers clips of old material so that people can make mash-ups, perhaps inserting their own pet in the killer rabbit scene from *Monty Python and the Holy Grail*."[28]

Ancillaries regarding books are much more common than musicals. Most major films have "novelizations" of the movie that bring in material revenues, and are planned to hit shelves within the marketing window of the related theatrical release. Of course, a movie based on a book or series of books (e.g., *Lord of the Rings, Harry Potter*) has a built-in audience and if successful will cause an uplift in existing book sales. If a franchise is big enough, it may spawn spin-off books (as distinct from novelizations of a particular film) that are an extension of the film's universe or characters, exploring different tangents or time periods (such as the young adult series of

Young James Bond novels). Star Wars is again a prime example, with countless *New York Times* bestselling books branded with Star Wars and grounded in the films' iconography, but not directly related to a particular movie. In all cases the producer or copyright owner may secure an advance for a license to the book based on its brand, and then earn negotiated royalties after the publisher has recouped any initial advance/minimum guarantee.

When speaking of ancillary revenues, the line becomes blurred between what may be referred to as an "ancillary" revenue stream and what is classic merchandising. The previous discussion regarding books is generally considered a merchandising exploitation as are video game sales, whereas live stage productions and licensing of film clips tend to fall into the ancillary basket. This simply punctuates the importance of clearly defining rights and distribution channels, because deals for books, video games, and live stage rights have little in common other than the root ability to license the exploitation right to each category based on the underlying intellectual property rights in the originating film or TV production. Managed carefully, each of these rights can yield in the millions of dollars and are anything but "ancillary" to the entities tailoring the exploitation of these rights within their discrete markets.

And, if there is a distribution/revenue opportunity and it has not been exploited (e.g., a Batman musical?), you can be assured that it has been discussed, analyzed, and someone has made an offer for the rights. The danger with ancillary exploitation is that it crosses over into brand management, and it can sometimes be just as important to a franchise what opportunities it turns down as what to license/exploit. For every Disney On Ice there is a disaster on ice looming.

Hotel and Motel

The hotel and motel window is just as it sounds: this is the service you see when in a hotel room, and typically have a choice of several first run movies that can be ordered (with payment simply added to your hotel bill). All studios offer their first run movies to the various providers, and the window is typically "triggered" by notifying the provider of a film's availability. This notification will usually be several weeks prior to availability, as the services need to program available "slots."

As an interesting, and not unexpected anecdote, this is a distribution window where "adult entertainment" paces the field. Although statistics are not readily available, the buy rate for adult programming is a significant multiple of the average buy rate for a top Hollywood title (e.g., more than 5×). Hotels wised up several years back changing the billing to simply "film" or "movie" regardless of the program purchased, easing corporate expense accounts (and significant others) of the burden of questioning the details of the charge on the $300/night hotel bill.

Size of Market and Window

This is a market (US) of a few million hotel rooms that are serviced by various providers, although given the relatively small scale a few providers have historically dominated the market (e.g., LodgeNet and On-Command).

As with other distribution windows, the hotel/motel window is jockeying for its exclusive bite of the entertainment pie. Traditionally, this window has been slotted between the theatrical release and the video release. Regarding theatrical, the concern is to capitalize on the exposure in theaters and the awareness generated by the theatrical marketing campaign, while not taking any business away from the theaters. Accordingly, the window generally started in the range of 8–12 weeks from the theatrical release. Very few movies today remain in theaters for this long, however, and to the extent the films are playing out that far the locations and screen counts have diminished to a marginal number. The issue then is what is "marginal," and would the availability of the film in a hotel detract from potential box office. Most theatrical executives would argue no, and the window from theatrical has been growing shorter over time.

A key factor influencing the timing is also seasonality, as hotels have peaks around holiday times, especially in the summer. Accordingly, July and especially August tend to be peak months. While the rhythm of the market used to be monthly, even the hotel/motel market is impacted by changing technology and the switch to digital media. With the ability to deliver and program digitally (vs. physical tapes), hotels can now switch out programs with ease. Hotels with this capacity are now able to rotate in new programming more frequently, and in the last few years it has become possible for movies to have variable start dates (as opposed to the historical pattern of first of the month rotation tied to physical elements). It would not surprise me to see more diverse availability patterns rather than the rigid beginning and mid-month cycles. In fact, it is likely that a form of pay per view (PPV) will fully cannibalize the hotel window, and

366

THE BUSINESS OF MEDIA DISTRIBUTION: MONETIZING FILM, TV, AND VIDEO CONTENT this revenue cycle will be absorbed and consolidated into a VOD/pay per view revenue pattern.

Finally, the length of the window is variable, but in cases can run several months. Intuitively, this is longer than one would expect, because it cuts into the video window. To permit a longer window it is therefore fair to posit that the distributor (1) will assume the impact on video will be nominal (reasonable if viewed as an impulse buy, and non-substitutional if assuming you would not rent a video out of town) and/or (2) has a compelling economic justification, such as receiving an advance guarantee (which if high enough needs time to be earned out).

Economics

Hotel/motel revenues are obviously dependent on guests paying to view a movie, and the frequency of ordering a program in the hotel is labeled the "buy rate."

In terms of pricing for buys, the average consumer price is at a slight premium to a theatrical ticket price and can be even higher for a hot new title (e.g., $11.95). Pricing in this window, unlike theatrical pricing, has a fair measure of elasticity; the cost may be less for an average title or discounted when a title plays later in the availability cycle. In summary, the overall pricing range is on the high side both because the audience is relatively captive (stuck in a hotel room) and because the availability is early; namely in advance of any other in-home/in-room availability such as on DVD. The resulting revenues are then split between the distributor and the service provider in a negotiated formula (e.g., sliding scale), which no doubt takes into account anticipated buy rates, the speculative nature of buys, and the limited peak window.

The total amount of money generated in this window is small when compared to the major revenue streams of theatrical, video, and television; hence, this is a classic "ancillary" revenue source. The order of magnitude for gross revenues (buy rate times amount charged) on a major title should in theory be capped in the few million dollar range given the relatively limited points of access.

Let us assume that one room is available for 90 days (e.g., 6 months with a turnover frequency of every other day), which means 5 buys equates to 5.5%. Compared to redemption rates, which tend as a general rule to be in the low single digits for most coupon type offers, this buy rate appears high and this in turn supports the argument of a capped range on the revenue stream. Continuing a simple

367

example, a 5% buy rate against 2 million rooms with an average price per transaction of $10 would yield $1M of gross revenues (100,000 transactions × $10). And remember, this is gross revenue; net revenue to the distributor will be based on a split, which may be low if a guarantee is applied. If, for example, a film has grossed $3M (triple the previous example) and the weighted average take from the distributor was 40%, then the net revenues would be $1.2M. This is a fair example in terms of how the revenue stream should be viewed: if a successful film can earn a million dollars or more, and a lesser title a few hundred thousand, that is enough revenue to be worth the effort yet not enough to be a driver of windows or a major source. Hence, we circle back again to the classic ancillary stream.

International

The international market is not as mature as the US market. The issue here really is scale, for with the US market being marginal in scale versus other revenue streams, the issue of resources versus return becomes a material concern internationally. The international market is fragmented, and turning a profit within a particular territory with a smaller population (and modern hotel infrastructure generally less sophisticated than the US) becomes a challenge. While the international theatrical, television, and video markets have become major revenue streams, and in some cases surpassed the US market, the same cannot be said of hotel/motel windows. In fact, this revenue stream/window is insignificant (and often non-existent) for most theatrical fare. As for the future, I would argue that rather than seeing a maturation it is likely that PPV and VOD opportunities are more likely to flourish and supplant what would have otherwise been a hotel window.

PPV (Cable) and Transactional VOD

With the advent of digital downloads and streaming services online the notion of what is "VOD" is blurring. The changes enabled by download devices/stores (iTunes, Zune) together with VOD streaming services (e.g., Amazon Video-on-Demand and Netflix electronic delivery) are discussed in Chapter 7, while this chapter outlines the roots of PPV and the associated economics and timing of its distinct window. Additionally, the following discussion is limited to so-called transactional VOD via cable and satellite, where a consumer pays for access, as opposed to emerging free VOD applications, including

Internet-based advertising supported VOD (e.g., Hulu, YouTube; see earlier chapters, including Chapter 7, for free VOD discussion).

PPV and VOD Roots

While PPV has been around for years, until recently being enabled by digital cable set top boxes, it never matured beyond a relatively small ancillary market. Whether this was due to clunky technology, limited offerings, or simply a market that was not ready for the model, it was clear that the new pay for sampling or viewing world is changing the historical pattern of consumption.

In the early phases of growth, the limited ability of servers to hold and download programming (both the number of programs and the speed of delivery) created hybrids that were clearly intermediate technologies. What grew up were variations of PPV such as Near Video On Demand (NVOD), which were euphemisms for technical delivery. Historically PPV was an event platform, perhaps most notably associated with sports such as boxing (and fights and out-of-market sports league packages are still a driver of classic PPV). If you want to watch the fight, pay $X and you will have access — no other way to see it. It then evolved into also showing movies that cycled; like watching a movie in business class on an airplane, every time the movie started again you could tap in and watch/buy it. The more servers, the more times a movie could cycle through, which allowed the chance to opt in more frequently.

This gradation of when a viewer could access programming, which was inherently a technical limitation, defined the window or right. If a viewer could gain access only periodically (e.g., live event basis), then it was PPV. If a viewer could gain access frequently (e.g., every 5 minutes), but not immediately, then it was defined as NVOD (imagine a back room of a 100 VCRs all playing a tape of the same film so that the movie could start anew every few minutes). Anything accessed with nominal waiting time came to be classified as VOD, which clearly over time would come to simply mean instant access.

Residential VOD: The Virtual Video Store

Residential VOD had long been hyped as the ultimate consumer service: the technology promised the potential of a virtual video store environment unburdened by inventory costs, stocked with a catalog of limitless titles that were always on the shelf, and accessible with the click of your remote. This ease of access to non-scheduled

369

programming was a clear threat to the traditional broadcast television landscape, and added another challenge to a model that was already struggling to address consumers skipping the advertising that funded their production.

Domestic

In broad concept, there is little material difference between PPV and VOD. In both cases, a consumer is able to pay to watch a program through his television at home. A flat fee is charged, and the program is available for viewing for a limited time. Historically, the movie once ordered would run like a live TV broadcast; however, with the advent of TiVo, similar digital virtual VCR devices, and digital rights management systems, the programming can be accessed and played over an allotted period such as 24 hours from purchase.

As previously described, the principal difference between PPV and true VOD is that PPV services have specific start times. In contrast, VOD allows the customer to select a film and start it whenever they want. Taking a step back, and forgetting the continuum of whether start times are less frequent to absolute, what these services offer consumers is access to a kind of video store via their bedroom television remote control. This represents the ultimate couch potato: not only are you watching in bed, but you have not even risen to visit the video store.

Historically, backend technology limited the selection of content accessible, making the range of movies available via PPV/VOD a fraction of the inventory a customer could find at his local video rental store. With technology improvements, such limitations are quickly disappearing and conceptually PPV and VOD services are already able to fulfill the digital consumption mantra of consumers being able to download what they want when they want. As technology continues to enable scaling, and memory and ability to simultaneously provide multiple simultaneous feeds cease to pose a limiting factor, the distinctions will dwindle and everything will consolidate into virtual video store like access. Once this line is blurred the only remaining delineating factor is the window. The window limits access overall, defined by when content is made available to the VOD service.

Providers

Like the hotel market, this similarly limited revenue stream has been dominated in the United States by a few players (e.g., "In Demand" owned by a consortium of the leading cable providers, including TimeWarner, Cox, and Comcast). (Note: the direct-to-home-satellite market, which is dominated by Direct TV, largely parallels the cable VOD market, and accordingly macro numbers should capture both platforms.) Around 2005–2006 this market started to take off, as digital cable boxes enabled simple access to content. Gross revenues continue to increase, justifying aggressive marketing via cable systems such as Comcast (e.g., "Comcastic" slogan). The new level of marketing was a clear signal that the market, which had been relatively flat for years, was entering a phase of potentially explosive growth.

Window

The window for residential PPV/VOD has historically been post video release, in part because in-home viewing of a film in a manner characterized as via a virtual video store is threatening to video sales. Because the PPV/VOD providers want to capitalize on awareness, which has waned significantly since the theatrical release and then received a jolt of life from the video marketing campaign, they naturally want the window to be as early as possible. If they had their druthers, the window would replace the hotel/motel window. Protecting the more lucrative video window has been the key priority, so the next best time is as close to the video release date as possible.

371

The window used to be several months after video, but as video has matured from a rental to sell through business, and as the preponderance of DVD sales have become frontloaded, the residential PPV/VOD window has become accelerated. The window keeps inching forward, moving from a distant six months to three months and now often a month post video; it would not surprise me by the printing of this book if the window has crept even further forward, as VOD will inevitably become synonymous with "rental" and therefore be available with the video release. (Note: A few years ago Disney, when it was experimenting via its MovieBeam service [before it divested the company], fully collapsed the window offering consumers certain movies on-demand the same day they would be released on video/ DVD; MovieBeam was further experimenting with pricing, differentiating between new and library films.) (See also Chapter 1.)

Again, lurking behind this window is a fear factor that VOD will cannibalize DVD sales. This fear seems to be going away, with studios working harder to harmonize these streams (leveraging one off the other) than they are to fight off cannibalization. To some degree, what synergies are best realized may turn on which division the rights are coupled with: some studios place VOD under the video group, while others bundle these rights with the TV group, and more specifically pay TV. The pay TV grouping occurs because on the flip side of the window is pay television, coming several months following VOD. As the pay TV window tries to similarly accelerate to come closer to the video window, VOD has to fight to keep its positioning: close enough to video to capitalize on the marketing spend and corresponding awareness, and short enough with enough space to allow the larger pay TV provider to appear as fresh and early as possible. Because the consumer is only vaguely aware of all this timing, the segmentation works and the revenues are maximized. This is another illustration of the interplay of Ulin's Rule factors.

Finally, coming back to the traditional/historical window, it is worth noting that because of this squeezed timing (between the larger revenue streams from preceding video availability and subsequent pay TV exposure) the advertising of PPV/VOD availability to customers is in very close proximity to the actual availability date. While improved marketing efforts (such as by the key cable operators) and the maturing market are likely to change awareness levels, historically relatively few people are aware that a title will be coming to VOD, as opposed to awareness of video availability. This historical lack of marketing, combined with VOD lending itself to a browsing pattern, means that VOD purchases tend to be impulse buys.

I have not seen specific market research on this issue, but I would speculate that most consumers traditionally ranked VOD as a default choice, scanning VOD availability when they were dissatisfied with the other choices on TV. Perhaps the VOD/PPV operators should be paying Bruce Springsteen for his lyrics "57 channels and nothing's on," for it is the dissatisfied channel surfer already tuned to his TV who is most likely to divert to the VOD tangent and be swayed to plunk down a few dollars for instant gratification (if not literal salvation from the negative experience of not finding something on TV that excites them). As the market matures, and as VOD becomes more of the norm, then it is fair to expect the consumer pattern to shift and VOD to become the first menu scanned. Arguably, this will be the tipping point for window changes.

I asked Jamie McCabe, Fox's Executive Vice President Worldwide VOD and EST, what he saw as the tipping point for the market's maturation, and he advised:

The promise of VOD has always been there, but until recently, the networks, technology and services have been unable to live up to the concept. As these challenges are met, we are seeing VOD usage climb significantly.

Networks around the world are being built faster and faster as a result of government sponsored initiatives and/or competition between cable and telephone companies. Technological advancements in video compression, cheap memory and processing power have made the devices at the end of the network more capable of receiving and displaying high quality video and graphics, in the home and on the go.

The most challenging piece of the business, once the technology catches up, is to aggregate compelling content and present it simply and effectively to the consumer. Content discovery tools and user-specific recommendations, combined with more traditional "push" marketing, help increase the usage of the services and boost the perceived value of the VOD offering generally. Once given the benefits of choice, control and instantaneity, users are very satisfied and the VOD habit is formed.

Economics

The PPV and VOD markets tend to work on straight buys, which makes sense given the general impulse purchase. This construct then lends itself to a revenue sharing, or sliding scale model (akin to hotel/motel), with the content provider in position for a larger share absent minimum guarantees. Without an advance, the VOD service can be viewed as simply a pipe or a location for access like a movie theater, with a form of sharing matching relative risks taken and the unpredictability of direct consumer consumption.

In terms of macro values/revenues, this window is also truly an ancillary stream when compared with video, TV, and theatrical revenues. The money, however, can be significantly more than hotel/motel and as an order of magnitude a strong title properly positioned should theoretically be able to earn a multiple of the money earned from hotels. This bump versus hotel makes sense, for the universe of customers is larger, and the larger base directly corresponds to greater consumption. The driving factor (or in this instance limiting) beyond market size (base) tends to be timing, as the further out exposure is from the video marketing campaign, the less "fresh" a title seems and the buy rates tend to diminish.

Pricing to the consumer is less expensive than to buy a movie in a hotel, arguably because (1) it is not a captive environment like a hotel room and (2) the PPV/VOD window is significantly later in the life cycle than the hotel/motel window. When a customer has already been able to access a film via video rental, it is hard to charge significantly more than the rental fee. There may be some premium for the in-home convenience, but the elasticity for convenience apparently is not that great. Accordingly, the charge to the consumer for viewing the same film at home via VOD may be less than half of what it would have cost to see the same film a few months earlier in a hotel room. As forms of VOD come to supplant video rental then it also makes sense to see a harmonizing of the VOD charge and video rental fee — a convergence that is already happening.

Next Generation: Subscription-Video-on-Demand and Internet VOD

Subscription-Video-on-Demand (SVOD) is a relatively new application that can be applied in a few flavors. One variation is simply a functionality improvement on an existing service. This may be the case with a pay TV service that allows its subscribers to access programming at any time as opposed to the scheduled broadcast times. Accordingly, if HBO were to start a show at 9:00 pm on Monday, an SVOD application of its service would allow customers to access and watch the program at a time of their choosing (usually any time after the initial scheduled showing). Basically, it is converting a limited selection of programming, such as HBO's content for a month, to VOD access functionality.

Another variation of SVOD is via a computer. In this application, a service will allow a subscriber to download a show to its computer (with the transfer enabled by a security link or closed loop Internet system). To the extent the residency of the program on the computer is time limited (e.g., a rental), then it is a type of VOD, as opposed to a permanent download (i.e., ownership), which is then a form of electronic sell through.

A further SVOD application is when program access is via a pay channel provider's set-top box (e.g., as occurs in various European markets). Certain highlighted content may be automatically downloaded/resident on the box (so-called "pushed"), while other content needs to be accessed and then downloaded to the consumer ("pulled"). In the end, whether pushed, pulled, or otherwise, the goal of SVOD is improving the consumer's pay TV experience by making paid for premium content accessible at any time. One can therefore envision SVOD supplanting pay TV (in terms of films this is merely an aggregation of content that could be available sooner except for the window); the question is really whether the customer will pay to have a subset of content available via their TV at an earlier date.

To the extent this is all about the window timing, then the relevancy of pay TV channels comes into question. The pay TV services that have focused on original programming may end up protecting their brand based on differentiating content, for the repurposing of theatrical content that helped build their channels is unlikely to survive in an à la carte, on-demand world providing access on or close to the video window. Pioneering new applications by Amazon and Netflix (see Chapters 5 and 7) are already enabling this vision, which in theory has to pose a serious threat to pay services. For the content supplier, this presents a Hobson's choice: failure to favor VOD may not give the consumers what they want, but failure to favor pay TV would give up guaranteed, very large revenue streams (see Chapter 7).

Given this conundrum, it is worth quickly revisiting (see also Chapter 7) how Amazon and Netflix are aggressively moving into the space, challenging cable's historical dominance in the VOD market. Amazon Video-on-Demand allows customers to watch any of 40,000 titles instantly, with the first couple of minutes streaming immediately for amazon.com users; in essence creating an online application comparable to cable VOD services, but with a much expanded offering of titles.[29] The other innovation by Amazon is the storing of the purchases remotely. When you buy a title, it can reside remotely in an Amazon digital locker (called "Your Video Library"), where a consumer can access it from anywhere, anytime, any computer. Netflix, for its part, started its transition from a hybrid order-online-and-receive-by-mail service by allowing its subscribers to instantly watch select videos on their PCs via clicking on a "Watch Now" button.[30] It then partnered with a variety of device manufacturers (Xbox, Roku, TiVo) whose boxes integrated Netflix functionality allowing movies and TV to be streamed by Netflix directly to consumers' TVs. Amazon too partnered with the Roku Digital Video Player, meaning those with a Roku box have the choice of streaming content on-demand from Netflix on a subscription basis or from Amazon on an à la carte rental basis. The ultimate vision of companies marketing boxes that can interface with the TV (e.g., iTV, Xbox, Roku) is to bypass cable and allow any video available (whether via a service such as Amazon or Netflix, or more generally via the Internet) to be streamed and watched over your TV.[31]

375

Window and Economics

The window and economics for SVOD simply track the underlying basic rights; namely, the window for an SVOD application of pay TV rights would mirror the consumer's pay TV subscription (although generally with no access to a show until it has been premiered on the service in its scheduled slot). The one exception to this would be to the extent parties want to limit viewing (protecting the value of pay exhibitions), where SVOD availability could be windowed only to provide "catch-up" access. In this instance, the SVOD availability for a particular piece of content may be limited to a set period post the initial broadcast of the content.

International

Unlike the hotel market, with the larger residential VOD consumer base available to be tapped, the international VOD market is growing faster and is generally exploited on most major studio product.

Similar to the United States, the maturation of this window had been held back both by waiting for available technology to execute efficiently and the overriding paranoia of negatively impacting the immensely valuable and (until recently) expanding video market. Also, paralleling US trends, with the maturation of the sell through video market VOD availability has been perceived as less of a threat. As a result, the standard window for VOD in most major international markets has also been creeping forward toward the video availability date. Eventually, like the United States, the VOD window is apt to become simultaneous with video and become the face of rental.

One interesting difference that may differentiate economics, is that while non-Internet VOD in the United States has been dominated by cable, in many global markets where satellite delivery (rather than cable) is the norm the set-top boxes tend to be part of/distributed by the pay TV services. Accordingly, content suppliers diversifying their deals with pay TV channels to also license VOD rights will naturally look to pay TV structures. Pay TV licenses, however, are premised on minimum guarantees (tied to subscriber bases) whereas VOD deals tend to be structured as revenue shares because of the uncertain buy rates from customers. One can expect that as these markets mature, business models will shift with them; deals may first start with guarantees to acquire content (mimicking pay TV structures, and providing an incentive to content owners reluctant to license in the face of potential video cannibalization), and then over time either adjust to reflect the value of buy rates, or change to a revenue share basis dovetailing with the à la carte nature of impulse buys.

Complicating the picture is the fact that in some territories broadband and phone company providers are aggressively entering the market; leveraging online delivery/access systems, these companies are trying to co-opt the VOD market by converting their subscriber base and directly competing with the pay services. Accordingly, in some markets phone company affiliates are battling the pay services (e.g., France, Germany); in others it is broadband services versus pay TV providers, and in some markets cable, broadband, phone, and pay services are all competing for VOD (e.g., Japan). The one common thread is that everyone seems to acknowledge that VOD, grounded in the new on-demand, more open access to content psyche, is among the next great frontiers.

Airlines

Market

The airline market, often referred to in the trade as In Flight Entertainment (IFE), has been relatively static compared to the explosive growth of video and recent activity in the VOD/PPV sector. While there have been improvements in presentation quality and diversification of delivery systems to allow personalized choice, the economics of growth are somewhat capped. There are simply so many flights and a fixed capacity of premium priced seats that can generate additional revenue. An airline is a bit like a theater chain. There is a fixed inventory of seating, and while investment can be made to upgrade the experience while in-seat, beyond the key driver of filling capacity the elasticity for revenue increases is (1) limited by the ability to increase ticket prices and (2) dependent on the ability to add variable charges (or bundle in charges in premium priced tickets) for ancillary items (e.g., concessions at a theater, drinks/food or personal VCR with business/first class on airlines).

The most significant change in the market has been the addition of personal screens as well as personal video systems to complement the overhead projected main screen. While the main economy cabin will still exhibit a film in a manner very similar to what was utilized 20 years ago, virtually all airlines offer a premium movie service in business and first classes. These premium services include distributed, on-demand, and personalized video systems: these systems all afford passengers greater choice and in cases flexibility in viewing.

A distributed system offers a series of programs (e.g., eight choices) that are cycled through, repeating at fixed intervals. A true on-demand system will offer a menu of films, akin to a virtual video store, and the passenger can select from a wide variety of films to play on their individual screens; such a system may offer both additional choice, as well as flexibility incorporating DVD player functionality (e.g., ability to pause/fast forward). Finally, some airlines will literally offer a personalized player — mini-digital video players, where a stand-alone machine and a tape or DVD are brought to the seat. This is the equivalent of the "old days" at rental stores, when you could rent the hardware and software together.

Because of this variance in delivery systems, formats and materials are similarly diverse. Some airlines utilize tape-based legacy systems, while others use high-end digital-based systems. As noted previously, some carriers even maintain a physical inventory of individual portable mini-players that can be loaned out to seats.

It should be noted that as a corollary to the expansion of "channels," more titles can be accommodated; further, this breadth allows for catalog product, making the menu of options parallel that from on-demand carriers. This is a boon to studios that are dependent on catalog churn, and as technology continues to grow the capacity for more product, the ability to license hits/classics as evergreens is likely to expand.

Finally, although picture quality on personal screens is sharper than tape projected onto a big screen, and headphones have been improved, the viewing experience on airplanes still remains inferior to other traditional viewing platforms. Moreover, as some form of entertainment has become standard on longer flights, certain carriers such as Virgin have installed systems also capable of playing games, and services such as In Motion Video offer in-terminal DVD rentals for viewing on laptops. Access to programming has therefore become more of an expectation than an optional item, and seemingly fewer passengers pay extra for watching in-flight films. While the audience is uniquely captive and it should therefore be theoretically possible to charge disproportionate fees, there are both competitive and practical boundaries that have kept pricing to consumers relatively flat. In essence, the improvements in quality, choice, and flexibility have become necessary simply to keep pace with consumer demand and expectations, and there is little premium that trickles down to producers from these platform enhancements.

378

Window

Most airlines want films before the video release, and to some degree match a hotel window: far enough from initial theatrical release that viewing does not materially cannibalize the theatrical run, and before the video release to maintain some measure of quasi exclusivity. The window is usually short, and can be as short as a couple of months. The squeezing of this window parallels the discussion regarding the historical VOD window. As a true ancillary, the window will be dependent upon the proportion of revenue driven relative to the revenue from juxtaposed windows.

Economics

License fees can still be structured in what seems a bit of an archaic manner: flat fees per film per flight. While general pricing has been relatively flat for years, differential pricing has evolved where there may be a charge for the main screen plus an incremental amount per flight for the on-demand systems. Fees overall can reach a reasonable number because licenses are usually non-exclusive; accordingly, while the price per film/flight may be relatively low, there is a significant multiplier effect (times number of flights, and then times number of airlines). Nevertheless, the ultimate revenues are not likely to approach the multi-million dollar levels of other revenue streams.

379

For a studio that is regularly licensing a few films/month to an airline, the relatively small per film revenues can add up over time. Airlines are thus another classic "ancillary," for even though the revenue is small and incremental, it is still significant enough to maintain and exploit the niche.

Non-theatrical

Non-theatrical rights refer generally to the projecting of a movie on screen to an audience in a venue other than a movie theater. The easiest frame of reference for most people is a college film night: Remember the film club or society that would show movies in a hall on Saturday night using an old 16 mm projector? Although it is no longer as common to project a 16 mm print, exhibiting prints at universities remains a staple source of revenue for non-theatrical business. Other common outlets are ships at sea, libraries, and prisons.

Window

Non-theatrical rights are often exploited in the period just before home video, trying to take advantage of the hiatus between theatrical and home video exploitation. This is especially true in the fall when summer movies have had their run, the films are being readied for the big fourth quarter video push, and colleges are back in session. To some, this is the ultimate time for film clubs to show the hot movies from the past summer.

Beyond this narrow window, non-theatrical rights are often exploited ad hoc, such as when a specific institution requests a one off screening of a picture. There are niche distributors who specialize in booking movies in this market (sometimes offering classics, which can often involve the body of work of individual directors), and work with a network/circuit of outlets such as bicycling to various universities. The tail of the window is therefore somewhat indefinite: non-theatrical exhibitions/licenses can arise 10 or 20+ years after a release, and the availability is only limited by whether the picture continues to be in demand.

Economics

Non-theatrical exploitation does not yield much revenue relative to other exploitation outlets. Perhaps more than the money, this distribution outlet recognizes that films are an art form that are in demand, and this avenue helps ensure that films can reach the widest possible audience. In essence, this fulfills a niche satisfying additional demand, almost for the sake of satisfying demand as an end, over and above pure economic concerns.

To the extent revenues are generated, the model is usually for the niche distributor to charge a distribution fee based on the revenues generated. In the university circuit, the splits are a bit like theatrical with the caveat that there is usually a single tier rather than a sliding scale. Accordingly, a non-theatrical split is likely to be straightforward (e.g., 50/50); of course, in some cases there can be different deals cut and guarantees paid, but the market is small enough and the distribution specialized/targeted enough that negotiations at the margins take a backseat to securing quality distribution in the channel. Outside of universities (e.g., to prisons) I admit to having no idea how revenues are truly calculated, nor do I probably want to know! (Although my assumption is that the deal is a similar simple split.) Most licensors are simply happy to know that they are exploiting this additional channel, focus on the breadth of distribution to universities (and perhaps ships at sea), and have an overall number they target based on comparable films and rentals.

Online Impact

- The online world is not so much changing the notion of product merchandising, but rather the range of merchandise offered and the outlets available to acquire product:.
  - Avatars, which are now popular surrogates for your own persona (e.g., for instant messaging, on social networking sites), and their accessories are an example of digital merchandise (e.g., users can buy digital merchandise, such as weapons or clothes, for their digital character).
  - Toys come with codes to unlock Web-based virtual worlds.
  - Video games are now being created in downloadable form, and in some cases networked such as via Xbox Live.
  - Film and TV Web sites often combine or link to e-commerce applications.
  - Secondary markets, such as for collectibles, have grown exponentially with online marketplaces, such as eBay.
  - Ringtones (e.g., theme music) are just one example of translating film and video elements into digital merchandising bits.
- VOD is by its nature now becoming commonplace online, and is likely over time to eclipse or become the new face of video rental.
- SVOD and VOD applications are changing the nature of pay TV services, and pose a long-term threat to pay TV channels—à la carte access challenges the aggregation model upon which pay services are built.

381

CHAPTER 9

Marketing

Marketing and distribution work hand in hand (or at least they should), with the line often fuzzy. Technically, distribution involves the sales, physical manufacture (or access if online), and delivery of goods for sale, such as a film print, DVD, or television master. For each category of media that a piece of intellectual property is licensed, distribution addresses how it is consumed and monetized: what is the price, where and how is the product sold (or leased), how many units are being made, how is inventory managed, and what are the costs of goods. Marketing, in contrast, focuses on awareness and interest. Marketing is to some measure the business and art of driving a consumer to consumption by making them aware that the good is available and creating the impulse to watch, buy, or borrow it. In summary, as noted in Chapter 1: *marketing focuses on awareness and driving consumption, whereas distribution focuses on maximizing and making that consumption profitable.*

Back to Experience Goods

In Chapter 3 I discuss the problem of predicting the success of a film or TV show (i.e., experience goods) given the factors of imperfect information, cascades, and infinite variety. While it may not be possible to predict the outcome, marketing by its nature is an attempt to influence the outcome. Accordingly, marketing comes to the rescue of the experience good quandary and tries to put some experience into that good; the viewer, without having actually consumed the end product (which per an experience good is the only way to know whether you really like/want it), is helped to make up his own mind.

Marketing through trailers, posters, press, reviews, Web sites, seeded blogs, advertising, etc., is bombarding the consumer with inputs to influence the selection of a film, TV show, or video in an environment stacked with an infinite variety of creative product. And the most effective marketing may be that which makes you feel you have already (to a degree) experienced the film/show. If a trailer is a microcosm of the experience, and the trailer is well directed to a consumer demographic, then it may seduce that target consumer to see the film, explaining in part the unique frustration of having felt hoodwinked if the movie did not fulfill the expectations engendered by the trailer signal.

Accordingly, beyond marketing helping to build a brand for distribution windows, it is interesting also to view these activities in the economic context of differentiating information inputs; those inputs, heavily influenced by marketing, are uniquely important in selecting a product you cannot know whether you will like until you have so-called consumed it.

It is further interesting to speculate how the online world will impact these traditional patterns and the positioning of inputs. Is there a difference in utilizing Rotten Tomatoes (www.rottentomatoes.com) which cumulates all critics' picks into a single scorecard — does "fresh" (greater than 50% positive reviews) really mean it is a good picture, or are variations and cascades baked into the equation such that you have no better reference from the overall verdict versus an individual critic where you have sorted out an internal mechanism to map their biases onto your own? Do social networking sites, where you affiliate with friends, provide a better predictor and negate cascade behavior or do they exacerbate the problem? Do recommendation engines really work to defeat the inherent uncertainty in consuming an experience good, and do references to "others who bought X also bought Y" further work to defeat the risk of unwisely committing one's time? In the media and entertainment industry, the online world is making the whole concept of marketing a lot more entertaining.

Strategy (Film)

Marketing strategy is impacted by several factors, including the budget, target audience (demographics), timing, talent involved, and partners.

383

Budget Tied to Type and Breadth of Release: Limited Openings, Niche Marketing, and the Web's Viral Power

For a film, the marketing budget is the most significant cost item outside of making the picture. While there is no exact rule, it is common for the marketing budget (inclusive of prints and advertising) to equal a significant percentage of the cost of producing the film. A film that costs $75M may, for example, have a domestic marketing budget of $35M+, inclusive of the following line items:

- Media/Advertising
- PR
- Web site
- Travel

As discussed in Chapter 4, the amount spent to open a film is disproportionately large because the theatrical launch of a film is the engine that drives all downstream revenues. Accordingly, the money spent up front marketing a film, creating awareness, develops an overnight brand that is then sustained and managed in most instances for more than a decade. In extreme cases, marketing costs can equal or exceed production costs. The *Wall Street Journal* noted of the March 2009 release of *Monsters vs. Aliens*, which was trying to expand the market for 3-D films: "DreamWorks Animation spent upwards of $175 million to market the film globally, more than the $165 million the studio used to make the movie."[1]

Word of Mouth Limited Openings and Niche Marketing

Not all films, of course, can sustain a marketing budget in the tens of millions of dollars, which forces distributors/studios to employ a variety of strategies for launch (see also Chapter 4 and the section below on Press and PR). One strategy is not to open a film in a wide, big-bang fashion. Opening a film in a nationwide and worldwide manner is the most expensive avenue, requiring national media and costs that make the launch an event. As touched on in Chapter 4, if a picture is opened in limited release, targeting critics and key cities and hoping that reviews and word of mouth will create momentum, the costs are dramatically reduced. This is a typical pattern for art-type movies, and movies that may appeal to an intellectual base (e.g., Woody Allen) where openings in, for example, New York, Los Angeles, and a few other select locales will draw avid moviegoers and start

384

creating buzz. The risk factor with a staged release pattern is obviously that the reviews or performance will not meet expectations and the film could struggle to gain a wide release (that perhaps could have been achieved if the movie opened day and date nationwide).

Another strategy to open a film with limited marketing dollars is to focus on niche marketing. A perfect example of niche marketing are campaigns targeted at colleges. Distributors will try to tie-up with local on-campus film groups, etc., to get the message out on a film that they believe will appeal to this demographic. These types of campaigns can include posters, Internet components, sponsored events with film clubs, etc.

Sometimes niche campaigns may be referred to as "underground campaigns" or "guerilla marketing," which by their very nature can be difficult to orchestrate. There is a bit of inherent hypocrisy for a studio to try and stimulate a grassroots campaign with an expressed goal of creating a hip factor. This is because what the studio is doing is seeding a bit of money to try and create a groundswell while really saving money. (Note: This generalization is a bit unfair, as given the profile of the niche film in question and resources there probably is little money available for marketing; nevertheless, perception matters, and studios as the masters of perception could be accused of an end run even if under the circumstances they may be orchestrating the most viable strategy.)

As a component of a lower budget campaign, viral campaigns are becoming more popular. These are Internet-driven campaigns using Web sites, blogs, and teasers. The goal of these campaigns is that the film or an element within it will simply "catch on." One of the most frequently cited examples is *The Blair Witch Project*, a low budget film that leveraged viral marketing to garner $140M at the US box office.[2] Lots of people like to point to *The Blair Witch Project* as proof of a strategy, but seldom is it mentioned that the odds of success here are no better than in other areas; namely, there are many more wannabes than *Blair Witch* successes.

Is Viral Messaging on the Web Always a Good Idea?

In the zeal to point out that the Internet's democratization of access affords a platform where anyone can have a shot, it is easy to forget that the Web is the essence of clutter. Gaining impressions and buzz amid the infinite choices online may actually be a longer shot statistically than a low budget grassroots campaign. The intersection of execution and luck is not magically better online. Additionally, while there are certain tricks of the trade and optimization strategies that can be employed, any viral campaign ultimately relies on sharing and peer-to-peer excitement. Moreover, in this context "messaging" is no longer captive, and online users, unabashed in giving opinions and feedback, can be brutal. It is hard to control spin once material is unleashed into the blogosphere, and any campaign needs to be careful about opinion potentially turning negative. There is no guarantee that positive comments, downloads, and buzz will materialize, and as people continue to learn and experiment, this avenue could be a risky awareness strategy (even if compelling) when compared to a traditional media blitz.

Shift of Dollars to Online Tempered by Market Still Evolving

Despite these risks, the Web is no doubt a boon to marketers, and money spent to stimulate viral buzz is both tempting and often productive; moreover, the Web allows unique targeted marketing, and as technology and advertisers become more sophisticated more dollars will shift online given the inherent efficiencies of better matching expenditures and messaging to narrowly defined consumers. As the shift in marketing dollars suggests, this is already starting to happen. However, until Internet spending grows exponentially from its current levels it will still be dwarfed by traditional media spends.

Further, the world of online is still evolving (with new formats available, and video advertising strategies being tested), and creative breakthrough ads are challenging; generally speaking, as of today online marketing alone cannot create mass awareness.

Timing, Seasonality, and Influencing External and Internal Factors

Timing of a campaign is critical, and again it depends on several moving parts. Sometimes, it can be an effective strategy to say very little, allowing symbolism and mystery to create buzz. One of the best examples of this was the 1989 release of the first Batman movie starring Michael Keaton and Jack Nicholson. Months before the release the Batman logo/symbol was simply plastered around the world: consumers could see it on posters, on buses, and on phone booths in London.

I asked Michael Uslan, who launched the *Batman* film franchise and has served as executive producer of all of the *Batman* films (including most recently *The Dark Knight*), how he had seen marketing evolve in the roughly 20 years between the first *Batman* and *The Dark*

386

Knight, and in particular how the Internet was influencing campaigns. He noted:

When our first, revolutionary "Batman" film was released in the summer of 1989 by Warner Bros., I considered it the best marketed film in history. In New York City, you could not walk one block without running into someone wearing a Bat T-shirt or hat. That iconic black and gold bat symbol was everywhere. Movie posters were being stolen from bus shelters and theatre lobby displays. People were paying to walk into movies showing the "Batman" trailer then leaving before whatever feature was playing came on. Pirates were selling that brief trailer at comic book conventions for $25 a pop. When the Berlin Wall came down, kids were coming through to freedom already wearing Batman caps. But marketing via an Internet strategy didn't exist. Today, it's completely different. You cannot successfully and fully market any comic book or similar genre movie in this day and age without a viral campaign on the Net starting ten months to a year prior to release if your intention is to build a franchise and market a brand. "The Dark Knight" had, perhaps, the best viral campaign ever. Fans of comics, movies, science fiction and fantasy, manga and anime, animation, horror, etc. must be engaged early on and "courted" for they have the capability to make or break a movie by their support or the lack thereof. Studios now bring their filmmakers and stars to the bigger comic book conventions to pay homage to the fans they know they must ultimately win over. There are currently so many dozens of key fan-sites on the Internet with millions of people trolling them all day and late night. It is a bonded community where word spreads like lightning. The Internet is not only important to market a genre film domestically and internationally today, it is essential.

I will come back to Web sites and online later, but I want first to continue my focus on timing; the matrix of elements associated with timing can profoundly impact a marketing campaign. When it may be best to launch a film is driven by both "internal" factors related to the inherent/specific elements of the property as well as "external" events that impact consumer's consumption patterns but are otherwise unrelated to the film at hand.

Internal Factors

The most important element of timing is that external events are as influential, and arguably much more influential, than direct elements ("internal") driven by the film/property. By internal, I mean particular relevance of the property that dictates specific optimal release timing. Perhaps the best example of this are films with holiday themes. A Christmas-themed movie, such as *Christmas with the Cranks*, *Four Christmases*, *Polar Express*, or even *Chronicles of Narnia* should be released during the year-end holiday period to optimize interest. Similarly, movies with beach themes (e.g., surfing related) are clearly a more natural fit in the summer. Occasionally, there are movies with literal direct tie-ins to dates, such as *Home for the Holidays* (starring Holly Hunter), which involves family coming home over Thanksgiving, Independence Day (about science fiction and not about July 4th), which had a clear marketing hook on July 4th, Halloween (and other thrillers) around Halloween, and sports movies that revolve around the sport currently "in season" (such as *The Rookie* or *The Natural* during baseball season, or *Remember the Titans*, *Leatherheads*, or *Friday Night Lights* during football). When listing just a few of these tie-in categories there becomes a larger overlap with theme and timing than one would likely identify without reflection.

Because people are looking for films with "the Christmas spirit" in December, about love at Valentine's Day, about the beach during the summer, and about baseball during baseball season, it is obvious to find films with these themes releasing in these time frames. Simply, the themes of these types of films are top of mind; important for marketing, they also create an alternative reference (vs. key word genre categories such as action, romance, thriller, drama, chick-flick, etc.) that subliminally or probably overtly drives interest.

External Factors

By external events, I mean outside factors wholly unrelated to the film that have a material impact on people paying money to go to the theater. The four principal elements are (1) events of national or international importance, (2) holidays, (3) competition, and (4) economic events.

Events of national importance, while obviously a broad category, generally means major events known about significantly in advance, such as political elections or major sporting events. Not only do these

388

events draw attention away, making it harder to compete for viewing, but these events drive up the price of media. On the sports side, distributors take into account dates for the Olympics, the World Cup, and major sports playoffs and championships (whether Formula 1 events in Europe or the Super Bowl in the United States). For politics, the concerns may be more limited, but periodic major events such as presidential elections will dictate timing. Again, this is driven as much by having to compete with an external event perceived to be monopolizing (or at least drawing) target consumers' attention as with the corollary impact of the cost of media. Having to buy media time during a presidential election when key outlets are able to sell spots at a premium (and when inventory may even, in some cases, be sold out) simply drives up budgets with no fringe benefits.

The second external category, holidays, is important not because holidays can get in the way (as in the case of an election or sporting event) but because they create free time. The entertainment business is at the heart of the leisure industry, and the more people have free time the more likely they are to consume an entertainment product. Accordingly, the biggest release dates of the year are around Memorial Day weekend (commencement of summer break), July 4th, Thanksgiving, and Christmas. Movies are a social experience, and film marketing tries to drive a truck through the gates held open by the dual forces of getting together and compulsory free time. Box office is largely driven by weekends and in terms of marketing opportunities key holidays are nothing short of weekends on steroids.

For kids, the summer season is the most critical release period of the year; having extended periods of free time while being out of school drives up weekday box office numbers, validating the holiday/vacation relationship (see also Chapter 4).

The third external category is competition, perhaps the most overlooked and yet at the same time arguably the most influential factor in terms of attracting an audience. Competition can be subdivided into a couple of categories: direct competition among films for market share, and competition among studios and rivals (which can at times add an emotional and even irrational component). Regarding direct competition, distributors will always be looking for the so-called cleanest window. Would you want your next film to be opening against the next *Spider-Man*, *Shrek*, or *Star Wars*? Certain event films can literally suck so much of the box office out of the market that it becomes questionable whether other films can perform simultaneously. Studios perform sophisticated analysis on the market size, and what portion of a demographic they want to attract, but whether the

389

market can expand to handle certain capacity is always a tricky calculation.

Studios therefore jockey for release dates and try to put a stake in the ground early to ward off would-be competitors. Sony and Marvel, for example, in early 2009 announced it would release *Spider-Man 4* on May 6, 2011, securing the pole position in the summer box office race, a position Marvel covets and is similarly trying to secure in 2010 with the slotting (more than a year in advance) of *Iron Man 2* on May 7, 2010.[3] With summer weeks and holiday weekends at a premium, it has become commonplace to map out release date schedules years in advance.

One of the most time-consuming and important parts of the art of theatrical distribution is trying to track the matrix of competitive titles, and both schedule and protect release dates. As a result, dates are either universally known and touted (to ward others off) or guarded with strict secrecy to keep competitors guessing. As dates get close, the cat is of course let out of the bag and lots of last minute jockeying takes place. The most intense poker game is played in the summer (the busiest time of year) since a new tentpole film is releasing virtually every week.

In terms of efficiency, it would be simpler and better for all involved to work through a trade association and schedule dates, eliminating the secrecy and politics, and allocate slots in a fashion that would optimize the pie. This practice, however, is deemed collusive and violates anti-trust and international competition laws. I was once involved with a case in Europe alleging collusion among studios in setting release dates, a case that was ultimately dismissed but still sent a chill through the spines of the parties involved.

I would argue that while collusion is possible, and would create more efficient economics, the fact remains that the film business is cutthroat: the desire to best a rival dwarfs the forces of collusion and ensures true and vibrant competition. And remember, this can be a business driven by irrational competition — people's jobs and star can rise and fall by rankings and even perception. There is more than an ego element to where a studio falls in terms of box office rank (e.g., top distributor of the year). With so much riding on a film's performance and its opening, paranoia comes into play. No matter what a film's marketing budget is, there is always fear that the budget of a competitor's title is higher. Add to this equation the fact that when the marketing budget and decisions are being mapped out the film may not be finished (or the people doing the planning may not have even had a chance to see it), and that no matter what the questions may be about your picture you are going purely on hearsay regarding the competition. This is not like marketing one brand of soap against another. This can be a last minute chess game involving the blind leading the blind. Driven by emotion, imperfect information, extremely high stakes, and fierce competition, passions can run high.

Moreover, given this hyper-competitive environment, a studio may try to maximize results by counter-programming (a strategy that may draft off of increased in-theater foot traffic, target a different demographic than is drawn to a new blockbuster picture, or simply address the too much product, too few weekends challenge). An extreme instance of counter-programming is to spend with the intent of crushing a competitor's film. In the context of battling brands, it can be as much of a success to undermine a key competitor's film as to launch one yourself. Of course, no one will admit to this, but it can be gleaned in the marketplace when there are obvious rivals or niches to protect.

I will label the final key external category as economic events. While this can sound a bit amorphous, marketing at its most base level is trying to encourage people to spend money. Just like periods of holiday that create free time, there are periods that stimulate so-called free money. Pay days and bonus periods can become catalysts for planning product releases (and conversely, tax day, April 15th is probably a time to avoid). In certain countries there are traditional bonus periods, and in some countries bonuses are either legally or culturally built into salary structures, such as a "13th month" of pay. This factor is much less influential in terms of planning a theatrical release, because the relative cost of a movie ticket is low. If the price of admission is not a barrier to entry on a weekend, then it is hard to argue that a release should be planned around a bonus period. This timing tends to be much more pivotal at retail (e.g., for DVD release), and is something likely tracked by the Wal-Marts of the world; a study of product releases to paydays (1st and 15th of month) would probably yield a closely mapped curve. Perhaps, this is over-analyzing, for the likelihood is that in most cases this factor happens to dovetail with other elements, such as year-end bonuses overlapping holiday periods.

Day-and-Date Release

It used to be the pattern that a film would open in the United States and then be released subsequently in international territories. This

391

had multiple advantages including (1) saving money on prints by being able to reuse prints and send them to a different territory when one territory wound down (so-called "bicycling of prints," which is of course limited to common language territories); (2) allowing talent to travel to staggered premieres; (3) enabling the heat from the US release (e.g., box office, reviews) to spread to the rest of the world; (4) allowing the marketing department to learn from the US release; and (5) simply allowing time to complete international versions (e.g., subtitles, dubs). As discussed in greater detail in other chapters (see Chapters 2 and 4), however, piracy and other pressures have led to studios now favoring day-and-date releases (especially in the context of event films), which simply means near simultaneous release of the picture in all territories.

Reducing the impact of piracy has grown in importance because with the combined forces of a global economy and easy Web access distributors run the risk of a picture illegally showing up in a territory before its scheduled opening. Day-and-date releases are the best prevention against piracy; the pattern also yields the biggest worldwide box office number the quickest. In terms of economics, the calculation is whether the accelerated international release will bring in more money (than would otherwise be lost to piracy) than the incremental costs associated with simultaneous release (e.g., extra prints, overtime to rush international versions). (Note: This is an even more difficult equation in practice because inevitably a simultaneous release means that in some territories, given cultural patterns, seasonality, outside events, etc., the timing will not be optimal.) The elimination of the chance to learn from and tinker with earlier marketing strategies is an intangible that will not lead the decision, especially since global marketing is driven off the US campaign.

Third-Party Help: Talent and Promotional Partners' Role in Creating Demand

Talent Involved

Nothing sells a property like a star, and the magnitude of the star and their willingness to promote the film can be a significant factor in the overall strategy. This is a double-edged sword, however, for talent can be unpredictable — both in terms of dedication to the project and timing — and very expensive (think entourages, first class travel, and accommodations). Much needs to be put in motion in advance of the release, and the mechanics of production are such that most big stars are well into other projects by the time the prior film has completed post production and entered its marketing and release phase. Accordingly, while personal commitment, emotion, relationships, and ego are gossiped about, the fact is that time management can be the paramount concern. Even if a star is committed to promoting a film and willing to travel for publicity, they could be tied up with another project (worse if on location) and simply have limited availability.

The advantage to using talent/stars to promote a film is the enormous amount of free publicity that can be generated. The talk show circuit, ranging from morning shows (e.g., *The Today Show*), to afternoon talk shows (e.g., *Oprah*), to late night programs (e.g., *The Tonight Show*), generates significant exposure and tend to foster other appearances and press opportunities. The downside to using stars (beyond costs) is lack of control.

Unlike a trailer or advertisement, a star as a spokesman may or may not put on the appropriate spin. Given, however, that the preeminent concern at this phase is awareness the risk is usually worth taking. Stars are paid enormous sums and that premium is largely for awareness: people want to see them, know about them, go to their films. They are a presumed built-in draw, the so-called sure-fire way to entice the consumer to pay money to go see the product (though statistically, this has been proven a fallacy). Famously divorced from Nicole Kidman, engaged to Katie Holmes, and often front page news for his promotion of Scientology, Tom Cruise had achieved as many headlines for jumping on a couch during the *Oprah Winfrey Show* and behaving erratically as anything else during the promotional window for *Mission Impossible III* — the public perception was starting to turn from golden boy to eccentric. Shortly following *Mission Impossible III's* failure to meet certain expectations, Paramount ended its long-term deal with Cruise's production company, with Sumner Redstone (chairman of Paramount's parent, Viacom) publicly mentioning Cruise's personal behavior among the reasons for its decision (sending some shockwaves through the industry). At this point, many were questioning whether the star's appearance would help the picture, or whether the risk of negative publicity may hurt it.

Stripping away the artistic element, and whatever life and magic they breathe into the end product, at its most base level stars are a vehicle for instantly branding a film. An unknown product, for which hundreds of people have spent months of their lives, becomes a such and such film. Given this inherent branding, whether fair or not, it is economically wasteful not to use that branding in turn to create branding and awareness by association for the film. If a movie has lots of talent involved, such as a famous director, then there are simply multiple hooks to exploit.

Promotional Partners

Promotional partners can on occasion influence timing and positioning. A cereal company or fast food company may be willing to create product tie-ins, and even pay for advertising. An advertisement by a cereal company, Burger King, or McDonald's can create huge demographic-specific awareness.

It is important here to distinguish between merchandising and promotional partners. A merchandising deal (see Chapter 8) is generally a licensing arrangement where a third-party company pays a fee to the property owner for the right to create certain goods featuring elements of the property. The end product is therefore a Batman action figure, a Spider-Man costume, or a Dora the Explorer backpack. In contrast, a promotional partner already has its own product; usually a very well-known branded product. What it is offering is a chance to tie-in its brand in a fun way utilizing elements of the film brand. Accordingly, a kids meal at a restaurant may be themed for the week using characters from the movie, or a character from the movie may appear on a box of a well-known cereal. These are instances of cross-promoting brands as opposed to creating a unique new product SKU designed solely around the elements from the film.

If a distributor is fortunate enough to have a property that lends itself to this type of tie-in (these opportunities are limited to big films), then lead time must be built in and limits on content may be imposed. The promotional partner, no matter how much they may like a film idea or property, is still self interested: they are simply trying to attract more consumers to their product by associating themselves with another property (brand) on the assumption that the tie-in will lead to a lift in sales. They are not willing to risk their own brand on a tie-in that could undermine their brand. Accordingly, violence and other content tied to age ratings is critically important. A tie-in partner such as a toy company, for example, targeting a kids demographic is likely going to be extremely concerned about content not being too violent or sexually explicit.

Assuming the content hurdle is cleared, then the next key issue is timing. Product development time lines are years out, and it is not uncommon for promotional partners to be locked in up to a couple of years in advance of a release, and for the partners to demand locked release dates. Given this time frame, promotional partners tend to align with known film brands. This creates a mutual comfort factor — both the product brand and film brand know what they are dealing with — and is also a practical necessity. At the time the partner tie-in needs to be locked, the film may not have even been started. How can a major corporation with a household brand commit to a tie-in and spending up to millions of dollars on blind faith? Only by associating with a known brand, and feeling as if there is only an upside.

One of the best known partnerships was a deal struck between Disney and McDonald's. Both companies agreed to a 10-year exclusive arrangement. It was a brilliant move by Disney, for in one stroke they gained exposure at the largest fast food retailer in the country and also excluded competition. At the time for McDonald's, Disney was considered the only "studio brand," and as a consistent family friendly brand it meant a high-quality, safe association.

Going back to the example of the summer of 2007, various partners were being simultaneously courted by different studios. With *Spider-Man 3*, *Shrek 3*, *Pirates of the Caribbean 3*, *Bourne 3* and *Harry Potter 5* all coming out, together with *Fantastic Four II* and *Transformers*, there was fierce competition for limited major partners. There are only so many large packaged food companies, soft drink companies, fast food outlets, candy companies, etc., and everyone wants to affiliate with the market leader. Moreover, not only do they want the market leader to associate with their film, but they want that market leader to help brand the film by spending their own advertising money and creating unique in-store displays. A successful campaign spreads the message over the airwaves and at retail, creating millions of impressions and potentially exponentially increasing the media weight behind a campaign. Table 9.1 lists some of the partners lined up for summer 2007.

Product Placements — Finance, Not Marketing Driven
Product placements are similar to promotional partner tie-ins, but are generally distinguishable in that the third-party promotional partner will also advertise outside of the film/property; hence, such third party will leverage its brand in retail together with the tie-in film. A pure product placement will only involve integrating a consumer brand into a film, television, or online property, where there is an indirect association. Examples of a product placement are the judges on *American Idol* drinking a coke (with the Coca-Cola bottle and logo prominent), or as discussed in Chapter 3, with the financing of

395

Table 9.1 Promotional Partners

Film	Promotional Partners	Details and/or $
Spider-Man 3	Burger King, General Mills, Kraft, Comcast, 7-Eleven, Wal-Mart, Target, Toys-R-Us	• ~$100M in media, mainly on commercials • General Mills promo involved 20 brands in 12 categories, putting the film on ~100 million packages • Kraft — 10 product brands
Pirates 3	Volvo	• 4-week game online to find a buried SUV
Transformers	Burger King, Mountain Dew, General Motors	
Shrek 3	Sierra Mist, Snickers, M&Ms, Kellogg, McDonald's	• McDonald's was a global partner, promoting the film and characters in more than 100 countries • Multiple Kellogg cereals and products
Bourne 3 (Ultimatum)	Volkswagen, MasterCard, Symantec, American Airlines, Banks (ABN-AMRO, HSBC, Barclays)	• $40M value across partners; VW alone committed to ~$25M (Touareg2 featured in film action sequences) • Symantec's Norton Antivirus "Protect Your Identity With Norton" tie-in campaign

Note: *Bourne* stats "Major brands get behind 'Bourne,'" *Variety*, July 12, 2008; other titles "Sequels Spur Spending Spiral," *Variety* May 14–20, 2007.

certain online originals having a character wear a particular brand of shoes. In both of these cases the viewer is drawn to the product, with the character (or in the case of the reality program or contest, the judge or host) using the product as the marketing hook. There is no direct tie-in between the brands. The lines here can be quite fine, as a car used in a film (e.g., a special sports car in a James Bond film) is a kind of product placement; however, because in these types of cases there may also be off-film marketing ("see …. in the James Bond film…") the deal may be better characterized as a promotional partner tie-in.

Another way to distinguish between these types of arrangements is that promotional partner deals are generally designed to add marketing weight and promotion to a show or movie. In contrast, product placements do little to promote the show, but create a separate revenue stream (basically in-show advertising) that can be viewed as defraying production costs (i.e., a method of financing) or a revenue stream helping to recoup production costs. It is for this latter reason that several online original programs, unable to secure enough revenue from new advertising markets, have utilized product placement opportunities to help finance production (again, see Chapter 3). The challenge with product placements is that creators often bristle that they undermine the integrity of the show, and the brands that are usually prominently featured (to justify the fees paid) may date the shows in the long tail.

One way to defeat these problems is to create a product placement that has functional relevancy. This, however, is difficult to execute creatively, for the product needs to be built into the show and integrated at an early stage. I recently saw an example in the online context that may be an ideal model for utilizing product placements. The online social network Gaia Online, which allows people to build environments and socialize via avatars in a virtual world, has innovated a clever way to integrate product placements that goes beyond simply seeing the visual. As has fast become a trend, users can buy virtual goods to dress up their characters, and in this instance, can buy Nike shoes. What is different is that when the character wears those shoes they go faster, creating a relevancy and functionality that creates more value for the brand and does not detract from or compromise the underlying content. In this example, the Internet has taken product placement to another level.

Theatrical Marketing Budget

The marketing budget is the largest cost outside of physical production impacting the P&L of a film. Given the increasingly competitive nature of the marketplace, and the compressed periods of theatrical release (see Chapter 4), the costs of marketing have spiraled to almost unimaginable highs. As already referenced, the average domestic cost for an MPAA member studio to market a film in 2007 was $35.9M.[4]

Direct Costs

By far, media is the largest cost category. Media costs and strategy involve mapping placement to demographic targets and achieving a certain reach and frequency. This is often expressed in terms of percentage of target reached, such as 70%, and how many times that grouping is hit with impressions (such as one, two, or three times). Media buys are then made on the basis of impressions. The end goal is to achieve a certain awareness level, which then hopefully translates into consumption.

Media buys are aggregated in four principal areas: television and radio, print, outdoor, and online. These categories are exactly what they sound like. TV and radio are simply commercial spots of varying lengths. Outdoor ranges from billboards to sides of buildings to buses and phone kiosks. Newspaper/print involves advertisements that can differ by size, prominence, color, etc., and like TV can be executed locally, nationally, and to finely tuned demographics (e.g., women's magazines). Online is a catch-all encompassing everything relating to the Web. There is no magic formula, and different marketing gurus will allocate different weights depending on their experience and to some degree gut feeling. Some believe that with increasing media diversity and competition that the middle is disappearing; namely, either spend modestly and targeted, or spend big enough to rise above the clutter.

Allocation of Media Costs

TV advertising alone can often account for more than half of the total media marketing costs. The allocation of costs is a picture-by-picture decision, but almost invariably the largest costs are first for TV advertising, next for newspaper advertising, and then the balance of the pie divided among Internet, outdoor (e.g., billboards, buses), and radio advertising.

These are difficult costs to track in the aggregate, but the following MPAA chart (Figure 9.1) gives a snapshot as to the prominence of TV spending and the relatively small amounts of advertising committed online.

It is also useful to look at the breakdown on a per film basis (Table 9.2). In 2007, the following are select examples across key titles from a variety of studios, as referenced in the *Hollywood Reporter* (note, all figures in $M).[5]

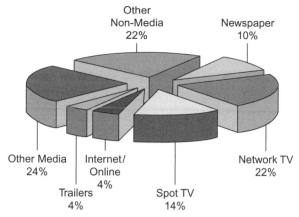

Other
Non-Media
22%

Newspaper
10%

Other Media
24%

Internet/
Online
4%

Trailers
4%

Spot TV
14%

Network TV
22%

MPAA 2007 Entertainment Industry Market Statistics

Figure 9.1 MPAA Theatrical Marketing statistics: MPAA Member Company Average Distribution of US Advertising Costs by Media, Motion Picture Association Entertainment Industry Market Statistics–2007, www.mpaa.org/researchStatistics.asp. [Note: Other media includes cable/other TV.]

Because media costs are frontloaded to open a film, pursuant to the compressed theatrical box office curve, if a film underperforms it is too late to adjust. Accordingly, for films that do not achieve box office numbers greater than $100M, the percentage of marketing costs relative to box office can be a frightening number. This was the case with *Music & Lyrics* starring Hugh Grant where the marketing costs were more than 70% of the total box office (and remember, rentals are roughly half the box office, meaning that the marketing costs significantly exceeded the revenues taken in by the distributor at this stage).

Internet Impact

The power of the Web to target messages to specific demographics is a marketer's dream, and the budgets for online advertising continue to grow. However, the percentages spent online and the migration of marketing dollars has not been as great or fast as one may expect. Contrary to most expectations, the percentage amount spent by the studios in 2007 was actually down a fraction from what they spent in 2006.[6] How can this be the case?

Arguably, this is due to a couple of factors. First, the market is still struggling with experimentation and standardization. When the types of advertisements are evolving, as is the method of integration, there are inherent limits on spending. More than once I have been involved

Table 9.2   Select Films by 2007 Movie-Ad Spending

Studio and Distributor	Domestic Box office	Total Media Marketing Costs	Network TV	Cable TV	Newspaper	Radio	Magazines	Spot TV	Internet
Enchanted (Disney)	$127.8	$44.6	$11.7	$11.6	$6.2	$0.1	$0.1	$13.0	$0.2
Shrek the Third (Dreamworks/Paramount)	$322.7	$45.1	$20.6	$11.6	$4.7	$0.1	$0.1	$5.2	$0.4
I am Legend (Warner Bros.)	$256.3	$39.8	$21.7	$6.8	$4.4	$0.0	$0.0	$4.0	$0.1
Spider-Man 3 (Sony)	$336.5	$41.7	$17.7	$9.5	$4.9	$0.6	$0.3	$5.1	$2.1
The Bourne Ultimatum (Universal)	$227.5	$36.9	$10.2	$10.0	$5.5	$0.5	$0.1	$2.8	$4.8
Live Free of Die Hard (Fox)	$134.5	$33.6	$14.0	$9.0	$3.9	$0.5	$0.0	$4.0	$0.1
Music & Lyrics (Warner Bros.)	$50.6	$35.7	$15.5	$6.5	$5.2	$0.0	$2.1	$3.3	$0.4

with great marketing ideas, only to be held up because the type of advertising contemplated either did not exist, or if it did exist was new enough that people were unsure of how to price it, or serve it, or measure it.

Second, some argue that the nature of the Web enables users to find what they want without marketers having to pay for it; basically, if it is available and compelling it will be found. A trailer that is released virally can be accessed from thousands of points. As a studio, if your best message is the visual, and online distribution of a trailer is free, then why additionally pay for advertisements? This theory is buttressed by the nature of experience goods. As earlier discussed advertising helps the consumer feel as if they have experienced the film; the consumer then creates signals that may lead to cascade behavior, which may be further accelerated by viral sharing among users frequenting social networking sites. Of course, this information flow and result can also turn negative, which is a complicated way of saying that whether a trailer is compelling is now even more important in the online world.

I asked Tom Warner, a marketing executive who has managed releases of blockbuster films such as the Star Wars prequels for Lucasfilm and *Kung Fu Panda* for DreamWorks Animation, how he viewed the current climate for using the Web to market film and TV content:

There is no question more and more people are online, and the Internet has become an important part of the marketing mix. It is a great and efficient way to reach specific targets. That said, the Internet is still a young medium and changing daily. Unlike television, which has created a standard ad unit with the :15 and :30 second spot, online is still the Wild West. In the beginning, it was all about the banner ad. However, the banner ad is very limited creatively and not that effective. Now, it is all about integrating your message within the content of the site and tailoring the message to speak to that audience.

To the question of whether there would be a natural leveling off of allocation between online and TV spending for marketing, or are we likely to see experimenting for a number of years, Tom added:

I think we are still in the infancy of the Internet and experimenting will continue for years to come. Advertisers will continue to experiment and adapt as the Internet evolves.

Perhaps because of these current limitations spending online relative to traditional offline media is still a very small fraction of the overall media budget. Nevertheless, the promise of direct marketing, inherent efficiencies of reaching an exact demographic, the ability to report precise 1:1 metrics, and the inevitable maturation of the space mean that allocations will continue growing.

Correlation of Marketing Spend to Success

While William Goldman is correct that "nobody knows anything," and most statistical correlations of top box office stars to movie performance evidence that stars in fact do not guarantee a project's success, at least one popular benchmark seems true: bigger budget movies tend to yield the best return on investment. Despite the seemingly bigger risks (if we assume higher marketing costs go somewhat hand in hand with higher budgets), the most costly films are on average the most profitable, with an SNL Kagan study finding that of all films with wide releases (i.e., more than 1,000 locations) between 2003–2007, "the two priciest segments surveyed showed the best profitability...80 films costing more than $100 million to produce showed average profitability of $282.3 million."[7]

402

Trailers

The goal of the trailer is obviously to entice interest in viewership, and hopefully to create awareness through both direct viewing and word of mouth. The problem with the creative is that the trailers often have to be cut before the film is completed, and this is almost always the case with teaser trailers (which further means there are instances where scenes in the trailer may not make it into the final cut of the movie). This problem is exacerbated by effects-laden films where shots may be filmed in front of blue or green screens and effects shots then created and integrated into the frame. The job of cutting/creating a trailer is simply to do the best with what you have available.

For the distribution budget, the cost is in creating the negative and then printing the physical trailers for distribution. Although the trailer itself is short, the number of copies can be in the several thousands as the goal is to achieve the broadest possible market coverage. Trailer costs can therefore be significant when adding up the several line-item categories.

- Creative and mastering
- Focus group testing

- Physical prints
- Cans for shipment
- Freight and transport

There are accordingly economic decisions regarding trailering, as the distributor needs to judge how many versions of a trailer to make (if the film warrants targeting to different demographics, such as a love angle geared toward women and action sequences skewing toward men) and how many copies to print. Complicating these decisions is the fact that there is no guarantee as to how many of those copies will actually be shown — it is up to the discretion of the local theater what trailers will be played. In some cases, a certain number of limited trailers will be attached to the front of the film print, thereby somewhat guaranteeing placement. These attached trailers are precious real estate, and the decisions of what is trailered with what, and what is attached, will even go up to the head of the studio.

The placement of trailers, and direct linking where possible, is critical because everyone wants to have their trailer attached to the film(s) with the best demographic overlay to the target market for the future film. One can imagine the politics of this choice, with different investments in different films, lobbying by directors and producers, key relationships with clout... Everyone wants to be on the front of the next blockbuster, and competition will be fierce to piggyback on event films.

The studios will receive reports of trailer coverage after the weekend, which is the ultimate gauge of whether the right range of copies was produced and shipped. Of course, all of the previous discussion addresses physical trailering, but as earlier noted trailers will also be posted online and can potentially achieve greater reach and frequency via the Web and viral sharing. Trailers, in summary, receive so much attention because, by their nature (including their ability to solve the experience good problem), these visual teasers continue to be among the most efficient of marketing tools both on and offline. Interestingly, they are an example of a practice as old as films that has found a way not only to survive but even grow in importance in the Internet age.

Teaser and Launch Trailers

Tentpole level films typically have a teaser trailer six months or so in advance of release, and then a launch trailer a couple of months in advance of the release date.

Because of the limited material available for teasers, they tend by their nature to be short at around a minute in length. Taking into account lead times, for a summer movie teasers will often release in the fourth quarter of the prior year, taking advantage of the holiday box office season and the large audiences that will be attending theaters. Similarly, teasers for holiday films will often accompany summer releases. This is a relatively efficient way for a distributor to start spreading word about an upcoming blockbuster.

A launch trailer, by comparison, is a very different animal. The launch trailer, released much closer to the theatrical release, will usually be much longer (e.g., 2-minute range as opposed to 1 minute), and rather than so-called "teasing" will give the audience a better sense of the story/what to expect in the movie. Many people often complain that "the best scene was in the trailer or commercial," but it is hard for a marketing executive not to cull from their best assets to entice people into the theater.

Posters

Posters, or in film parlance "one sheets," have been around as long as movies, and to some are even considered a distinct form of art. The poster is simply a single static image used for the same purposes as the trailer. Knowing that the poster may have more visibility than any other piece of artwork in promoting the film, it needs to convey a succinct and compelling message. This will be the piece most likely picked up by the press for initial coverage, and the enduring image at the box office.

The economics of the poster is similar to trailers, just less expensive (usually). Posters are less costly to manufacture and distribute, but interestingly the creative can be much higher. Because movie posters are often deemed works of art, and the commissioning of artwork simply put can be as expensive or inexpensive as the budget can bear, this is an area of both real and niche celebrities. The subjective nature of posters also lends itself to focus group testing, as messages can range from direct to mysterious. Additionally, as sometimes happens with high-profile films, posters may mimic trailers, such as when a unique teaser poster accompanies the teaser trailer, and a release poster dovetails with the launch trailer messaging. It is all about what will draw in the audience, and the answer may not be the most clever or creative. This is an area that can be lots of fun, and truly lets creative marketers have a significant impact on the film.

One final item to mention about posters is that they can be sold, thereby creating an ancillary revenue stream not available with trailers. In general, however, these sales are incremental to other merchandise and it would be rare to factor this revenue into the equation. In fact, the marketing department will have the task of delivering posters within a budget range, and will likely never know anything about the revenues, if any, earned from later sales.

In-Theater

A related element to posters is in-theater advertising. At the simplest level, in-lobby posters provide direct marketing to those making their decision what to see once at the theater. This element has grown in importance with the expansion of multiplexes, and is critical in enticing would-be customers making an impulse decision once already at the theater. In-theater advertising may also involve more elaborate marketing, such as standees, additional signage, branded concession items (e.g., cups), and even billboard-type advertising outside.

Commercials (Creating) and Creative Execution

Creating advertisements for a property is similar to the process of cutting trailers, in that for bigger films there may be multiple versions generated. Commercials can be tailored to targeted demographics (e.g., playing up action scenes to a hard core male audience) and then the media bought accordingly. Hence, there can be a very significant range, from very targeted ads to workhorse broad demographic spots.

405

In addition to the multiple versions, each version may be edited for different lengths. Commercials can range from a tag of a few seconds, up to a minute, with most spots cut to 15 or 30 seconds. Again, what will work best is a gut creative call or based on overall budget (although, budgets permitting, distributors will test the spots on focus groups to optimize the outcome).

Finally, there is an economic call regarding the extent to which the process is managed in-house versus outsourced. Given the volume of product and challenges it is common for studios to work both with advertising agencies as well as trailer specialists. Only in Hollywood, though, could a trailer specialist become a main character, such as Cameron Diaz' role in the 2006 Christmas release *The Holiday*.

Creative Execution

Although it may sound like a truism, the quality of the creative is a critical factor in the success of a commercial, as well as all the other marketing elements discussed. The same problems that lead to challenges with creative goods underlie the creation of marketing materials, though smaller in scale and tempered by the fact that the creative is derivative of another property (i.e., the film). Commercials win awards too, and whether commercials or other marketing materials achieve their goal of creating awareness and stimulating consumer interest may be subject to the intangible of creative execution.

Press and PR

Press and PR can form a major part of the overall marketing campaign, and few realize both how complicated and time-consuming orchestrating all the elements of PR can be. Areas that PR has to manage include (1) press kits, (2) press junkets (both long and short lead), (3) reviews, (4) talent interviews and management, (5) tie-ins/placements on other media such as TV shows, and (6) screenings (in coordination with distribution).

Press kits traditionally included fact sheets, press releases, slides, and some glossy photos. Today, they can still include these elements, and are supplemented with online elements; in fact, online press kits (i.e., electronic press kits; EPKs) are already the norm. They are vital in terms of key messaging, and making available images to be used in print, television, and online coverage. A good press kit is engaging and informative, and also has direct messaging—the film if not already a brand will hopefully become one, and staying true to a brand requires concise and bounded messaging. Everyone wants to write the review and article, and the press kit gives the journalist hold of the driving wheel and a guided map. How and where they then drive and chronicle the journey is out of PR's control, but a good press kit guides the less adventurous driver along the scripted route.

Handouts are limited in a business of glitz and images, and studios therefore choreograph press junkets. These interactive sessions will allow invited journalists to talk with key talent, learn about unique production elements, and taste a bit of the film. The cost of junkets can be high, involving renting and decorating venues, catering parties, creating custom reels, flying in and putting up talent/celebrities, and creating takeaways/goodies. Against this budget the marketing department needs to place a value on the level of awareness and hype that the journalists will ultimately create. What is the value of a good piece on *Entertainment Tonight* or a story in the *Chicago Tribune* versus the cost of a 30-second commercial? Press is at some level just another angle and tactic to create interest that will spike awareness and attract consumers.

406

Beyond the tried and true press kits and junkets/press conferences, good PR will take the film into another media space and create tie-ins. Convincing *Saturday Night Live* to have the star of the film host is a good example of this strategy. (Do you think it is a coincidence that Steve Martin happens to host the week his *Pink Panther* movie is opening?). Similarly, a star of an upcoming film may make a special guest appearance on a scripted TV show, creating buzz and interest; not so surprisingly, vertical integration between network groups and studios allow this. Everyone loves seeing a character out of context in a cameo appearance, and on occasion such as when a Desperate Housewife shows up in a locker room for a sports promo, the media attention can reach a frenzy. Can there be better publicity than being written into a *Simpsons* episode, even if the character or person may be the subject of a witty slander?

Finally, PR is the group that manages talent interviews. Every outlet wants time with the director, producer, or star, and PR orchestrates the maze of interviews. It is PR that has to manage who has an exclusive, whether there is a press embargo (granting information in advance for stories under the pledge that a story will not run before a specified date), and when and where talent will be available. Although talent will have agents and managers, it is the studio machine that will set in motion the blitz of appearances on talk shows. Basically, PR often functions as the gatekeeper to talent, and manages access to talent in a way that at once is hopefully respectful to people's time (and for talent, time is money) and maximizes positive exposure for a film/property.

For all of the above, take this task and then expand it to a global scale. One day TF1 in France wants to interview on location, the next ProSieben from Germany, and the following NHK from Japan. To handle the world there will often be regional press junkets, which may mean at least one in Europe and one in Asia in addition to those in the United States. Requests will be coming in from thousands of newspapers and television stations. And worse, if they are not coming in, it is the job of PR to drum up interest and make them come in, whether that means seeding stories, pitching angles to publications and journalists, or creating special tie-ins. All of this activity needs to happen on a massive scale in a compressed time frame. The incremental budget costs are labor and travel.

In the end, with the global reach of the Internet, and so many new applications in the digital age such as EPKs, it is fair to ask the question whether overall the Internet is a friend or foe to PR. It is a valid concern, given the danger of leaks that can lead to ubiquitous access and news versus the ability to disseminate a message almost instantly to everyone simultaneously around the globe. I asked Lynn Hale, George Lucas' head of PR at Lucasfilm since the 1980s, what she felt about the Internet on balance:

> It cuts both ways, although overall I would say that the Internet is a friend. On the one hand, the Internet makes it impossible to keep secrets. I doubt that George could have ever pulled off the surprise of Darth Vader's revelation if *The Empire Strikes Back* were released today, or if the Internet had been around in 1980. But on the other hand, the Internet has given us an instant worldwide platform to immediately disseminate news. Lucasfilm learned early on the power of the Web, and we embraced it. As early as 1998, we were reaching out directly to our fans, providing information that wasn't necessarily of interest for conventional news outlets. Back when we were releasing Episode I, Starwars.com listed theater locations that would be showing the teaser trailer. Fans flooded into theaters in such huge numbers that it became news. Local stations reported on it, and even the late night shows—like Letterman and Leno— included comments in their opening monologues. It was unprecedented at the time, but now movie studios rely heavily on the Internet to create excitement around a film's opening. It's another piece of the puzzle, and another tool at our disposal.

408

Screenings

To make sure that influential people can be impressed by the film and help spread the word, PR will work closely with distribution regarding screenings. Screenings have a wide range (charity, partners, press, critics, word of mouth, theater chains) and PR has the direct responsibility for ensuring that press screenings are effective. These screenings tend not to involve additional expense beyond the screening costs, but it is important to make the best possible impression on the critics/audience who will be reviewing (and potentially writing about) the film. Accordingly, efforts may be made to ensure high-quality venues, with good sound, picture, and ambiance. PR can only do so much to influence reviews, but at its core one of the jobs of PR is to try and positively influence the outcome and put the film in the best possible light.

Media Promotions

Another category driving awareness is media promotions. This can involve a variety of stunts or giveaways, with radio station contests (and film-based prizes) a common vehicle. The key with these types of promotions is to secure additional media weight, and thereby impressions, by creating a contest, quiz, or similar interactive event engaging consumers with the property.

Exhibitor Meetings

The distribution and exhibition communities have two major conventions per year, Show East (Orlando and moving in 2009 to Miami) in the fall and Show West (Las Vegas) toward the end of March. Distributors use this opportunity for a dog-and-pony show for theater owners, getting them excited about their upcoming releases. If a producer or studio has already released its trailer, it may use this opportunity to create a separate short piece to show the theater owners.

These markets provide a significant marketing opportunity for the distributor, and depending on the film either the director, producer, or key stars will attend to introduce the movie. This can be "showbiz" at its best: packed audiences waiting for a first look at a film, with press clicking photos of the stars present just to create chatter and excitement.

In the Spring of 2005, the atmosphere was electric at Fox's presentation between the photographers' feeding frenzy clicking pictures of Brad Pitt and Angelina Jolie walking out together to promote *Mr. & Mrs. Smith*, and the entrance of Storm Troopers together with George Lucas to highlight the release of the final Star Wars movie. (Note: Of late, and especially influenced by the severe economic downturn starting in 2008, these annual events have been significantly toned down by many studios.)

Film Markets and Festivals

There are a variety of major international festivals, which serve as outlets to debut films, gain publicity, and screen films for potential distribution pick up/acquisition.

There are literally markets all the time, but those shown in Table 9.3 are examples that have risen to "major" status (timing is approximate as dates tend to shift over time):

Table 9.3 Festival Locations and Timing

Festival	Location	Timing
Sundance	Utah	Winter
AFM	Los Angeles	Fall
Cannes	France	May
Venice	Italy	Fall
Toronto	Canada	Fall

The impact of independent festivals is significant, as they provide an outlet beyond the studio gatekeepers, and have proven their ability to launch directors, stars, and hits. It is now 20 years since Steven Soderbergh debuted *Sex, Lies and Videotape* at Sundance (winning the dramatic Audience Award), prior to the film going on to win the Palm d'Or in Cannes and catapulting both the director and actress Andie MacDowell into stardom. More recently, *Slumdog Millionaire's* best picture award in Toronto was a precursor to its capturing the Golden Globe for Best Picture and winning the Oscar for Best Picture (2009). Part of the problem with success is that what were once independent festivals intended to provide opportunity and expression for independent filmmakers have become so influential and competitive — with studios trolling to pick up properties for distribution — that the festivals have been swamped with submissions and inadvertently become another kind of gatekeeper.

Web Sites

In addition to impacting advertising (online expenditures and targeted campaigns), PR and trailer exposure, the digital and online worlds are profoundly influencing marketing efforts via project-specific Web sites. Now, not only do producers need to think about reserving titles, but as soon as a project matures it is wise to reserve the related domain name (a common word or title may be translated into a phrase such as XYZmovie.com).

Web sites need to be built, and the timing of launch, sophistication of site, and budget will all influence the end product. For an event-type movie, there may even be pressure to build the site well in advance as a place for fans to visit during production. This can seed interest and create early buzz. If a director is willing, the Web site can even be a place for production journals or a regular director blog from the set, as was the case with Peter Jackson during the making of the *Lord of the Rings* films.

As with a trailer, however, building a Web site in advance of a release can be challenging, for there may be little or no new material to post initially. When *Indiana Jones and the Kingdom of the Crystal Skull* was announced, there was enthusiasm for updating the older Indiana Jones site; however, until new production commenced there were few new key assets that could be posted. Nevertheless, the site became (as are all film sites) a place to post new news, the oldest and simplest function of film/TV sites.

As noted earlier, it is now commonplace to be able to go to a film or TV show's Web site and see the trailer or other preview of the product. Moreover, the trailer is now "networked" such that it can be found not only on the film's dedicated Web site, but linked to review sites and theater listings. A few years ago if you missed a trailer in theater you may never see it, but today you can catch it in a variety of locations, replay it, and even link it/e-mail to a friend via a social networking site creating a viral network buzz. For every studio executive complaining about the availability of its programming on video sites without authorization, there seems a counterbalancing marketing guru eager to take advantage of the platform to widen distribution of trailers, etc. The potential to distribute trailers to target demographics and allow sharing of trailers (or even elements thereof) on social networking sites adds another toolset to the marketing executive (see further discussion in the section Online Marketing Expanding the Toolset).

411

Beyond News and Trailers: Interactivity

A powerful feature of Web sites is their ability, beyond posting news and showing trailers, to market a property by more deeply engaging users/fans. Today, with video functionality common online, Web sites can host a variety of elements, including behind the scenes shots, interviews with key cast and crew, Web documentaries (e.g., of a making-of nature), Web cam feeds, and live chat video chats. For the last Star Wars film Lucasfilm created a series of Web documentaries, such as behind the scenes of creating light saber battles and the genesis of creating the villain General Grevious; these included footage of George Lucas approving iterative design elements, interviews with artists at Industrial Light & Magic, and shots of behind the scenes green-screen shoots.

In addition to video elements, Web sites may contain mini-games, links to e-commerce sites, links to promotions and promotional partner sites, and downloadable elements for instant gratification. Everyone loves free and often sites will allow certain downloads of screen savers, buttons, etc. The cross-promotion between online engagement and watching can be very significant for a franchise. Tom van Waveren, former head of Egmont Animation (Denmark), creator and producer of Cartoon Network hit *Skunk Foo*, and producer of hit animated reality show *Total Drama Island*, told me the following regarding the interaction of kids engaging online and watching *Total Drama Island*. (Note: The finale of *Total Drama Island* broke Cartoon Network records, including at the time setting a new record and becoming the top telecast among Tweens 9–14 for the network.)

What makes Total Drama Island unique is both its teen skew as an "animated reality show" and its online extension on Total Drama Island: Totally Interactive. On Total Drama Island: Totally Interactive, which was accessible on the CN website, each episode's challenge to the contestants is mirrored by a casual game and viewers can create their own avatar to play such games. Two things were remarkable about Total Drama Island: Totally Interactive. First of all, we were overwhelmed by the response we got to the site, and had two server crashes in the first week trying to match our capacity to demand of peaks of over 100,000 simultaneous users from the first month. By the time of the season finale over 3 million unique avatars had been created and being regularly used. And secondly, we could see a pattern evolving between the viewing figures on air and the activity peaks online. Comparing our data, we could see that 10% of the viewers were simultaneously watching a new episode and on-line playing the games with their avatar. This demonstrated that the world of Total Drama Island was, at least to 10% of our audience, a multi tasking multi platform entertainment experience instead of a TV show or an on-line game. One experience on several platforms simultaneously.

Trying to learn from this experience, we are looking at how we can create equally fluent transitions from one platform to the next with our other properties. This means that all the codes of the on air world need to be respected on-line and that the nature of the content offered on line is closely connected to the on air experience.

412

The search to create synergies by crossing over media, whether by interacting with content via the Web or a mobile phone, is now even driving the nature of the programming. When millions of viewers text message a vote on *American Idol* they are deeply engaged in the content, and producers are ever-seeking clever ways to add interactive components (e.g., text message, vote online) to linear programming.

Finally, one great benefit to Web site marketing is its duration: where most marketing comes and goes (e.g., TV spots), a Web site is persistent, reaching back in time before a show/film launches to help seed interest, reaching maturity during product launch and offering depth of content from trailers to interactive features, and remaining available through downstream exploitation allowing complementary marketing to long-tail revenue streams. Depending upon the size of the franchise, there may be periodic updates with key launches, such as with a video release (describing elements of bonus materials, and maybe even some extra features that can only be unlocked with the purchase of a DVD), or re-promotion of titles (e.g., box sets, TV specials).

413

Market Research

All studios track films, and try to benchmark interest and awareness both in terms of overall levels as well as within specific demographics. There are two primary measuring sticks: awareness (segmented into general awareness and unaided awareness) and interest (comparing definite interest and definitely not interested). General awareness will track the percentage of the sampled population that is aware of an upcoming release, and the person polled will be given a number of upcoming films including the one the studio is tracking (accordingly, it is a so-called leading question). Unaided awareness, which is a barometer of the heat of the film, tracks whether the person will cite the film that is coming up ("What films are you aware of opening soon, or in X week?") without the film's name being mentioned in the question. Definite interest/definitely not interested, beyond the obvious, is a yardstick as to the effectiveness of the creative messaging. Given that this messaging is designed to influence the input signals (i.e., it is the input), then for definitely not interested numbers to rise means that something has gone awry in the crafting of the signal.

The analysis is further broken down into demographics, such as the following:

All kids 7–14
- Boys 7–14
- Girls 7–14

All under 25
- Women under 25
- Men under 25

All 25–35
- Women 25–35
- Men 25–35

All 35–50
- Men 35+
- Women 35+

This segmentation will obviously allow targeting of demographics, and identify where a film is tracking particularly well or poorly. The tracking (which can be expensive) will further correlate to time out from release (e.g., 4 weeks out), and may additionally segment tracking into levels of interest such as definite or maybe. The further out the tracking, the more the information is driven by long lead press, expectations from fans that watch for "the next film by X or starring Y," and the impact of the theatrical trailers and online sources. The studio can then adjust the advertising spend to match where weaknesses occur. If the film is a romantic comedy and is tracking below expected levels among women, advertising may be adjusted to ensure that this key demographic is addressed in an attempt to raise awareness levels to a targeted range (similarly, buying incremental spots on football may be added if the target is males and numbers are low). If overall awareness is low, then it may make sense to buy a spot on a highly rated TV show to jolt the numbers (which is why ads on premium primetime programs, such as *American Idol*, can be so expensive, as a huge number of eyeballs can be reached instantly; this effect is still difficult to achieve online).

Beyond spending to counter tracking numbers that are below targets (or worse exhibit negative trends), another tactic that can be implemented is to change commercials (i.e., shift the creative messaging). If something is just not working, a new spot can be cut to attract viewers. This can be done to communicate more effectively within the original demographic targeted, to highlight an actor that may be coming off a recent hit, or in cases where there is real fear to switch tactics entirely. These strategies to try and adjust the dial to hoped for levels are feasible so long as tracking is far enough out to allow time to adjust; however, there are still limits, as marketing budgets are usually relatively fixed in absolute terms, and certain commitments will likely have been made weeks if not months in advance. This is, remember, a highly competitive market and another film is likely chasing the same audience and vying not just for end consumers, but also for space and tie-ins to attract those same consumers.

Finally, research will also track the film in question against other films — both past and present. Most important, given the competitive environment, is data regarding other films in the marketplace. Further, studios will model potential outcomes by benchmarking results against historical pictures where a comparison is useful. This may take the form of comparing against a genre, a prior film if the movie is a sequel, or a film driven by the same star (e.g., how did the prior Tom Cruise action picture track, or how did the prior film directed by Ron Howard open). The key Hollywood trades (i.e., *Variety*, *The Hollywood Reporter*) will now even regularly print charts comparing actor X's prior box office openings to targets for an upcoming release.

Indirect/Third-Party Costs

All of the previous categories discussed in conjunction with the theatrical marketing budget, whether hard direct costs or overhead, are costs borne by the distributor. If a property lends itself to becoming a major or even event-level release then there is the possibility of supplementing this budget with funds of third parties. There is nothing like, and in cases nothing harder than, finding other people's money. The two major categories are from promotional partners and from merchandising licensees.

Promotional Partners

As noted previously, promotional partners who tie into a property need to invest directly for the cross-promotion to be realized. The film's budget will not be used to advertise goods in a happy meal at McDonald's, or the character on a cereal or candy wrapper. The partners need to invest both in creative and in hard media dollars to make these programs work.

A snack food, beverage, or cereal company will need to create a specific new advertisement incorporating film elements/characters into its own brand. The trick here is to find an appropriate intersection of the brands, where the creative is positive to both brands, leverages one off the other, and creates something fresh and interesting that will attract consumers. In some ways, this is akin to a cameo appearance of an actor in another piece, except in this instance the cameo is into a branded product and the cameo has a theme tying the concepts together.

The economics are therefore the cost of the creative (the spot and related artwork); the cost to roll out the program to affiliates, product distributors, and franchisees; and the media costs for placing related commercial spots. The promotional partner will need to weigh these expenses against the anticipated uplift in sales, and arrive at a budget with a positive net present value weighing the campaign costs against the uplift in contribution margin. As part of this budget, the promotional partner will often offer and/or guarantee a certain amount of media weight/spend on the campaign. Accordingly, the studio knows it will spend $X million with its own ads, and can count on an additional $Y spend from its partners. These numbers can be difficult to quantify precisely, however, because they are frequently pledged in bulk value and may be difficult to track. Nevertheless, the commitments and impact are very real, and can account for a significant amount of the media weight for a campaign.

The distributor benefits from exposure on multiple fronts. First, there is incremental media advertising, thus helping drive awareness and impressions. Second, there are the in-store retail impressions from product on shelves, and in the best of cases dedicated displays and standees. Third, there is the impression from consuming the product, whether this is time spent reading details/information on packaging, using packed in premiums (find X inside marked boxes of ....), and spending time with the property/characters in the physical or online world by consuming/interacting with the tied-in product. If advertising is measured in impressions, and further if effectiveness is measured with time spent (impressions multiplied by time spent with the impression), then a good product tie-in can be worth gold. For the product partner, the same applies — if the tie-in helps improve sales, and if the attractiveness stimulates the consumer to spend more time consuming the product, then it is surely a net win for them as well.

Merchandising and Game Tie-ins
The second major category is advertising from merchandising partners. It is rare to see hats and T-shirts being advertised, but certain categories can bring valuable media weight. The most important,

416

arguably, is from toys pushed by one of the major toy companies (e.g., Mattel, Hasbro). Kids are fickle customers, but they are malleable targets and voracious consumers. Toy companies are significant spenders, and a new action figure, doll, or toy based on a major franchise will be a major driver of revenues. Accordingly, a leading toy company may create advertising for its product, and then place significant media behind it to stimulate awareness and sales. The formula is exactly the same as from the promotional partner. Every media dollar spent by the merchandising partner is an incremental dollar to the studio's media budget.

Additionally, as discussed in Chapter 8, it is common to launch video games related to the films, and the marketing of the game can also help broaden franchise awareness for the movie (and vice versa, the movie for the game). For this media weight to be effective, however, the game needs to be launched prior to or simultaneously with the film, which is often a difficult challenge given game development and production lead times.

Net Sum and Rise in Historical Marketing Costs

The true marketing budget for a tentpole type film may be as follows:

(1)   Distributor Media Budget
+ Promotional Partner Media Budget
<u>+ Merchandising Media Budget</u>
= Total Direct Media Budget

(2)   + Imputed Media Value from PR
= Total Media Weight

+ Distributor Direct Costs
(3)   + Distributor Incremental Overhead
= Total Marketing Budget/Costs

This is, of course, the ideal scenario. Most films do not benefit from merchandising or promotional partners and are focused on the direct media budgets and PR opportunities.

Over time, the total costs of marketing a movie have risen with the rise in negative costs. The MPAA published the following statistics (Table 9.4), evidencing marketing costs peaking in 2003 at \$39.5M/ MPAA member studio title (all costs below in \$M):[8]

Table 9.4   Negative Costs and Marketing Costs

Year	Negative Cost	Marketing Cost	Total Costs
2002	$47.8	$30.4	$78.2
2003	$66.3	$39.5	$105.8
2004	$65.7	$34.8	$100.5
2005	$63.6	$36.1	$99.7
2006	$65.8	$34.5	$100.3
2007	$70.8	$35.9	$106.6

The trend is not that different when looking at Member Subsidiaries/ Affiliates specialty divisions (e.g., Fox Searchlight, Miramax, New Line, Sony Pictures Classics). The shorter theatrical window and increased competition is forcing higher costs for these so-called smaller pictures to compete. These spiking costs perhaps were one of the reasons a number of the studios shuttered specialty divisions (e.g., Paramount Vantage) in 2008.

Video Marketing

Even though it is an ancillary market, in many ways video marketing more closely parallels theatrical marketing than television. Virtually every major category of costs comes into play in a video campaign for a major/tentpole film: trailers, posters, commercials, press/PR (and in rare instances, even promotional partners). Video marketing can be more complex because of the need for direct-to-consumer marketing (like theatrical) and the need to coordinate in-store retail specific campaigns (unlike theatrical) requiring significant trade marketing. While theaters may have posters, and an occasional standee, "in-theater" promotion tends not to be on the scale of campaigns run by major retailers like Best Buy and Wal-Mart.

Macro Level Spending/Media Plan and Allocation

The same type of media allocation graphs and charts as previously depicted in the theatrical context can be drawn for video. Paralleling theatrical campaigns, television spending is traditionally the dominant direct cost category. Near the peak of the DVD sales curve, this TV percentage dwarfed all other categories, with the *Hollywood Reporter* noting: "There is one thing on which most studios agree: Allocating marketing dollars to the small screen makes sense. Nearly 80% of video marketing expenditures last year were for television commercials, with broadcast and cable in the lead..."[9] Table 9.5 lists allocations for the years 2003–2005 near the peak of the DVD sales curve:

Table 9.5   Video Marketing

Year	Network TV	Cable TV	Spot TV	Syndi TV	Newspaper	Magazine	Outdoor	Internet	Radio
2003	43.4%	25.1%	6.5%	4.7%	1.4%	16.2%	0.6%	0	2.2%
2005	38.3%	32.1%	5.7%	2.8%	1.1%	14%	0.3%	2.1%	2.3%

2003 figures, HR "Video Marketing—By the Numbers" 8/10–16, 2005; 2005 stats HR "Video Marketing & the Media—Caught in the Web," 7-11-17, 2006.

In terms of percentage spend, as a rule of thumb marketing budgets will often be targeted in the range of ~10% of anticipated sales, and in cases can approach double that number. Of course, there ends up being an inverse relationship to sales, as big hits with higher unit volumes drive down the ultimate percentage, paralleling the trend with theatrical. For example, Disney spent $34M+ in marketing *Finding Nemo*, including $20M+ just for TV spots. While this represented the biggest video marketing campaign for a title that year, *The Hollywood Reporter* noted it was still but "a small fraction (6.4%) of the $536.7 million that Adams Media Research estimates the studio grossed from "Nemo" video sales." Similarly, Fox ended up spending only 6% of the $200M video revenues ($12.9M) on X2:X-Men United.[10]

As expected, and as the market has became more cluttered and competitive, expenditures rose and the allocation of media became more diversified. Big titles still need to hit threshold reach and frequency targets, but a variety of titles can be pitched into specialty markets, or in a more targeted manner, increasing the ROI for shifting some weight to the Internet and specialty cable. In 2005, again toward the DVD curve's peak, Fox reputedly spent 5% of its video marketing on the Internet, evidencing the new trend. Its SVP of Marketing Communications, Steve Feldstein, highlighted to *The Hollywood Reporter* that strategy had moved well beyond simply buying TV spots: "There are a lot of elements that go into making a release into an event—from publicity and promotional activities to generating in-store excitement—and with the Internet, it's all becoming much more direct consumer marketing."[11]

Commercials and Box Artwork; Retail Execution — Point-of-Purchase, Posters, Trailers

Again, like theatrical, significant effort and money is focused on branding the property and creating sales tools. Commercials are critical in a DVD campaign, and will need to be created just for this market— "buy it today…" Although not as common as with a theatrical release (and again limited to bigger titles), a variety of spots may be cut, with different lengths and targeted to different demographics. Trailers and posters do not play as prevalent a role and tend to be used more for trade and in-store marketing.

The most significant addition to the marketing arsenal is the box artwork, which almost always is a new design/image. Designing the artwork is tricky, because in one shot the image must be true to the property, remind people of why they liked the film (e.g., featuring a character), have a collectible appeal (the goal is to get people to buy it), and also appear fresh (time has passed, and people always want something new). Whereas movies come and go in theaters, this artwork/box will sit on shelves for months or even years as the continuing face of the brand to consumers long after the heat of the release. (Note: This same concept applies to TV box sets as well.)

Retail Execution — Point-of-Purchase, Posters, Trailers

Until the Internet's long tail takes over, shelf space is still supreme and gaining retail support is the lifeblood of any DVD campaign. This involves specific placement of titles, special merchandising opportunities (e.g., unique displays and standees in the form of specially produced corrugate), in-store events and signage (e.g., posters), and commitment to keeping the title in prominent positions. It also means outside of store advertising support, including in circulars and, if the property justifies it, in TV spots. Circulars are more important than most people recognize. Not only do they have very significant reach, but they are obviously directly tied to generating in-store traffic, the ultimate point-of-purchase (POP).

Beyond driving people into the store, campaigns are focused on capturing the attention (impulse buys) of consumers in-store, regardless of what brought them there to shop. In-store programs involve coordinating multiple placement opportunities such as front-of-store POP displays and signage, special in-aisle corrugate, near check out racks, end cap placements (e.g., in new release section), and in-line facings. Moreover, as the sales cycle continues there may be advance planning for subsequent waves, such as special positioning at holiday times and movement to studio sponsored call-out areas (e.g., the Y collection, best sellers).

To help distinguish in-store programs certain retailer exclusives may be offered. This often takes the form of premiums, such as stick-

420

ers/buttons/posters, but may also involve unique product SKUs (e.g., special artwork on box, packed in merchandise). All of these special features may incentivize a particular retailer to support a campaign. This support may be in the form of allocated placement in the retailer's catalog and circulars, in hard dollar expenditures on TV advertising, or extra in-store efforts and/or commitments. Money already exists to execute some of these activities from the co-op advertising and MDF allowances traditionally included within an overall marketing budget; the trick is to effectively spend these sums and earn an appropriate ROI.

Press, PR, and Third-Party Promotions

There is a halo effect from the theatrical release, which obviously benefits video, but as the stakes have grown DVD marketers have learned a second bite at the PR apple pays dividends. All the studios will hold retail focused summits building up their future releases, outlining marketing data, plans and tie-ins and even bringing in talent from big pictures to excite the buyers. Further helping generate buzz for the release, studios will sometimes even sponsor "launch parties," inviting key cast members and obtaining press coverage.

As DVD releases have become events, with trade awards for best DVDs (and like any awards, with multiple subcategories to spread the glory), there are major press opportunities beyond staged parties. To create interest, ideally there needs to be a bit of a new story, which leads many studios to focus on bonus features and navigation. As discussed in Chapter 5, fancy menus, director commentary, deleted scenes, documentaries, bundled games or demos, and even sneak peeks are examples of value-added material (VAM) typically produced for DVDs.

In terms of economics, it is fair to question the production costs for these elements, as it is a difficult call whether and how much of this material is essential to stimulating sales. Certainly, there is value for collectors and fans, which may be sufficient in cases to justify large expenses. However, I would argue that the bigger factor is media and press. These hooks help garner attention and interviews, gaining millions of "free" impressions that are additive to the hard media costs in terms of gaining awareness through targeted reach and frequency goals. Moreover, as discussed previously, a critical part of any DVD campaign is retail buy-in, and if you want the major chains to support a title, including featuring it in their own advertising, then you better be supporting the title yourself.

Third-Party Promotional Partners

The largest category of third-party media placement is retail spending to execute in-store and to advertise (e.g., circulars). In somewhat rare instances, a promotional partner may tie into a video release, similar to the theatrical context where McDonald's may theme in-store giveaways, or a cereal company will co-brand a popular item. Every studio video marketing head dreams of these opportunities, but also laments that they can count on their fingers the number of times they have been able to execute this type of partnership, which inherently also would come with a third-party marketing commitment for direct consumer advertising. The fact remains that despite the rise of the video market and millions of dollars spent on DVD releases, promotional partners tend to associate this as an "ancillary" and rarely bring the support that is associated with a theatrical release. Nevertheless, select hit and especially franchise titles are sometimes able to secure this type of support, such as tie-ins with Papa John's Pizza for the video releases of *Ice Age* (2002) and *Indiana Jones and the Kingdom of the Crystal Skull* (2008).[12]

Net Sum

The same type of analysis could be outlined here as with the theatrical market:

$$\frac{\text{Distributor Media Budget} + \text{Aggregate Retailer Media Budget}}{= \text{Total Direct Media Budget}}$$

$$\frac{+ \text{Imputed Media Value of PR} + \text{Imputed Media Value from Retailer Circulars}}{= \text{Total Media Weight}}$$

Television

In contrast to feature films and DVDs, there are several categories previously discussed that generally do not apply in the TV context: trailers, one sheets, posters, promotional partners, and merchandise on launch. In most cases, commercials and PR/press play a similar if not more important role given the more limited promotional vehicles available.

Direct Costs

Many of the direct cost categories from theatrical marketing apply to television: television media, radio, print (newspaper and magazine), outdoor, and online. More and more networks are turning to off-channel media to cross-promote programming. It is not unusual to see advertising on buses for TV shows, and even on billboards for a major launch such as a new season of *24* on Fox. Nevertheless, as with movies, the bulk of advertising and media dollars is focused on TV promotion.

Commercials and Opportunity Costs

As a bit of a truism, the most effective advertising for a TV show is on TV, and in particular on the network where the show is airing. The issue for a channel is balancing its commercial inventory—on the one hand, it wants to sell 100% of its inventory to garner the largest potential revenue, while on the other hand it needs to hold back a certain number of spots to cross-promote and advertise its own programming. Accordingly, it becomes an opportunity cost analysis as to how much time to reserve.

423

As discussed in Chapter 6, the situation is seemingly easier for a cable network, for it has 24/7 inventory to allocate as opposed to a network that is limited to commercial spots within the hours it programs in primetime. A cable station with only a few original series can therefore look to cross-promote shows across its entire schedule, and has enough inventory to literally carpet bomb a series. In contrast, a network has more limited inventory and has over 20 hours of original primetime programming to promote (e.g., ABC could not afford to devote the amount of cross-promotional time to *Lost* as USA can devote to promoting *Monk*).

Press and PR

Press and PR is very similar to the theatrical realm: press kits are created, talent is made available for interviews and live talk show appearances, and trade pitches are made at festivals and industry trade shows. Reviews and word of mouth are equally important here as in the theatrical market; while weekend box office may be the barometer of films, first and second episode ratings are no less forgiving. Simply, a show that is not pulling its weight will be pulled, and press/PR is a critical tool in helping build awareness and an audience.

There are even screenings. As discussed in Chapter 6, the so-called "LA Screenings" in May have become an annual pilgrimage for foreign broadcasters to screen pilots and episodes of shows various studios/producers are debuting in the fall. Each studio will take a "day," for example, and an acquisitions executive from Spain will spend one day at Fox, the next at Warners, the next at Universal and so on. During these periods the studios/networks will wine and dine guests, bring in producers/directors to talk about their new shows, and throw parties and usually screen one of their about-to-be-released summer films. (Note: To be fair, these events are more sales, than marketing, focused.)

Use of Programming Schedules/Lead-Ins

Finally, the inherent nature of a network schedule affords cross-promotional opportunities by leveraging one show against another. Networks are all about lead-ins and lead-outs, tracking what percentage of a show's audience will stick around for the following program. A network takes a hit series and uses its audience to lead into and build awareness for a new show. This staple launch platform guarantees a certain built-in awareness and audience, and it is simply up to the next show to hold or build onto the base. Once a show is established and has taken advantage of piggybacking, it may then be moved to a different time slot on another day, where the process starts anew: has the show held its prior audience, is it strong enough to be a platform to help launch another show around it, is the audience for the following show falling off or building on its base?

Because of this synergistic pull, it is typical to see the same types of shows follow each other. A sitcom following a sitcom will likely hold the prior audience more strongly than a drama following a sitcom (because the audience demographic/expectation will shift). This in turn leads to lineups where NBC may be themed around sitcoms/comedies on Thursday evenings, whereas one drama on CBS will lead into another drama. When people criticize television for being formulaic, it is because formulas work (see discussion Chapter 1) and like shows will hold similar audiences. It is as if in TV everything is a double feature—staying for the first film just is not good enough. When I once spoke to the CFO of one of the major networks he likened the process of ratings to receiving a report card every day: in the morning you know how you scored relative to the competition the night before. Leveraging one show against another to create a strong lead-in can by itself make the difference.

Online Marketing: Expanding the Toolset

As discussed previously in the theatrical context, online marketing today involves a spider web of options. First, producers and distributors can market via the TV show's dedicated Web sites. Sites range from relatively simple — where one can watch trailers, learn about the cast and crew, and be updated with PR-related news — to deep and sophisticated sites. A particularly rich site may include mini-games, e-commerce opportunities, specially produced content exclusives (e.g., talent interviews, behind-the-scenes footage, documentaries), downloadable goodies, chat rooms, blogs, interactive components (quizzes, mash-ups), and avatars, etc.

A second component enabled by the Web is online advertising, where banner and video ads are bought, and the media precisely targeted to narrow demographics. This can be elevated to a partnership level, where key portals may cross-promote properties both generally and within entertainment and appropriate key-word related links.

Social Networking

An emerging component of online marketing is to tap into social networking, seeding blogs, and trying to stimulate a viral effect. Toward this end more and more people are allowing content to migrate, such that you can embed video trailers, images, and other elements into your own space (e.g., a MySpace page) to share with friends. Not only can a network theme tie into a release, but to a lesser degree so can you — the goal of a viral campaign is for individuals to evangelize on their own.

Few people are aware of just how large the streaming of videos has become linked to social networking sites. I asked Peter Levinsohn, former president of Fox Interactive Media (parent to MySpace) and current president of New Media and Digital Distribution for Fox Filmed Entertainment, about what motivates people to view videos in a social networking environment as opposed to on a pure on-demand video-based portal or site. He noted:

Social networking sites like MySpace are fundamentally about self-expression, and what someone posts is to a degree a reflection of who they are. These sites create an environment for people to discuss a range of topics — a kind of virtual water cooler where friends gather to discuss whether they liked something about a particular TV show like *House*, or if they had seen a funny viral video that had been emailed around recently. Online video content has become a centerpiece of those conversations—in fact video has become such an important part of that dialogue that MySpace TV is now the #2 site on the Web for consuming video content.

What's more, these interactions benefit consumers, producers and advertisers, and the best part is that the virtual community can scale and expand beyond what would typically occur in the physical world, for example, an office suite, because the Internet has no geographical boundaries. It becomes a global, real-time conversation and online video is in many cases the catalyst that brings all these people together.

Case Study: Marketing a Mega-Film

Marketing a film involves all the elements described earlier in this chapter (e.g., Web sites, trailers, posters, commercials), but in the case of an event picture the palette may be expanded and marketing/PR can easily involve countless initiatives carefully choreographed over more than a year. It is therefore interesting to view the different elements in relation to a time line, which in general terms I will break down as follows (Figure 9.2):

Figure 9.2

The scope of the elements (discussed later) along this time line presupposes a tentpole level picture, such as a *Spider-Man*, *Harry Potter*, *James Bond*, or *Star Wars* sequel, or a brand with such assumed expectations (e.g., a new Pixar movie) that this level of activity can be justified.

As with all marketing, the goal of the pre-release and release windows is to start building awareness. Even with sequels, because every movie is unique, the distributor needs to craft a new strategy related to these periods: *Spider-Man* research may predict the base from action themes is solid but other demographics dependent on the love interest may be underperforming and need to be buttressed; *Harry Potter* focus group testing may reveal concerns about the key characters aging; and *Star Trek* marketers likely struggle how to re-launch the franchise to more than the core sci-fi crowed with a prequel featuring young, mostly unknown actors.

Moreover, there are frequently inherent elements in a project that marketing needs to address, such as preparing its loyal (hopefully) audience for when a character or tone changes and the built-in expectations may therefore not be in synch with the new film in the franchise. This often happens with sequels that strive to enrich a protagonist by adding complexity and emotional character depth (where the character had otherwise risen to household fame as a typical hero). To achieve this shift the previously family friendly film takes on a darker tone, as our hero wrestles with a flaw or other torment. Think about the difference between *Batman Begins* and *The Dark Knight* versus certain pictures in the middle of the franchise (e.g., Arnold Schwarzenegger portrays Mr. Freeze), the challenges Harry Potter faces as he matures to adulthood, or the darker James Bond played by Daniel Craig versus the more tongue-in-cheek persona branded by Roger Moore. With *Star Wars Episode III*, Lucasfilm had to manage a film where the bad guys win (Anakin Skywalker turns to the dark side and becomes Darth Vader), and most of the good guys die or are at best exiled in bitter defeat (one might even say "hopeless," were these not prequels and we did not already know about *Star Wars Episode IV: A New Hope*).

A good campaign will recognize, beyond the goal of pure awareness, the challenge of its particular release, what demographics need to be wooed, and what anchor themes will serve as the messaging around which a myriad of independent brand events will be balanced.

Pre-Release Window: Period Leading Up to Time ~30 Days Pre-Release

The following are some of the events that tend to fall into this window:

- Teaser trailer
- Teaser poster
- Long-lead press (e.g., magazine articles, retrospectives)
- Video re-releases
- Launch trailers
- Launch posters

- Press junkets
- Special events
- Seeded brand placements

There is no so-called magic formula and it is the job of marketing and PR departments to draw up innovative ideas and tie-ins. Trailers, posters, and press events are somewhat standard fare and, while elements of artwork and messaging are not taken for granted, the system is already geared up to ensure these items effectively communicate a core branding statement. What this long-lead period affords for a mega-picture, however, is an opportunity for out-of-the-box initiatives — promotions which while likely requiring extra resources, can still be extremely cost-effective in terms of seeding brand and/or film specific awareness.

One of my favorite tie-ins related to Star Wars was a unique baseball promotion. Yankees–Red Sox baseball games are among the most fabled sports rivalries of all time, and the teams were heading into another season-ending collision (as it so happens following a gut wrenching game 7 playoff loss by the Red Sox the year before, which was to be avenged the next year with a World Series win). Some sportswriters had started calling the Yankees the "Evil Empire" and marketing tapped into this Star Wars analogy. During the last regular season series between the teams at the end of September, with the outcome likely to decide the playoff picture, Fox Sports aired an opening montage about the two teams. The montage was interspersed with film clips and as an example the long-haired and bearded Red Sox center fielder Johnny Damon appeared followed shortly by the hairy Chewbacca. The Fox Sports headquarters announcers, after introducing the clip, even held up a copy of a newly available DVD, which had an ancillary benefit of helping seed the market for the upcoming new film. A highly rated sports game was thereby leveraged as a tie-in to the film franchise creating unique marketing exposure (in part because the network liked the idea and had fun with it, and also because of the common Fox ownership).

Sometimes film franchises with a specific fan base, such as Star Trek, may lend themselves to conventions or promotional opportunities at industry conventions such as Comic-con. Given the phenomenon of "trekkies" it makes sense to rally Star Trek fans in advance of the J.J. Abrams directed prequel (May 2009 release). This same strategy may not work on other sequels (e.g., Bourne films).

Finally, when a film is one in a series it may make sense to reinvigorate the brand in the video market by releasing special editions or collector sets. MGM has done this effectively with James Bond sets, augmenting anticipation for a new film with new DVDs of the prior features. Similarly, Paramount released prior Star Trek films and series on Blu-ray for the first time in advance of its new feature. All of these activities help generate awareness for an upcoming release, and if clever enough will prepare the audience for new themes in the continuing franchise, while not yet tapping the core of the marketing budget reserved for advertising and other promotion closer to a film's launch. (Note: Depending on strategy, such DVDs may be delayed until the release window to tie-in with other retail product launches.)

Release Window: ~30 Days Pre-Release Through First Two Weeks Post-Release

The following are elements often found in this window:

- Launch of related merchandise
- Commercials air/advertising in all media launches
- Promotional partners' products hit shelves (with related advertising)
- Media promotions (contests, giveaways)
- Related video games release
- Novelizations hit bookstores
- PR media blitz — talk shows, radio, review shows, stimulate blogs
- Screenings
- Prior films often play on TV
- Web sites ramp up, add features (e.g., sneaks, making of elements)

The most obvious and critical component in this window is advertising, which will saturate the market across all types of media. Beyond direct spending to achieve consumer impressions, this is also a time when marketing/PR will try to leverage other media or events (e.g., talent appearances) to the greatest extent possible. Guest appearances on late night and morning talk shows are an obvious staple of the trade; special appearances, such as hosting a show like *Saturday Night Live*, can further hype a release. Online efforts will attempt to push positive tidbits, enable sharing via social networking sites, support blogs, help spread favorable reviews from key influencers, and provide Web exclusives.

Also, this release window is when it is most likely that other parties will want to tie-in with the movie franchise and devote their resources to cross-marketing, leveraging the media awareness for the film to focus on its consumer product. Returning to *Star Wars Episode III* for another example, Cingular (phone company) ran one of my favorite third-party advertisements around the movie's release. In the commercial, Chewbacca was doing his signature howl in an isolation booth for a recording producer. The producer asks him to do it this way, then that way ("that was great, now can I have a little...") and Chewy repeats the only howl sound that we ever hear from him.

Finally, returning to Star Trek again, Burger King tied into the release of the prequel film (2009) and on the merchandising front new toys and games were set to launch in April, the month before the prequel film's release. Given the significance of the franchise, not only was merchandise hitting shelves, but the studio worked to leverage direct retail support: augmenting an array of action figures, comic books, and other products, Wal-Mart was selling a new line of Star Trek Barbie dolls.[13]

While on-shelf dates for merchandising can vary significantly, promoting toys and other product linked to a movie during this period has a twofold benefit similar to that found with promotional partners. On one level there is an uplift in product sales given the surrounding media; further, though, in terms of kindling interest to see the film, kids who play with characters and learn about their background, or immerse themselves in related games, help spread awareness and virtually guarantee a measure of related ticket sales.

Post Release Window: ~30 Days Post-Release Through DVD+

By this period, activity has waned and the number of initiatives launched is a fraction of those found in the pre-release and release windows. Nevertheless, there are still a number of elements likely to be launched, such as:

- Sustain advertising
- Special promotions
- DVD release(s)
- Award campaigns (e.g., Oscars)

Once sustain advertising—taking advantage of reviews ("best of...") and awards—has run its course, the focus of the post-release window is not converting awareness into box office, but rather converting box office into DVD sales. As noted in the video marketing section, DVDs do not have the same promotional tie-in potential as theatrical releases, but in instances with a big enough film (e.g., Papa John's pizza and *Ice Age*), it is possible to diversify a campaign beyond traditional DVD retail marketing. Also, because of the size of the DVD market, this affords another opportunity to trot out stars for press junkets, tapping PR one last time (unless Oscar calls) before the activity winds down and marketing hibernates until long-tail re-promotion opportunities arise. When these new promotional opportunities do mature, it is often to help launch awareness for the next title in the franchise, starting the described cycle over again.

Online Impact

- Virtually all movies and major TV shows have Web sites that cross-promote the program/film and provide value-added information and content (e.g., talent interviews, documentaries, mini-games).
- Online venues allow consumers to see trailers, which previously were only available in theaters and on TV as commercials/advertisements.
- An increase in online piracy has been an impetus for the global day-and-date releases of content.
- Online sites provide social networking abilities to chat, blog about, or identify with the characters and broader brand-sharing interest, videos, reviews, recommendations, or critiques with friends and virally to wider circles.
- Increasing amounts are being allocated to online campaigns, targeting specific demographics.
- Review sites aggregating critics' opinions, which serve to accelerate and homogenize the "verdict," typify a range of new information that could impact consumption choices.
- Content producers are striving to find ways to add interactive components to linear programming (text messages, vote online) and stimulate crossover online/offline engagement.
- Online sites are creating new opportunities for product placements, which in addition to serving as sources of financing may allow new types of functional integration (to the extent an avatar/character is changed by associating with the product).

CHAPTER 10

Making Money—Net Profits, Hollywood Accounting, and the Relative Simplicity of Online Revenue Sharing

More content from this chapter is available on
www.businessofmediadistribution.com

"Hollywood accounting" has become a somewhat infamous phrase, but in practice it simply takes effort to understand the jargon and rules. The greatest single area of confusion is the fact that the term "net profits" has no correlation to the concept of net profits that most companies use in a typical corporate income statement. Rather, the term net profits used in Hollywood contracts is a carefully crafted and defined term of art.

Because most people fail to peel back the onion and learn the nuances (which can be frustrating, and appear unfair devoid of context), an element of prejudice has been affixed to the calculation of profits in Hollywood contracts. There is a pervasive feeling that the studies and networks are so-called "cooking the books": how else can a project earn over $100M at the box office, sell successfully into large secondary markets such as TV and video, and be in the red? The answer is that under traditional income statement and/or tax accounting the project may in fact be profitable, but that pursuant to a contractual profit sharing definition (somewhat unfortunately also labeled net profits) the project still posts a loss.

This gulf creates the common perception that the accounting system is either rigged or unfair. In fact, the system by many accounts is very fair, if not generous. From the standpoint of the studio or network that would be paying out net profit participations, it is sharing the upside even though it may have taken all or most of the risk. In what other business proposition would you find the following formula: Party A takes on 100% of the financial risk, Party A knows that on the majority of its projects it may lose money, Party A takes no defined or preferred return on its investment before other participants share in the upside, and Party A shares 50% of the profits after a defined breakeven point with its partner in the project? Nowhere.

This is the context behind why studios and networks have created padded profit sharing definitions to protect the recoupment of their investment and build in an internal ROI factor before actually paying out profit sharing. It is simply unfortunate that the resulting payout comes under the heading of net profits, for the use of the phrase is misleading relative to common sense and commonly applied methods of calculating profits in other business contexts. As far as a profit sharing mechanism that protects the investor first, and shares an upside with the people that helped make the project a success, it makes perfect sense; the only debate, then, is whether the profit sharing scheme is a good or poor one. The best way to understand "profits" definitions is to acknowledge that any reference to net or gross profits is a misnomer and instead refers to contractually defined schemes of contingent compensation. (See Figure 10.1 depitcting general structure.)

If the system was not already confusing enough, the introduction of online revenues has the potential of creating another level of nuance—simply read the new talent guild agreements (see Chapter 7) where certain residuals are calculated as a percentage of "Distributors Gross Receipts" and are applied, for example, on a sliding scale basis tied to download volumes (with different tiers tied to different types of content such as TV vs. features). Because the online world has evolved a relatively straightforward system of revenue sharing and is not beholden to the arcane Hollywood net profits

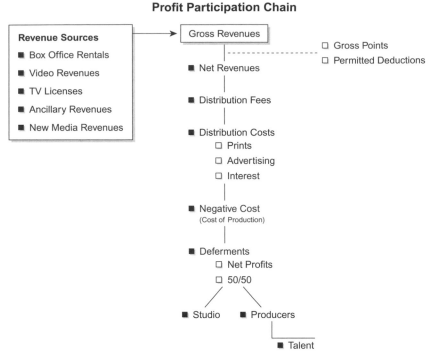

Profit Participation Chain

Revenue Sources
- Box Office Rentals
- Video Revenues
- TV Licenses
- Ancillary Revenues
- New Media Revenues

Gross Revenues
- Gross Points
- Permitted Deductions

- Net Revenues

- Distribution Fees

- Distribution Costs
  - Prints
  - Advertising
  - Interest

- Negative Cost
  (Cost of Production)

- Deferments
  - Net Profits
  - 50/50

- Studio   - Producers
  - Talent

434

Figure 10.1

system, the methods of calculating relative shares are on a collision course. I will discuss some of the implications later, and argue that the root of the problem is trust: net profits has become shackled and institutionalized by feeding on lack of trust between parties, while online revenue sharing has become commonplace and accepted because of the trust engendered by detailed, by-click, electronically tracked metrics. Is Hollywood more likely to challenge the revenues from online clicks by Google, or are the Googles of the new millennium more likely to challenge the perceived revenue sharing smoke screen thrown up by convoluted net profits definitions?

Finally, given the complexity of profit accounting, the following discussion primarily focuses on the context of film; nevertheless, the same general principles can apply to a network's profit participation accounting to a TV producer or a video on a made-for-video production.

Profit Participation Accounting

Profit participation accounting, which I need to emphasize is not "accounting" in the sense of GAAP or tax books, is simply a contractual revenue sharing arrangement negotiated between parties; what started out as a rational basis of sharing risk is now usually discussed in pejorative terms (aka Hollywood accounting), and over time has evolved into a bit of an arcane science that I will try to decode.

One threshold point worth mentioning is that all participations are phrased in terms of "X% of 100% of Y" such that 5% of net would contractually read 5% of 100% of the net profits of ..... This is because net and gross profits are artificial methods of dividing up certain revenue streams and are based on limited pools of receipts and costs. To avoid ambiguity, the definitions are careful to stipulate that the percentage tapped into is 100% of the defined pool described — not just of the profits of the contracting party. If party X were contracting for 10% of the profits, and the contract referenced profits as the share of financing entity party Y (e.g., studio) that had 50% of the profits (with the balance going to the talent/production entity), then party X would find they only had 5% of the total pool; whereas, if the contracts of party X and party Y both referenced a defined profit pool (100% of net profits, out of which they may share differently), then party X's 10% stake is preserved.

Because the pool is shared by multiple people, and the calculations of different individuals are impacted directly by the participations of third parties, it is possible to only share in part of the pool; as described later, and making things even more complicated, it is further possible to share in only part of the revenues in part of the pool.

History of Net Profits

Whether or not true, Hollywood lore attributes the genesis of net profits to a deal made between Jimmy Stewart and Universal Pictures on the film *Winchester '73* in the early 1950s. Jimmy Stewart was already a major star, and his customary fee was deemed too high for the budget that Universal was willing to approve. Stewart's agent, Lew Wasserman, purportedly struck a deal that granted Stewart a share of the film's net profits in lieu of his customary above the line guaranteed fixed compensation/fee; in essence, Stewart became a partner with the studio, sharing the profits equally with the studio once the film had earned twice what it cost to make.

The key phrase is "in lieu," for in the original concept the sharing was a parceling of risk where the actor risked his salary and on success reaped a large upside. Today, much if not all of that risk has been eliminated and major profit participants get large up-front fees plus share in a big chunk of the upside.

The trend started by Lew Wasserman is a bit ironic vis-à-vis his career. Wasserman, regarded as one of the true Hollywood moguls alongside the likes of Jack Warner and Louis B. Mayer, started the talent agency MCA, becoming an enormously powerful agent and defining the type of clout that is now taken for granted when referring to agencies like CAA, ICM, and WME. Wasserman's agency later took over Universal, and Wasserman ran Universal as the last of the original Hollywood moguls until the sale of the company to Matsushita (Panasonic) in the early 1990s. (Note: Since then, Universal has changed hands several times, next to Seagrams, then to Vivendi, and most recently to GE to form the combined NBC Universal). In his capacity as chairman of Universal, he sat on the other side of the table. One can only imagine what he thought about profit participations when Universal struck deals with leading talent, such as Steven Spielberg and Amblin Entertainment for *Jurassic Park*.

Net profits seemed to take a public turn in the 1990s with the cost of talent and budgets growing at an unprecedented pace. Maybe it was the combined growth of the video market, the international free TV market, and the global pay TV markets that gave participants a wake-up call: How could this avalanche of ancillary money be rolling in and pictures seemingly performing well still post losses? Whatever the reason, the concept of net profits or lack thereof seemed to start making its way into the headlines and reached a peak with Art Buchwald's lawsuit against Paramount Pictures over his rights and participation in the film *Coming to America* starring Eddie Murphy.

Celebrity Lawsuits Spotlight Accounting Practices

Seemingly every few years a new lawsuit brought by a celebrity alleging mistreatment in their profit participation catches media attention. On occasion, some of these suits delve into the nitty-gritty of net profits.

Art Buchwald vs. Paramount in Case Involving the Film Coming to America

Probably no case has reached the fervor of *Art Buchwald vs. Paramount Pictures*, a case in the 1990s that dragged on in the media and courts for several years. In his suit, Art Buchwald very publicly asked the question: How can this picture have grossed hundreds of millions of dollars and lose money? His claim and the underbelly of Hollywood's net profit accounting system were played out on the front page of *Variety* over the course of the trial. When Eddie Murphy referred to net profits as monkey points during the litigation, it tainted the perception of net profits as never before.

The case involved a treatment that Buchwald, a famous columnist and humorist (arguably the most famous humorist/political humorist at the time), wrote called "King for a Day" and optioned to Paramount (the development of which at the time fell, at least in part, under Jeffrey Katzenberg). The same studio went on to produce the Eddie Murphy vehicle *Coming to America*, which Buchwald argued was based on his treatment. The court found that *Coming to America* was indeed based upon Buchwald's treatment, and then reviewed in detail the intricacies of net profits in the so-called accounting phase of the trial. Among the reasons the case became a cause célèbre, is that in the context of this mega hit film that grossed over $350M, where Buchwald was initially paid no participation and the studio argued was in the red, the court found "that certain provisions of Paramount's net profit formula were unconscionable."[1]

437

The book, *Fatal Subtraction, How Hollywood Really Does Business*, written by Buchwald's legal team after the case, is a roller coaster ride through the trial, and is about as entertaining a read as one is likely to find concerning the world of net profits.[2]

Sahara Case — *Clive Cussler vs. Philip Anschutz Company*

More recently, Clive Cussler, a best-selling author who had 19 consecutive *New York Times* bestsellers, was embroiled in a case over the movie *Sahara*, based on his book of the same name. The case, against Bristol Bay, one of the film companies within the Anschutz Film Group controlled by mogul Philip Anschutz (who also controls Regal Entertainment Group, consisting of Regal Cinemas, United Artists Cinemas, and Edwards Theaters, and *Chronicles of Narnia* producer Walden Media), was primarily about Cussler's claims regarding his creative rights in the film. However, because of the people involved and the losses reported, the nature of net profits was again put in the limelight. All of the pieces were there for media drama: two high-profile stars in Matthew McConaughey and Penelope Cruz, a famous author in Cussler, a reclusive billionaire financier in Anschutz, an award-winning screenwriter, and even Michal Eisner's (former Disney CEO) son, Breck Eisner, as the director.

The *Los Angeles Times* wrote an exposé, with the headline: "How Do a Bestselling Novel, an Academy Award-winning Screenwriter, a Pair of Hollywood Hotties, and a No. 1 Opening at the Box Office Add Up to $78 Million of Red Ink?."[3] What it detailed was simply how a movie with revenues of over $200M was projected to lose ~$80M. Table 10.1 is a high level summary of the net loss based on the numbers highlighted in the article:

Table 10.1 Expenses and Net Loss (Based on Projections for 10 Years, Through 2015)

Negative cost	$160M
Print and advertising	$61M
Home video costs	$21.9M
Distribution fees	$20.1M
Other	$18.2M
Total expenses	$281M
Total revenue	$202.9M
Net loss	$78.3M

The grist for the media was the public listing of star salaries and excesses on the film, but it again thrust the nature of Hollywood profit accounting into the public eye.

Peter Jackson vs. New Line in Lord of the Rings Claim

Although it never led to the publishing of figures as resulted in these cases of Buchwald and Sahara, the nature of net profits was thrust onto the front pages when Peter Jackson sued New Line Cinema in 2005. Fresh off his Academy Award wins and having catapulted into the superstar league with his *Lord of the Rings* Trilogy films, Jackson alleged that he was underpaid $100M in net profits from the block-buster trilogy which grossed nearly $3B collectively. One eye-catching part of the claim was the argument that the studio used "pre-emptive bidding" allowing divisions within the vertically integrated corporate Warner Bros. group to obtain related rights (e.g., books, DVDs) rather than put them out to the competitive market. The battle, which became a public saga, and held up Jackson's willingness to be involved with a planned *The Hobbit* film, was eventually settled.

In the context of the lawsuit, the *New York Times* quoted former Carolco Pictures CEO (*Rambo* films) Peter Hoffman as follows: "Once upon a time, Hollywood studios paid a lot of money to net profit participants, and it was a fair deal...Then the studios got greedy and stopped paying, and now we have gross players who used to be net players fighting over vertical integration. The studios brought this problem on themselves."[4]

Why So Complicated — Endemic to the Talent System?

At some level, it is possible to argue that the complexity of profit definitions is a necessary outcome of needing to negotiate individual talent agreements. If talent were merely a commodity, akin to an assembly line input, and wage rates could be fixed then everyone would accept a level of standardization; this is, in fact, what happens with most labor union contracts. However, there is a profound difference when dealing with experience goods of infinite variety with a parallel infinite range of variance in creative input. This is even harder than sports, which in many ways is the most similar market. At least in sports it is possible to measure an individual's performance via objective metrics such as batting average, points per game, or tackles. With experience good entertainment products, there is such a complex matrix of inputs and variable results that individual contributions are more subjectively measured. Key creative talent is therefore not considered fungible, and cannot easily be homogenized into standard compensation schemes. Even if this was not the case, ego and agents would argue that an individual's value is unique and must be measured on a one-off negotiated basis.

439

The result of one-to-one varied deals is not efficient for either side. It creates delays for talent who are usually anxious to close deals rather than postpone them (as virtually all employment is on a project basis, and insecurity regarding landing the next project and/or being replaced the by the new, younger, hotter X runs high). On the producer/distributor side, negotiating each deal not only creates an up-front overhead burden (plus the political anxiety of haggling with agents/lawyers that can point fingers when deals fall through), but in accounting for contingent compensation they frequently have to customize reports and construct a labyrinth of deductions where one person's share is dependent on another's and another's....

I asked Jim Mullany, managing director of Salem Partners LLC, a Los Angeles-based investment bank and wealth management/advisory firm primarily involved in media and entertainment M&A advisory transactions and library valuations, if he ever envisioned a more simplified system, especially in light of new, growing revenue streams from new media and technology distribution platforms. He noted the following in confirming the underlying pressures that shape the current system:

> While participation accounting is brushed off as a "Hollywood Accounting" implying the worst meaning of the phrase, each participation statement that is rendered has to reflect the financial terms of the talent and financial contracts: the revenue and expense definitions, and the order and priorities of cost recoupment are spelled out in the negotiated contracts.
>
> The accounting systems required to create monthly, quarterly, semi-annual or annual participation statements (the timing of which is also contractually set out) are so massive and complex that many accounting departments have to revert to preparing statements manually using reported data from financial reporting systems from the various divisions (domestic and international) of the distribution company. Sometimes, the participation accounting department will have accumulated the unfiltered financial numbers for revenue and expenses, and must begin the manual customization of reports for each contractual party. They have to take into account:
>
> - The many different definitions of what is reported as revenue, and what is reported as deductible or recoupable expenses
> - The variable distribution fees per source of revenue
> - Calculation of contingent compensation paid to other participants are deducted if the contract specifies that priority
> - The addition of studio overhead surcharges to various expense categories, or not
> - Surcharges on other costs and fees are to be included or excluded
> - Home video revenue is typically defined as a 20% royalty on gross adjusted wholesale video revenues; or an alternative for financial partners is to calculate video revenue as wholesale revenues less an allowance for returns, and then deduct costs of manufacturing, packaging, and shipping video units

440

It is not uncommon for each member of the creative and financing team of a television or film project to have a different set of definitions for reporting revenue and expenses deducted, before the defined profitability is declared.

In an ideal world, a studio would insist on standard contract terms with uniform definitions for all contracts entered into by the studio. Unfortunately, those fixed carved-in-stone standard terms would hold only until the studio tries to sign an "indispensable" talent element, and waives policy to craft an individualized contract reflecting more favorable terms negotiated by the talent agent or lawyer representing the indispensable creative talent. The contact terms would be negotiated section by section. The formerly standard template of participation accounting for back-end purposes and payment of contingent compensation would be modified henceforth.

Gross and Net Profits: How are They Defined and Calculated?

All studios and networks have similar gross profits and net profits definitions, but it is critical to remember that these vary by contract and are not fully standardized. The following parameters are industry custom, and have become so-called terms of art, but nuances exist and any profit participation can only be understood and administered by reference to its defining document.

Included and Excluded Revenues

A key to understanding net profits is to understand the baseline of what revenues are included in the calculation, and which revenues are excluded: *not all revenues are counted.* Film, video, and television revenues are all included in gross and net profits calculations; however, which specific revenues are captured (e.g., film rentals or box office), at what point are they captured (on television sale or broadcast) and what portion of revenues are counted (e.g., video wholesale or video royalty) are issues defined by contract.

Fully Included Revenues (A)

With respect to theatrical revenues, 100% of film rentals are included (see Chapter 4); no revenue retained by the exhibitor, even if the theater is an affiliate or directly owned by the studio, is included. Revenues from sales of films to television are similarly accounted for at 100%.

Allocations and Timing   A wrinkle on the inclusion of TV sales revenue is that it was (and still can be) common practice for films to be sold in packages. A studio will combine, for example, 15 to 30 films and receive an overall fee for the entire package. What revenue should be attributable to any particular film within the package (see also Chapter 6)? This can be a hotly contested area, for allocations can swing revenues on a picture millions of dollars and the interests of the studio and producer may not be aligned.

In addition to allocation issues, television revenues can be subject to timing delays, setting back when revenues are accounted for and shrinking the up-front pool of revenues upon which profits are calculated. Whoever is responsible for paying participations (e.g., studios) may not be apt to adopt the GAAP revenue recognition rules (which accelerate the reporting of revenue over the term of the license in year one, as discussed in the following section). Instead, they will take the logical position of recognizing advances once holdbacks have expired and match the revenues to the term of the contract. Money in hand may not be counted until downstream when the broadcast it has secured takes place.

Partially Included Revenues (B)

Video revenues are included, but only a fraction of the actual video receipts are customarily put into the pot. As discussed in Chapter 5, video revenues are typically accounted for at only 20%, equating to a royalty on the gross revenues. Beyond segmenting only a fraction of video revenue for inclusion in profit calculations, the video revenue number is further reduced or delayed by the calculation of return reserves (see also Chapter 5). These reserves set back revenues, and only if and when they are liquidated are the amounts put into gross revenues (off of which the royalty will then be calculated).

Excluded Revenues (C)

Revenues from merchandising and theme parks are generally not included. Also, the following items are usually referenced as simply being excluded: theme park royalties, music and record royalties, books, and royalties derived from derivative works or the underlying material.

$$A + B + C = \text{Baseline Revenue for Calculating Net Profits}$$

Merchandising and Other Revenues as a "Separate Pot"

Sometimes certain ancillary revenues, such as from merchandising, will be put into a separate pot. In this instance, the participant will receive a separate accounting statement tracking the definition of revenues of that single revenue stream; a distribution fee may or may not be charged, and the timing of payment may be linked directly to the right or may tie into a separate definition (e.g., 5% of 100% of merchandising receipts, but only after such point as.....). If there is a separate pot, these revenues need to remain separate, and not be included in the definition of revenues for net profits; otherwise they would be double counted.

Certain Costs Always Deducted

Certain costs are almost always deducted as "off the top" expenses for all participants. Even in the context of "gross" or "gross revenues" these terms are actually net of off the top expenses; the amount remaining after the off the tops are sometimes conceived of as "gross" in terms of the revenue line from which all participants then look to apply deductions or percentages of revenues. The following are standard categories of off the top expenses.

Trade Fees and Dues

The studios are members of trade associations that lobby on their behalf and also fight common issues such as piracy. The most well known group, as referenced in several instances throughout this book, is the Motion Picture Association of America (MPAA). The MPAA maintains affiliated regional offices throughout the world, and plays a key role in lobbying foreign governments on laws impacting piracy and the protection of intellectual property (see Chapter 2). Another association is the Association of Motion Picture and Television Producers, Inc. (AMPTP). This organization, including all the major studios and independents, negotiates union agreements with the various Hollywood guilds (see Chapter 7 for discussion of new media residuals impacting SAG and WGA negotiations, and leading to strikes). Associations such as the MPAA charge dues and assessments that cover legal and administrative costs, and the studios recoup this money by charging these costs back to pictures as an off the top deduction.

Checking

Checking here means costs borne by the studios to send "auditors" out to theaters to ensure that box office receipts (given the predominantly cash nature of the business) are accurately reported. Depending on clout, these costs are often capped. (Note: Cost of collecting money due is also typically an off the top.)

Duties, Tariffs, and Licenses: Conversion

These involve costs incurred to permit the exhibition of the picture in foreign territories and the associated costs to convert foreign currency to US dollars, including related costs of converting and transmitting restricted funds (restricted funds are less applicable today given the global economy).

Residuals

These are the payments (see Chapters 2 and 7) required under union collective bargaining agreements (e.g., Screen Actors Guild, Writers Guild of America, Directors Guild of America) for use of the picture in media post its initial release medium (e.g., such as television following theatrical).

444

Taxes

This does not refer to income tax, but rather taxes of whatever nature that may be levied on the picture (e.g., relating to the exhibition).

Distribution Fees

Distribution fees are the not-so-hidden charges that compensate the distributor for its work in selling the picture and managing the license (including collections, delivery, and all related back-office functions). Rather than charging a mark-up on a per product basis, the distributor charges a percentage on the revenues (akin to an agency fee). This percentage, in theory, is designed to (1) cover the distributor's overhead cost of its sales and distribution infrastructure (including people/salaries and offices as outlined in Chapter 1) and (2) provide the distributor a profit margin for its work (though many will argue it is only intended to cover costs).

Range of Fees

Distribution fees are charged on theatrical, non-theatrical, television, video, and merchandising receipts. The standard fees, although they will vary by distributor, tend to be in the following ranges:

Revenue Stream	Distribution Fee
US theatrical	30%
Foreign theatrical	40%
US network TV	25%
US cable and syndication	35–40%
Home video	30–35%
Merchandising	50%

When looking at these fees, it highlights the importance of below market fees discussed in Chapter 3. If Producer X benefits from a 10% fee, then on $100 million of revenues it bears only $10 million versus a party with a standard fee of 30% that would bear $30 million.

Subdistributors and Affiliates: Fees as Overrides

With respect to foreign exploitation, studios that do not have captive subsidiaries within a territory will distribute via an independent subdistributor or an affiliate. The subdistributor is a full-fledged distribution company, and will charge a distribution fee for its service. The corresponding risk is that the studio may receive a net amount that it reports as its gross receipts, and then charges its own fee on this sum. For example, a subdistributor in Asia charging studio X a fee of 20% receives $500,000; it would remit $400,000 to studio X, who in turn would charge 40% ($160,000). The net into the pot is $240,000, even though $500,000 was taken in at source. Many contracts will accordingly negotiate either (1) that the studio fee is inclusive of all subdistributor fees or (2) that the studio takes a smaller override fee on receipts from the subdistributor.

The concept of an override needs to be carefully defined. Depending on interpretation it could mean a fee charged on the net amount remitted (akin to a commission) or a fee in addition to the subdistributor's fee such that there is a cumulative fee; in the latter instance the contract would define the total fee to be inclusive of any subdistributor's fee.

The following is an example of how this subtle distinction can vary the participation:

	($millions)	Assumptions
Box office gross	20.0	
Rentals	10.0	@50% of box office
Sub fee	2.5	@25% fee
Distribution expenses	4.5	
Revenue remitted	3.0	
Override commission	0.3	@10%
Net receipts	2.7	

	($millions)	
Box office gross	20.0	
Rentals	10.0	@50% of box office
Sub fee	2.5	@25% fee
Override	1.0	@10%
Distribution expenses	4.5	
Revenue remitted	2.0	Revenue remitted = Net receipts

At the Source Recognition

In the context of revenues that are earned in one locale and then remitted upstream, it is vital to pinpoint where and when revenues are captured. A simple example of how this can vary accounting is to consider how an advance is treated. A participant with clout will want to ensure that they are not disadvantaged by a subdistributor guaranteeing an amount that ends up higher than the receipts taken in (this can occur when a guarantee is credited but not ultimately earned out), and having the reporting only reflect the actual territory receipts rather than the higher amount received by the studio. (Note: This scenario also raises timing issues. It can be debated whether the guarantee should be recognized when committed, paid, or earned out.)

Second, beyond an advance/guarantee scenario, a participant will want to account for revenue "at the source" simply to ensure it is capturing the greatest amount of revenue. The important rule when capturing items at a certain tier of distribution is to ensure symmetry, such that if costs are applied are at the source, so are revenues.

In the case of a third-party foreign distributor (as opposed to a branch of the studio), the studio will report 100% of revenues received from the foreign distributor and take a fee on this "gross." In reporting to a participant, however, the cash to the studio is less than at the source gross, because (1) the foreign distributor may deduct its distribution fee and expenses, with the net amount remitted to the studio being considered the gross receipts and (2) there may be withholding taxes that further reduce the cash amount tendered. The amounts accounted for become exponentially skewed if there is more than one level of subdistribution, which can occur absent contractual caps and prohibitions.

To account at the source, the revenues received by the subdistributor from exploiting the property would be considered gross and then any deductions would be applied from this point. Accordingly, if there were a distribution fee applied it may be aggregated with any fee of the studio (capped so that the aggregate fee is no greater than X); alternatively, the studio may simply apply an override to subdistributor remittances.

Expenses should be treated in a similar manner, such that if receipts are captured at the source then expenses are applied at this level as well. A corollary to this issue is how costs of affiliates are treated; some may argue that these are not arm's length transactions and the studio can arbitrarily elect to use its own affiliates at rates it establishes. There is of course danger for abuse, but checks and balances can be put in place such as requiring the same (or no worse than) rate card pricing as charged to unaffiliated third parties.

Distribution Costs and Expenses

The "off the tops" described previously are simply a subset of the overall category of distribution expenses that are deducted by the distributor. In general, the distributor will be allowed to deduct any and all expenses relating to the distribution and exhibition of the picture. This will be expressed contractually in a catchall phrase covering monies paid, advanced or incurred by the studio "in connection with the distribution, exhibition, marketing and exploitation of the Picture." The only carve out is that these costs relate to the sale of the Picture and are not part of the costs of making the Picture. While this sounds straightforward, as mentioned earlier issues can arise such as whether trailers are a production or distribution expense (although the foregoing is routinely accepted as a distribution cost). The principal costs other than off the tops are in the following sections.

Prints and Physical Materials

The costs of prints, duplicate prints, masters, etc., are obviously a large and legitimate expense (and, as discussed in Chapter 4, part of the impetus for D-cinema, which holds the promise beyond presentation improvements of eliminating the bulk of these costs). The key here is to capture the actual costs, which when charges go down to the level of tape stock (which may not be easily separable on a per film basis) can be tricky.

Advertising

This is perhaps the largest single cost relating to distributing a film. "Advertising" is a catchall for advertising, marketing, and promotional costs, and includes subcategories such as the following:

- Publications, including local and national trade and consumer press (e.g., newspapers)
- Television, radio, and online advertising
- Screenings
- Artwork
- Promotional materials (e.g., free giveaways)
- Trailers
- Travel and entertainment costs of marketing executives

Negative Cost

"Negative cost" means the cost of creating the finished product; namely the cost of production through to the final delivered film negative. When people are asking the simple question: "What did it end up costing?" the answer will be the negative cost was X. As mentioned in a few sections, what costs are included in negative cost can be subject to debate. For example, should advances against gross participations be included in costs, and again where is the line between production costs and distribution costs (e.g., a foreign language master)?

Other Distribution Costs

Other distribution costs may include the following:

- Dubbing and subtitling costs for foreign versions
- Shipping and delivery costs (significant in delivering prints to theaters)
- Insurance
- Copyright registration and protection costs and expenses
- Litigation related to the property/picture (e.g., copyright infringement claims)

Gross Participations, Deferrals, and Advances as Cost Items

Deferments

A deferment is simply a payment that is agreed to be made in the future, but is tied to the occurrence of a specified event. That event could be something like box office reaching two or three times the negative cost, or when a breakeven point with a specified fee (e.g., imputing a reduced distribution fee) occurs. Deferments are a type of contingent compensation since they are not guaranteed, but are usually structured to kick in a point deemed more certain than the point at which net profits would be due.

Deferments are also a way to skirt budget items, as certain compensation to above the line talent may be taken out of the budget to hit a magic mark for greenlighting the project, while promising the dollars at a point that everyone expects to attain. If there is a perceived risk involved, then the deferment will likely be higher than the up-front guaranteed compensation would have been (this also makes sense, since the payment is also delayed).

Gross Participations as a Cost Item

Participations payable before net profits are due, such as gross participations, may sometimes be added into the cost of production and treated as part of the negative cost for the purposes of calculating net profits. As further illustrated, this can obviously have a profound impact on net profits ever being realized.

Advances

Advances are often lumped in with deferments, but are different because a deferment generally refers to the timing of paying a fixed sum, whereas advances are tied to a variable contingent element. The contingent element is the backend, and by paying a portion of that contingent backend as a non-refundable advance the scheme of Hollywood accounting basically turns a contingent payment into a guarantee. A star, for example, may take a budgetary cash fee of $2 million, which is structured as an advance against his backend. While this methodology may have no ultimate impact on the participant (other than accelerating compensation), it can have a profound impact on third parties whose participations are subject to recoupment of production costs; as discussed further, by accelerating the payment, the $2 million goes into the salary/production cost line, thereby increasing the production costs that are then further increased by both overhead and interest, setting back the point of recoupment for all non-gross participants.

Imputed Costs: Production and Advertising Overhead, Interest

Advertising Overhead

Salaries of studio personnel working on advertising and marketing for the picture are not allowable charges. However, it is customary to add an advertising overhead charge (e.g., 10%), which is a gross up of the total advertising costs deducted. Some may find this unfair, and argue that the studio's distribution fee is supposed to cover overhead costs, but the advertising overhead fee is generally accepted as a standard provision in net profits definitions.

Interest on Negative Cost

In addition to the negative cost and the administrative fee, the studio will also charge interest on the cost of production from the time the costs were incurred until the production costs are fully recouped. This interest cost is charged whether or not monies are actually borrowed to make the film. Often studios will self-finance, but the argument is there was an opportunity cost and that the studio has in effect loaned the money to itself.

Interest costs can add up quickly because costs of production are so high: 7% on $50 million is a large number, and interest continues to be recalculated on the unrecouped production costs and then becomes an additional cost to be recouped. Because interest is recouped first (banks are usually at the head of the line), there is a compounding effect of interest delaying recoupment: interest continues to accrue on unrecouped production costs, such that receipts may pay down interest charges but during the same period new interest is accruing on the production costs. This interest treadmill is made more cumbersome from the participant's standpoint to the extent interest is also charged on the overhead added to production costs; further, timing issues can exacerbate interest charges. Does interest accrue from the time expenses are committed or actually paid, and similarly are advances counted into receipts to pay down/stop interest or only recognized when earned?

Overhead Gross Up

In addition to the actual costs, it is customary to add a standard gross up to cover elements of studio overhead, similar to the advertising

450

overhead fee discussed previously. Here, the net profits definition will invariably state that an administrative fee of 15% of the cost of production (excluding this fee) will be added to the cost of production. Accordingly, the negative cost is really the cost of production plus 15%.

Phantom Revenues: Allocating Taxes and Other Non-Picture-Specific Items

Allocations are always a hotly debated element given the tension between subjective calls inherent in the nature of allocations and what participants want to believe are "exact" costs in accounting. When properties are bundled and fees and/or costs need to be apportioned, what should the formula be (e.g., straight-lined based on relative box office, or another formula)?

Rebates

In the case of rebates, these may be part of a multi-picture deal, where a supplier may grant preferential terms to a customer based on a variety of factors, including length of term and volume of business. Most will consider overall incentive deals as part of the cost of doing business and not allocable on a line-item basis; however, others will dispute this and argue that any rebate incentive must be pro-rated or otherwise allocated back on a by-title basis and passed along.

451

Taxes/Tax Credits

Many countries impose withholding taxes on remittances of royalties (e.g., Japan), which are triggered because the intellectual property basis of the content means payments are remitted via a license. Moreover, these taxes can be challenging to assess because their application involves both the individual picture and the ultimate tax position of the entity bearing the withholding tax. When withholding taxes have been applied against a specific picture attributable to a specific license, then arguably a corresponding matching tax credit ought to be applied to the picture (the concept being that per tax treaties a party should not be "double taxed" such that if you bear the tax locally it should be offset by a tax credit on your corporate taxes). The problem is the utility of such tax credit is tied to the company's overall tax situation, and whether it avails itself of that tax credit is dependent on its corporate tax profile and not the individual transaction.

If, for example, a $1 million license is subject to a 10% withholding tax given the tax treaty between the United States and country X, such that only 90% of the license fee is remitted and 10% is captured via a tax credit matching the deduction (i.e., a $100,000 tax credit), should the licensee that has 90% of the cash reported be grossed up to 100%? While the answer may seem a simple yes, issues of "if and when" are significant because at the time of remitting the 90% the distributor/licensor may not know whether it will use the corresponding tax credit. The decision will be determined by unrelated factors, including whether it is even eligible (it needs sufficient overall profits to claim the credit in the first place) and then if eligible what strategy is deployed in its overall corporate tax planning. For its part, the content owner bearing the 10% withholding tax is likely to only account for the 90% received, arguing it has no control over the withholding (governed by law/tax treaty) and it may or may not use the tax credit (a likely scenario if high production costs/investment and revenues are not matched in timing).

Net Profits: An Artificial Breakeven Point and Moving Target

Net profits are the point at which gross receipts have recouped (1) distribution fees; (2) distribution expenses; (3) interest on the cost of production; (4) the negative cost, including the studio's overhead fee; and (5) gross participations and deferments payable prior to net profits.

Net profits basically track the definition of initial actual breakeven (see later): the point at which gross receipts, from the sources of revenues that are counted toward gross receipts, equals the total costs on the project, including any imputed costs that are included in the definition of costs. The difference between net profits and initial breakeven is that with net profits there is no fixed stopping point; new distribution costs and fees paid or incurred are applied with each accounting period, and continue to "roll" forward. Accordingly, with each accounting period additional costs, fees, and revenues are thrown into the equation, and the "net profit" line calculated anew. Table 10.2 is an example.

Gross Participations/Profits

There are multiple types of gross participations, but in general a gross player receives money at a defined point prior to net profits. It could

Table 10.2 Net Profit Calculation A

Revenues and Costs	Assumptions	Net Profit Calculation (in millions)
Cost of production	$35 million	
Box office	Gross box office	$200
Film rentals	Assume 50% of box office	$100
Distribution fees	Assume 35% on average	$35
Distribution costs:		$45
Prints	Prints — $10 million	
Advertising	Advertising — $35 million	
Interest on negative cost	Assume 10%	$3.5
Total negative cost (cost of production + overhead allocation)	Cost of production + 15% studio overhead on costs	$40
Profit/loss		($23.5)

be as early as "first dollar gross," which means participating at the same time that the studio takes money without deductions (although even in this rare case, individuals are still customarily subject to the "off the top" deductions detailed earlier).

The key to gross participations is that distribution fees, print and advertising costs, and costs of production—the major expense categories in making and releasing a film—are not deducted. Individuals participating in true gross profits literally earn a percentage of the defined gross revenues with hardly any deductions at all.

Table 10.3 is an example, comparing the previous net profit participation scenario to one where talent has a 10% gross participation.

Impact of Categorizing Costs as Production vs. Distribution Costs

Timing

As discussed in the section Advances, as well as what charges are included within the negative costs, the line between what is a production versus distribution cost may be dependent on timing and contractual definitions; this is because the line is not always clear. Is

Table 10.3 Net Profit Calculation B

Revenues and Costs	Assumptions	Net Profit Calculation (in millions)
Cost of production	$35 million	
Box office	Gross box office	$200
Film rentals	Assume 50% of box office	$100
Gross participant	Assume 10% gross points	$ 10
Distribution fees	Assume 35% on average	$ 35
Distribution costs:		$ 45
Prints	Prints —$10 million	
Advertising	Advertising — $35 million	
Interest on negative cost	Assume 10%	$ 3.5
Total negative cost (cost of production + overhead allocation)	Cost of production + 15% studio overhead on costs	$ 40
Profit/loss		($33.5)

a trailer a production item? Are certain masters or prints such as foreign language versions properly distribution cost items? If talent delays payment to the backend, are these fees part of the cost of the picture, and is it fair that advances against a backend instead are categorized as production costs that then are grossed up by an overhead component and are subject to interest?

In general terms, timing can create a relatively clear line—any costs to get to a finished negative can be construed as a production, and all subsequent costs (foreign masters, dubbing, etc.) for other versions would be distribution expenses.

Online Accounting: Simple Revenue Sharing and the Net Profits Divide

Gross is Gross and Net is Net — Sort of

The online world has not yet descended into the complexity of net profits seen in film and TV, and to date employs relatively straightforward definitions of gross and net revenues. In the context of sorting out what sources of advertising maximize the value of their content, this new breed of distributor (whether online ad streaming or downloads) has been first grappling with what is an appropriate revenue split of the resulting advertising mix. To a degree, the corollary question of how a participant (e.g., writer, director) is compensated from this pot has been deferred because the participant in this case is more often than not simply the producer, and the revenue share and participation one and the same.

As far as gross and net are concerned, there are few exclusions from "gross." However, it is possible to segment a Web site and exclude certain sections or categories (e.g., Yahoo! News could be treated differently from Yahoo! Sports); similarly, certain overall revenues, such as run-of-site advertising, may not be counted on a particular subsection of a Web site where the revenue sharing/deal is focused on targeted revenues from that discrete area of the site. When thinking about this question, it is easy to postulate how much more complex it could grow, but the dissection has not yet occurred and generally "gross is gross."

In terms of calculating net profits, there will be various contractual deductions from gross, but again this area has not evolved excruciating complexity. It is more typical to find limited deductions, such as for direct third-party costs incurred (e.g., ad serving fees), but also typical to employ a catchall percentage deduction from gross to capture the basket of administrative and third-party costs incurred in serving, hosting, tracking, and reporting revenues. Paralleling the treatment of gross revenue recognition, costs are lumped in a rational range and not re-allocated back on a line-item basis and subject to allocation scrutiny. Therefore "net is net" and more generally accepted given parties believe the ability to track by impression results in accuracy and transparency. The question is, however, is that really the case when baskets of costs are lumped together?

What has happened is that the ability to track costs and revenues at a more detailed level has engendered a culture of trust, even though the ultimate reporting often does not reflect the greater level of detail that the metrics conceptually enable. In the end, actual participant reporting can be just as detailed (if not more so) in film and television even though the information being cumulated is less precise. It will be interesting to watch whether this anomaly continues.

Revenue Sharing

Regarding how to split the revenue, the issues are not dissimilar to the economic analysis in determining what percentage of video revenues should be paid—either as a profit split or royalty—to the content owner/producer (see Chapter 5). What has started to evolve in the online space is a formula of revenue sharing, where parties negotiate a split such as 60/40 or 70/30, with the majority to the producer if the site's share is deemed tantamount to a distribution fee. In the video context, one of the issues in setting formulas is whether true net revenues (so-called off the top revenue splits) can be tracked and audited, and licensors often default to a royalty basis to approximate what they expect a split to be given the easier monitoring and auditing. The online world, however, is premised on detailed metrics (cost per click, CPM, unique visitors, etc.) and the ability to drill down and share true, actual revenues and costs is assumed.

Again, this underlies one of the fundamental differences the online space is forging: because of the detailed metrics there is implicit trust in the system, and the accuracy (even arguably veracity) of the revenue splits. Simply, people trust and accept revenue sharing. This is in stark contrast to the traditional media world, where skepticism of profit splits and accounting has evolved the byzantine system of net profits discussed throughout this chapter and provided a subtext to the 2007–2008 Hollywood guild strikes and stalemates. Actors and writers, in an attempt to provide certainty in the context of where they mistrust accounting, want guarantees of what they will be paid online as well as assurance that the accounting includes revenues attributable to online usage of their work. Revenue sharing is anathema if some of the revenues to be shared may not be included in the pot in the first place.

Is all this trust properly placed when in fact there are a myriad of issues that can arise online, ranging from fraudulent clicks/impressions to allocations of delivery/bandwidth costs? There are only two logical next steps: either online revenue sharing which to date has been relatively straightforward becomes more complicated (e.g., "gross revenues" are more finely sliced, and delivery and infrastructure costs allocated) or everything becomes simpler and the "trust in revenue sharing" spreads from Silicon Valley to Hollywood and everyone accepts simple division of the pie (e.g., 70/30 split of gross revenues, where gross retains its common sense, all in, meaning).

What I believe is likely to develop is a hybrid weighted toward the current Internet structure: the Internet world will not stand for a convoluted net profits system, and economic reality is that "gross" and "net" are not as simple as "gross" and "net" and there will be

456

important and legitimate tweaks that need to be made in accounting. I believe this is already taking shape in deals with a Web component and a simplified system, premised on revenue sharing of a straightforward definition of net profits, will become the de facto standard.

I turned again to Jim Mullany (from Salem Partners) for his opinion regarding what I am labeling the net profit divide. In terms of whether there would be an element of convergence in accounting given new media delivery systems, he noted that in terms of downloads-to-own, online viewing services such as Hulu, and yet to be invented services, there would be a shift in the revenue versus expense construct; namely, the costs to generate revenues (e.g., advertising, usage fees, subscription fees) would be nominal because only a digital version of the program needs to be provided to the host service, no physical good is delivered to the end consumer, and nothing is manufactured (and therefore not subject to packing, shipping, and inventory logistics). However, he advised that this shift would not so easily lead to a shift in how profit accounting is treated, given the incentives and strong institutional forces at play:

This streamlining of the distribution process should help simplify financial participation reporting for revenue and costs for these sources for a studio or property owner's financing partners and creative talent involved in the project, who have a stake in the "back end" (contingent compensation) based on the terms of their employment contracts—whether it be a percentage of adjusted gross revenue or adjusted gross proceeds, or a percentage of a defined Net Profit.

The reality, however, might be different.

- The company providing the delivery service (Netflix, Hulu, Amazon, Comcast, et al.) in the current and announced projects (other than the network Web sites), will take a fee from gross revenues for providing their delivery service.
- There is no uniform standard digital format requiring the preparation of multiple digital masters.
- Depending on the contractual agreement with the delivery service there may be a reimbursement or recoupment of

the service provider's advertising and promotional costs, along with amounts or percentages for operating overhead.

- There will likely be recoupable costs associated with the sale and collecting of advertising revenues.
- SVOD has inherent tracking and reporting problems in the fair/contractual allocation of subscription revenues to suppliers of product.
- It is also conceivable, and now probable, that the company owning the "pipe" that provides the signals to the home or business will take a slice of gross revenues generated from the consumer and/or the delivery service as a fee for providing the DSL or wireless signal, and allowing the delivery service to provide a high-quality signal or priority streaming access.

However, assuming all the above issues didn't exist—if the revenue streams were very easy to track and collect, the idea of simplifying the profit participation equation is counter to the usual way that studios and/or distributors operate. Typically, the more complicated (causally defined as "creative") the structure of the cash flow waterfall, and opaque the definitions of standard terms, the better.

Accordingly, an industry observer can easily conclude that it is in the studio's best financial interest to keep the contract process and the reporting as complex and opaque as possible. Participation accounting for new streams of revenue and related costs therefore will be interpreted and inserted into templates already established, until a talent guild negotiates different contract terms with the distributors/studios that will define it otherwise. That is why video-on-demand (whether it be from downloading, streaming or other delivery variations), pay-per-view and other new media utilized for home viewing of filmed entertainment will be considered as "home video" revenues for participation reporting purposes rather than "television" revenue. These revenue streams will be calculated to the studio/distributor's benefit as a 20% royalty based on gross adjusted revenue, rather than a gross revenue subject to deduction of identifiable costs.

Variations of Profit Participation

Types of Breakeven

Breakeven in theory is the point of recoupment of all actual costs expended in making and releasing a picture. Depending on the definition, a participant may receive funds with or without additional charges applied. There are at least three types of breakeven concepts routinely utilized.

Initial Breakeven (aka Initial Actual Breakeven)

Conceptually, initial breakeven is the point at which costs are initially recouped, or in other words, the point when gross receipts equals the aggregate of expenses on the project. The expenses that need to be recouped have all been previously discussed: (1) distribution fees; (2) distribution expenses; (3) negative cost, including the studio's overhead fee and interest on the cost of production; and (4) gross participations and deferments payable before or at initial breakeven. Initial breakeven is essentially the same point at which net profits are first due.

This creates a trigger point defining which costs are subsequently deducted; for example, a participant that has a right to gross proceeds kicking in once initial breakeven is reached will not have additional distribution fees or expenses (save standard off the tops) deducted. Essentially, the adding on of additional costs and fees stops at initial breakeven for participants that have a gross participation or deferment starting at initial breakeven.

Cash Breakeven

Cash breakeven differs from initial breakeven in that there will often be a reduced negotiated distribution fee; this is, in theory, because the distribution fee includes a profit margin element that is backed out with a reduced fee. Since cash breakeven is only granted to players who command a participation in something better than net profits, gross participants and deferments are generally not deducted. Cash breakeven is reached when there are gross receipts available to recoup (1) the distribution fee, (2) distribution expenses, (3) interest, and (4) the negative cost, including the studio's overhead fee. Similar to initial breakeven, once this point is reached no further distribution fees and expenses are charged. Although at one level it may seem cash breakeven ought to exclude imputed overhead and a distribution fee, some distribution fee and overhead charge needs to be factored in to cover the costs of distribution and production management; the studios are carrying real and significant overhead to bring the product to market.

Talent that receives a participation at "cash breakeven zero" bears no distribution fee (i.e., the zero fee), and are pushed back only by the film's cost and its distribution expenses (P&A). To the extent they are also not bearing any gross players, and talent has taken a reduced fee betting on their backend gross points, there may be some juggling. For example, if an A-level star who customarily receives some form of gross participation takes a small cash fee in the budget (e.g., to help get the picture made), then for the purpose of someone else's cash break zero deal there may be an amount imputed to the budget on the theory the budget is artificially low; namely, the studio needs to account for the fact that it is paying out significant sums to talent, which need to be deducted at some level before the other participants.

Adjusted Gross and Rolling Breakeven

Adjusted gross refers generically to an intermediate type of participation, which has elements worse than first dollar gross and better than net. This can mean that there has been a reduced negotiated distribution fee, including a zero fee; typically, however, adjusted gross means that (1) there is a modified distribution fee and (2) major distribution expenses, including print and advertising costs, are deducted.

Online Supplementary Material

For additional discussion of adjusted gross, rolling breakeven, how net profits may be modified by over-budget penalties, and schemes applying box office bonuses in lieu of profit participation, please refer to the online supplemental material. This supplementary material also includes a section on how producers' shares may be reduced by bearing participants (applying hard and soft floors), as well as a section on how GAAP and tax accounting (e.g., capitalization rules) differ from profit participation accounting.

Online Impact

- Online contracts tend to employ simple revenue sharing models, rather than complicated net profits.

- Online metrics directly track revenues, by click or impression, without allocations; if allocations are applied, they tend to be off the top percentage fees to capture costs of ad serving and related third-party costs.
- The culture of online contracts tends to grant much less audit protection/rights: trust the clicks and metrics. Will this continue? It remains to be seen whether online metrics are quite as trustworthy as they appear.
- Online revenue share splits tend to track distribution fee splits (e.g., distributor retains 30%, content owner 70%), where content owner's share is treated as gross vis-à-vis sharing percentages with third-party contributors (if there are participants).

461

References

Chapter 1

1. Motion Picture Association of America Theatrical Market Statistics-Worldwide Box Office Reaches Historic High, www.mpaa.org/researchStatisitics.asp; Motion picture theater industry statistics 1965–99, Chapter 2, Movie macroeconomics, *Entertainment Industry Economics*, by Harold Vogel, Cambridge University Press, 5th ed., copyright 2001.
2. *The Da Vinci Code's* International box office as a percentage of the worldwide total of 71.3% pursuant to boxofficemojo.com/alltime/world.
3. "Hollywood Studios Fined for Price Fixing," *Variety* 5/11/2006.
4. "Studio 3 Networks Announces epix, the New Brand in American Consumer Entertainment," Reuters, 1/27/09.
5. "Glut of Films Hits Hollywood," *Wall Street Journal*, 9/3/08.
6. "Label-it Is," *Variety*, 3/19–25, 2007.
7. *Variety*, "Label-it Is," 3/19/07.
8. www.mpaa.org/researchStatistics.
9. "White-Knuckle Summer," *Variety*, 1/22–28/07.
10. *Hit & Run*, by Nancy Griffin & Kim Masters, Simon & Schuster, copyright 1996.
11. "Movie Biz on the 'Bubble' — 'Bubble' Triple Bow Biz Inconclusive," *Variety*, 1/30/06.
12. "Window Treatments," *Variety*, 3/1/06.
13. Comcast Press Release, "Comcast and IFC to Offer On-Demand Day and Date Premieres of Independent Theatrical Films," 2/28/06.
14. *USA Today*, "Morgan Freeman Movie Might be Coming to a PC Near You," 2/8/06.
15. "European Movie Chains Boycott Major Releases," *Arts Technica*, 2/6/07; "British Exhibitors Shut 'Museum' — Fox Punished for Breaking Window," *Variety*, 2/1/07.
16. What's Driving the Box Office Batty — Hollywood is Pushing Movies to DVD and Video Faster — and Theaters Feel Squeezed," *Business Week*, 7/11/05.

Chapter 2

1. William Goldman, *Adventures in the Screen Trade*, Warner Books, copyright 1983.

2. Catmull, Ed, "How Pixar Fosters Collective Creativity," *Harvard Business Review*, 9/08.
3. "NBC Pulls the Plug on *Quarterlife*," *Variety*, 2/28/08.
4. Leamonth, Michael, The Business Insider, Silicon Valley Insider, "ABC Gives Web Moms a Chance At the Tube," 5/19/2008, itm.abc.go.com.
5. US Constitution, Article 1, Section 8.
6. Title 17, US Code, § 102.
7. Title 17 United States Code, § 106.
8. Title 17 US Code, Section 107.
9. Grokster p. 10, citing See Sony Corp. v. Universal City Studios, supra, at 442.
10. Grokster, pp. 23–24.
11. "What are Patents, Trademarks, Servicemarks, and Copyrights?" and sub-heading "What is a Trademark or Servicemark?," http:/www.uspto.gov/web/offices/pac/doc/general/whatis.htm.
12. Anti-Piracy Tab: Who are They?, mpaa.org.
13. Piracy Data Summary, mpaa.org/researchStatistics.asp. 2005.
14. Stetler, Brian and Stone, Brand "New Wave of Pirates Plunders Hollywood — Streaming Videos are the Latest Threat," *International Herald Tribune*, 2/6/09.
15. Anti Piracy Tab: Piracy and the Law, mpaa.org.

Chapter 3

1. US Theatrical Market Statistics, mpaa.org, 2007.
2. "A $500 Million Film Ain't What It Used to Be," *USA Today*, 1/13/06.
3. "White-Knuckle Summer," *Variety*, 1/22–28/07.
4. Lieberman, David, "Marketing Gold Could be Found in Web Video," *USA Today*, 4/4/08.
5. Sweney, Mark, "Bebo's Online Drama Fans in for a Shock," 1/16/08. guardian.co.uk.
6. Richard Caves, *Creative Industries*, Harvard University Press, p. 179, 2002.
7. Richard Caves, *Creative Industries*, pp. 178–179.
8. De Vany, Arthur and Walls, David, "Uncertainty in the Movie Industry: Does Star Power Reduce the Terror of the Box Office?" *Journal of Cultural Economics*, 23: 285–318, 1999, ©1999 Kluwer Academic Publishers. Printed in the Netherlands.
9. "Other People's Money," *International Variety* 1/23–26/06.
10. "Other People's Money," *International Variety*, 1/23–26/06.
11. *Wall Street Journal*, 4/29/06.
12. *Wall Street Journal*, 4/29/06.
13. *Wall Street Journal*, 4/29/06.
14. *Variety*, 5/16/06.
15. *Variety*, 5/16/06.

16. *Variety*, 5/16/06.
17. "Old Studio Moguls Find New Future in Hedge-Fund Financing," *International Herald Tribune*, 11/20/06.
18. *International Herald Tribune*, 5/18/2006.
19. PR Newswire, DreamWorks release, 8/26/02.
20. "Old Studio Moguls Find New Future in Hedge-Fund Financing," *International Herald Tribune*, 11/20/06.
21. "Can Polar Express Make the Grade?," *Business Week*, 10/20/04.
22. Barnes, Brooks, "As Others Shun Hollywood, FedEx Founder Bets on Movies," *International Herald Tribune*, 7/22/08.
23. Grover, Ron, "As Lucas goes Digital, Will He Ditch Hollywood?," *Business Week*, 4/27/01; Brennan, Judy "Fox Feels the Force," *Entertainment Weekly*, 4/17/98; www.ew.com.
24. Grover, Ron, "As Lucas Goes Digital, Will he Ditch Hollywood?," *Business Week*, 4/27/01.
25. SEC S-1 Filing: The primary result of giving pro forma effect to the Distribution Agreement as of January 1, 2003 is that we recognize revenue net of (i) DreamWorks Studios' 8.0% distribution fee and (ii) the distribution and marketing costs that DreamWorks Studios incurs for our films, 7/21/04.
26. "Spielberg Severs Paramount Ties," *International Herald Tribune*, 10/07/08.
27. "DreamWorks in Deal with Universal," 10/14/08; www.nytimes.com.
28. Barnes, Brooks and Cieply, Michael, "DreamWorks and Disney Agree to a Distribution Deal," 2/10/09.
29. www.the-numbers.com/movies/2006 and www.abc.net.au/news, 11/1006.
30. "International Treaties," Special Section, *The Hollywood Reporter*, 11/2008.
31. "States' Film Production Incentive Cause Jitters," *New York Times*, 10/12/08.
32. "States' Film Production Incentive Cause Jitters," *New York Times*, 10/12/08.
33. "States' Film Production Incentive Cause Jitters," *New York Times*, 10/12/08.

Chapter 4

1. mpaa.org/researchstatistics.
2. box office from boxofficemojo.com.
3. Movie Theater Deal: When Genius Merged, Forbes.com, 6/22/05.
4. Movie Theaters of the Absurd, Forbes.com, 3/2/2001.
5. "The Phantom of Megaplex," *CFO Magazine*, 1/1/2001.
6. "Megaplex Mania," *USA Today*, 11/17/05.

7. The Phantom of the Megaplex, CFO.com, 3/2/2001; Movie Theaters of the Absurd, Forbes, 1/1/2001; "The Multiplex Under Siege," *The Wall Street Journal*, 12/24–45/2005.
8. "D-Cinema Grows Under Carmike, Christie Pact," *The Hollywood Reporter*, 12/20/05.
9. "D-Cinema Grows Under Carmike, Christie Pact," *The Hollywood Reporter*, 12/20/05.
10. "Crunch Time — 3-D Handbook Special Report," *The Hollywood Reporter*, 10/10/08.
11. "Can This Man Save the Movies? (Again?)," *Time*, 3/20/06.
12. "Can This Man Save the Movies? (Again?)," *Time*, 3/20/06.
13. DiOrio, Carl, "3-D day — D'Works Ani 'Monsters' is Biggest Push into New Realm," *The Hollywood Reporter*, 3/25/09.
14. Barnes, Brooks, "Theaters Slow to Warm to 3-D, Dispute Over Upgrades Threatens Hollywood's Big New Bet," *Los Angeles Times*, 1/13/09.
15. DiOrio, Carl, "3-D day — D'Works Ani 'Monsters' is Biggest Push into New Realm," *The Hollywood Reporter*, 3/25/09; Schuker, Lauren, "Strong 'Monsters' Feeds Hollywood's 3-D Hopes," *Wall Street Journal*, 3/30/09.
16. Movie Theaters of the Absurd, Forbes.com, 3/2/2001.
17. "Apple Turns to Indies to Buoy iTunes Film," *International Herald Tribune*, 10/24/07.
18. "Apple Turns to Indies to Buoy iTunes Film," *International Herald Tribune*, 10/24/07.
19. "'Madagascar,' downgrades slow DWA," *The Hollywood Reporter*, 6/1/2005.
20. Four-day opening box office, www.boxofficeguru.com.
21. www.boxofficeguru.com.
22. "'Sith' degrees of Separation," *Variety*, 5/30/05.

Chapter 5

1. Ault, Susanne, "Studios' Digital Revenue Will Grow 15% a Year," *Video Business*, 5/20/08; Chmielewski, Dawn, "Studios Editing Video Strategy," *Los Angeles Times*, 6/16/08; 2004 home video sales accounted for 51% of studios top line revenues, Kagan Research estimates.
2. Media Control GfK International estimate, as quoted in *Video Business*, 11/21/09; Magiera, Marcy, "Worldwide packaged media up 6% in 2008."
2a. www.museum.tv/archives/etv/H/htmlH/homevideo/homevideo.htm.
3. *Sony Corp. v. Universal City Studios* 464 U.S. 417, 104 S. Ct. 774, 78 L. Ed. 2d 574 (1984).
4. A History of Home Video and Gaming Retailing, The Entertainment Merchant Association, www.entmerch.org/industry_history.html.
5. A History of Home Video and Gaming Retailing, The Entertainment Merchant Association, www.entmerch.org/industry_history.html.

6.   "'Lion King' Rules at Retail," *Billboard*, 10/18/2003.

7.   "'Finding Nemo' DVD/Video Sales Reach 20 Million," *USA Today*, 11/17/2003.

8.   *Communication Technology Update*, 11th edition, by August E. Grant and Jennifer H. Meadows, Focal Press, Chapter 14, "Home Video," 2008.

9.   "2004 Video Wrap," *The Hollywood Reporter*, 1/19/05.

10. wikipedia.org/wiki/List_of_Disney_direct-to-video-films.

11. "Scorpion 2 Latest Direct-To-Video Prequel," Reuters, 8/7/08.

12. *International Herald Tribune*, 12/31/07–1/1/08.

13. "Sony Prevails in Format War," *International Herald Tribune*, 2/20/08.

14. "Sony Prevails in Format War," *International Herald Tribune*, 2/20/08.

15. Communications Technology Update, Chapter 14 Home Video, p. 197, citing, K Gyimesi (2006, December 19). Nielsen study shows DVD players surpass VCRs. Nielsen Media Research. Retrieved March 12, 2008 from http://www.nielsenmedia.com/.

16. entmerch.org/industry_history.html.

17. www.mania.com, 11/6/01, Big Green for SHREK Vid.

18. "Video Slips as DVD Market Matures," *USA Today*, 1/4/06.

19. "Year End Wrap," *Variety*, 12/26/05–1/1/06.

20. "Studios Editing Video Strategy," *Los Angeles Times*, Business Section, 6/1608.

21. Szalai, Georg, "DVD Market Down 5.7% in 2008," *The Hollywood Reporter*, 1/14/2009.

22. "Year End Review," *Variety*, 12/26/05–1/1/06.

23. "How DreamWorks Misjudged DVD Sales of Its Monster Hit," *Wall Street Journal*, 5/31/05.

24. "Netflix Delivers 1 Billionth DVD," Associated Press, 2/25/07; also, www.entmerch.org/industry_history.html.

25. "What's Driving the Box Office Batty—Hollywood is Pushing Movies to DVD and Video Faster—and Theaters Feel Squeezed," *Business Week*, 7/11/05.

26. "British Exhibitors Shut 'Museum': Fox Punished For Breaking Window," *Variety*, 2/1/07.

27. "How DreamWorks Misjudged DVD Sales of Its Monster Hit," *Wall Street Journal*, 5/31/05; see full article in Appendix.

27a. *Video Business*, Carl DiOrio, June 2, 2005.

28. "Feds Shred 'Shrek' Prove," *Variety*, 5/5/06.

29. "End of the DVD Party? First DreamWorks' *Shrek 2*, now Pixar's *The Incredibles*. Retailers are Shipping Back Scads of Unsold Copies. A Bad Plot Twist for Tinseltown," *Business Week*, 7/2/05.

Chapter 6

1.   FCC's Review of Broadcast Ownership Rules, as outlined in a Consumer acts summary on the FCC Web site www.fcc.gov/ownership.

1a. http://en.wikipedia.org/wiki/List_of_United_States_over_the_air_television_networks.

2. Martin, Denise, and Dempsey, John, "Spike's 'Star' Wattage — Cable Net Pays Up to $70 Mil for Six Franchise Pics," *Variety*, 10/19/05.

3. "Nets Share Window On 'Worlds,'" *Variety*, 2/26/06.

4. Pilot Programs, The Museum of Broadcast Communications. www.museum.tv/archives/etv/P/htmlP/pilotprogram/pilotprogram.htm.

5. Museum of Broadcasting, Pilot Programs, www.museum.tv/archives/etv/htmlP/pilotprogram/pilotprogram.htm.

6. Andreeva, Nellie, "Focus: 2009–10 Pilot Season — Back on Auto Pilot," *The Hollywood Reporter*, 3/6/09.

7. "He Has a Hot TV Series, a New Book — and a Booming Comedy Empire," *Time*, 9/28/87.

8. http://www.fundinguniverse.com/company-histories/The-Carsey Werner-Company-LLC-Company-History.html.

9. "Sopranos and Sex and the City Estimates," *Broadcast & Cable*, 1/11/07.

10. "'Office,' 'Earl' Land at TBS," *Variety*, 6/21/07.

11. http://www.museum.tv.archives/etv/F/htmlF/financialint/financialint.htm.

12. http://www.fundinguniverse.com/company-histories/The-Carsey Werner-Company-LLC-Company-History.html.

13. "Digital Media Brings Profits (and Tensions) to TV Studios," *New York Times*, 5/14/06.

14. "Cable Hits the Wall," *Variety*, 7/9-1507.

15. "Nets Face Muddled Metrics — Upfronts Unsettled By Ad Agony," *Variety*, 4/2–8/07.

16. http://www.nielsenmedia.com.

17. http://www.nielsenmedia.com.

18. http://www.nielsenmedia.com.

19. "New Rules Roil the Ad Biz," *Variety*, 7/9–15/07.

20. "New Rules Roil the Ad Biz," *Variety*, 7/9–15/07.

21. "New Rules Roil the Ad Biz," *Variety*, 7/9–15/07.

22. "A Game-Changing Season," *Ad Age*, 8/6/07; www.mediakid.adage.com.

23. "Nets Face Muddled Metrics," *Variety*, 4/2–8/07.

24. "As Seen on TV," *Wired*, 10/08.

25. "As Seen on TV," *Wired*, 10/08.

26. "Fox Feeds HBO's Film Fix," *Variety*, 7/9/07.

27. "Fox Feeds HBO's Film Fix," *Variety*, 7/9/07.

28. "Scouring the Vaults," *Variety*, 10/2–8/06.

29. "Pro7 Inks Deal with WBITTV," *The Hollywood Reporter*, 2/23/07.

30. "Private Equity Firms Win German TV Bid," *International Herald Tribune*, 12/15/06.

31. FT-Orange Lures Auds to Pay TV, www.variety.com, 3/4/09.

467

32. http://www.answers.com.com/topic/taurusholding-gmbh-co-kg Encyclopedia of Company Histories: TaurusHolding GmbH & Co. KG.
33. "Kirch Creditors Line Up for First Payments," *The Hollywood Reporter*, 1/23/07.
34. "How the Mighty Fall," *Time*, 4/15/02.
35. European Cover Story, "The Fall of Leo Kirch," *Business Week*, 3/11/02.
36. "How the Mighty Fall," *Time*, 4/15/02.
37. European Cover Story, "The Cartoon King," *Business Week*, 5/10/99.
38. International Edition Cover Story, *Business Week*, 5/10/99.
38a. "German Firm to Buy Henson for $680 Million," *Los Angeles Times*, February 22, 2000.
39. "Zounds! EM.TV Slips on Ice (International Edition)," Business Week Online, 11/6/00.
40. European Cover Story, "The Fall of Leo Kirch," *Business Week*, 3/11/02.
41. "Private Equity Firms Win German TV Bid," *International Herald Tribune*, 12/15/06.
42. "Europe Flick TV Switch," *The Hollywood Reporter*, 2/12–18/06.
43. http://www.dtv.gov/consumercorner.html.

Chapter 7

1. "At Stake in Viacom vs. Google Lawsuit: Future of Media — Defining Ownership in an Age of Fluid Content," *Ad Age*.
2. Internet to Revolutionize TV in 5 Years, Reuters via Yahoo! News, 1/27/07.
3. "The Wired Guide to the Online Video Explosion," *Wired*, 5/06.
4. comScore Video Metrix: comScore Press Release, "Number of Hulu Video Viewers Increases 42 percent in February, according to comScore Video Metrix," 3/24/09.
5. "Sneak Preview of PC Film Fight," *International Herald Tribune*, 2/12/07.
6. "Four Guilty in Web Piracy Case," *Wall Street Journal*, 4/18/09.
7. Arango, Tim, "Music Deal Fails to Lift Sour Mood on Apple," *New York Times*, Global Edition, 2/2/09.
8. Sandoval, Greg, Report: Studios Want Interoperable DRM, CNET News, August 26, 2008.
9. "Movie Studios Expand 'Download To Own' Services in U.S.," *International Herald Tribune*, 4/4/06.
10. "Blockbuster Uploading MovieLink," *Variety*, 8/9/07.
11. "Apples' Eye on Movies," *The Hollywood Reporter*, 9/13/06.
12. "Wal-Mart Sees Download Upside," *Variety*, 11/29/06.
13. Zune Eats Creative's Meager Lunch, Grabbing 4 Percent of MP3 Player Market, www.Wired.com, 5/12/08.

14. www.netflix.com and www.hackingnetflix.com.
15. "Wal-Mart Sees Download Upside," *Variety*, 11/29/06.
16. "In Hollywood, the Picture Blurs for Studio Profits," *Wall Street Journal*, 9/5/06.
17. "In Hollywood, the Picture Blurs for Studio Profits, *Wall Street Journal*, 9/5/06.
18. Wal-Mart's Movie Download Service Passes into Ignominy," *International Herald Tribune*, 1/1/08.
19. "Movie Studios Expand 'Download To Own' Services in U.S.," *International Herald Tribune*, 4/4/2006.
20. "Sneak Preview of PC Film Fight," *International Herald Tribune*, 2/12/07.
21. "Google Channels YouTube," *The Hollywood Reporter*, 10/10–16/06.
22. "Google Channels YouTube," *The Hollywood Reporter*, 10/10–16/06.
23. "Universal Nears Victory in Battle Over Royalties," *International Herald Tribune*, 2/13/07.
24. "Universal Nears Victory in Battle Over Royalties," *International Herald Tribune*, 2/13/07.
25. "Universal Nears Victory in Battle Over Royalties," *International Herald Tribune*, 2/13/07.
26. Viacom in $1 Billion Copyright Suit versus Google, YouTube, Reuters, 2/13/07.
27. "Small Screens, New Programs," *International Herald Tribune*, 1/29/07.
28. Marissa Mayer on Charlie Rose: The Future of Google, Future of Search, www.techcrunch.com, 3/6/09.
29. "Disney Will Offer Many TV Shows Free on the Web," *Wall Street Journal*, 4/10/06.
30. "20ᵗʰ, NBC Unfurl Digital Deal for 'Earl'," *Variety*, 2/20/07.
31. Rose, Frank, "As Seen on TV," *Wired*, 10/08.
32. "Hulu Guru, Kilar Vision," *Future Media*, 4/08; "Less is More on Video Web Site," *International Herald Tribune*, 10/30/08.
33. "Less is More on Video Web Site," *International Herald Tribune*, 10/30/08.
34. Hulu's Online Video Explosion, Julia Boorstin's report of her interview with Hulu CEO Jason Kilar, quoting ComScore numbers, www.cnbc.com, 11/11/08.
35. Nielsen Media Research as referenced in Video Sites Duke it Out for Content: YouTube, Hulu React to Sign Deals for Movies, Shows That Draw Advertising, www.wsj.com, 4/17/09.
36. ComScore Press Release, "Number of Hulu Viewers Increases 42 percent in February, according to comScore Video Metrix," 3/24/09.
37. "Disney Joins Hulu as Equity Partner," *The Hollywood Reporter*, 5/1/09.
38. Rose, Frank, "As Seen on TV," *Wired*, 10/08.
39. Video Sites Duke it Out for Content, www.wsj.com, 4/17/09; "Disney's TV Unit Will Make Short Videos Available on YouTube," *New York Times*, 3/31/09.

40. "Google Pulls the Plug on Online Video Sales, Rentals," *Wall Street Journal*, 8/13/07.

41. "Google Acts to Make YouTube a Cash Cow," *International Herald Tribune*, 8/23/07.

42. Hayes, Dade, "Albie Hecht Keeps an Eye on Web—Spike TV Founder Balances New and Old Media," *Variety*, 5/1/09.

43. "The Hollywood Treatment," *Wired*, 8/08.

44. "Amazon Video Gets 'Pipeline' to TV Sets," *International Herald Tribune*, 7/18/08.

45. Netflix and TiVo to Partner on Movies, www.nytimes.com, 10/30/08.

46. Joint Microsoft and Netflix Press Release, "One Million X-box LIVE Members Download and Activate Netflix on Xbox 360," 2/5/09.

47. "WGA Negotiations Set to Start," *Variety*, 7/11/07.

48. "Hollywood Executives Call for End to Residual Payments," *New York Times*, 7/11/07.

49. "Producers Make Dramatic Call for Residuals Revamp," *Broadcasting & Cable*, 7/11/07.

50. "WGA Negotiations Set to Start," *Variety*, 7/11/07.

51. "Producer's Make Dramatic Call for Residuals Revamp," *Broadcasting & Cable*, 7/11/07.

52. Special Bulletin, Contract 2008 TV/Theatrical Negotiations Update, www.sag.org/files/documents/SAG_Contract_2008.pdf.

53. Special Bulletin, Contract 2008 TV/Theatrical Negotiations Update, www.sag.org/files/documents/SAG_Contract_2008.pdf.

54. Special Bulletin, Contract 2008 TV/Theatrical Negotiations Update, www.sag.org/files/documents/SAG_Contract_2008.pdf.

55. The Nielsen Company, Nielsen Three Screen Report, 5/08.

Chapter 8

1. Toy Makers Bet on Blockbuster Films for Sales, Reuters, 6/6/06.

2. "A New Way to Use the Force," *Wall Street Journal*, 8/22/06.

3. Hager, George, "Disney to Purchase Fox Family for $3 Billion," *USA Today*, 7/23/01; Saban Capital Group, Inc. Press Release, "News Corp and Saban Reach Agreement to Sell Fox Family Worldwide to Disney for $5.3 Billion," 7/23/01.

4. "H'W'D'S Musical Mania," *Variety International*, weekly edition, 10/6–12/08.

5. Figures in '000s. 2004 Annual Report, discussion of "4Kids TV Broadcast Fee under Item 7.

6. 4Kids Entertainment 2004 Annual Report, Notes to Consolidated Financial Statements Years Ended December 21, 2004, 2003, and 2002; Advertising Media and Broadcast under Item 1. Description of Business.

7. Item 7, 4 Kids TV Broadcast Fee.

8. "Remember Squirtle and Jigglypuff? They're Back," *New York Times*, 8/7/07.
9. "Gotta Catch The Pokémon Pirates Nintendo Goes to Court in Crackdown on Fakes," *New York Daily News*, 11/09/99.
10. "Elements of Style," *KidScreen*, 5/07.
11. "Elements of Style" *KidScreen*, 5/07.
12. "'Spider-Man,' 'Transformers' and 'Pirates' Toys Battle for Boys' Attention," *Los Angeles Times*, 6/12/07.
13. Toy Story by Georg Szalai, *The Hollywood Reporter*, 2/13/09.
14. "Now Playing: H'w'd's Toy Ploy," *Variety International*, 6/11–17/2007.
15. "Spider-Man,' 'Transformers' and 'Pirates' Toys Battle for Boys' Attention," *Los Angeles Times*, 6/12/07.
16. "Company News: Hasbro Extends Deal on Star Wars Toys by 10 Years," *New York Times*, 1/31/2003.
17. "Hasbro Gets Toy and Game Rights to Marvel Heroes," *New York Times*, 1/9/06.
18. "Hasbro Profit Falls on Charge," *New York Times*, 7/23/07; "Hasbro's Net Income Drops 82% On Charge Tied to Warrants," *Wall Street Journal*, 7/23/07; Hasbro Press Release, "Hasbro and Lucas Extend Star Wars License Through 2018," 2/30/03; www.secinfo.com/d1dzf.2d.d.htm.
19. "'Spider-Man,' 'Transformers' and 'Pirates' Toys Battle for Boys' Attention," *Los Angeles Times*, 6/12/07.
20. "Strong Sales for Licensed Merchandise," *USA Today*, 4/15/08.
21. Szalai, Georg, "Toy Story," *The Hollywood Reporter*, 2/13/09; itemizing annual consumer product retail sales for Disney, Warners and Viacom as respectively $30 Billion, $6 Billion and $5 Billion.
22. "'Spider-Man,' 'Transformers' and 'Pirates' Toys Battle for Boys' Attention," *Los Angeles Times*, 6/12/07.
23. Szalai, Georg, "Toy Story," *The Hollywood Reporter*, 2/13/09; box office from boxofficemojo.com.
24. Szalai, Georg, "Toy Story," *The Hollywood Reporter*, 2/13/09.
25. "Playdate for H'wood Toys," *The Hollywood Reporter*, 2/15–17/08.
26. www.webkinz.com.
27. "$2B Estimate, the Webkinz Effect," *Wired*, 11/08/.
28. "Silly Walking onto the Web," *International Herald Tribune*, 9/8/08.
29. "Amazon Video Gets 'Pipeline' to TV Sets," *International Herald Tribune*, 7/18/08.
30. Netflix Press Release, "Netflix Offers Subscribers the Option of Instantly Watching Movies on their PCs," 1/16/97, www.netflix.com/MediaCenter?id=5284.
31. Reardon, Marguerite, Rok Adds Amazon Video on Demand, CNET News, 3/3/09.

Chapter 9

1. Schuker, Lauren, "Strong 'Monsters' Feeds Hollywood's 3-D Hopes," *Wall Street Journal*, 3/30/09.
2. www.boxofficeguru.com.
3. DiOrio, Carl, "Marvel's Date Shake Slows Super Releases," *The Hollywood Reporter*, 3/13/09.
4. www.mpaa.org/researchStatistics.asp.
5. Galloway, Stephen, "Special Report: Movies & the Media, Slim Pickings," *The Hollywood Reporter*, 5/30/08.
6. Galloway, Stephen, "Special Report: Movies and Media, Slim Pickings," *The Hollywood Reporter*, 5/30/08.
7. "Money Buys Happiness," *The Hollywood Reporter*, International weekend edition, 10/3-5/08.
8. www.mpaa.org/researchStatistics.asp.
9. "Video Marketing- By the Numbers," *The Hollywood Reporter*, 8/10-16/04.
10. "Video Marketing- By the Numbers," *The Hollywood Reporter*, 8/10-16/04.
11. "Caught in the Web." Video Marketing & the Media Section of DVD Special Report, *The Hollywood Reporter*, 7/11-17/06.
12. Ault, Susanne, "Papa John's Partners on Indiana Jones Promo," *Video Business*; www.pizzamarketplace.com, 11/7/02, "Papa John's Launches First Movie Tie-in with 'Ice Age' Promotion."
13. Fernandez, Jay A., "Enterprise Marketing," *The Hollywood Reporter*, 2/20/09.

Chapter 10

1. Superior court of the State of California, for the County of Los Angeles, Art Buchwald, et al, Plaintiffs. V Paramount Pictures Corporation, et al, Defendants, Statement of Decision (Third Phase), 3/16/1992.
2. *Fatal Subtraction*, by Pierce O'Donnell and Dennis McDougal, Doubleday, Copyright 1992.
3. "How do a Best Selling novel, an Academy Award Winning Screen writer, a pair of Hollywood Hotties, and a No. 1 opening at the box office add up to $78 million of red ink?" *Los Angeles Times*, 4/15/07.
4. "The Lawsuit of the Rings," *New York Times*, 6/27/05.

Index

478

479

481

485

YouTube acquisition, 318–320
YouTube *vs.* Viacom, 320–321
Google Video, 296t–297t, 305, 319
Gorilla clauses, 263
Government involvement, 114–117
Grammer, Kelsey, 28
Grant, Hugh, 399
Grant of Rights, 64
Grazer, Brian, 18–19
Grisham, John, 26t
Grokster, 66–68, 166, 180, 300–301
Gross participations
  as cost item, 449
  licensing royalties, 356–357
  types, 452–453
Gross profits
  cost deductions, 443–444
  definition and calculation,
    441–454
  vs. net, 454–455
  types, 452–453
Gross revenues, 434f
Gross up, 450–451
Grouper, 327–328
Guaranteed weeks, 130
Guarantee licensing programs,
    354–358
Guerilla marketing, 385
Gun Hill Road, 89–90
Gun theaters, 142–143

H

Haffa, Thomas, 285
Hale, Lynn, 408
Hamill, Mark, 27
Hancock, 79
Handout marketing, 406
Hanks, Tom, 89, 98, 157
Harry Potter franchise
  ancillary revenue, 364–365
  bargain bins, 207
  branding, 26t
  budget, 22–23
  decay curves, 154
  distribution considerations, 7–8
  international market, 270–271
  life cycle, 29–30
  mega-film marketing, 426
  promotional partners, 395
  sequels, 27t
  source material, 26t, 40t
  window patterns, 230

Hasbro
  licensing programs, 359
  merchandising, 344, 416–417
  toy-film-toy cycle, 360–362
  toy mega deals, 359–360
  video market, 184
HBO
  aftermarkets, 42
  DVD rentals, 186
  financing, 104
  first run TV series, 237–238
  original programming, 249, 266
  output deals, 261–262
  pay TV output deals, 262
  as pay TV player, 258
  as premium channel, 227, 258
  SVOD, 374
  and syndication, 245
  window patterns, 229
HD-DVD *vs.* Blu-ray, 184–186
HD Net, 33–34
Head Case, 266
Heaven's Gate, 52
Heavy.com, 76
Hecht, Albie, 329
Hedge fund financing, 85–89, 87t
Hedges, Jim, 106–107
Henson, Jim, 285
Hepburn, Audrey, 28
Herskovitz, Marshall, 54–55
Higglytown Heroes, 52–53
High budget, definition, 22
High School Musical, 307, 345
Hip factor, 385
The History Channel, 41t
Hitachi, 166
Hitch, 232t
HIT Entertainmnt, 361t
Hit & Run, 23
The Hobbit, 438
Hoffman, Peter, 438–439
Holden, William, 28
Holiday-themed films, 388
Holiday weekends
  blockbuster decay curves, 149
  decay curves, 148
  marketing factors, 389
  release strategies, 138
  theatrical booking frenzy, 143
"Hollywood accounting"
  Art Buchwald v. Paramount Pictures,
    436–437

486

489

495

501

502

504

506

508

509